# Neither poverty
# nor riches

Titles in this series:

NEW STUDIES IN BIBLICAL THEOLOGY

*Series editor: D. A. Carson*

# Neither poverty nor riches

## A BIBLICAL THEOLOGY OF MATERIAL POSSESSIONS

## *Craig L. Blomberg*

APOLLOS

APOLLOS (an imprint of Inter-Varsity Press),
38 De Montfort Street, Leicester LE1 7GP, England

*First published 1999*

**British Library Cataloguing in Publication Data**

A catalogue record for this book is available from the British Library.

ISBN 0–85111–516–0

Set in Times New Roman

Printed and bound in Great Britain by Creative Print and Design (Wales), Ebbw Vale

*To the memory of William Collitz*

All royalties received from sales of this book will be donated to Christian organizations of the author's choice that are currently implementing significant aspects of the biblical themes surveyed here.

# Contents

# Series preface

*New Studies in Biblical Theology* is a series of monographs that address key issues in the discipline of biblical theology. Contributions to the series focus on one or more of three areas: 1. the nature and status of biblical theology, including its relations with other disciplines (*e.g.*, historical theology, exegesis, systematic theology, historical criticism, narrative theology); 2. the articulation and exposition of the structure of thought of a particular biblical writer or corpus; and 3. the delineation of a biblical theme across all or part of the biblical corpora.

Above all, these monographs are creative attempts to help thinking Christians understand their Bibles better. The series aims simultaneously to instruct and to edify, to interact with the current literature, and to point the way ahead. In God's universe, mind and heart should not be divorced: in this series we will try not to separate what God has joined together. While the notes interact with the best of the scholarly literature, the text is uncluttered with untransliterated Greek and Hebrew, and tries to avoid too much technical jargon. The volumes are written within the framework of confessional evangelicalism, but there is always an attempt at thoughtful engagement with the sweep of the relevant literature.

Dr Blomberg's volume is an extraordinary achievement. With remarkable compression, this book not only guides the reader through almost all the biblical passages that have a bearing on poverty and wealth, but weaves the exegesis into a biblical theology that is simultaneously faithful to the historic texts and pastorally sensitive to the immense issues facing today's church. Dr Blomberg cannot simplistically condemn wealth: he has learned from Abraham, Job and Philemon. Nor can he exonerate acquisitiveness: he has learned from Amos, Jesus and James. The result is a book that is, quite frankly, the best one on the subject. It will not make its readers comfortable, but neither will it make them feel manipulated. Read it and pass it on.

*D. A. Carson*
*Trinity Evangelical Divinity School, Deerfield, Illinois*

# Author's preface

Ironically, this is a book by the rich for the rich. This is not a comment about the precise net worth of either the author or the readers, but merely an observation that scholars, theological students and the educated public, for which a work of this nature is intended, comprise, by global standards, part of the small percentage of the socio-economic elite in our world today. As a member of that cadre of scholars myself, I am very much aware of how easy it is to skew the interpretation of the biblical data so as to console myself that my current economic status and practices fit comfortably with Scripture's teaching about material possessions. To try to combat this tendency, I have read widely from authors of many different theological, ethnic and economic perspectives. I have tried to weigh heavily those few but significant experiences throughout my life of travelling and interacting first-hand with people in communities of acute poverty, both in North American urban centres and internationally. And I have listened particularly carefully to the voices of colleagues and students who have read the manuscript in its current or previous forms who themselves represent marginalized communities at home and abroad.

One of the significant dynamics of being poor, of course, is the sense of powerlessness that often accompanies economic poverty. While I cannot claim to have experienced this kind of powerlessness, I have had somewhat comparable experiences as a result of various physical afflictions. Right in the middle of the research for this volume, I contracted a repetitive stress injury, which a series of doctors thought was thoracic outlet syndrome, though no-one ever diagnosed it definitively. As I dictate this preface and get ready to send in the final draft of this book in manuscript form, I have participated in a regimen of physical therapy, swimming, weightlifting and other stretching exercises for nearly a year and a half, and for the first time since the onset of the RSI, I can now write or type up to perhaps seven or eight pages consecutively before needing to take a break. For many months, even one page brought on considerable pain. This disability has made the completion of this book much more challenging, but, thanks to a variety of friends and technology, it has become possible. Even as the RSI improves, however, my right knee, which has not had proper amounts of cartilage in it since surgery following an injury that I sustained when I was nineteen, is becoming increasingly arthritic. The doctors tell me I am too old for a cartilage transplant and too young for knee replacement surgery, so I must rely on further exercises, a knee brace, medication and a generally sedentary lifestyle for the time being. The sense of helplessness which both of these injuries have at times engendered in me I suspect is not entirely different from the powerlessness that the economically impoverished often feel. Nevertheless, it is important for me at the outset of this book to admit frankly that I am not poor economically and that I realize this does limit my ability to understand the topic of this book to a certain extent.

Many people merit my heartfelt thanks for their help in producing this volume. Pride of place goes to Mrs Jeanette Freitag, who has transcribed the dictated drafts of this book with great speed and accuracy. I must also express my gratitude to Mr Russ Bruxvoort, who read and summarized numerous works for me during a quarter-long research assistantship; Mrs Esther Kissel and Miss Karen Fisher for their help in typing the bibliography; Professor Elodie Emig for painstaking checking of quoted sources to ensure accuracy of their citation; and to my editors, Dr D. A. Carson of Trinity International University, and Dr Mark Smith of IVP in the United Kingdom. Having taught two elective courses based on this material, I am also grateful to two classes' worth of students for their interaction with my thoughts on the topic, including my wife, Fran. I must also express appreciation to Denver Seminary for granting me a sabbatical term during the spring and summer of 1997, enabling me to complete the research for this project, and to the libraries of Denver Seminary and Tyndale House in Cambridge, England, for their friendly help and efficiency in numerous details of the project. Hopefully sparing me unnecessary gaffes in my treatment of the Old Testament material, my colleagues Dr Daniel Carroll R. and Dr Richard Hess both read and commented in some detail on my chapters treating the contribution of the Hebrew Scriptures to the theme of material possessions.

All Scripture citations are taken from the New International Version (inclusive language edition). Quotations from the Apocrypha have been taken from Bruce M. Metzger's edition of the *Oxford Annotated Apocrypha* (Revised Standard Version; New York: Oxford, 1977). For pseudepigraphical material, I have used the edition of James H.

Charlesworth (*The Old Testament Pseudepigrapha*, 2 vols. [Garden City: Doubleday, 1983–85]). For material from Qumran, I have quoted the edition of Florentino García Martínez (*The Dead Sea Scrolls Translated* [Leiden: Brill, 1994]). For other ancient Greek and Roman sources, I have cited the translations from the Loeb Classical Library.

Finally, I should like to dedicate this book to the memory of my maternal grandfather, Mr William Collitz (1900–84). As a young adult, he emigrated from Germany to the United States and spent his working years as a grocer in Muscatine, Iowa. Like so many hard-working Christians of his era, but perhaps more successfully and consistently than most, he embodied many of the scriptural principles that this book highlights with respect to wise savings and investment, frugal spending on himself and generous giving to others. As the generation of Americans who lived through the Great Depression is dying off, may their stories and legacies inspire younger generations to imitate their models of wise and compassionate use of material possessions.

*March 1998*                                                    *Craig L. Blomberg*

# Abbreviations

| | |
|---|---|
| *ABR* | *Australian Biblical Review* |
| *AJT* | *Asia Journal of Theology* |
| *ASTI* | *Annual of the Swedish Theological Institute* |
| *AUSS* | *Andrews University Seminary Studies* |
| *BA* | *Biblical Archaeologist* |
| *BBR* | *Bulletin for Biblical Research* |
| *Bib* | *Biblica* |
| *BibTod* | *Bible Today* |
| *BJRL* | *Bulletin of the John Rylands Library* |
| *BSac* | *Bibliotheca Sacra* |
| *BTB* | *Biblical Theology Bulletin* |
| *BZ* | *Biblische Zeitschrift* |
| *CBQ* | *Catholic Biblical Quarterly* |
| *CSR* | *Christian Scholars' Review* |
| *CT* | *Christianity Today* |
| *CTM* | *Currents in Theology and Mission* |
| *CTQ* | *Concordia Theological Quarterly* |
| *CTR* | *Criswell Theological Review* |
| *DownRev* | *Downside Review* |
| *EJT* | *European Journal of Theology* |
| *EQ* | *Evangelical Quarterly* |
| *ERT* | *Evangelical Review of Theology* |
| *ET* | *Expository Times* |
| *ETL* | *Ephemerides Theologicae Lovanienses* |
| *ETR* | *Etudes thèologiques et religieuses* |
| *FN* | *Filología Neotestamentaria* |
| *GTJ* | *Grace Theological Journal* |
| *HBT* | *Horizons in Biblical Theology* |
| *HeyJ* | *Heythrop Journal* |
| *HTR* | *Harvard Theological Review* |
| *HUCA* | *Hebrew Union College Annual* |
| *IBMR* | *International Bulletin of Missionary Research* |
| *IBS* | *Irish Biblical Studies* |
| *IEJ* | *Israel Exploration Journal* |

| | |
|---|---|
| Int | Interpretation |
| IRM | International Review of Mission |
| ITQ | Irish Theological Quarterly |
| JAAR | Journal of the American Academy of Religion |
| JANES | Journal of the Ancient Near Eastern Society |
| JAOS | Journal of the American Oriental Society |
| JBL | Journal of Biblical Literature |
| JETS | Journal of the Evangelical Theological Society |
| JNES | Journal of Near East Studies |
| JQR | Jewish Quarterly Review |
| JR | Journal of Religion |
| JRE | Journal of Religious Ethics |
| JRS | Journal of Roman Studies |
| JSNT | Journal for the Study of the New Testament |
| JSOT | Journal for the Study of the Old Testament |
| JSP | Journal for the Study of the Pseudepigrapha |
| JTS | Journal of Theological Studies |
| Neot | Neotestamentica |
| NESTTR | Near East School of Theology Theological Review |
| NovT | Novum Testamentum |
| NTS | New Testament Studies |
| PRS | Perspectives in Religious Studies |
| RB | Revue Biblique |
| RefJ | Reformed Journal |
| RefTR | Reformed Theological Review |
| RelStud | Religious Studies |
| RevExp | Review and Expositor |
| ScripBull | Scripture Bulletin |
| SJT | Scottish Journal of Theology |
| ST | Studia Theologica |
| SvExÅrs | Svensk Exegetisk Årsbok |
| SWJT | Southwestern Journal of Theology |
| TB | Tyndale Bulletin |
| ThBeitr | Theologische Beiträge |
| TrinJ | Trinity Journal |
| TS | Theological Studies |
| TT | Theology Today |
| TZ | Theologische Zeitschrift |
| WTJ | Westminster Theological Journal |
| ZAW | Zeitschrift für die alttestamentliche Wissenschaft |
| ZNW | Zeitschrift für die neutestamentliche Wissenschaft |

# Introductory considerations

## A sampling of statistics

At least one billion out of the more than five billion people in our world today fall below any reasonable poverty line. Within a few years, the percentage is estimated to top 25% of the global population. While indigence, false religion and corruption certainly account for some of this plight, many of the poor are the victims of natural disasters, famine or drought. Overseas farmers often cannot make an adequate living from their small and infertile fields. Many in the cities are chronically unemployed in places where there are no jobs or are underemployed in jobs which do not pay adequate wages (see further Oxford III Conference 1995: 13–14). In addition to suffering sheer lack of income, the poor are often uneducated or afflicted with physical sickness, political oppression and/or religious persecution. The majority of the world's impoverished live in rural areas or villages, particularly in the so-called '10–40 window' (i.e. 10°N – 40°N latitude). Countless others have left the countryside for the burgeoning megalopolises of the Two-Thirds World in hopes of a better life, but only a handful ever find it. Instead, huge sprawling slums and shanty towns surround the peripheries of most major cities in Asia, Africa and Latin America. Terrorism and civil war cause additional misery, leading to 20 million refugees outside their countries of origin, and another 24 million people displaced within their own nations (Nicholls 1996: 2–5).

Two million children die every year from easily preventable infectious diseases. The number of people who lack access to safe drinking water is estimated at 1.3 billion.[1] Poor nations amass enormous debts they cannot possibly repay, while trade deficits ensure that they will continue to export what wealth and natural resources they have to benefit the rich nations even though their people grow poorer. Innocent children always suffer the most. In 1994 it was calculated that the

[1] For these and related statistics in a systematic overview of global poverty research, see Øyen, Miller & Samad (1996).

wealth of the world's 387 billionaires equalled the combined incomes of the bottom 45% of the entire world's population, or about 2.5 billion people (Marty 1995: 2). Yet already more than a decade ago, nearly 200 million of the world's poor professed some form of Christianity (D. Barrett 1982: 5). And, to the extent that they become aware of our lifestyles through television or foreign visitors, they often wonder why we in the West seem to care so little about their plight.

The major cities of the Western world present various parallels, although levels of suffering are not as extreme. Nevertheless, the gap between rich and poor in the United States and in the United Kingdom has been growing steadily over the last twenty-five years, irrespective of the political parties in power or the policies they have advocated (R. Sider 1997: 143–144).[2] For several years, the infant mortality rate in the USA has been the highest in all of the so-called 'developed' nations of the world (Ronsvalle & Ronsvalle 1990: 160). Increasingly, this disparity runs along racial lines, with the percentages of impoverished blacks, Hispanics and native Americans far outstripping those among whites and Asians (cf. R. Sider 1997: 178–179). Attempts at 'affirmative action' programmes to create equal opportunity for employment among minorities have met with only minimal success. Yet the highly publicized and politicized examples of 'reverse discrimination' have so alienated the majority of Americans that these policies and laws are being rescinded – a situation bound to exacerbate the disparity between the 'haves' and the 'have-nots'. So, too, a certain conservative mind-set toward illegal aliens or immigrants has led to a clamping down on public benefits that these people are eligible to receive, with innocent children again being the most tragic victims. And the nation as a whole suffers from a certain collective amnesia, forgetting the fact that a huge percentage of current Americans descend from peoples who, from the native American perspective, were once illegal immigrants themselves.

In both North America and Western Europe, three economic impasses suggest the failure of all major social and political proposals or systems to date. First, poverty is increasing, with average income levels falling, gaps between the rich and poor widening, and personal and national indebtedness rising, all despite significant increase in per capita production. Second, notwithstanding the efforts of various

---

[2] For current information on the North American and Western European scenes more broadly, see G. Riches (1996). Cf. Geiger (1995: 19–20): 'Developed countries which are most zealous in pursuing a free-market economy, like the United States and Britain, are experiencing increased income inequality and poverty.'

environmental groups, including some who gain notoriety because of their idiosyncratic protests or connection of ecological issues with 'earth-worship', all of the following problems have grown worse: the depletion of the ozone layer, global warming, acid rain, the loss of biodiversity and farmable land, the amount of toxic chemical waste, deforestation, pollution of the sea, depletion of available energy resources and the overall deterioration of human health. Third, again irrespective of the major political systems and despite temporary local reversals, the number of unemployed people, particularly in Europe, continues to skyrocket.[3]

Given all these alarming and discouraging trends, it is astonishing to see what Westerners spend their money on. A survey of expenditures in the late 1980s and early 1990s demonstrated that Americans spent annually twice as much on cut flowers as on overseas Protestant ministries, twice as much on women's sheer hosiery, one and a half times as much on video games, one and a half times as much on pinball machines, slightly more on the lawn industry, about five times as much on pets, one and a half times as much on skin care, almost one and a half times as much on chewing gum, almost three times as much on swimming pools and accessories, approximately seven times as much on sweets, seventeen times as much on diets and diet-related products, twenty times as much on sports activities, approximately twenty-six times as much on soft drinks, and a staggering 140 times as much on legalized gambling activ-ities (Ronsvalle & Ronsvalle 1992: 53–54).[4] And in 1995 worldwide expenditures for advertising, designed largely to convince us that all of these and similar items are necessities, amounted to $385 billion (R. Sider 1997: 21). As for church construction, between 1984 and 1989 American Christians spent $15.7 billion (R. Sider 1997: 89). Suter (1989: 649) puts it pointedly: 'In its most dramatic and obscene form, the question is whether the labour and resources of the Third World nations should contribute more to the opulence of America's cats and dogs than to the elementary good health of Third World humans.'

Meanwhile, the amount of American giving to charitable organizations of all kinds remains relatively constant at somewhere between

[3] For details of all three of these themes, see Goudzwaard & de Lange (1995: 6–36).

[4] The Ronsvalles give the net figures. Since some of these statistics are starting to be a little dated, I have converted them into percentages that are less likely to have changed as much. Legalized gambling, in fact, has dramatically increased, both in the US and in the UK. For a graphic pictorial comparison of the material possessions of a representative family from each of thirty different countries from all continents of the globe, and for various statistics about the wealth or poverty of each, see Menzel (1994).

1.6 and 2.16% of a family's income (Stafford 1997: 21–22). American *Christians* do only slightly better, averaging somewhere around 2.4% of the national per capita income (R. Sider 1997: 205). And consistently, Americans with lower incomes give more of their earnings to religious organizations than those with higher incomes (Ronsvalle & Ronsvalle 1990: 154). There are also noticeable generational disparities. Senior citizens in the US today form the age-group that consistently gives the most generously to explicitly Christian causes. The so-called 'baby boomers' have typically amassed so much debt that they have less disposable income, despite their greater overall earnings. And the so-called 'Generation X' or 'baby busters' are quickly realizing that on average they cannot expect to replicate the wealth or lifestyles of their parents, although that has not, in general, stopped them from trying. Hence, levels of personal indebtedness soar even higher (on all three groups, *cf.* further Sine 1991: 143–164.) In most affluent or suburban Western communities, it is impossible to detect any outward differences between the expenditures of professing Christians and the religiously unaffiliated who surround them in their neighbourhoods. Suter (1989: 645–648) suggests that John Wesley's epigram ('Gain all you can, save all you can, give all you can')[5] has been replaced with 'Money will solve all your problems,' 'Go with the flow to make the dough,' and 'Spend all you can.' As for our governments, the US ranks last among the eighteen major Western donors of foreign aid in terms of percentage of GNP, while the UK comes in twelfth (R. Sider 1997: 31).

Many of these trends are present but not as extreme in Western Europe.[6] But percentages of church-goers and evangelical believers are noticeably lower than in the US. A recent survey of 'the gospel, the poor and the churches' in Britain demonstrated that few of those surveyed articulated a distinctively *Christian* response to world poverty, and that the entire spectrum of suggestions for the causes of poverty was represented in every socio-economic bracket and religious denomination. What influenced the variation in attitudes stemmed rather from one's perception of the church's mission and one's personal experience, if any, with poverty. Bible passages most likely to be cited were Mark 14:7 and Matthew 25:31–46, and then, more often than not, they were misinterpreted (Rowland 1995).

---

[5] Lawfully and sensibly, that is.

[6] To take just one example, in Western Europe since the 1940s, 'Nutritional diseases have been those due not to deficiency but to excess' – of food intake, sugar consumption and animal fats (Grigg 1993: 256).

# Christian response

What should a genuine Christian response to all of these trends be? Historically, Christians have distinguished themselves considerably from their surrounding cultures by championing concern for the poor of their world in ways that other world religions and ideologies typically have not. In fact, it is arguable that almost all of the major attempts to alleviate poverty and human suffering have a Christian foundation at one level or another: monasticism, with its emphasis on simple living and giving to the poor; socialism or communism, given Marx's reliance on Christian ethics and ideals even if divorced from their theological underpinnings (see, *e.g.*, K. Bockmuehl 1980); capitalism, with its frequent dependence on the so-called 'Protestant work ethic' (see, *e.g.*, Catherwood 1987); and numerous other mediating systems.[7]

Following the Second World War, however, North American and Western European countries (those with the greatest modern legacy of Christian values) experienced unprecedented rates of economic growth and affluence. The decades of the 1950s and 1960s would sow the seeds of a considerable shift in thinking and practice with respect to material possessions (McClay 1995). Whereas many who had lived through the Great Depression and two world wars were sympathetic to Wesley's approach (see previous page), patterns of both saving and giving began to erode. Meanwhile, the world's population was also growing at unprecedented rates, leading to an alarming increase in the magnitude and visibility of world poverty.

The first major new Christian response to these shifts began in 1968 with the epoch-making Roman Catholic council, known as Vatican II, which spawned an enormous amount of theological literature that came to be known, following Gustavo Gutiérrez' pioneering work, as 'liberation theology' (Gutiérrez 1968). In the face of frequent Roman Catholic neglect of the structural issues preserving poverty among the masses in predominantly Catholic countries, especially in Latin America, liberation theology developed a three-fold method which began with the experience of massive global injustice and suffering, moved to an analysis of the causes of poverty and then promoted what it believed would be the most helpful corrective measures. The use of the Bible came into play primarily only in these last two stages. The published form of many liberation theologies actually reveals a more complex dialectic than might be suggested by

---

[7] For good surveys of the history of Christian thinking in this area, see González (1990); Gordon (1989); Santa Ana (1977); and Countryman (1980).

the simple methodological affirmations of the theologians themselves. The language of subsequent Roman Catholic documents, beginning with CELAM III (the Latin American Council of Bishops) in Puebla, Mexico, in 1979, bequeathed to the religious world the conviction that God has a 'preferential option for the poor' (for the specific texts, see Karris 1990: 13–15). In other words, 'God sides with the oppressed against their oppressors and calls believers today to do the same in working for a more humane society on this earth' (Klein, Blomberg & Hubbard 1993: 451).

Initially, the most famous forms of liberation theology appropriated Marxist analysis and methods, sometimes calling for violent rebellion against political or religious oppressors. The earliest stages of liberation theology were also characterized by, and criticized for, their lack of serious biblical exegesis. One important exception was found in the works of a writer who was also one of the most outspoken advocates of viewing the Bible as promoting communism, José Porfirio Miranda (see esp. Miranda 1982; cf. also Croatto 1981). Throughout the 1980s, however, a second phase of liberation theology emerged which was more tied to the biblical text, employed a viable hermeneutic and relied less on Marxism and/or violent revolution. Perhaps the most detailed example of careful exegesis with respect to the historical Jesus is the work of Juan Luís Segundo (1985); for an example of more balanced theological reflection, one may profitably consult the African Bakole wa Ilunga (1984).[8]

Evangelical response to liberation theology was at first largely one of neglect and more recently one of relatively unsophisticated and one-sided critiques (e.g., Nash & Belli 1992; McGlasson 1994). Notable exceptions have emerged mainly from those who have been career missionaries or indigenous Christian leaders in the very locations that spawned liberation theology. Here one thinks particularly of the work of the long-time British missionary to Latin America, Andrew Kirk, and his North American counterpart, Thomas Hanks (see e.g., Kirk 1980; Hanks 1983; cf. also Nuñez 1985; Nuñez & Taylor, 1996). One critique of all major phases and forms of liberation theology, however, has remained relatively constant, namely, its underestimation of the role of

---

[8] For other examples of sophisticated liberationist exegesis, see the summaries in Rowland & Corner (1989); and for larger trends, including the two phases of liberationist thought more generally, see McGovern (1989). Cf. also Carroll R. (1992: 112–113, 312–319). Of course, since the fall of the Iron Curtain in 1989, liberation theology has entered another mode altogether as it takes the near-global triumph of capitalism over communism into account.

life in a world to come, with or without Christ, determined by one's response to the gospel. This criticism has at times been exaggerated. Gutiérrez' foundational work clearly enunciates the spiritual dimensions of salvation (1988: 25) but proceeds to make little of them – an understandable procedure in trying to swing the pendulum back from an extreme over-emphasis on a heavenly future without a corresponding emphasis on social justice in this world. But it is not clear if all of Gutiérrez' followers can be excused as easily.

All of these developments in and theological reflection on current realities in the world at large set the stage for one of the most influential catalysts among British and North American evangelicals to help them finally come to grips with global poverty: the publication by Ronald Sider in 1977 of *Rich Christians in an Age of Hunger*. Sider built on scattered evangelical realizations that the gospel offered a more holistic liberation of body and soul than was commonly enunciated by conservatives, particularly in the US, at least since the so-called fundamentalist–modernist controversy of the 1920s.[9] Sider produced a work which has gone through three subsequent revisions, the most recent one being a twentieth-anniversary commemorative edition. Sider began with a barrage of statistics highlighting the plight of the poor in the world today and the disparity between the 'haves' and the 'have-nots'. Then he used several chapters to engage in serious biblical study thematically arranged; offered a sharp critique of capitalism, a largely unprecedented evangelical focus on structural evil and a call for appropriate, though relatively modest, state intervention; and provided detailed suggestions for applications of the biblical material to contemporary Christian living, including the concept of a graduated tithe. Sider has been active, too, in the leadership of Evangelicals for Social Action, the journal *Transformation: An International Dialogue on Evangelical Social Ethics* and numerous related international conferences and symposia,[10] particularly in conjunction with the Oxford Centre for Mission Studies.

Sider's work also spawned several extremely conservative responses. One of the most direct, polemical and ill-informed was David Chilton's, which parodied the title of Sider's work: *Productive Christians in an*

---

[9] The most notable predecessor was the International congress on World Evangelization in Lausanne in 1974; a congress which unfortunately had far less impact on evangelical thinking inside the US than outside it.

[10] Particularly significant for our theme was the conference that generated the Oxford Declaration on Christian Faith and Economics in 1990.

*Age of Guilt Manipulators* (1981).[11] Chilton blamed poverty primarily
on laziness and non-Christian religion, accused Sider of creating false
guilt among the industrious Christians of the West, reread the relevant
biblical data through the eyes of postmillennial reconstructionism and,
in general, disagreed with virtually every point Sider made. Only
slightly less opposed, though considerably less antagonistic in tone,
has been the ongoing work of Ronald Nash. Among other recurring
themes, Nash finds the problem with the Western world not in too much
but in too little capitalism. He identifies American government and
economy as interventionist rather than capitalist, promotes an extreme
right-wing form of libertarianism and highlights the so-called 'suc-
cesses' of a more 'pure' form of capitalism internationally, particularly
in the East Asian countries (while largely ignoring its failures, as in the
great disparities of wealth created in Latin American countries where
multi-national corporations pay far less tax than in the North and the
West). His hermeneutical system is not as untenable as Chilton's, but
serious biblical exegesis occurs only very sporadically in his writings
(see esp. Nash 1986; 1987). So, too, E. C. Beisner (1988) has produced
a helpful thematic treatment of 'prosperity and poverty', highlighting
the idolatry of mammon and the need for biblically based stewardship.
But when he addresses systemic evil, his solutions are again clearly
libertarian.

A more recent, balanced and significant counterpoint to Sider appears
in the work of John Schneider (1994). Provocatively entitling his study
*Godly Materialism*, Schneider engages in considerable, careful, biblical
analysis to stress the potentially positive roles of money and wealth
among God's people. Like Chilton, his major concern is to avoid
imposing false guilt on affluent but godly Christians. He believes such
guilt runs rampant among Christian professionals, and he epitomizes his
concerns by describing his desire to enjoy, without any sense of guilt, a
recently constructed cedar wood deck in his backyard and an outdoor
barbecue on a summer evening, as he watches his children play in
innocence and safety on their oak-lined lawn. Schneider defends the
thesis that what counts for believers is a spirituality of love, not some
particular level of income or its charitable disposal. It is arguable that
Schneider's concerns are real ones but that the number of affluent
Christians imposing a false guilt on themselves is far smaller than he
imagines. In light of the statistics on the paucity of charitable giving

[11] Startlingly, the cover is designed to mirror the first edition of Sider's work; the
author's name is cleverly hidden and the subtitle, 'A Biblical Response to Ronald J.
Sider', typeset so that at first glance it appears that Sider authored the book.

(above, pp. 19–20), it would seem that there is a genuine guilt that too few middle-class believers in the North and the West experience.

Also of note among recent evangelical publications are two works by Gene Getz (1990a; 1990b). One of these is a thorough survey of New Testament teaching on material possessions, arranged in canonical sequence, but turned into a series of more than one hundred principles for contemporary Christian application. The work is somewhat mis-leadingly entitled *A Biblical Theology of Material Possessions*; only one short initial chapter surveys the Old Testament, and it is unduly truncated because of dispensational presuppositions. The second work is a shorter, thematically arranged popularization and application of the first. In general, both of Getz's works move too quickly from texts to principles without sufficient analysis of the historical and literary contexts of each passage or any detailed exegesis.

While not based on serious scholarship, concurrent with all of these developments, largely though not exclusively in charismatic circles, has been the continuation, and even growth, of the so-called 'health and wealth gospel' or 'prosperity theology'. High-profile proponents have included the evangelists Oral Roberts, Kenneth Hagin, Kenneth and Gloria Copeland and Benny Hinn. Thus, one influential wing of global Christianity continues to promise its adherents unlimited levels of material prosperity, if only they have enough faith and are prepared to 'name it and claim it' in prayer.[12] But such 'theology' can be developed only by ripping text after text from its context and by making applications that would seem ludicrous in most Two-Thirds World settings, in which it is clear that all the faith one can muster gives few people a chance of significantly bettering their material lot in life. Unfortunately, such theologies at times actually garner significant followings and offer great hope in contexts of impoverishment, precisely because people's circumstances are so drastic. But ultimately their failures either create great guilt complexes in the followers of such movements or engender great disillusionment with Christianity in general. John Stott has not overstated himself when he declares, 'We have to have the courage to reject the health-and-wealth gospel absolutely. It's a false gospel' (McCloughry 1996: 29).

Also prevalent at the popular level of evangelical writing today are numerous books on a Christian approach to stewardship, money matters and the workplace. But the vast majority of these deal exclusively with individual Christian behaviour, highlighting work and the owning of

---

[12] See Barron (1987) for a good overview and a relatively sympathetic critique of the 'health and wealth' gospel.

property as appropriate Christian activity, and the responsibility of employees to witness to their friends in the workplace about their faith. In general, they present a concept of Christianity as utterly privatized. Business ethics are seldom addressed in detail. Money, at worst, is seen as a neutral entity, and structural evil is seldom discussed (Witten 1995).[13] For treatments of the church as counter-cultural community, one has to turn primarily to sources influenced by the Mennonite and Anabaptist traditions.[14]

Indeed, the spectacular collapse of communism in much of the world in which it once held sway has led to the hegemony of capitalism as the worldwide economic system of a dawning new millennium. This implicit triumph of the world-view often held in Western evangelical circles as the most compatible with Judeo-Christian foundations makes the need for serious biblical critique all the more crucial. Various symposia and debates have made it clear that no single modern economic system can be equated simplistically with 'the biblical model' (see Clouse 1984; Gay 1991). Thus if one economic system is to prevail for the foreseeable future, the ways in which it is or is not compatible with biblical teaching become all the more critical to explore (Campolo 1997).

Unfortunately, in the process of such critique, thoughtful studies mediating between classic capitalist and socialist models, like the very helpful recent one by Goudzwaard and de Lange (1995; cf. Goudzwaard 1979) appear to have had little impact, especially in North America. This Dutch study proposes that Christians work towards 'an economy of care', focusing on the creation of small local groups of a cross-section of the major political, economic and religious leaders of individual communities, taking the needs of their local settings into their own hands, as an alternative both to the impersonal and often ruthless policies of the multi-national corporations that dominate global capitalism and to the large interventionist and statist machines that often characterize Western and particularly European governments (Goudzwaard & de Lange 1995: esp. 47–48). Indicative of a handful of

---

[13] A key exception is J. White (1993), with his blistering attack on materialism in our churches, especially considering our budgets and building programmes, but he offers little constructive advice for individual members' own lifestyles. Ellul, over a decade ago (1984), and Foster a little more recently (1989), have written important studies of the potentially diabolical seduction of material possessions, but these works have not commanded nearly the following that they deserve. On American attitudes to 'ethics in the workplace', see esp. Wuthnow (1994: 79–115).

[14] See esp. Hauerwas & Willimon (1989); for a thoughtful Christian approach to economics, cf. Halteman (1995).

similar Christian studies, Goudzwaard and de Lange articulate a 'theology of enough', challenging Christians to establish a voluntary consensus on both minimum levels of income and resources below which people should not be allowed to fall and maximum levels of consumption and expenditure on self, above which people ought not be allowed to continue.

With similar motivation, but following slightly different procedures, numerous holistic missions movements overseas are enabling impoverished people to create small self-sustaining businesses, teaching them literacy and marketable skills in the name of Jesus, and in conjunction with the proclamation of his gospel (see esp. Nicholls & Wood 1996). In the American inner cities, the movement of the Christian Community Development Association and like-minded organizations has implemented similar initiatives (see esp. J. Perkins 1993).

Neglected in almost all of the literature discussed in this introduction thus far, however, is a revolution in New Testament studies provoked initially by a burgeoning sociological analysis of Scripture. Major studies of the socio-economic world into which Jesus and Christianity were born, of the probable socio-economic standing of Jesus and his disciples themselves, as well as of the spectrum of individuals who were converted to Christianity in its first generation, all point to a full range of poor, 'middle class' and well-to-do believers. Already twenty years ago, Malherbe (1977: 31) could speak of a 'new consensus' on this point, as over against an older, generally exaggerated emphasis on the poverty of Jesus and his first followers. So, too, an analysis of the various New Testament documents and their ethical instruction, against these more nuanced historical and social backgrounds, has led to an appreciation of the diverse and at times seemingly competing themes of the Bible with respect to God's people and their material posses-sions.[15] Yet, as often happens, a revolution in scholarly biblical studies takes considerable time to filter down to popular literature and theologizing.

Thus, in the flurry of all of the publishing on Christians and money matters, there is still a major gap in the current literature. When I decided to teach an experimental elective course at the seminary level in the spring of 1995 on a biblical theology of material possessions, the only book in print that attempted any detailed, sequential survey and

---

[15] For a brief introduction, see Klein, Blomberg & Hubbard (1993: 443–445), and the literature there cited. The most recent and relevant studies will appear throughout our discussion below.

discussion of the major biblical data was that of Getz described above (1990a). Yet, as mentioned, it is more a list of principles, potentially derivable from the text, than a genuine 'biblical theology'. Still lacking are works which interact with any kind of hermeneutical sophistication with the Christian use of the Old Testament in the New Testament age, with the use of historical narrative for theology or with the application of occasional epistolary literature in a later time and culture. In addition, all of the major developments in biblical scholarship just noted, dealing with the socio-economic standing and practices of the early Christians, have yet to be integrated into a theology of wealth and poverty.

Like Getz, therefore, I set out to write a 'biblical theology' of material possessions, but with much more detailed attention to Old Testament and intertestamental foundations, and with more attention to historical backgrounds, literary context, the unique genres of each portion of Scripture and the key hermeneutical issues attaching to a contemporary application of the biblical data. I was convinced by my preliminary study that syntheses of these data in light of these numerous exegetical concerns led to conclusions that charted a middle ground between Sider and his critics.[16] I was also very aware of how readily interpreters read their own personal and cultural experiences into Scripture in studies dealing with a subject as volatile as 'money', and I knew that I needed to read extremely widely so that my own presuppositions, conscious or unconscious, could stand the best chance of being challenged.

Since I embarked on this project, Schneider's work has filled at least a small portion of the gap I perceived.[17] But his is still somewhat more of a popular-level study not conversant with the full breadth of the most relevant scholarship, and I am convinced that he remains a bit too optimistic about the goodness of wealth among affluent Westerners. Plus, a more comprehensive survey of the biblical data is needed than he provides. From a non-evangelical, though still very centrist perspective across the whole theological spectrum, Sondra Wheeler (1995) proves helpful, but she focuses on a detailed investigation of only a handful of representative texts from the various New Testament corpora. And she brings to her study certain historical-critical

[16] Given Sider's successive revisions of his views over the years, along with the increasingly right-wing shift of much contemporary American evangelicalism, those syntheses are now considerably closer to Sider's than to many of his critics. But when one takes appropriate New Testament use of Old Testament teaching into account, it is still not clear if Sider's approach to structural evil can be fully sustained.

[17] Its copyright date is 1994, but it was not available from the publisher until May 1995.

assumptions and methodological limitations on ethical application that I cannot share.[18] So it seems that the need for a work such as I envisaged remains.

The New Studies in Biblical Theology series attempts to renew a viable evangelical, biblical theology after the discipline as a whole fell on hard times, especially due to rampant assumptions about the disunity of Scripture or the lack of its authority, or due to an inability to agree on the nature of that authority (for overviews, *cf.* Childs 1992: 3–51; Hasel 1995). The editor of this series, D. A. Carson, sets out the parameters and options for such a biblical theology in a helpful article. Our study falls under the particular category of tracing an important biblical theme throughout the major biblical corpora and agrees with Carson's conclusions about the assumptions essential to doing biblical theology today: a dependence on reading the Bible as a 'historically developing collection of documents'; presupposing 'a coherent and agreed canon'; demonstrating 'a profound willingness to work inductively from the text'; seeking 'to make clear the connections among the corpora'; and calling 'men and women to knowledge of the living God' (1995: 27–32; *cf.* also Hasel 1996). In the context of a theology of material possessions, we might add 'and to an obedience to the commands of that living God'. In *The Gagging of God*, Carson elaborates on several of these themes, particularly the need to keep the biblical data surveyed in any thematic analysis tied to the major story-line of Scripture, including their relationship to the most dominant theological emphases in any given context. This better enables readers to recognize what is central or what is peripheral at any given point. In an age of growing biblical illiteracy, even among church-goers, this need has become that much more acute (Carson 1996: 193–314).

This present study did not begin by presupposing what levels or amounts of unity and/or diversity would emerge from analysis of scriptures relevant to the theme of material possessions. But in light of the study, what has emerged, I believe, is a series of relatively consistent themes and emphases across all the biblical corpora in the midst of other diversity. These themes are summarized in my concluding chapter. The general hermeneutical methods adopted correspond to those laid out in detail in Klein, Blomberg and Hubbard, especially in our final chapter on moving from text to application (1993: 401–426). In brief, the key to making such a move can be summarized in terms of

---

[18] A slightly older work with many of the same strengths and weaknesses is the even more narrowly focused study on 'asking for money in the New Testament' by Bassler (1991).

levels of abstraction and specificity. In the case of the Old Testament, one must run each passage through a grid or filter of its 'fulfilment' in Christ (Matt. 5:17) to see how, if at all, its application is altered in the New Testament age. For all texts in both Testaments, one must often relate situation-specific mandates to broader, more timeless, categories. Particularly with respect to ethical issues, the interpreter must look for ways in which the principles of the original texts can be practised in changed contexts (C. Wright 1995: 114–116). Hays (1996) helpfully distinguishes rules, principles, paradigms and symbolic worlds in the biblical texts, developing different kinds of contemporary applications for each. The closer the situation in any given portion of our contemporary world corresponds to the features – in this case the socio-economic features – of the world behind any given biblical instruction, the more straightforwardly one can transfer the principles of those texts to our modern age. The less the correspondence, the higher one has to move up the 'ladder of abstraction', to look for broader principles that may transcend the uniqueness of specific situations (cf. also I. H. Marshall 1978).[19]

The format of this book, then, is a survey in roughly historical sequence of the contributions of the major biblical witnesses to a theology of material possessions for God's people in the church age – that is, from Pentecost onward. Chapters 1 and 2 survey the most relevant Old Testament backgrounds. Because we proceed more rapidly at this point than in the chapters dealing with the New Testament, we group material together largely according to the major canonical divisions: first the Torah, followed by the so-called historical books, in chapter 1; then the poetic and wisdom literature, along with the major and minor prophets, in chapter 2. We comment in passing on questions of historicity and historical sequence, but the theological conclusions derived are largely independent of debates on these issues.

Chapter 3 turns to the intertestamental period and surveys historical trends, the plethora of Jewish literature (both from the so-called Apocrypha and Pseudepigrapha and from the Dead Sea Scrolls), various sectarian and philosophical developments in Judaism and in the Greco-Roman world immediately preceding the birth of Christianity, and the relevant evidence from the Gospels themselves pertaining to the socio-economic standing of Jesus and the people who interacted with him.

---

[19] The Protestant canon forms the body of literature assumed to be uniquely authoritative for the believer, but the inclusion of the Old Testament apocrypha among important intertestamental background literature should enable Catholics and Orthodox to profit equally from our survey.

Chapters 4–7 then turn exclusively to the New Testament. Again, assumptions about the historical trustworthiness of this material will be discussed briefly, but will not prove essential for agreement on the theological emphases with respect to material possessions. Chapter 4 surveys the teachings of Jesus in the Synoptic Gospels, first in the parables and then in other non-parabolic teachings. Chapter 5 turns to the data from the epistle of James, arguably the earliest New Testament letter and one which emerges out of a primitive Jewish-Christian milieu with much significant teaching on our topic. Chapter 6 will also survey the book of Acts. The vast majority of information on wealth and poverty in Acts comes in the first 'half' (Acts 1 – 12) dealing with the early Palestinian and Jewish stages of the nascent Christian movement, and hence roughly contemporaneous and homogeneous with the community and contribution of James.

Chapter 6 proceeds to a survey of the data of the epistles of Paul, treated in chronological sequence as best as we can reconstruct it. It includes a major section on the single longest sustained and most significant portion of biblical teaching on our topic, Paul's treatment of the collection for the poor in Judea (2 Cor. 8 – 9). Chapter 7 then gathers together the remaining New Testament material, often held to be the latest chronologically (although more conservative datings would allow some of this literature to overlap with the latest letters of Paul). This chapter divides into two major sections: first, a return to the data of the Gospels and Acts, this time with a view to discerning the redactional emphases of the synoptic evangelists; then a look at the remaining New Testament documents. By including here for the first time the Gospel of John, we are not presupposing the common notion that it is largely unhistorical, but we do recognize the difficulty of separating Johannine tradition from redaction. Given the thematic links between John's Gospel and the remaining Johannine literature often assumed to be the latest New Testament documents, we have chosen to include the Fourth Gospel at this point. The second major section of chapter 7 also focuses on the epistles not attributed to Paul, James or John (Hebrews, 1 and 2 Peter, Jude), as well as on the book of Revelation. Here the canonical sequence of books may, at least roughly, correspond to their order of composition.

Chapter 8 recapitulates the major conclusions of each previous chapter and summarizes the distinctive characteristics of each biblical corpus. It draws additional connections among the major sections of Scripture and reflects on the significance of the Bible's emphases for Christian discipleship in the contemporary world. Here I disclose some of our own family's practices, hopefully to encourage others that significantly improved stewardship can occur even with very modest efforts, but I also allude to the more radical ideas and practices of others.

The research which has gone into the production of this relatively slim volume has involved wide reading at all levels of the discussion, from extremely technical scholarship to very popular-level writing. But, in keeping with the goals of this series, I have tried to be relatively succinct in my presentation and have aimed at a level that can be read easily by the introductory theological student and thoughtful layperson alike. For those who wish to pursue the scholarly debates in more detail, the fairly ample documentation and bibliography point them to most of the significant literature. Indeed, I have tried to include all the works I have surveyed and found relevant to part of our discussion, in either a parenthetical note or a footnote at some point in the book itself, so that the bibliography is limited to giving the full documentation for literature cited in abbreviated form in the text proper. But whether one reads with an eye for minute detail or simply to observe the broad contours of the biblical information, I hope that all readers, and particularly those who share my Christian commitment, may realize the substantial disparity between the biblical mandates and contemporary Christian practice. I hope, too, that all may be challenged to address the issues of stewardship of material possessions in their own lives, joyfully, not out of a gloomy sense of externally imposed guilt, but in recognition that a large part of our world today, not least within the church, may well be called to repent of past apathy and self-centred indulgence. In fact, whether or not one adopts the agendas of the so-called 'left' or 'right', the increasingly acute needs of the poor worldwide, including hundreds of millions of poor *Christians*, may well demand nothing less than a significant change of spending priorities on the part of many affluent Westerners.

# Chapter One

# The Old Testament and material possessions: the historical books

## From Eden to Sinai

Both Jews and Christians have consistently viewed the period from creation to God's giving the Law to Moses as the first major era in history. The biblical account of this era spans from Genesis 1 to Exodus 19. This material, in turn, subdivides into three discrete sections. Genesis 1 – 11 narrates the creation of the world and primeval human history, highlighting in particular the fall of humanity into sin. Genesis 12 – 50 forms the patriarchal narratives, in which God begins to fashion a uniquely chosen people, the Israelites, by promising the land of Canaan and its blessings to Abraham and his offspring. Through this people, spiritual and material blessing would ultimately flow to all the world (Gen. 12:3). Exodus describes the fledgling people of God enslaved in Egypt and narrates their liberation under Moses' leadership, roughly 400 years later. Chapter 19 ends with the Israelites' arrival at Mount Sinai, from which God would reveal his Law and inaugurate a covenant with the people of Israel that would remain in force until the coming of Messiah.

Of all the major periods of Old Testament history, this first one discloses the least amount of detail about the role of material possessions in the life of God's people, but it does present several foundational principles that dare not be overlooked. We may survey this material under the three headings corresponding to the three periods of time just noted.[1]

## *Genesis 1 – 11*

The most important observation about the material world to emerge

---

[1] The theological emphases of the 'historical' material in the Pentateuch are generally agreed upon irrespective of one's analysis of the literary forms or tradition history of the constituent elements. Nevertheless, there is support for the use of very ancient (*i.e.*, pre-Mosaic) sources throughout Genesis (Garrett 1991; Wiseman 1977) and increasing evidence for the historicity of major swathes of the patriarchal narratives (Millard & Wiseman 1980; Hess, Satterthwaite & Wenham 1993).

from the creation account in Genesis 1 is that God initially created it good. Seven times throughout the chapter, after each major stage of creation, the refrain recurs, 'and God saw that it was good' (Gen. 1:4, 10, 12, 18, 21, 25, 31). The blessing and abundance of the garden were created for humans to enjoy. This emphasis contrasts sharply with beliefs in various other ancient religions, most notably in later Hellenistic thought, that the material world was corrupt from its inception (C. Wright 1995: 181–187). In distinction from the rest of the created order, God fashions humans uniquely in his own image (1:26–27) and gives them dominion, or stewardship, over all the earth (1:26, 28).

> Because man is created in God's image, he is king over nature. He rules the world on God's behalf. This is of course no license for the unbridled exploitation and subjugation of nature. Ancient oriental kings were expected to be devoted to the welfare of their subjects, especially the poorest and weakest members of society (Wenham 1987: 33).

Again, unlike many Greco-Roman religions, Judaism and Christianity portray work as part of God's good design for his people from the outset of human history.

As the only part of creation fashioned in God's image, humans are far more than simply the most advanced species of animal. The immediate context of Genesis never defines what the image of God involves, although the concepts of dominion over creation and differentiation by gender appear juxtaposed with it. Jews and Christians alike have therefore regularly associated image-bearing with ruling over God's material world and having a qualitatively unique capacity for interpersonal relationships, with the most perfect and intimate approximation of relationships within the Godhead being modelled in human marriage.[2] The fall of humanity into sin (Gen. 3), Cain's murder of Abel (Gen. 4) and the destruction of most of the human race in the flood (Gen. 6 – 8) demonstrate how corrupt God's image in persons quickly became. And as part of God's judgment against Adam, work now proved burdensome (3:17–19). But the prohibition against murder and the introduction of capital punishment as its penalty in Genesis 9:5–6 show that the image of God still remains even in fallen humanity:

[2] For an excellent Jewish discussion, see Sarna (1991b).

'Whoever sheds human blood,
　　by human beings shall their blood be shed;
for in the image of God
　　has God made all people.'

(Gen. 9:6)

The New Testament continues to affirm that all people are born with God's likeness (Jas. 3:9) and understands the process of redemption to correspond to the renewal of the image of God in a person (Col. 3:10; cf. Eph. 4:24). Thus, a crucial requirement for the *imago Dei* also involves our capacity for a relationship with God that is shared by no other life-form (Wilson & Blomberg 1993).

Two opposite, extreme applications of this theology must both be avoided. On the one hand, humanity must never be reduced to the *merely* material. Modern ideologies that protest against 'speciesism' either ignore or reject this biblical distinction. On the other hand, the dominion over creation granted to humans does not confer on them the right to rape the environment or to show cruelty to animals, but gives them the responsibility to take care of all of the rest of the created order.[3]

## Genesis 12 – 50

As God singles out one individual, Abram, to become, as it were, the father of a new country, he promises him,

'I will make you into a great nation
　　and I will bless you;
I will make your name great,
　　and you will be a blessing.
I will bless those who bless you,
　　and whoever curses you I will curse;
and all peoples on earth
　　will be blessed through you.'

(Gen. 12:2–3)

These promises, with some variation in wording, are repeated throughout Genesis (esp. 12:7; 15:18; 17:8; 22:17), not only to Abram,

---

[3] The whole issue of ecology and the environment lies outside the scope of this volume, but there are many principles transferable from the stewardship of material possessions to the stewardship of the earth. For representative, balanced study, see Young (1994); Granberg-Michaelson (1987).

but to his son Isaac and grandson Jacob. Early on, 13:2 describes how wealthy Abram became as the first provisional fulfilment of this promise. The rest of the book of Genesis unfolds as a narrative of the various steps and obstacles to inheriting the promise, including the important material portion of that promise, the land of Canaan (Clines 1978). Along the way, the riches amassed by the patriarchs are highlighted several times (cf. 20:14–16; 24:35; 26:13; 30:43; 47:27). Abraham, Isaac and Jacob all take turns sojourning in Canaan, but none is allowed to remain there permanently. Jacob's son Joseph, because of the treachery of his brothers, finds himself in Egypt, even in prison. But ultimately God blesses him materially, too, as Pharaoh makes him second in command in all the land.

The wealth of the patriarchs must therefore be understood within its clear covenantal context. This wealth is tied directly to God's plan to give his people a special land. In the Christian era, in which believers do not live in a uniquely promised land, we must take care not to assume that wealth necessarily, or even frequently, represents God's blessing.[4] What is more, Genesis also consistently stresses that the patriarchs gave generously of their wealth. Abram allows Lot to choose the more fertile land (Gen. 13). This act 'is recognized by most commentators as being set out as a model for his descendants to imitate' (Wenham 1987: 299), given the Lord's immediate confirmation that he will make what is left for Abram into the land of divine promise (cf. Gen. 13:1–13 with 13:14–18). After defeating five kings of Canaan in battle, Abram gives a tithe of his spoil to the high priest of Salem, Melchizedek (14:20), and refuses to accept any possessions that would enable the king of Sodom to boast that he made Abram rich (14:23).[5]

Jacob's mixed track record of obedience to God scarcely makes him an exemplary model of receiving riches as a reward for faithfulness, although Genesis 31:38–42 does remind us of the extent of his sacrifice in working for Laban.[6] More noteworthy, however, are Jacob's lavish gifts to his estranged brother Esau (32:13–16), intended as an informal

---

[4] Kidner (1967: 35) adds that the exceptional blessings of the patriarchs are perhaps 'a fleeting foretaste of the general blessing which was promised to come to them in the end: nothing less than the lifting of the curse and the undoing of the Fall'.

[5] V. Hamilton (1990: 413–414) observes that Abram's tithe is a gift and not an obligation and that his subsequent refusal of gifts follows royal etiquette closely paralleled at Ugarit.

[6] Wenham (1994: 278) comments that 31:42 is a 'summary of the whole story of Jacob's life, at least in Harran,' and that 'here Jacob confesses that his preservation and his wealth are all due to God's power overriding the meanness of his uncle Laban; the Lord is a God who enriches his people even in their oppression'.

peace-offering and thus given partly in the interest of self-preservation. These gifts nevertheless testify to Jacob's generosity with the riches he had amassed. In 33:11 Jacob declares, 'God has been gracious to me and I have all I need.'

Finally, Joseph comes to power in Egypt precisely to be a good steward of its rich grain harvests in preparation for the years of famine ahead (Gen. 41). But he had previously also languished in prison through no fault of his own. Joseph's distribution efforts during that famine demonstrate one early fulfilment of God's promise that his people would prove a blessing to the nations: 'And all the countries came to Egypt to buy grain from Joseph, because the famine was severe in all the world' (41:57).[7]

The preservation of the patriarchs throughout Genesis 12 – 50 is never an end in itself, or primarily a response to their levels of obedience to God, but rather God's sovereign method of fulfilling his promises to gather a unique people together in a unique land. Those promises seem to be in jeopardy as the book of Genesis closes, but the next major stage in bringing them to fulfilment will comprise the story-line of the second book of the Pentateuch, Exodus.

## Exodus 1 – 19

As the centuries passed, a new king arose 'who did not know about Joseph' (Exod. 1:8). The harsh labour inflicted on God's people stemmed from this change in pharaohs and was unrelated to any change in the Israelites' obedience.[8] The bulk of the first half of Exodus, of course, tells the story of the liberation of God's people under the leadership of Moses. The exodus forms a prominent theme in many modern liberation theologies, and it provides an important corrective for those who think of 'salvation' in either Testament as solely 'spiritual.'[9] Still, Exodus is clear that this liberation is holistic. Physically oppressed people are being physically liberated, but with an unambiguous spiritual objective – to let everyone know that Yahweh alone is God (Exod. 6:7;

[7] V. Hamilton (1995: 513) sees Joseph as an antitype of Noah, adding, 'the storehouses of Joseph ... are for the survival of the masses', as the famine threatens the whole of the Middle East.

[8] Pleins (1994: 283–284) stresses that the distinction between Israel's good fortune under Joseph and bad fortune later is due to the difference between good and bad pharaohs, not between one illegitimate form of government and another divinely ordained one.

[9] For an entire commentary on Exodus from a liberationist perspective, see Pixley (1987). *Cf.* also Croatto (1981), who relies on Exodus to develop 'a hermeneutics of freedom'.

9:16) and to create a covenant community of followers who will serve him by obeying his laws (Exod. 20 – 40). *Contra* much liberation theology, the people of Israel do not stay and revolt, but leave for a new land to which God has called them.[10] And Exodus 13 introduces the consecration of the firstborn, beginning a tradition of giving that which is most valuable as an offering to the Lord. We may not keep and do as we please with all the good gifts God has given us.

Plundering the Egyptians shows that God wants his people to go into their new land with a measure of wealth (Exod. 11:2–3; 12:35–36). Some of this wealth would later be used to build the tabernacle. But it is this very cache of precious metals that also quickly lures the Israelites into idolatry. While Moses is receiving the Law on Mount Sinai, Aaron is leading the people below in fashioning the golden calf (32:1–6). In fact, the dominant method of providing physical sustenance for God's people in the desert prevents them from becoming too well off. Introduced in 16:16–18 is the daily provision of manna. Individuals will collect varying amounts, based on their abilities, but God will ensure that no-one ever has too much or too little.[11] Exodus 16:19–21 demonstrates that hoarding proves impossible; the manna simply spoils. But verses 22–30 show God's miraculous provision on the sixth day of the week so that the food can be preserved over the Sabbath, and the people will not have to work by collecting their food on that day. Both of these phenomena ensure that they will remain wholly dependent on God for their needs, although not all of the people immediately accept these stipulations (16:20, 27–30). As Durham (1987: 226) summarizes,

> Yahweh provides for physical needs each day, only to have some of his people attempt to hoard for the next day. Yahweh provides for the spiritual growth of his people by setting one day apart as special, only to have some lose the benefit by ignoring the day.

Of course, this arrangement is temporary, even in the history of Israel. It ceases with their entry into Canaan (Josh. 5:12). But the apostle Paul, centuries later, will find timeless truths here about avoiding extremes of

---

[10] A point Lohfink (1987: 51) argues is not really accounted for in most liberation theologians' uses of the exodus. It is not always observed in other brands of theology either!

[11] It is not clear if this 'evening out' takes place miraculously, or if the text means simply that the Israelites 'pooled the manna collected, and each kept the agreed ration of an omer per head' (Cole 1973: 132). The rabbis usually assumed the former; since Calvin, the latter has increasingly proved popular.

riches or poverty in the Christian community as richer believers share with poorer ones (2 Cor. 8:15). We are reminded also of the fourth petition of the Lord's Prayer: 'Give us today our *daily* bread' (Matt. 6:11), and of Jesus' warning to let the day's own trouble be sufficient for the day (Matt. 6:34 and par.).

## From Sinai to Canaan: the Law of Moses

From the middle of Exodus to the end of Deuteronomy, the compiler of the Pentateuch narrates the Israelites' wilderness sojourn. Into this historical framework, he inserts major sections dealing with the laws God gave his people in the covenant at Sinai.[12] The Mosaic Law will form the legal charter for the children of Israel from this point forward until the coming of Messiah. New Testament writers consistently maintain that the Law is fulfilled in Jesus, who is that Messiah (*e.g.*, Matt. 5:17; Luke 24:27, 44; Gal. 6:2; Col. 2:17; Heb. 8). No command issued to Old Testament followers of Yahweh necessarily carries over into the Christian era unchanged, but every command reflects principles at some level that are binding on Christians (2 Tim. 3:16; *cf.* Klein, Blomberg & Hubbard 1993: 278–283). With respect to laws affecting material possessions, one may distinguish two somewhat balancing themes within the Torah. On the one hand, the ownership of property enshrines a fundamental Judeo-Christian value. On the other hand, numerous safeguards relativize turning the ownership of property into an absolute value or into an excuse for selfishness. Tellingly, this second theme finds far more detailed elaboration than the first. Our survey of both themes can only highlight main passages because of the pervasiveness of the relevant legal material.[13]

---

[12] Tradition criticism, of course, regularly debates the origins of all these laws, assigning various portions to dates anywhere from the time of Moses to the post-exilic era. Certain lines of historical development of the legal material can then be postulated, often based on perceived discrepancies among laws on a similar topic. While there is no doubt that Deuteronomy often revises earlier Pentateuchal legislation to prepare the Israelites for sedentary existence in their land and anticipates events of later centuries, we see no reason to engage in the standard tradition-critical speculation here. The second millennium BC treaty form argues for a very early historical core for Deuteronomy, and the book itself regularly presupposes and reuses the preceding four 'books of Moses' (*cf.* LaSor, Hubbard & Bush 1996: 9, 116–117; Dillard & Longman 1994: 47–48). At any rate, as background for a New Testament theology of material possessions, what counts is the theological unity of the Torah widely perceived in Judaism by the time of Jesus.

[13] For a thorough study, see C. Wright (1990), who stresses how God intends Israel's relationship to the land to be a paradigm of human stewardship of the whole earth. For the close relationship between property and individual families, see Westbrook (1991).

## Ownership of property

The very fact that God has promised Israel the land of Canaan, with its abundant natural resources, demonstrates his commitment to providing the blessings of the material world as a pre-eminent, good gift for his people (see, e.g., Num. 14:8; Deut. 6:3; 8:18). Numbers 26:52–56 further demonstrates the principle that all families and clans should receive an allotment of property proportionate to their size. In other words, 'to a larger group give a larger inheritance, and to a smaller group a smaller one; each is to receive its inheritance according to the number of those listed' (Num. 26:54; cf. Josh. 13 – 19).[14] This ideal contrasts markedly with arrangements in other feudal kingdoms near Canaan in that day, in which by far the more common pattern was the concentration of vast tracts of land among the royal and aristocratic elites, leaving a majority of the people in considerable poverty (Brueggemann 1975: 354). At the same time, a text like Leviticus 25:23 reminded the Israelites that all their possessions ultimately belonged to the Lord and were merely leased to the people so that they might be good stewards of them.

The Ten Commandments themselves stress the immorality of theft and covetousness (Exod. 20:15, 17), and these short prohibitions are considerably expanded elsewhere in the Law (e.g., Exod. 22:1–15). Related laws designed to preserve private property intact include the regulation of boundaries of fields (Deut. 19:14; 27:17); the insistence on inheritance rights, particularly for the firstborn (Deut. 21:15–17); the importance of preserving honest scales in weighing produce during community transactions (Lev. 19:35–36); and the injunction against accepting bribes (Exod. 23:8; Deut. 16:19). In addition, there is a long history of Christian interpretation of the sixth commandment (against theft) as applying also to the excessively rich, inasmuch as they are stealing from the poor who have no access even to a basic standard of living (Gnuse 1985: ix).

The various Mosaic laws on ownership of property stand behind the Western ideal of every family being able to purchase its own plot of land, but this ideal cuts in two different directions. Those already possessing property are entitled to protect it, but they must continue to work for opportunities for all others to own property and take care lest

---

[14] Numbers 26:55–56 insists, however, that the division shall be by lot. Commentators who assume that the editor of this paragraph did not see the two points as flatly contradictory usually resolve the tension by assuming that the area of the land for each tribe was decided by lot, 'whereas the size of the tribal inheritance within that general area was proportional' (Ashley 1993: 538).

their own use of capital stand in the way of this good or even exploit the less well-to-do (Hartley 1992: 448). The sociology of the law codes in ancient Israel has been summarized thus: 'In such a society private property is never used to oppress the neighbor, or as is the case in a capitalistic order of society, as means to come to more property. Instead it is used generously to entertain guests and to help the poor' (von Waldow & Eberhard 1970: 186). Unlike neighbouring cultures, Israel's law tended to place a higher priority on people than on property or social class (Gnuse 1985: 31).

## Safeguards relativizing the ownership of property

Numerous additional sections of the Mosaic Law advanced the theme that property rights might not be considered absolute. Indeed, the entire system of offering unblemished animals as sacrifices served as a reminder of the costliness of sin (*cf.* Exod. 34:26 on the principle of firstfruits). The Israelites had to give up something of substantial economic value to secure their atonement. But in addition to this general system, we may focus on four more specific types of laws that relativized property rights: 1. laws against interest; 2. days and years of rest (Sabbath, sabbatical year and Jubilee); 3. taxes, tithes and offerings; and 4. other laws concerned with justice for the poor.

### Laws against interest

Three specific passages forbid Israelites to loan money to one another at interest: Exodus 22:25–27; Leviticus 25:35–37; and Deuteronomy 23:19–20.[15] Two difficult interpretive questions surround these three texts. The terms in Hebrew translated 'interest' or 'usury' (*nešek* and *tarbît* – from 'bite' and 'increase', respectively) have been taken either as referring to any kind of interest on any kind of loan or as merely prohibiting *excessive* interest (NIV mg.).[16] The ancient Jewish and Christian commentators until the 1500s uniformly interpreted these texts as prohibiting all charging of interest (Gordon 1982; Nelson 1949). But by the time of the Reformation, European economic systems had become sufficiently 'capitalist' that these laws no longer seemed

---

[15] The Elephantine papyri and other Jewish literature show that the Jews at times broke their own laws.

[16] Hebrew scholars, however, are largely agreed on the former interpretation. Where they disagree is over the significance of the individual terms. Some think *nešek* refers to interest deducted before a loan is granted, while *tarbît* refers to an additional sum beyond the principal repaid to the creditor (so *e.g.*, Neufeld 1955 and S. Stein 1953). Others see *nešek* as interest on any kind of loan, particularly of money, with *tarbît* as interest on loans of food (so, *e.g.*, Gamoran 1971 and Loewenstamm 1969).

enforceable. More recent commentators who have tried to tone down the prohibition probably reflect this frustration with implementing such bans in contemporary society rather than an accurate explication of the texts' original intent. Either way, Maloney (1974) notes that Israel was unique among its neighbours in adopting any prohibition against interest and gives examples of the exorbitant interest rates of other Ancient Near Eastern cultures.

In Deuteronomy 23:20, however, the text itself makes one exception to the prohibition against interest-taking. This exception played a significant role in the history of Judaism and, indeed, fostered severe anti-Semitism in later medieval Europe: Israel was allowed to charge interest on a loan to a foreigner! This distinction suggests a third possible interpretation of the laws against usury. Ancient Israel prior to the monarchy formed almost exclusively a peasant and agricultural society and rarely entered into internal commercial loans. Rather, commercial loans in Israel would have been drawn up almost always in the context of trade with other more mercantile nations. Internally, loans were granted primarily, if not exclusively, to the poor. Commentators have regularly concluded, therefore, that God wanted to distinguish between the economics of the business world and the principles God's people employ in lending to each other (Porteous 1966: 31). Churches to this day in various countries of the world sometimes insist on interest-free loans between Christian organizations, even as they acknowledge the legitimacy of moderate interest rates in banking and business.[17] At any rate, the Exodus and Leviticus passages clearly refer to not hurting the poor, so however one interprets this legislation, loans and their repayments must never worsen the plight of the destitute. Sadly, on both personal and international levels today, this is often precisely what does occur, as poor individuals and countries incur greater and greater debts that become ever harder to service.

## Sabbath, sabbatical year and Jubilee

Once a week, the Sabbath was to be a day on which the Israelites performed no work. Similarly, one year in seven was to be a sabbatical year of rest, and after forty-nine years the Israelites were supposed to celebrate a Jubilee year with added distinctives. Clearly each of these institutions limited the amount of material possessions one could

---

[17] *Cf.* Sarna (1991a: 139). Ballard (1994) goes farther and tries to find ways Christians can avoid all interest-taking situations, believing that usury remains as sinful as ever. But he fails adequately to address the hermeneutical issues involved in moving from an Old Testament agrarian world to our globally interconnected, capitalist context.

accumulate, simply by shortening the length of time one was allowed to work (Exod. 23:12). Additionally, while workers rested and fields lay fallow, the poor were allowed to glean from the crops that remained in the field (Lev. 19:9–10; 23:22). The farmers and their families were also allowed to eat from the residual growth of the fields during the fallow year (Exod. 23:10–11; cf. Lev. 25:1–7). These laws were relatively unparalleled in the Ancient Near East and thus marked Israel off as a distinctive people and potentially less productive in comparison with the 'competition'.[18]

The origins of the Sabbath of course go back to the days of creation. Just as God rested on the seventh day, so his people must cease from labour at the end of each week (Exod. 20:8–11). The origin of the sabbatical year is less certain. At first it may have corresponded to the seventh year from when any individual farm was first cultivated (C. Wright 1984: 130–131). Exodus 23:10–11 could be so interpreted. But in the legislation in Leviticus, the years are apparently to be coordinated nationwide (Lev. 25:1–7). Leviticus 25:21–22 further recalls the principles associated with God's provision of manna in the wilderness: 'I will send you such a blessing in the sixth year that the land will yield enough for three years. While you plant during the eighth year, you will eat from the old crop and will continue to eat from it until the harvest of the ninth year comes in.' Once again God's people are encouraged to trust him for their sustenance and not to attempt to hoard or accumulate wealth for the long term (Gerstenberger 1996: 376).

Besides affording rest and limiting material accumulation, the sabbatical years offered opportunities for the freeing of Hebrew servants, who because of debt had sold themselves into slavery to their own kinsmen (Exod. 21:1–11; Deut. 15:12–18). One way in which Deuteronomy 15 clearly goes beyond Exodus is in insisting that the freed slave should not be sent away empty-handed (15:13).[19] Because the fledgling nation of Israel was at first composed exclusively of freed slaves, it was not to tolerate permanent slavery in its midst. Closely related is the cancellation of debt (Deut. 15:1–11). Some writers think that debts were merely postponed during sabbatical years, since the land

---

[18] Hartley (1992: 445) comments: 'Greed prevents a person from enjoying what he has, for it drives one to spend all one's energy on getting more. Conversely, if a person can learn to live with what one has and to take periodic times of rest away from work, that person has time to enjoy and appreciate what one has gained with a thankful attitude.' For a study of the calendar of ancient sabbatical years, see Wacholder (1973–74).

[19] For the various options of relating the different manumission laws in the Torah, see Japhet (1986).

was not tilled, making it difficult to earn further income (*e.g.*, C. Wright 1984: 136; Craigie 1976: 236). But the text reads more naturally as referring to cancellation, and this is the way the ancient rabbis understood it as well. The Deuteronomy 15 passage does not refer to any point after the seven years at which repayment resumes, and the concern that some might not grant a loan to a needy person because the sabbatical year loomed near (15:9) makes little sense if the debt repayment was merely postponed rather than cancelled (Merrill 1994a: 243; Mayes 1979: 247–248). Parallels in more urban, 'capitalist', Ancient Near Eastern societies demonstrate that the principle of cancelling part or all of the debts of the poor was not limited either to Israel or to this period of history (J. Hamilton 1992: 45–72; for the hermeneutical moves and timeless principles necessary to determine contemporary applications, see pp. 139–158).

Deuteronomy 15 also discloses an interesting progression from the idealistic to the realistic. In verse 4, we read, 'However, there *should* be no poor among you, for in the land the LORD your God is giving you to possess as your inheritance, he will richly bless you.' But verse 5 acknowledges that this blessing is contingent on obedience, while verse 7 recognizes the possibility that poverty will remain: '*If* there are poor among your people in any of the towns of the land that the LORD your God is giving you ...' And because Israel never fully obeys, by verse 11 the writer declares flatly: 'There *will* always be poor people in the land.' But far from offering any excuse for not helping the poor, this verse goes on immediately to command God's people 'to be open-handed towards those of your people who are poor and needy in your land'.[20]

The celebration of the Jubilee year is shrouded in obscurity.[21] On the one hand, Leviticus 25:8–55 outlines in considerable detail the stipulations related to it (and *cf.* the passing reference in Num. 36:4). But it is uncertain whether this special sabbatical year was ever observed. Leviticus 26:35–36, 43 and 2 Chronicles 36:21 suggest that the land was never able to 'enjoy' its sabbaths until the Jews went into exile. Jeremiah 34:8–16 describes a proclamation of freedom for slaves in conjunction with a sabbatical year, but both were quickly rescinded.

---

[20] Houston (1995: 307–308) notes a consensus, with which he agrees, that sees these verses as fundamentally contradictory, but it is not at all obvious why this should be so. For the logic of this entire paragraph, see Tigay (1996: 146–147).

[21] Hartley (1992: 427–430, 430–431) has helpful excursuses on the origins of the Jubilee and on its relationship with the texts on fallow years and freeing slaves. Fleming (1995: 145) gives evidence for a similar festival at Emar.

1 Maccabees 6:49 and 53 refer to the practice of the sabbatical year in the second century BC (cf. the earlier promise in Neh. 10:31), but no comparable text ever refers to the celebration of the Jubilee, even in the intertestamental period (see Fager 1993: 34–36 for other relevant evidence).[22]

Whenever it took place, however, the Israelites were to 'proclaim liberty throughout the land' (Lev. 25:10), a call which was enshrined on the American liberty bell still housed in Philadelphia, and which was highly influential in the revolution against Great Britain. Ironically, some of the most stalwart contemporary defenders of American freedom miss entirely the larger context in which this proclamation is embedded and the distinct significance of the Jubilee. Here, if ever, is the ultimate relativization of private property. On average, each person or family had at least a once-in-a-lifetime chance to start afresh, no matter how irresponsibly they had handled their finances or how far into debt they had fallen. At first glance, the freedoms granted in each sabbatical year seem to render the Jubilee legislation unnecessary. But it may well be that the bulk of Leviticus 25 deals with more serious situations than were covered by the sabbatical years. Chirichigno (1993: 351–542) discerns four increasingly severe stages of deprivation dealt with in this chapter (cf. also Levine 1989: 175–181). In Leviticus 25:25–34, the debtors sell part of their land. In verses 35–38, they become dependent on charity or interest-free loans from others. Verses 39–40 find them selling themselves as hired workers, though not as slaves, to fellow Israelites. But in verses 47–54, they sell themselves with their families to foreigners. Throughout, these verses describe a variety of options for 'redemption' (the buying of a slave's freedom). But even if none of these occurs, 'they and their children are to be released in the Year of Jubilee' (Lev. 25:54).

The possibility that the Jubilee was rarely, if ever, implemented makes it no less God's will for Old Testament times. While not applicable in all its detail to Christians in the New Testament age, New Testament allusions to the Jubilee (esp. Luke 4:16–21) demonstrate that certain principles underlying this legislation still remain in force (C. Wright 1995: 197–212), and these challenge all major, modern economic models. The Jubilee suggests 'a sharp critique of a) statism which disregards the precious treasure of personal rootage, and b)

---

[22] Also unclear is whether the fiftieth year that was to be consecrated was the same year as the seventh sabbatical year (in a sequence of forty-nine years, counted inclusively) or was part (so, e.g., Hoenig 1969) or all (so, e.g., the Talmud) of a second consecutive sabbatical year.

untrammelled individualism which secures individuals at the expense of the community' (Brueggemann 1975: 360).[23] It supports the family, unites worship and social concern, and reminds one that ultimately all property belongs to the Lord. The principles of sabbatical year and Jubilee further stress the major threat to social good that debt creates (Hartley 1992: 444), a threat which remains at least as insidious today.

*Taxes, tithes and offerings*
The number and origin of the Jewish tithes are also somewhat cloaked in mystery. Leviticus 27:30–33 mandates that a tenth of all the produce of one's land and all of one's flocks should be given to the Lord. Numbers 18:8–32 explains that these offerings were to be given to the Levites (see esp. 18:21), who otherwise had no source of income, and who in turn would tithe to the priests (18:26–28). Even 'full-time religious workers' were subject to the laws of tithing.[24] In Deuteronomy 14:22–29, a tithe of one's produce and flocks was to be eaten at the central sanctuary, or, if transportation proved prohibitive, exchanged for currency, which could then be used to purchase foodstuffs at the place the Lord would choose for his central dwelling. Every third year, however, the tithes would go to the local storehouses so that they could be distributed not just to the Levites but also to other poor and marginalized people: 'the aliens, the fatherless and the widows' (Deut. 14:29). Ahlström (1993: 666) defends the view that the cult centres were administrative tax-collection centres during the monarchy. Deuteronomy 26:12–15 reproduces for the most part these same provisions in abbreviated form. Originally, there may have been only one tithe intended (Craigie 1976: 233–234), but the harmonizing Jewish mind-set quickly solved the apparent contradictions between the passages by identifying at least two separate offerings. And by New Testament times, most Jews had come to interpret the every-third-year offering for the poor as above and beyond the other two tithes (Tobit 1:7–8; Josephus, *Antiquities* 4.8.22). Pro-rated annually, these added up to a 23.3% 'tithe'.[25] Of course, 10% apparently went to one's own festival

---

[23] *Cf.* also Wenham (1979: 323–324): the Jubilee principles oppose equally 'the monopolistic tendencies of unbridled capitalism and thorough-going communism'; and North (1954: 175): 'Where communism decrees "None shall have property", Leviticus decrees, "None shall lose property;" but both are against unhealthy latifundism.'

[24] Contrast R. Allen (1990: 857): 'There is a tendency, then and now, for persons to believe that if their lives are spent in the Lord's work, then they are exempt from contributing to that work.'

[25] For more detail on these various tithe laws and their relation to one another, see esp. McConville (1984: 68–87).

celebration, a further reminder that God does not require unmitigated asceticism.

A different type of tax appears in Exodus 30:13. Moses commands the Israelites that, after crossing the Jordan and occupying the Promised Land, they must each contribute half a shekel to be used for the service of the tabernacle (cf. also 30:16). Here is a flat tax that is not a percentage of one's income, a tax which verse 15a stresses should be identical for rich and poor. A fixed-rate tax symbolizing atonement for one's life (30:15b) suggests the equality of all persons before God (Durham 1987: 403). After the construction of the temple under Solomon centuries later, this tax would become annual and be used to care for God's holy house in Jerusalem (2 Chr. 24:6–9). In Nehemiah's day, as the temple was being rebuilt, the tax is described as a third of a shekel (Neh. 10:32), perhaps due to variation in the value of the currency. By New Testament times, the half-shekel tax would be roughly equivalent to two days' wages (i.e. two denarii). Reference to this tax appears in Matthew 17:24–27. The flat rate ensured that even the poorest, who might not be required to give nearly so much via the various tithes, would have to give sacrificially at least here. It also reminds us that some disparity in economic status remained even during the wilderness wanderings (Cassuto 1967: 394).

A summary of all the taxes and tithes prescribed at one point or another in ancient Israel is somewhat staggering: forced labour under the monarchy, royal taxation, emergency tribute in wartime, the temple tax, the gleaning to be left during sabbatical and Jubilee years, firstfruits and other voluntary offerings, and the mandatory 'triple tithe' (for details and references, see Oden 1984). One can hardly claim that God's people were free to enjoy unbridled prosperity from their material resources. Still, the juxtaposition of a tithe one could consume oneself in celebration and community alongside the offering for the poor points out a balance even in this seemingly burdensome legislation (Gitlin 1963: 579–580). As for the unlikelihood that one's family could consume 10% of a year's produce or its equivalent at one feast, Douglas Meeks (1989: 88) reminds us, 'the abundance of the feast is meant for sharing with the stranger and sojourner, as well as the widow, the orphan, and the servants'.

*Other laws concerned with justice for the poor*
Numerous other commandments throughout the Pentateuch demonstrate God's concern for the needy. The practice of gleaning was based on

God's laws that farmers should not continue to harvest their fields to gather all the leftovers, but should allow the poor to come and collect what the harvesters missed on their first trip through (see, *e.g.*, Lev. 19:9–10; Deut. 24:19–22). Meeks (1989: 87) observes, 'Gleaning rights are not voluntary acts of charity of the rich toward the poor; they are the poor's right to livelihood.' On the other hand, Deuteronomy 23:24–25 protects the farmer from others who might try to glean too much too quickly.

Second, numerous passages require God's people not to mistreat the foreigner or alien in their midst. Exodus 22:21; 23:9 and Leviticus 19:33–34 explicitly support this command by appealing to the fact that the Israelites were aliens in Egypt. Frequently, the alien is grouped with other paradigms of powerlessness in the Ancient Near East – the widow, the orphan and the poor in general (*e.g.* Deut. 14:29; 16:11, 14; 26:12, 13). Indeed, virtually all the cultures surrounding Israel agreed that these kinds of people should be cared for. Patterson (1973: 233) wonders if the early predominance of similar legislation in antiquity 'might not have been a primeval reflection of God's own self-disclosure as being the Redeemer of the helpless. Its very antiquity may be accounted for because it speaks of man's helpless position before God right from the beginning. '

Additional texts on the theme of the alien include Numbers 15:15 (apply the same laws to the Israelite as to the alien), Deuteronomy 10:17–18 (God shows no partiality) and 24:17–22 (do not deprive aliens of justice).[26] In our contemporary world, in which governments make the distinction between legal and illegal aliens, Christians are polarized and emotions run high as to what responsibility, if any, governments or churches have toward the illegals. It seems arguable, however, that because God uniquely bequeathed the land of Canaan to the Israelites, in a manner unlike his allotment of the lands of any other nations, all aliens at one level were illegals. So, without necessarily calling into question the wisdom of modern distinctions between legal and illegal aliens for legislative purposes,[27] it would seem unconscionable that any *Christian* should ever support efforts to withhold basic human services from the neediest in any land, regardless of their country of origin (*cf.* Olson 1986).

Third, a 'sliding scale' for offerings and sacrifices was instituted (Lev. 5:7, 11; 12:8; 14:21–22). In other words, the poorest who could not

---

[26] For a thorough study of the alien in Israelite law, see van Houten (1991).

[27] *E.g.*, it would seem highly unpractical to do away with all regulations as to who could or could not emigrate from one country to another.

afford to sacrifice livestock such as sheep were permitted to replace them with doves or young pigeons. If even these proved prohibitive, an offering of fine flour could substitute.[28] Other laws that provided alternative means of compliance for the poor included the penalties for theft (Exod. 22:2), the payment of a vow (Lev. 27:8) and the celebration of the Passover (Exod. 12:4) (Brin 1994: 74–82).

Fourth, Deuteronomy 24:6 insisted that one could not take another person's livelihood as a pledge, that is, as collateral in a court of law. This verse speaks of a millstone; verses 12–13 refer to a cloak that a person needs to have for sleeping. 'Such equipment was absolutely essential to survival itself' (Merrill 1994a: 319). (One could require lesser deposits, however; cf. Exod. 22:25–27; Deut. 24:10–13.) For the same reason, wages had to be paid on time and not withheld (Lev. 19:13; Deut. 24:14–15). Workers often depended on their daily pay to provide food for themselves and their families on that very day.

Finally, impartiality, especially in the law courts, proved crucial. Leviticus 19:15 and Exodus 23:3 forbid partiality, not only in favour of the rich, as has been the temptation in most societies, but also in favour of the poor. These verses directly refute the slogan made famous by post-Vatican II theologians, especially of the liberationist stripe, that 'God has a preferential option for the poor.'[29] Reverse discrimination may be as immoral as the initial discrimination it seeks to rectify. None of this, however, necessarily commits one to opposing all forms of 'affirmative action', because it is arguable that a certain amount of apparent favouritism to the marginalized is needed in any society merely to create the *equal* opportunities for all that then enable laws against partiality to be implemented fairly.

## Conclusion

Because God intended Israel's Law to enlighten the nations (Deut. 4:5–8), its principles should find some application in all cultures. Christopher Wright (1993: 162–165) highlights four transcultural values of 'redeemed economics' which also helpfully summarize the major thrusts of the Law that we have surveyed above. First, there was to be shared access to the land and the use of its resources by the distribution to family, clan and tribe. Second, all able-bodied Israelites had the right and responsibility to be productive workers. Third, economic growth and material goods were both validated and put under careful constraint

---

[28] Wenham (1979: 100) and Hartley (1992: 69) note that the sacrifices referred to in these texts were obligatory rather than optional; hence, these provisions.

[29] A refutation repeatedly stressed throughout McGlasson (1994).

and critique. Finally, a major concern permeating the Law involved justice in the use and distribution of the products of the economic activity of God's people. With J. M. Hamilton (1992: 135–138), I would agree that the quality of this justice determines God's evaluation of any given society, inasmuch as God is the advocate of the powerless.

## In the Promised Land: cycles of obedience and disobedience

After the Pentateuch, the so-called historical books of the Old Testament cover the period of Israel's entrance into Canaan, the conquest and allotment of the land, the chaotic period of the judges, the united and divided monarchies, exile, the return to the land and the rebuilding of Jerusalem and its temple. The motif of material possessions *per se* does not dominate this material, but a major preoccupation certainly involves Israel's request to occupy the land in peace and prosperity. The governing theme of the 'Deuteronomistic' history that unites many of these books is that each generation will inherit God's promises to the extent that it obeys his covenant stipulations.[30]

As God's people completed their forty years of wilderness wanderings and prepared to enter Canaan to occupy the land that God had covenanted to give them, both promises and pitfalls lay before them. In the wilderness, they were forced to rely on God's miraculous provision; now they would enter a land rich enough in natural resources to tempt them to rely on themselves.

> Land folk want to pretend that life is not precarious and history is not contingent. In the land of sureness there are no risks to be taken, but only modest taxes to be paid. In the land of sameness there are no newnesses to be faced or hoped for but only institutions to honor. In the land of closedness there are no unexplained dimensions which may yet reach us, but only rituals to perform. There is only complacent self-indulgence or there is uneasy despair, or perhaps there are both (Brueggemann 1977: 58).

[30] Debates about the extent of the writing of the so-called 'Deuteronomic' historian and about whether the Chronicler is also responsible for Ezra and Nehemiah need not detain us here. The further along one proceeds in Old Testament history, the greater the number of scholars who are prepared to grant a substantial measure of historicity, at least to the major contours of the events narrated.

Or put more succinctly, 'the central temptation of the land is coveting' (Brueggemann 1977: 59).[31]

At the same time, obedience to God's laws could provide the Israelites collectively with great material prosperity (see, *e.g.*, Lev. 26:3–5, 9–10; Deut. 11:26–32; 28:1–14; 30:11–20; Josh. 8:30–35). Wealth *can* be a sign of God's blessing, even if it is not always related to an individual's or a nation's obedience. But the unique covenantal arrangements between God and Israel prevent us from generalizing and saying that God *must* materially reward his faithful people in other nations or eras. And, of course, one sad feature of biblical history is that throughout the Old Testament period more often than not Israel proved more faithless than faithful.[32]

Soon after entering the Promised Land, Achan's sin in hiding forbidden spoils from the battle of Jericho led to the defeat of the nation at the smaller Ai (Josh. 7). (Compare the episode with Saul failing to wait for Samuel and obey his orders in 1 Samuel 15.)[33] Later Hannah would recognize that

'The LORD sends poverty and wealth;
he humbles and he exalts.
He raises the poor from the dust
and lifts the needy from the ash heap.'

(1 Sam. 2:7–8)

This 'psalm' would prove influential in Mary's 'Magnificat' (Luke 1:46–55) centuries afterwards (*cf.* further Hoppe 1987: 43–45). But Hannah's grandsons would seek inappropriate profit from their work as judges, accepting bribes and perverting justice (1 Sam. 8:2–3), all of which led to the country's ill-advised request for a king (8:4–9). And the Israelites persisted in this request even after Samuel clearly

[31] A drastic rewriting of Israel's socio-economic history was made popular by Gottwald (1979), who saw the Israelite conquest of Canaan as a peasants' revolt, overthrowing great feudal city-states. But his model is highly speculative and receives little direct support from biblical or extra-biblical material, as is increasingly being recognized, even in very critical circles (*cf.* Lemche 1985 with T. Thompson 1994). For an evangelical summary and critique, see C. Wright (1995: 147–178).

[32] An excellent survey of six models of Old Testament thinking on the land appears in Habel (1995): a source of royal wealth and power, an undeserved gift from Yahweh, a domain promised to the ancestors, a personal allotment, an extended sanctuary and an inviting world of opportunity.

[33] The purpose of these 'bans' is not directly related to the goodness or wickedness of material possessions, except that 'God, not man, receives glory and profit' (Butler 1983: 71).

explained the personal and economic cost it would entail (8:10–22). 'Taxation, which had been unknown [sic], would become increasingly oppressive, until the people were virtually slaves, and cried out for liberation. But having made a deliberate choice of this form of government, Israel would have to live with its restricting demands' (Baldwin 1988: 85).

We turn, therefore, to the age of the monarchy. There is no doubt that Kings David and Solomon, and many of their successors, became enormously wealthy, in part due to their covenant faithfulness. But much of the lavish riches of the monarchy were bound up with the construction and operation of the temple, with its distinctive sacrificial cult, which is fulfilled and superseded in Christ (Heb. 4:14 – 5:10; 7:1 – 10:18) and thus not directly transferrable to Christian worship. Ironically, the post-Constantinian church, as exhibited in countless European cathedrals, often reverted back to this Old Testament model. Historically, Protestant places of worship have been far less lavish than Roman Catholic or Eastern Orthodox, although today's evangelical, suburban, Protestant subculture in the United States offers one major exception. Additionally, the passages speaking of the gifts given to furnish the temple, like the tabernacle before it, consistently stress the voluntary nature of the offerings (Exod. 25:2; 35:5; 1 Chr. 29:6, 14). Exodus 36:5 adds that the people were bringing more than enough.

Solomon's prayer of dedication makes it clear that a stunningly ornate temple appropriately testified to the world of God's majesty and covenant love (1 Kgs. 8:22–61), provisionally fulfilled in the Queen of Sheba's visit (1 Kgs. 10:1–13; cf. 10:23–25). Solomon also proves generous with his wealth (10:13).[34] Later when Joash would repair the temple, money was collected not for luxuries but only to pay the workers to make basic restorations (2 Kgs. 12:13–14). The integrity of this enterprise is stressed by the fact that no accountants were required (12:15; cf. 22:7 with similar repairs under Josiah).

Still, the wealth associated with the sacrificial cult brought both blessing and ruin. At its zenith in the final years of the united monarchy (see esp. 2 Chr. 8 – 9), 'the suggestion must be that as Solomon had been willing to channel these resources [wisdom and wealth] into the building of the temple, so now he was rewarded with an even greater abundance of these selfsame gifts' (Williamson 1982: 233). To his credit, Solomon did not seek wealth when God offered it to him but asked for wisdom instead (2 Chr. 1). Nevertheless, with his wealth,

[34] 'Solomon gives the queen tangible gifts to supplement the intellectual and spiritual gifts he has given her' (House 1995: 162).

much of it brought from foreign nations, came additional wives and concubines, who ultimately led Solomon into idolatry in his old age (1 Kgs. 11). The unrestrained lavishness of Solomon's court (1 Kgs. 4:20–28; 10:14–29) resembled the profligacy of other Ancient Near Eastern monarchs more than the divine ideal (Deut. 17:14–20, esp. 17:17). Material wealth clearly corrupted the first kings of the divided monarchy. Rehoboam's greed led him to alienate his people through increased forced labour, while Jeroboam repeated the sins of Aaron and the Israelites in the wilderness by fashioning *two* idolatrous golden calves (1 Kgs. 12:25–33). Later, Jehoshaphat imitated Solomon by becoming increasingly richer and more powerful as he devoted himself to the Lord (2 Chr. 17 – 18). But the powerful circles into which he was introduced (through an alliance with the ungodly king Ahaziah) eventually compromised his devotion (2 Chr. 20:35–37).

The little book of Ruth introduces us to a pair of marginalized women, Naomi and her daughter-in-law. The well-to-do Boaz proves to be a compassionate and generous rich man by leaving extra leftovers in his fields for the gleaners and by paying special courtesies to Ruth. No doubt, too, the price he paid to buy back Naomi's property and to acquire Ruth as his wife involved considerable sacrifice, explaining in part why the 'nearer kinsman' was unwilling to pay the needed amount (Ruth 4:6).[35] Centuries later, the Jewish girl Esther would rise from obscurity to wealth and power in Persia through no particular merit of her own, but to be the instrument of God's sovereignty in rescuing his people (book of Esther).

In striking contrast to all these characters, Ahab in 1 Kings 21:1–16 illustrates the depths to which the covetous can fall. Already reigning with far more wealth than he could ever want or need, he still tried to purchase the ancestral land of the neighbouring vineyard owner, Naboth, and then pouted when Naboth would not sell his property. Thus his wicked wife Jezebel had the man executed in order to acquire the land, flagrantly violating the principles of Leviticus 25 on ancestral lands remaining within families.[36] Elijah had already prayed for drought to demonstrate Yahweh's superiority over Ahab's and Jezebel's god Baal and had rescued the widow of Zarephath and her family from the

---

[35] For more on the economic practices presupposed in this book, see R. Hubbard 1988; for a creative retelling of the story, stressing more typical attitudes between rich and poor in situations parallel to Ruth's, see Wood (1996).

[36] 'With the loss of land would have gone the loss of position and before long Naboth and his posterity would have been reduced to the status of royal pensioners' (DeVries 1985: 256).

famine it caused (1 Kgs. 17; *cf.* the story of Elisha and the widow's oil in 2 Kgs. 4:1–7). Now he has to pronounce God's death-sentence on Ahab and Jezebel for their unbridled greed (1 Kgs. 21:17–24).

One may generalize from these examples and observe that as the loose confederacy of Israelite tribes turned into a familial monarchy under Saul, David and Solomon, and the divided kingdoms which followed them, the prophecies of 1 Samuel 8:11–18 were fulfilled. Kings would conscript the sons of Israel's families into their armies and take their servants and daughters to be perfumers, cooks and bakers. The monarchy would also co-opt the best of the fields, vineyards and groves of the land and demand a tenth of the produce and flocks, so that in essence God's people would become slaves of the king. The shift from an agrarian to an urban culture made Israel's economic profile resemble the surrounding nations: a greater disparity between 'haves' and 'have-nots', with large amounts of wealth concentrated in the hands of the few and the majority of the people eking out a subsistence-level income (Neufeld 1960). By Solomon's time, policies of taxation and servitude closely paralleled Egyptian practices (Redford 1972).

Eventually the divided kingdoms of Israel in the north and Judah in the south would both fall. First Assyria and then Babylon would send many of God's people into exile, and it was not until the sixth and fifth centuries BC that Jews under the Persian empire would be allowed to return to their ancestral homeland. Once again work on the temple would resume with great material wealth (Ezra 1 – 2). But the final passage from the historical books of significance for a survey of the Old Testament's teaching on material possessions sounds a different note. Ezra and Nehemiah have led the returning emigrés to rebuild both the temple and the walls of Jerusalem. Despite their attempt to amass as many provisions as possible, the temple is rebuilt on a much smaller scale than its Solomonic predecessor, and, commendably, Nehemiah pays much more attention to the poor. When he learns of the plight of the taxation and indebtedness of his countrymen (Neh. 5:1–6), he rebukes those who are charging interest and impoverishing fellow Jews (5:7–10). Specifically, Nehemiah commands them to return the pledges on mortgaged properties (5:11). The people respond with repentance, promising to redress the wrongs that they have committed (5:12–13). Nehemiah goes on to cite his exemplary model of caring for the poor by refusing to tax the people for his own personal luxury (5:14–19). In passing, this text shows that 'the lending of money was itself no evil; better that a man should be in debt than that he should have to beg his bread. Nehemiah shows no remorse for having been a money lender'

(Clines 1984: 166; *cf.* pp. 165–170 for the details of the economic arrangements here).[37] Instead, he focuses on the usury. The drastic circumstances require extreme measures; Nehemiah 10:31 will reflect a less temporary arrangement as the people promise to resume keeping Sabbaths and sabbatical years, complete with their cancellation of debt. Nehemiah's model, as governor, exceeding what was required by law, reminds us 'of the obvious truth that leadership means going further than those one is leading' (Williamson 1985a: 246). Christian leaders today need to model generosity in their giving, so that the average church-goer, whose offerings prove paltry in comparison, can see that greater sacrifice is both possible and necessary.

## Summary and conclusions

God created the material world wholly good but sin has corrupted it along with humanity. In the first stages of God's plan for redeeming his creation, he chose a man (Abram) from whose family would come a uniquely chosen nation (Israel) which was to be a blessing to all the world. God gave first the patriarchs and then the Israelites unique promises about enjoying a special land (Canaan) in prosperity whenever they obeyed him adequately. This arrangement was made with no other nation or people, and not until the time of Moses and the exodus would the Israelites even begin to approach the fulfilment of this promise.

At Sinai, God gave his people laws which would typify universal principles of liberty and justice. The right of families and clans to own property played a central role within this Law, but far more commonly enunciated were restrictions to prevent the abusing of this privilege. God was particularly concerned lest some of his people amass so much wealth that it became impossible for others, including foreigners, to receive the same blessing. With the later development of the monarchy, the gap between the 'haves' and the 'have-nots' grew, and more often than not those with wealth gained it at the expense of the powerless and needy in the land.

Clearly, even under the strictures of the Mosaic covenant, the data are too complex to conclude that material blessing is always a reward for obedience or poverty a punishment for disobedience. Wealth can turn

---

[37] But the NIV translation of Neh. 5:10 may mislead. Instead of 'let the exacting of usury stop' (*cf.* also 5:7, 11), Fensham translates, 'let us absolve this loan' (1982: 193). Presumably Nehemiah would not have commented on his own behaviour in this way if he himself had been breaking the laws against charging interest.

one's heart from the Lord, one may exploit the poor in order to gain it, or one may give of one's riches generously and compassionately to glorify God and help the needy. Extreme wealth and extreme poverty both appear undesirable. But the faithfulness of a covenant-keeping God to people who are frequently faithless overshadows any concerns with *merely* socio-economic issues.

# Chapter Two

# The Old Testament wisdom and prophetic literature

The previous chapter surveyed Old Testament material spanning almost the entire period of time covered by the literature of the Hebrew canon. When we arrived at the book of Nehemiah, we were well into the middle of the fifth century BC. The earliest known Jewish testimony to the date of the last written book of the Old Testament appears in Josephus, assigning the end of prophecy to the reign of Artaxerxes who died in 424 BC (*Against Apion* 1.8.40–41). Malachi may well have been written in 433 BC (Verhoef 1987: 160). The last 'half' of the Old Testament in the canonical sequence of English translations, therefore, does not move us chronologically forward. Instead, it collects together writings from numerous centuries covered by the historical books of the first 'half' belonging to two major genres of literature: 1. poetry and wisdom, and 2. prophecy. Much appears on the theme of wealth and poverty in these books, which this chapter will survey.

## Poetry and wisdom literature

The poetry and wisdom literature comprised the books of Job, Psalms, Proverbs, Ecclesiastes and Song of Songs. The origins of Job are unknown, although some would date the story-line to as ancient a time as the age of the patriarchs (Alden 1993: 26). The remaining books are all traditionally associated, at least in part, with either David or Solomon. They may thus offer important reflections on riches and poverty from the perspective of the enormously rich. At the same time, the proverbial nature of much of this literature may well have initially stemmed from popular lore (Whybray 1990: 5), and it transcends cultures and socio-economic brackets.[1] Four of these books may be dealt with briefly: Job, Song of Songs, Psalms and Ecclesiastes.

---

[1] Thus the debates regarding Davidic or Solomonic authorship of the material attributed to them recede somewhat for this study and will not detain us here. Whybray actually believes that Proverbs reflects several different socio-economic contexts.

We will consider the first two of these books separately, as they are each notable for distinctives of their own. Then we will look at themes that Psalms, Proverbs and Ecclesiastes share, as they stand out as having much in common. Finally, a more intensive study of Proverbs will follow, inasmuch as it is the biblical book that devotes the largest proportion of its teaching to explicit instruction about wealth and poverty.

## Job

Job, from the otherwise unknown land of Uz, is described at the outset of the book bearing his name as 'the greatest among all the people of the East' (Job 1:3). He had amassed enormous wealth and yet 'feared God and shunned evil' (1:1). The bulk of the work describes the results of God allowing Satan to test Job by removing first his wealth and then his health. Satan insisted that Job would surely curse God to his face (1:11). While Job at times comes close to doing this, he steadfastly refuses to reject God altogether. In the process of dialoguing with his four would-be comforters – Eliphaz, Bildad, Zophar and Elihu – he raises all the classic questions of theodicy. He insists until the end that, sinner though he may be, he has done nothing to deserve the severity of his suffering. In short, the book of Job stands as a massive counterpoint to the Deuteronomistic cycles of blessing and deprivation based on obedience and disobedience. This would remain true, canonically if not historically speaking, even if Job pre-dated the Law and/or were not Israelite in origin. Within certain parameters and within the Mosaic covenant, it may be true that faithfulness brings peace and prosperity, while faithlessness leads to exile and ruin. But these patterns cannot be generalized as typifying human experience everywhere (cf. esp. Job 21:7–21 with 24:1–12). Unseen forces, whether divine or demonic, may well be at work in human affairs in ways people will never understand this side of eternity (cf. Witherington 1994b: 52; Scott 1965: 140).

Of special interest for a study of material possessions are the repeated references by Job to his exemplary concern for the poor during the period in which he was materially blessed. Job rescued the poor, fatherless, widowed, blind, lame, needy and stranger (29:12–16). Verse 17 ('I broke the fangs of the wicked and snatched the victims from their teeth') demonstrates that 'he was not just a protector but militantly opposed the wicked' (Smick 1988: 981). In a barrage of conditional sentences, Job asks if he has ever unreasonably denied helping any category of destitute (31:16–23). He recognizes that then God should have judged him severely:

> 'If I have put my trust in gold
>     or said to pure gold, "You are my security,"
> if I have rejoiced over my great wealth,
>     the fortune my hands had gained ...
> so that my heart was secretly enticed ...
> then these also would be sins to be judged,
>     for I would have been unfaithful to God on high.'
>
> $(31:24-28)^2$

But Job maintains his innocence of these sins (*cf.* also 30:25). Instead, his self-portrait 'is one of tenderness, generosity, service, justice, and bravery, an admirable assortment of attributes that all God's people would do well to own' (Alden 1993: 284).

The ending of Job provides important support for those who stress riches and wealth as good gifts from God to those he loves. After Job faithfully withstood temptations that would have overwhelmed almost everyone else, 'the LORD blessed the latter part of Job's life more than the first' (42:12). The remaining verses of the book describe the restoration of Job's property, his animals and numerous additional children. But we have every reason to believe that God knew that Job would be as generous with these provisions as he had been with his earlier ones. The model that we saw with the patriarchs repeats itself. God's people may at times be enormously wealthy, but a major purpose of God granting them that wealth is that they may share it with those in need. Job 1:21 retains abiding significance:

> 'Naked I came from my mother's womb,
>     and naked I shall depart.
> The LORD gave and the LORD has taken away;
>     may the name of the Lord be praised.'[3]

## The Song of Songs

The Song of Songs describes a wealthy king as the lover in whom a

---

[2] Hartley (1988: 390–391) notes that these disavowals are consistent with the Ancient Near Eastern pattern for generosity by ideal kings and other wealthy individuals.

[3] Clines (1989: 36) correctly observes that the idea of wealth as a reward for piety stands in tension with that of death as the great leveller of persons. Job's words here reflect neither fatalism nor despair but rather a 'boundary situation', from which 'the rest of life is evaluated'.

Shulamite girl delights. Five times in the book and three times in rapid succession in 3:6–11 this king is identified as Solomon (*cf.* also 1:1 and 8:12). There is considerable debate as to whether these references to Solomon are to be taken literally and even as to whether the king and the woman's lover refer to the same person. But there is no question that the language of love on the lips of both bride and bridegroom regularly appeals to the beauties and delights of earthly possessions. Weddings to this day, as in the ancient world, are often once-in-a-lifetime occasions for particularly lavish expenditures, and this is not necessarily bad. But the main thrust of this short book is not to teach prescriptively about the right or wrong use of earthly goods but to celebrate the love that lies behind the luxury.[4]

## Psalms, Proverbs and Ecclesiastes

Two of the themes of these three books stand in a certain tension with each other. On the one hand, the 'prosperity gospel' of the Deuteronomist is preserved. Industry and faithfulness lead to God's covenant blessings, including material well-being (Pss. 112; 128; Prov. 12:11; 13:21; 21:5). On the other hand, continuing the theme of Job, these wisdom writers recognize that many of the poor and suffering in this life never find relief for their lot, while many wicked rich people continue to flourish (Ps. 37:16–17; Prov. 15:16–17; 16:8).[5] Although it is debated to what extent these books envision a full-orbed future life, some resolution of this tension clearly appears in the theme of justice in a coming world (Ps. 49:10–20).[6]

Meanwhile, numerous texts warn the well-to-do about the transience of earthly riches. At one level, the entire book of Ecclesiastes contributes to this theme. One may profitably compare Psalm 39:4–7 ('You have made my days a mere handbreadth …') with Proverbs 23:4–5 ('Cast but a glance at riches, and they are gone …'). As a result, God's people must put their trust in him, not in whatever measure of earthly resources he has granted them or that they might wish he had granted them (Ps. 52:7; Prov. 3:9–10). Those with abundance must help the needy generously (Prov. 29:7). Above all, the godly king will free the poor person who calls to him and will have pity on the feeble (Ps. 72:4). In fact, the 'poor' feature directly in thirty-three different psalms – as people in some low position, often weak or socially

---

[4] For the most detailed survey of these and related issues, see Pope (1977: 17–229).
[5] On this tension, contrast Coggins (1987) and Weir (1988).
[6] On the afterlife in the Psalms, see esp. Alexander (1987).

oppressed (McPolin 1989: 81–83).[7] They are those to whom God shows special compassion (see esp. Pss. 9:18; 68:5–6; 113:7–9), while godly persons 'lend their money without usury' (Ps. 15:5). And various psalms closely resemble the Law with its concern for social justice. For example:

'Defend the cause of the weak and fatherless;
maintain the rights of the poor and oppressed.
Rescue the weak and needy;
deliver them from the hand of the wicked'
(Ps. 82:3–4)

The Psalms also disclose the beginning of a periodic equation between the materially poor and the pious person (e.g., Pss. 40:17; 86:1; 109:22). 'The psalmists were deeply convinced that God was concerned not only about the alleviation of all aspects of material deprivation, but also for the relief of the deep religious needs which the vicissitudes of life presented. They saw quite clearly that physical and spiritual well-being before God were two sides of the same coin' (Gillingham 1988: 19). Psalms 9 – 10, perhaps originally a single acrostic poem, clearly illustrate the theme of God exalting the poor and oppressed who trust in him (Hoppe 1987: 121–122). In a striking example, even the rich king David could recall times in his life when he seemed 'poor' – that is, physically and spiritually at risk (Ps. 34:6).

Claims like those of Psalm 37:25 ('I have never seen the righteous forsaken or their children begging bread') raise serious questions. One can spiritualize such verses or interpret them as an ideal to be realized only in the life to come. But it is probably best to take them as a simple description rather than an absolute promise. Nevertheless, that even one psalmist could make this observation stands as a challenge to God's people of all times as to how the community of the redeemed can function (see esp. G. A. F. Knight 1982: 180–181). Meanwhile, the injustices that Psalm 73 so poignantly epitomize probably reflect the more common experience of God's people.

Ecclesiastes continues the theme of 'protest literature', begun in Job, by stressing the vanity of trusting in transient riches (see esp. Eccles. 5:8–17; 6:1–12). The author's 'grand experiment' with fabulous wealth

---

[7] The key terms are *'ānî* (literally, one who is bowed down); *dal* (a weak or frail person) and *'ebyôn* (originally, the one who asks [for alms]). Depending on the context, any of these terms could refer to either material or spiritual poverty, or both.

and indulgence is a 'total failure' (Garrett 1993: 270). 'Time and chance happen to them all [the swift, strong, wise, brilliant and learned]' (9:11). Interestingly, despair can often arise out of circumstances of plenty without an eternal perspective on life and death (Yancey 1990: 16). The milieu of the author, consistent with though not requiring Solomonic authorship, is one of 'a world, or more precisely a class, of financial high-rollers', 'a class of entrenched wealth' most concerned with a possible fall from their luxurious state (Kugel 1989: 46).

The book closes with the injunction to fear God and keep the commandments as the sum total of the matter (12:13), thereby relativizing whatever temporary happiness material possessions may have granted. Yet at the same time, the book of Ecclesiastes is punctuated with statements about the appropriateness of enjoying God's good gifts as long as they remain in the context of dedicated service to God (see esp. 5:18–20; cf. also 2:24–26; 3:12–13, 22; 8:15; 9:7–10; 11:9 – 12:1). Ecclesiastes 7:11–12 suggests that an ideal life combines wisdom and wealth, while 11:1–6 enjoins diversification of investments.[8] Because of the apparent tension between all these passages and the major theme of the letter, it is often insisted that Qoheleth ultimately rejects the perspective put forward in these asides, but there is no literary or textual support for this perspective. It is better, therefore, to see these as genuine commands to enjoy the material world (or the 'wife of one's youth'!) from within an eternal framework that keeps life's transience in perspective (Garrett 1993; Eaton 1983). One can enjoy creation without worshipping it, especially by keeping the life to come in clear focus (3:21; 12:7).[9]

## A more intensive focus on Proverbs

The genre and contents of Proverbs closely resemble those of a variety of other works of Near Eastern literature, most notably the Egyptian proverbs of Amenemope.[10] The theology of individual proverbs is seldom explicitly tied to the unique covenantal arrangements between God and Israel. While often assumed to be the teaching of the rich for the rich (a natural assumption if one accepts Solomonic authorship of the majority of the book), a close study of the proverbs' point of view

---

[8] 'Cast your bread upon the waters' (11:1) refers to 'the risk involved in sea-trade' (Whybray 1989a: 159). Thus, it is not a call to charity, as often assumed.

[9] If one follows the Masoretic text, contra the ancient versions, 3:21 can be rendered as 'Who knows the spirit of man which goes upward, and the spirit of the beast which goes down to the earth?' (Eaton 1983: 87–89; Kaiser 1979; AV; NASB).

[10] For a detailed comparison of wealth and poverty in the instruction of Amenemope with the same theme in the Hebrew Proverbs, see Washington (1994).

has convinced some that at least a good number of them are 'commenting on the two social and economic extremes [rich and poor] from the outside' (Whybray 1989b: 334). A certain 'middle-class' ideal may be present, and if many proverbs reflect commonly held wisdom, this theory of their origins is still consistent with some Solomonic appropriation of them. For both of these reasons, therefore, the Proverbs are arguably the most generalizable and timeless of the Old Testament teachings on material possessions. On the other hand, the very genre of a proverb suggests that it expresses a principle or generalization that often proves true but that may not be taken as an absolute. At any rate, the sheer amount of material in Proverbs on money and material circumstances merits our taking a closer look at the teaching of this book.[11]

To begin with, Proverbs has much to say about how to acquire possessions or to avoid losing them. Righteousness and humility form important prerequisites (10:3; 22:4).

> Good people leave an inheritance for their children's children,
> but a sinner's wealth is stored up for the righteous,
>
> (13:22)

while

> The righteous eat to their hearts' content,
> but the stomach of the wicked goes hungry.
>
> (v. 25)

Second, one acquires possessions by diligence, vigilance (21:5; 27:23–24) and plain hard work (12:11; 14:23). Most famous here is 6:10–11 (cf. 20:13):

> A little sleep, a little slumber,
> a little folding of the hands to rest –
> and poverty will come on you like a bandit
> and scarcity like an armed man.

Conversely, the hurriedly gained inheritance is less likely to be appreciated and preserved (20:21). Several of these proverbs seem to depict an idealized view of the world that has at times been falsified. There is no doubt that many poor people are lazy but many others are victims of

---

[11] A helpful topical survey of Proverbs appears in Kidner (1964: 31–56).

circumstances outside their control. For these proverbs to remain true even as generalizations, one must have general control over one's work, life and family, with no severe systemic social problems (Witherington 1994b: 73–74), situations which apparently obtained for at least short periods of time in the life of ancient Israel.

At the same time, Proverbs stresses a theme we have seen throughout the Old Testament thus far, that the righteous rich also give generously to the Lord and to the needy.

> Honour the LORD with your wealth,
> with the firstfruits of all your crops;
> then your barns will be filled to overflowing,
> and your vats will brim over with new wine.
>
> (3:9–10)

> Do not withhold good from those who deserve it,
> when it is in your power to act.
> Do not say to your neighbour,
> 'Come back later; I'll give it tomorrow' –
> when you now have it with you.
>
> (3:27–28)

A text that could equally well have appeared in the Law reminds us to defend the rights of the disadvantaged:

> The righteous care about justice for the poor,
> but the wicked have no such concern.
>
> (29:7)

Similarly, the righteous king 'judges the poor with fairness' and 'his throne will always be secure' (29:14). The virtuous and noble wife of Proverbs 31:10–31, clearly enjoying at least a 'middle-class' standard of living, 'opens her arms to the poor and ... the needy' (31:20).[12] Conversely,

> If you shut your ears to the cry of the poor,
> you too will cry out and not be answered.
>
> (21:13; cf. also 11:24–26; 22:16)

---

[12] Verses 19–20 together form a chiasm and appear at the climactic centre of the entire poem of vv. 10–31, thus pairing hard work and generosity to the needy as the twin emphases of these verses (Lichtenstein 1982).

More common than direct commands or threats, as in these verses, are simple descriptions such as

> The lips of the righteous nourish many,
> but fools die for lack of judgment.
>
> (10:21; *cf.* 14:31; 19:17)

Passages that may or may not promise *material* reward for generosity to the poor include 22:9 and 28:27.[13] Gottwald (1985: 573) observes that fewer than one third of the proverbs dealing with rich and poor teach that people get what they deserve, whereas the rest recognize the presence and problem of socio-economic injustice.

Also relativizing material wealth as an absolute good is a series of proverbs that compare the value of riches with wisdom, knowledge, honour, a good name, fear of the Lord, love, righteousness, peace and safety. For example, God's Wisdom personified cries out to the people of the streets,

> 'Choose my instruction instead of silver,
> knowledge rather than choice gold,
> for wisdom is more precious than rubies,
> and nothing you desire can compare with her.'
>
> (8:10–11; *cf.* 3:13–16; 16:16; 22:1)

A number of these proverbs take the form 'Better a little with ... than wealth with ...' For example,

> Better a little with the fear of the LORD
> than great wealth with turmoil.
> Better a meal of vegetables where there is love
> than a fattened calf with hatred.
>
> (15:16–17; *cf.* 16:8; 17:1; 19:1; 19:22; 28:6)

In fact, G. H. Wittenberg (1986: 73) points out that a majority of the 'better than' proverbs deal with issues of wealth and poverty and commend poverty with righteousness rather than riches with injustice. A final reminder of the transience and therefore of the lesser value of

---

[13] Giese (1992: 409–417) notes that several verses in the LXX Proverbs reveal a stronger component of compassion for the lowly than is found in the MT. Prov. 22:9 is one of these, adding an extra couplet in the Greek: 'He that gives liberally secures victory and honor; but he takes away the life of them that possess them.'

riches, compared with character qualities which last for ever, appears in 23:4–5:

> Do not wear yourself out to get rich;
> have the wisdom to show restraint.
> Cast but a glance at riches, and they are gone,
> for they will surely sprout wings
> and fly off to the sky like an eagle.

When one includes proverbs that are descriptive rather than prescriptive, much additional teaching on wealth and poverty emerges.[14] This collection of proverbs comments ironically but factually on the temporal power and security riches can provide, without commending their acquisition. For example, the wealth of the rich is their fortress, while 'poverty is the ruin of the poor' (10:15). The poor are hated even by their neighbours, while many people love the rich (14:20; though *cf.* 14:21b: 'blessed are those who are kind to the needy'). That these descriptive proverbs do not reflect God's ideal is apparent in 18:11:

> The wealth of the rich is their fortified city;
> *they imagine it* an unscalable wall.

So, too, in 28:11 'the rich may be wise *in their own eyes*', but the poor with discernment see how deluded they are. Other descriptive proverbs commenting on the friends and power that the uncaring wealthy amass appear in 18:23; 19:4; 22:7; 28:3, 8.

Still another collection of proverbs stresses the coming of judgment day, in which the wrongs of this world will be righted. Thus, 11:4 reminds us that

> Wealth is worthless in the day of wrath,
> but righteousness delivers from death.

So, too, in 11:28,

---

[14] Wittenberg (1986: 58–59) sees many of these as part of 'act–consequence' proverbs which he thinks may have a different tradition-critical origin than other forms. But recognizing a distinction between descriptive and prescriptive forms seems to alleviate the need for such proposals.

> Those who trust in their riches will fall,
> but the righteous will thrive like a green leaf.

People who mock the poor reproach their Creator and will not go unpunished (17:5). One must not rob the poor or crush the afflicted, because the Lord will plead their case (22:22–23), while God continues to oppose those who hasten to get rich or show partiality (28:20–22). Whether in this life or in the next, it remains true that

> Dishonest money dwindles away,
> but whoever gathers money little by little makes it grow.
>
> (13:11)

Two somewhat miscellaneous proverbs reflect the levelling that comes from considering this life from God's perspective. The rich and poor have a common bond because 'the LORD is the Maker of them all' (22:2), while the poor and the oppressor have one thing in common; 'the LORD gives sight to the eyes of both' (29:13).[15]

One passage on material possessions in the book of Proverbs stands out as unique in seemingly commending a middle-class ideal. Among the sayings of Agur, we read in 30:8b–9,

> '… give me neither poverty nor riches,
> but give me only my daily bread.
> Otherwise I may have too much and disown you
> and say, "Who is the LORD?"
> Or I may become poor and steal,
> and so dishonour the name of my God.'

Whybray (1989b: 334–335) suspects that the socio-economic standing of the author of this proverb differs from that of all the rest in the canonical collection, but he also recognizes that a middle way between vast wealth and destitution is being idealized. *Contra* many, Garrett (1993: 238) believes that the falsehood and lies of Proverbs 30:8a are enunciated in verse 8b. The two requests of verse 7 are not 'Keep falsehood and lies far from me' (30:8a) and 'Do not let me be rich or

---

[15] Wittenberg (1987) takes these two as his starting point for traditio-historically dissecting the proverbs into those that promote industrious agricultural living – *i.e.*, in which amassing wealth righteously is viewed as at least neutral and often good – and those that seemingly equate the rich with the wicked, reflecting the inroads of corrupt urban commercialization.

poor' (30:8b). Instead, the two requests are 'Do not give me poverty and do not give me wealth.' The latter 'convinces one that God is not necessary'; and the former, 'that either he is of no help or that his laws are impossible to keep'. Verse 9 additionally 'reveals a marked fixation on the glory of God (rather than personal needs) as the prime motivation for the requests'.

Chutter (1982: 28) recognizes the difficulty of summarizing Proverbs' teaching on material possessions under one main heading, but agrees that the book protects against extremes of wealth and poverty and commends an intersection 'somewhere within the boundaries of an adequate standard of living'. This still allows for a variety of lifestyles of wise accumulation and disbursement, so long as prosperity is yielded to devotion.[16] Although it is premature to speak of summarizing pervasive patterns throughout both Testaments, one of the theses of this volume is that the avoidance of extremes of wealth and poverty is a consistent, recurring biblical mandate. Of course, before we too readily label this a 'middle-class' ideal and content ourselves that we fall within this range, we must remember two things: first, polls consistently suggest that more than 80% of Westerners consider themselves middle-class, thus largely evacuating the term of any meaning; and second, the nature of the 'middle-class' ideal of Proverbs 30:8 is defined by the clause, 'give me only my daily bread', a far lower standard of living than that to which most people calling themselves middle-class today aspire. Nevertheless, Gowan (1987: 350) appropriately generalizes:

> [The Old Testament] assumes throughout that there will always be some with relatively more possessions. This is no scandal, for wealth is to be prized as one of the good gifts of God (Prov. 22:4). What is a scandal, as many texts have shown us, is when those who do not have so much are deprived of what is rightfully theirs by those whose consciences do not bother them. Perhaps the closest the Old Testament comes to a desire for a 'middle way' is put in individual terms rather than as a plan for society.

By way of contemporary application, Aitken (1986: 190) adds, 'If individuals and nations were thus contented, two-thirds of the world's population would not be living in poverty.' As we will note below

---

[16] Guinan (1977: 35–36) is more confident: 'The balance of the reflections of the wise is well summed up in Proverbs 30:7–9 ... Extreme poverty and extreme wealth both have their problems in leading us away from Yahweh. The words of the wise recognize and warn against them.'

(pp. 249–255), this contentment could still allow most 'middle-class' Westerners a reasonably comfortable lifestyle.

## The Prophets

The final major section in the canonical sequence of the English Old Testament is the collection of books from the 'writing prophets' spanning the eighth to the fifth centuries BC. Although each prophet addresses distinct and at times unique historical circumstances, there are numerous themes, not least with respect to material possessions, that justify our treating this material together as one, admittedly heterogeneous, unit of God's Word.[17] As we saw in chapter 2, economic life for Israel had already substantially changed under the united monarchy in the eleventh and tenth centuries BC. Previously, 'the Israelites defined themselves not only in opposition to the great empire of Pharaonic Egypt, but, also, against the highly centralized and bureaucratized states that they were to dispossess'. Again, 'Israel was not a state like the Canaanite states, but, rather, a collection of riff-raff (*erev rav*, Ex. 12:38) without a central government, a capital city, a professional army, a class of charioteers. It was a group of alienated peasants with no stake in the stratification of Canaanite society' (Levenson 1976: 232). As a result, they had to trust in God as their sovereign in the suzerain–vassal relationship of their covenant treaty.

All this was abandoned in the time of the kingship, and, despite the ideal of a generous and benevolent king, by the period of the divided monarchy during which the writing prophets ministered, much had changed for the worse. Indeed, the prophetic denunciations against Israel can be connected directly 'with the development of class distinctions under the monarchy, the appearance of a commercial, moneyed class and the growth of a patriciate who lived a life of luxury and self-indulgence and gave not a thought to the miseries of the poor who toiled for them' (Porteous 1966: 34). Again, the loss of ancestral properties to wealthy aristocrats who bought up vast tracts of land for ever altered the economic landscape and widened the gap between rich and poor. The concomitant and 'growing love of luxury, pretentiousness and ostentatiousness was in striking contrast to the simple,

---

[17] Here, too, we reach the one major Old Testament corpus where the historical settings of each biblical book can, with only a few exceptions, be determined with relative confidence. Even most critical scholars generally assume that at least a core of the teachings attributed to a given prophet do go back to that historical figure.

unsophisticated and natural life, traditional to old pre-monarchical Israel and still fully maintained in the villages' (Neufeld 1960: 44).

The covenant rewards of peace and prosperity for obedience can still be detected during the reigns of occasional good kings, almost exclusively in the south in Judah, and most notably with Hezekiah (2 Kgs. 18 – 20) and Josiah (2 Kgs. 22:1 – 23:30). The fall and rise of Daniel, closely mirroring the career of Joseph centuries earlier, further demonstrates that power and wealth can be used appropriately by God's people and can even be used for strategic socio-political purposes. But also like Joseph, Daniel repeatedly finds himself in more austere circumstances, even in danger of losing his life. But the text gives no hint that he is any less faithful to God during these hard times; indeed his suffering stems directly from his faithfulness to Yahweh.[18]

What the writing prophets are most known for, however, is their 'radical' bent in boldly denouncing the sins of their society. Clearly, ethical issues, including the use of one's material possessions, rank among the major topics of prophetic rhetoric. But one has only to read in its entirety virtually any book of prophecy at random to see that at least as serious as the Israelites' ethical sins was their idolatry. Theological and ethical defection from God's will consistently go hand in hand. Liberation theology has regularly taken its cue from these same prophets, denouncing the ways in which rich oppressors today exploit the poor (Boff & Boff 1987: 35). As noted in the 'Introductory considerations' (see above, p. 22), various liberation theologians have at times aligned themselves with Marxism and have called for violent revolution. But the model of the Old Testament prophets is diametrically opposed to such violence. God's people are never called to revolt, not even peacefully, against their foreign adversaries, but are warned about the violent ways in which God will use those nations to punish Israel for its sins. Nevertheless, the bold denunciatory rhetoric of the prophets against the sins of their people remains an important model for Christians today, especially when popular social sins in our cultures similarly and flagrantly contravene God's righteous standards. Such sins cut right across all of the conventional political agendas and range from the issues of the 'right', such as combating abortion and euthanasia, to the concerns of the 'left', such as rebuking the exploitation of the poor and outcast of our societies (*cf.* R. Sider 1987).

---

[18] In the Hebrew, of course, Daniel is included not with the 'Prophets' but with the 'Writings'; all the more reason why we cannot take his themes as representative of the core of Old Testament prophecy.

Distinctively, the prophets do not limit their rhetoric to Israel. They regularly lambast foreign nations, too, for the arrogance their wealth has engendered. The most striking examples of such pronouncements of judgment come in Isaiah 14, with its references to the Morning Star who has fallen from heaven, as part of a taunt against the king of Babylon (cf. Is. 14:4, 12), and in Ezekiel 26 – 28, in which a dirge song against the city of Tyre (Ezek. 26 – 27) gives way to a more specific prophecy against the king of Tyre (Ezek. 28, esp. vv. 11–19). In both the Isaiah and the Ezekiel passages, the language seems to surpass anything that could be predicated of earthly kings. This has led some interpreters, therefore, to assume that the fall of Satan from heaven is being described. Whether or not that interpretation is correct,[19] it points out the extent to which language of judgment against the oppressive foreigner can approximate to condemnation of the demonic. That the prophet often applies the same standards to foreign nations as he does to Israel further reminds us that the principles involving material possessions remain relevant to everyone in the world. Put simply, God may have made a unique arrangement with the people of Israel to bless them materially in response to their covenant faithfulness, but he calls all peoples to care for the needy, seek justice and use their wealth compassionately. But the primary emphasis in this survey, by the nature of the data, will have to deal with the prophecies addressed first of all to Israel. In fact, the standards according to which God, through his prophets, judges his people are regularly based on the Torah itself (see the helpful chart in Dearman 1988: 58–59). These data may be divided into two parts: what the nation has done wrong and what it must do right. More than in any other part of the Old Testament, the relevant texts prove so numerous that we can only sample a representative cross-section of them.

## The sins of Israel with respect to material possessions

At least five major categories of sins may be enumerated.

1. *Worshipping idols made of costly materials.* The close link between idolatry and the wrong use of material goods is evident

---

[19] Although both chapters are widely interpreted among grass-roots evangelicals as referring to Satan, scholarly evangelical commentators generally disagree. *E.g.*, Oswalt (1986: 310–326) sees the king of Babylon in Isaiah as typifying human pride and its destruction more generally. *Cf.* also Watts (1985: 212). On the Ezekiel reference, *cf.* L. Allen (1990: 93–96) and Taylor (1969: 195–198). Oswalt (1986: 320) also notes that while some Church Fathers found references to Satan in these texts, the Reformers generally did not.

immediately. Isaiah 2:7–8 hits home with its synonymous parallelism:

> Their land is full of silver and gold;
> there is no end to their treasures.
> Their land is full of horses;
> there is no end to their chariots.
> Their land is full of idols;
> they bow down to the work of their hands,
> to what their fingers have made.[20]

As part of Israel's judgment, Isaiah foretells ironically,

> In that day people will throw away
> to the rodents and bats
> their idols of silver and idols of gold,
> which they made to worship,
>
> (2:20)

because they are fleeing to caverns in the rocks to try to evade God's wrath (2:19, 21). Isaiah 44:12–20 sarcastically ridicules the futility of worshipping gods made by human hands, while Hosea 2:8 laments how Israel has not acknowledged God as the source of either its staples (grain, new wine and oil) or the wealth that it misused in its idolatry (silver and gold). But even when Israel used its precious metals for the temple, Haggai reminds them that '"The silver is mine and the gold is mine," declares the LORD Almighty' (Hag. 2:8).[21]

2. *Trusting in ritual rather than in repentance.* Equally biting in its mockery are the words of Jeremiah, who berates the people of Judah for shouting over and over again, 'This is the temple of the LORD', as if their regular frequenting of God's place of worship or reciting a liturgy would save them from his judgment (Jer. 7:4).[22] Rather, 'If you really change your ways and your actions and deal with each other justly, if

[20] Motyer (1993: 56) comments, 'The Bible has no animus against wealth (*treasures*) as such. All depends on how it is acquired (3:14), how it is used (5:8) and whether it is seen as an alternative security to trusting the Lord.'

[21] In context, Merrill (1994b: 211) suggests that v. 8 stresses the centrality of God's own glory in the otherwise comparatively sparsely furnished rebuilt temple.

[22] Craigie, Kelley & Drinkard (1991: 121) remark, 'They did not perceive the secondary role of the temple, nor did they understand that their own moral integrity was of far greater significance to God than simply the physical presence of a building.' Has the modern Western church learned this lesson?

you do not oppress the alien, the fatherless or the widow and do not shed innocent blood in this place, and if you do not follow other gods to your own harm, then I will let you live in this place ...' (7:5–7). Many church-goers today might do well to heed a New Testament equivalent of this teaching in Jesus' Sermon on the Mount: 'If you are offering your gift at the altar and there remember that your brother or sister has something against you, leave your gift there in front of the altar. First go and be reconciled to them; then come and offer your gift' (Matt. 5:23–24).

3. *Extorting, robbing and oppressing to gain more land.* Ezekiel 22:29, Micah 2:2 and Amos 5:11–12 are three of numerous passages that stress how the rich in Israel are trying to get richer at the expense of the poor. Instead of honouring the Torah's commitment that inheritance remain within families so that all can own at least modest amounts of property, numerous illegal and unethical manoeuvers are being concocted to concentrate wealth in the hands of fewer and fewer. Rent capitalism (the paying of rent to one or several owners of the various factors of production) has led to upper-class exploitation of the peasants. Urban luxury and extravagance are maintained at the expense of charging the poor prices that require them in extreme cases to sell themselves into slavery, even to foreigners (Lang 1985: 90–95).[23] Three specific techniques which are repeatedly denounced are the use of dishonest scales and prices in the market-place (*e.g.*, Ezek. 45:10–12; Hos. 12:7), foreclosing on unpaid debts (*e.g.*, Amos 2:6–8)[24] and defrauding labourers of their wages (*e.g.*, Mal. 3:5).

4. *Boasting in wealth.* Amos, in particular, proves unrelenting in his harsh rhetoric against those who believe themselves to be exempt from God's judgment in an age of relative prosperity, despite their callousness and crimes against the poor. Amos 4:1 addresses the wealthy women,

Hear this word, you cows of Bashan on Mount Samaria,
you women who oppress the poor

---

[23] *Cf.* also T. Finley (1985: 416), 'Rich and powerful people are becoming richer and more powerful at the expense of the poor and powerless.'

[24] Selling the needy for a pair of sandals can refer to a paltry sum, a bribe paid to a judge, or to debt slavery. The last of these seems most likely. See Andersen & Freedman (1989: 313).

> and crush the needy
> and say to your husbands, 'Bring us some drinks!'[25]

And the excessive luxuries of the notable men of the nation are equally lampooned in 6:4–6:

> You lie on beds inlaid with ivory
> and lounge on your couches.
> You dine on choice lambs
> and fattened calves.
> You strum away on your harps like David
> and improvise on musical instruments.
> You drink wine by the bowlful
> and use the finest lotions,
> but you do not grieve over the ruin of Joseph.

Gossai (1993: 272) comments, 'In examining the prophets' critique of the corrupting influence of affluence and luxury, it must be understood that the prophets are not members of a particular economic class at odds against another.' And 'it is certainly not the case that the prophets are placing the poor on a pedestal and proclaiming the advantages of being poor'. Still, 'it is the acquisition of wealth at the expense of the poor and the maligning of *sdk* and *mšpt* which come under attack.'

Habakkuk likens the evil people in his day to fishermen catching innocent fish with hooks and nets. Their idolatrous materialism is poignantly depicted:

> Therefore he sacrifices to his net
> and burns incense to his drag-net,
> for by his net he lives in luxury
> and enjoys the choicest food.
> Is he to keep on emptying his net,
> destroying nations without mercy?
>
> (Hab. 1:16–17)

In context these verses refer to the Babylonians, whom God has raised up to punish Israel. But given Israel's repeated imitation of the idolatry

[25] 'The sarcastic epithet *cows of Bashan* seems to refer both to the luxury that the wealthy women enjoyed and to a certain voluptuousness and sensuality which their extravagant life-style afforded them' (D. Hubbard 1989: 155).

of the pagan nations surrounding them, this passage vividly illustrates the 'boasting in wealth' that often afflicted God's people as well.

Even ordinary commerce and trade, which in themselves are neutral, regularly turn into a seduction to sin. Amos berates those who trample the needy and do away with the poor of the land because they ask,

> 'When will the New Moon be over
> that we may sell grain,
> and the Sabbath be ended
> that we may market wheat?'

> (Amos 8:5a)

They cannot wait for the day of rest to end so that they can go and make more money. The subsequent verse and a half makes it clear that they cheat the poor in the marketplace, on top of everything else (Amos 8:5b–6). In fact, the exile took place in part precisely as God's judgment for the Israelites' failure to observe sabbatical years (Jer. 34:8–22). Merchants cause problems in Zephaniah as well, probably reflecting the influence of foreign commerce and its dishonest practices (see esp. Zeph. 1:11–13).[26] And in Zechariah 11:5, those who buy slaves proclaim, 'Praise the LORD, I am rich!' as if God were the one who had blessed them with their wealth. But for Zechariah it is clear that the Lord will no longer pity people with such an attitude (11:6). As Baldwin (1972: 180) comments, 'Riches are no proof of the Lord's favour (Mk. 10:23), least of all when they are obtained by fraud.'[27] All these prophetic references, and especially the texts in Amos, should give well-to-do Westerners considerable pause, especially those who seem largely indifferent to the needs of the poor worldwide.[28]

5. *Financial motivation for leaders' ministry.* Perhaps no more tragic indictment against Israel occurs than in those passages that depict the corruption of the country's leadership. As both Testaments make plain, to whom much is given much shall be required (*cf.* Lk. 12:48). The sins of leaders, by virtue of their potential to lead the masses

---

[26] D. Baker (1988: 97). R. L. Smith (1984: 13) simply equates 'merchants' with 'the people of Canaan' in this context.

[27] Meyers & Meyers (1993: 255) wonder 'whether there is some subconscious critique of a market economy at work here. If buying and selling goods is a merismic construction representing the totality of economic dealings, then on a literal level the message is that such activity cannot have a positive outcome; whatever happens, the flock comes to ruin.'

[28] For a more detailed exegesis of Amos, and poignant sociological analysis with applications to contemporary Two-Thirds World realities, see Carroll R. (1992).

astray, prove that much more culpable (*cf.* Jas. 3:1). Micah 3:11 is representative:

> Her leaders judge for a bribe,
>    her priests teach for a price,
>    and her prophets tell fortunes for money.
> Yet they lean upon the LORD and say,
>    'Is not the LORD among us?
>    No disaster will come upon us.'[29]

Verse 12, however, immediately proceeds to predict that because of these leaders Jerusalem would turn into 'a heap of rubble'. Little wonder the later rabbis insisted that those who would teach God's word must earn their keep by a different trade (*e.g.* Aboth 2:2; Meg. 28a and Sot. 47b similarly protest against the acceptance of gifts and bribes by wise men). Bi-vocational ministry to this day is an economic necessity in many parts of the world. With New Testament precedent as well, it may be increasingly appropriate in our Western world that grows ever more suspicious of minsters' motives (see below, pp. 185–186).

Other Old Testament prophetic texts that condemn leaders who abuse material possessions include Micah 7:3 ('the ruler demands gifts; the judge accepts bribes') and Isaiah 3:14–15 ('the elders and leaders' have plundered the poor and crushed God's people). Isaiah 10:1–2 lays specific blame at the feet of the lawmakers

> ... who issue oppressive decrees,
> to deprive the poor of their rights
>    and withhold justice from the oppressed
>    of my people,
> making widows their prey
>    and robbing the fatherless.

In sharp contrast, the messianic Branch of 11:4 will judge the needy

> ... with righteousness ...
>    with justice he will give decisions for the poor of the earth.

---

[29] Mays (1976: 89–90) concludes, 'Probably it was not "the fee" for service or profit from work that Micah sees as hideous, but the fact that gain had become the overriding basis of the practices.'

> He will strike the earth with the rod of his mouth;
> with the breath of his lips he will slay the wicked.

Differing from the politicians in Isaiah's day, 'righteousness will be his belt and faithfulness the sash round his waist' (11:5). The covetousness and deceit of prophets and priests reappear in Jeremiah 6:13 and 8:10, with both texts supplying the refrain, 'from the least to the greatest, all are greedy for gain'. Here is clear evidence that the practices of the leaders eventually spread to all the people (cf. also Ezek. 33:31). In Ezekiel 22:6–12, it is the princes of Israel who oppress the alien, mistreat the fatherless and widow, and charge usury and (excessive?) interest – that is, unjust gain from neighbours by extortion. The term 'unjust gain' in verse 12 refers to that which is acquired by violence, plunder, injustice, selfishness, or by taking an additional cut of profits beyond otherwise legitimate earnings (Oswalt 1980; cf. Brown, Driver & Briggs 1953: 130).

## What Israel must do

What then does repentance for the Israelites look like with respect to material possessions? Perhaps no text is more famous or central than Micah's key summary:

> He has showed you, O people, what is good.
> And what does the LORD require of you?
> To act justly and to love mercy
> and to walk humbly with your God.
>
> (Mic. 6:8)

Again we may unpack these thoughts under five subheadings.

1. *Seek justice for the marginalized.* As in the Torah and wisdom literature, a recurring refrain throughout the Prophets calls on God's people to treat with justice the poor, oppressed, fatherless, widow and alien in the land. In Isaiah 1:17, what the NIV renders as 'encourage the oppressed' may more literally read 'put right the oppressor'.[30] Jeremiah 22:13–17 contrasts the one who amassed wealth while not paying his labourers with those who 'defended the cause of the poor and needy'.[31]

---

[30] Motyer (1993: 472). Cf. Oswalt (1986: 94) ('straighten out the ruthless'); and Watts (1985: 13) ('remedy oppression').

[31] In context probably a reference to Jehoiakim. Jeremiah 'knows that Judah's king is bound to observe the royal style of life which obtains for all kings. What offends him is

Gowan (1987: 341) refers to this text as 'an adequate, brief summary of the social message of the prophets' and 'the Old Testament's typical description of the nature of a healthy community'. Without the aid of a male head of household, widows and orphans in antiquity were often at a considerable socio-economic disadvantage. The 'poor' here refer not to the majority of the people eking out a subsistence-level income, but to those who were utterly destitute. As noted earlier, 'illegal alien' probably best captures for us today the social dynamic of the individual to whom various translations refer as a 'sojourner' (Gowan 1987: 343). What all the individuals mentioned had in common was an acute sense of powerlessness.

Even the gross sins of Sodom appear in a new light in the Prophets. Ezekiel 16:49 declares, 'Now this was the sin of your sister Sodom: She and her daughters were arrogant, overfed and unconcerned; they did not help the poor and needy.' Ezekiel is certainly aware of Sodom's and Gomorrah's reputation for gross immorality, including homosexual sin. Verse 50 immediately goes on to speak of the 'haughty and detestable things' they did 'before me', and 'detestable' (Heb. *to'ēbâh*) is an adjective regularly applied throughout the Hebrew Scriptures to gross sexual sin (*cf.* esp. Lev. 18:22 in the explicit context of homosexuality). But both sexual immorality and material selfishness stem from the same self-indulgent attitudes, and it is little wonder that the two increasingly appear together in our affluent Western world as well.[32]

Under the heading of the marginalized appear again the *'ănāwîm*, those both materially poor and spiritually pious to whom we were introduced in the Psalms. In this context the *'ănāwîm* are the impoverished Israelites struggling to rebuild their country. Isaiah 61:1 is the classic prophetic text:

> The Spirit of the Sovereign LORD is on me,
> because the Lord has anointed me
> to preach good news to the poor ...[33]

---

that Jehoiakim makes a show of kingship which he combines with a neglect of the fundamentals of good rule', especially with respect to social justice (McKane 1986: 531).

[32] Brownlee (1986: 247) believes that Ezekiel is exegeting Gen. 18:20–21 and 19:13 with their references to the 'outcry' (*sā'aq* and cognates) of Sodom, a term usually referring to the outcry of the oppressed.

[33] Watts (1987: 302) calls them 'the faithful who wait on Yahweh in spite of their personal distress'; here, 'the dispirited Jewish community around the ruins of Jerusalem before Ezra returned'.

Isaiah goes on to promise that the Spirit is binding up the broken-hearted, freeing the captives, releasing the prisoners from darkness and proclaiming the year of the Lord's favour (a probable allusion to the language of Jubilee) and the day of vengeance of our God, to comfort all who mourn (Is. 61:1–2).[34] Motyer's comments (1993: 500) comprehensively capture the implications of this passage, which he correctly takes as messianic in its original context: 'In review, the *good news* embraces personal renewal and restoration (bind up the *broken-hearted*), release from restrictions imposed by people (*captives* is a negative description of the creation of a harmonious society) and the rectification of circumstances (*release ... for the prisoners*).' In similar fashion, Isaiah 58:6–7 asks rhetorically,

'Is not this the kind of fasting I have chosen:
to loose the chains of injustice
    and untie the cords of the yoke,
to set the oppressed free
    and break every yoke?
Is it not to share your food with the hungry
    and to provide the poor wanderer with shelter –
when you see the naked, to clothe them,
    and not to turn away from your own flesh and blood?'[35]

The latter part of this quotation also combines with Ezekiel 18:5–9 as important background for the so-called parable of the sheep and goats in Matthew 25:31–46.

2. *Do not boast in riches but be generous in giving them away.* Yet another passage which the New Testament echoes is Jeremiah 9:23–24 (*cf.* 1 Cor. 1:26–29).[36] Here Jeremiah calls the wise not to boast in their wisdom, or the strong in their strength, or the rich in their riches, but to boast that they understand the Lord, who exercises kindness, justice and

---

[34] This text 'could well be used as a daily reminder of what the prophetic tradition is all about' (Everson 1978: 69).

[35] 'As the Lord demonstrates to Israel how their liberation manifests salvation, so are they to carry on God's own redemptive action in their liberation of one another' (Polan 1986: 208).

[36] J. Thompson (1980: 321) observes that in these verses, 'we have a succinct summary of the religion of Israel at its highest. Wisdom, strength and riches, however valuable they may be when properly used, are altogether subordinate to the knowledge of God. True religion consists in acknowledging the complete sovereignty of God in life and allowing him to fill life with those qualities of steadfast faithfulness, justice and righteousness which he possesses, in which he delights, and which he desires to find in his people.'

righteousness on earth, 'for in these I delight'. In one of the Old Testament texts most frequently quoted to encourage Christian giving, Malachi 3:8–10 describes how the children of Israel are robbing God by not donating the full amount of their tithes and offerings: 'Bring the whole tithe into the storehouse, that there may be food in my house' (Mal. 3:10). But this verse does not prove that tithes remain mandatory for believers in the New Testament era. Verse 10 immediately continues to speak of the floodgates of heaven from which God would pour out 'so much blessing that you will not have room enough for it'. Malachi clearly alludes to the covenantal arrangement unique to the nation of Israel. And verse 12 continues, 'then all the nations will call you blessed', an obvious reference to the distinctive promises to Abraham in Genesis 12:1–3. It is also important to remember the unique relationship in the Old Testament between tithes and offerings and the temple cult. Without a similar centre for bloody sacrifices today, one cannot simply transfer all principles for giving to God's sanctuary in the Old Testament to church budgets in the New Testament age (cf. further Verhoef 1974)! But we will have more to say about the tithe in today's world in subsequent chapters.

3. *Lament.* A third appropriate response as part of repentance is to lament one's sins and the horrible consequences that they generate. The entire book known as the Lamentations, attributed to Jeremiah, articulates this theme with numerous references to the material blessings that have been lost through the Israelites' wicked use of them. This language will provide important background to our later discussion of Revelation 18.

4. *Seek the welfare of the city.* A verse unique among all the prophetic literature is nevertheless recognized by most commentators as crucial to God's social ethic. To the astonishment and horror of many in his audience, Jeremiah 29:7 commands the Israelites to seek the good of the Babylonian oppressors among whom they will be exiled: 'Also, seek the peace and prosperity of the city to which I have carried you into exile. Pray to the LORD for it, because if it prospers, you too will prosper.' Jeremiah commands the Israelites 'to abandon hope in a "holy revolt" against Babylon, which had been inspired by the false prophets' promises that God would bring the exiles back in a short time and to place their hope instead in the Lord and a new way of life'.[37] Jeremiah is not just being realistic but is giving a small, vulnerable community a large missional responsibility. The Israelites are drawn into the public

[37] Keown, Scalise & Smothers (1995: 72). D. Smith (1989: 137) calls this 'nonviolent social resistance'.

process so as to avoid sectarian withdrawal (Brueggemann 1991: 32). One recalls New Testament texts such as Romans 12:20–21: 'If your enemies are hungry, feed them; if they are thirsty, give them something to drink,' and 'Do not be overcome by evil, but overcome evil with good.'

5. *Cling to promises of restoration.* Consistently throughout the Prophets, despite the frequent tirades against the sin and injustice of the day, there are promises of better days to come. God will not forsake his people; he will ensure that a righteous remnant always remains to whom he will one day restore the land. The exiles who returned after the edict of Cyrus, king of Persia, and rebuilt the temple and the city walls under Ezra and Nehemiah, experienced a partial fulfilment of this promise. Nevertheless, a majority of the prophets at one point or another look forward to a much more utopian restoration that must be equated with a millennial kingdom or new heavens and a new earth. Tellingly, these visions regularly describe the blessings that God's people will once again experience in terms of material prosperity (Is. 54 – 55; 60 – 66): abundant food to eat (Is. 25:6 – the origin of the New Testament references to a messianic banquet – *cf.* also Joel 2:23–27), sharing the wealth of the nations (Zech. 14:14), and the absence of corrupt merchants or traders in the house of the Lord (Zech. 14:21 mg.).[38] Even the vision of a new temple described in such detail in Ezekiel 40 – 48 fits into this category, although it is disputed whether this should be understood as a literal, rebuilt temple or not.[39] On any interpretation, its ideals of equity in land distribution, including land for the resident alien (Ezek. 47:21–22), stand as a sharp rebuke to most current socio-economic systems. And the messianic shepherd of Ezekiel 34 looks forward to plentiful material abundance (see esp. Ezek. 34:25–31), in a chapter that provides important background to the feeding miracles in the Gospels.

[38] The Hebrew literally refers to 'Canaanites', but the term had become equivalent to people of any nationality who made extortionary profits, because of the frequency of the practice among Israel's pagan neighbours (*cf.* Baldwin 1972: 208; R. L. Smith, 1984: 292). As late as the end of the first century AD, Josephus (*Against Apion* 1.12.60–61) could claim that Israel depended relatively little on exporting or importing, being still a predominantly self-sufficient agrarian society (*cf.* also Prov. 31:24; Neh. 13:16).

[39] There are four major interpretive options: 1. a prophecy of a literal rebuilding never obeyed; 2. a symbolic depiction of the church; 3. a literal rebuilt temple still to come in the future; 4. an apocalyptic picture of the coming perfection of God's plans for his people accentuating the centrality of worship, the presence of the Lord among his people and his blessing them with an orderly arrangement of their duties and privileges. L. Allen (1990: 214–215) opts for the first; Delitzsch (1983: 388–390), for the second; Cooper (1994: 353), for the third; and Taylor (1969: 253–254), for the fourth, which seems best.

## Summary and conclusions

Hebrew wisdom/poetry and prophetic literature enrich our understanding of God's revelation concerning material possessions and build
on the principles already articulated in the Torah and historical books.
Job and Ecclesiastes remind us that the reasons some are poor or
rich remain locked in the mysteries of God. The wisdom and poetic
literature more generally holds in a certain tension the twin themes
of material reward for righteous living and the oppression perpetu-
ated by the unjust rich. The book of Psalms introduces the $^{ca}n\bar{a}w\hat{i}m$ –
the materially poor and religiously pious who reappear again in the
Prophets, especially Isaiah. The dominant thrust of the Prophets,
however, is that God will judge the exploitative rich as part of his
eschatological plan to create a perfectly just society and redeemed
material world. Zechariah 7:10 enshrines a recurring theme that
aptly summarizes God's heart in the prophetic literature: 'Do not
oppress the widow or the fatherless, the alien or the poor' (Schwantes
1977: 84).

## Conclusions concerning the entire Old Testament and material possessions

'The Hebrew Bible does not automatically support one economic or
liberation analysis of poverty' (Pleins 1994: 280). Neither the amassing
of riches nor their lack is seen as a necessary good (or evil). The industriousness promoted by capitalism finds parallels, but the poor are by no
means seen as generally lazy. The relative equality promoted by socialism appears, too, but via individual and familial titles to property, not
via state ownership. The prophetic denunciation of social injustice
central to liberation theology permeates the Old Testament, but not once
is there a call for violent resistance to Israel's oppressors on these
grounds.

Instead, the Old Testament cuts right across all modern systems and
ideologies. It clearly presupposes both the right and the responsibility
of those who are able to work to provide for their own well-being. But
God does not promise that hard work automatically leads to material
blessing. In the framework of the unique covenant he arranged with
Israel, he commands obedience to the Torah, and it is within this
covenantal framework that the vast majority of Old Testament promises
of prosperity must be viewed. They are consistently tied to the
Promised Land and to the temple cult and its sacrificial form of

worship. Land and worship in the New Testament are both clearly 'spiritualized', at least during the church age. However one resolves the debates about a possible, literal future for Jews in Israel during a millennium, the material blessings of the covenantal arrangement between God and Israel are consistently 'christified' in the present age (see esp. Davies 1974). That is to say they are fulfilled in Christ in such a way that believers may not claim these promises in a literal, materialistic sense during the Christian era. John 4:24 denies any role for a temple or piece of property that is different from or holier than any other. Jesus' followers will worship God 'in spirit and in truth' wherever they may be. Paul regularly refers to our bodies individually, and the church corporately, as living temples and sacrifices (e.g., 1 Cor. 3:16–17; 6:19; Rom. 12:1–2). The psalmist promised the meek in Israel an inheritance in the Promised Land (Ps. 37:11); Jesus quotes this verse in beatitude form to bless all of his followers with the gift of the whole earth (Matt. 5:5). Colossians 2:16–17 and Hebrews 4:1–11 explain that the Sabbath rest is a shadow of the substance that was to come, which is Christ, and that living as Christians in this age and the next spiritually fulfills the sabbatical laws (cf. esp. Carson 1982). Wealth as a sign of God's blessing and as the reward for one's labour, then, are the two major strands of Old Testament teaching that for the most part do *not* carry over into the New Testament (see esp. Wheeler 1995: 123–127).

Even within the Old Testament economy, however, material blessing was never viewed as an end in itself. An abundance of resources was to be shared with the nations and particularly with the needy. The emphasis on property rights clearly cuts in two different directions. Since all, in theory, should have the opportunity to own at least a modest plot of ground, none should ever be permitted to have too much. The 'haves' and the 'have-nots' are interdependent. Brueggemann (1975: 355) sums up the key words here as 'respect and restraint'. Numerous commands enjoin voluntary generosity, while mandatory taxes and tithes are instituted to prevent extremes of riches and poverty from remaining. The institutional norms of the Jubilee create a halfway house between creation and kingdom ethics based on the value of interpersonal relationships and local communities. They are concerned with the depersonalization of both market forces and staterun societies (see esp. Schluter & Clements 1990). Proverbs 30:7–9 offers an unusually worded expression of this 'golden mean'. We must seek neither poverty nor riches. Those who have already been blessed with wealth must be generous and compassionate in using it. Interestingly, this mediating perspective will recur even more in the New Testament than it does in the Old.

The key to evaluating any individual church or nation in terms of its use of material possessions (personally, collectively or institutionally) is how well it takes care of the poor and powerless in its midst, that is, its cultural equivalents to the fatherless, widow and alien. This theme pervades the Law, the historical books, wisdom and poetry, and the prophetic literature. People always take priority over prosperity. Those in positions of power have no increased privilege, only increased responsibility (Gowan 1987: 353). The New Testament suggests that governments should promote justice, but it primarily emphasizes the responsibilities of the individual and the church.

Williamson (1985b) sums up the teaching of the Old Testament on the material world under three headings that closely resemble the points we have just made. First, the land and its produce are good. Dangers arise only when they are used for personal ends rather than for protection of those in trouble. Next only in importance to the promises to Abram in Genesis 12:1–3 is the Jubilee principle of Leviticus 25:23. Land may not be sold in perpetuity; it belongs to God, but he shares it with us and wants as many of us as possible to benefit from it. Second, the widow, orphan and immigrant are paradigms of the powerless. There is a partial alignment of poverty and piety but never any direct equation. Any system can and should be judged by what happens to the marginalized. Third, material blessings in the Old Testament confirm God's covenant to build a mighty nation out of Israel, who would then share its Law and its wealth with the world. This principle of generosity and compassion with one's material blessings pervades the Hebrew Scriptures and applies to everyone – from the grass-roots, rural-community level all the way up the social ladder to the king.[40]

With the exception of the promise of material blessings for covenant obedience or diligent industry, all of the major themes of the Old Testament teaching on material possessions reappear in one form or another in the New Testament. Many are applied even within the Old Testament to individuals (*e.g.*, Job) or to nations (esp. the enemies of

---

[40] More succinctly *cf.* George (1977: 21): the Old Testament reactions to poverty vary: 'Human wisdom sees in it [nothing but] the consequences of laziness or disorder; faith sees in it, each in turn, a divine punishment, a scandal, a call to discover certain religious values.' Ellis (1995: 4–14) sums up Old Testament teaching on stewardship under the category of God's gifts – creation, land and offspring – to which human response should be to manage the gifts under the sovereignty of God as their owner and in gratitude for them without pride or self-determination.

Israel surrounding her) in ways that make it clear that they are not limited to Israel. Christians should therefore take them very seriously and look for applications even in the changed cultures of modern society that permit those principles to be implemented.

# Chapter Three

# Additional historical background: between the Testaments

To understand the New Testament against its historical background, it is not enough simply to have surveyed the Old Testament teaching on a given topic. The nearly five centuries that constitute the so-called intertestamental period saw numerous historical, political, social, religious and economic changes in the Ancient Middle East. We will divide our study of this period into four parts: a survey of general socio-political developments during these centuries; an overview of the Jewish literature of this period; some generalizations about the differences among the Jewish sects and between Judaism and the Greco-Roman world; and information from the Gospels themselves bearing on the socio-economic status of their main characters.

## Socio-political developments[1]

As the Old Testament period drew to a close, Persia remained the dominant empire throughout the biblical world. In the late 300s BC, Persia gave way to Greece with the remarkable military exploits and conquests of Alexander the Great. Alexander's empire eventually divided in two, the northern half ruled by the Seleucids in Syria, and the southern half by the Ptolemies in Egypt. From roughly the 320s until the 160s BC, several generalizations held true about the empire that Alexander bequeathed to his successors (see esp. Jagersma 1985: 10–56). Resettlement and unification of the empire brought economic growth and prosperity to many places. What had largely been a rural-centred collection of provinces or territories quickly became highly urbanized. Hellenization, the spread of the influence of Greek customs and culture, also prevailed, causing no little turmoil for people who

---

[1] The most detailed and up-to-date overview of the entire Second Temple period, focusing on the significance of land in the economics of Palestine, is Pastor (1997). Much broader overviews of the social and economic histories of the Hellenistic world and Roman empires, now somewhat dated and with a periodic Marxist bias, are found in Rostovtzeff (1941 and 1957).

wanted to cling to their traditional customs, especially under the belief that they were God-given, as in Israel. To support imperial economics, the various Seleucids and Ptolemies increasingly taxed their peoples, and, when Antiochus III in 188 BC signed an ill-advised treaty with Rome promising large sums of tribute, the economic burdens on a province like Palestine increased markedly. These centuries brought the increase of latifundism, the dividing up of agricultural property into large estates, often owned by absentee landlords and run by slave labour. The Zenon papyri from the third century BC also disclose the rise of 'tax farmers', the middlemen who ensured that rents and taxes in both money and crops were paid to the estates' owners. Here lies the origin of the animosity between the typical peasant and what in the New Testament are often called 'tax collectors' or 'publicans' (although the two terms are not necessarily synonymous; see below, pp. 107, 140).

Antiochus IV (also known as Epiphanes) pushed the Jews in Israel to the point of revolt, because of his numerous oppressive laws and policies that virtually rendered the Jewish religion illegal. But there was also an economic dimension to the Jewish protest and a certain economic resourcefulness that, along with many other factors, enabled the Maccabean revolt of 167 BC to succeed despite the substantially greater size of the Syrian armies arrayed against them (for the story, see esp. 1 Maccabees). For the first time in centuries, God's covenant with Israel had again seemingly been vindicated. The Jews believed that God liberated his people because of their refusal to cooperate with the profane Hellenizers in their own country, and it was now incumbent on them to continue to obey his laws to retain their freedom. But the ideals and freedom promoted by the revolution increasingly deteriorated in subsequent decades. Rome continued to expand eastward, threatening menacingly on Israel's horizon, and was increasingly held at bay by taxes or tribute paid directly to the imperial coffers. While prosperity at first improved sharply under the Hasmonean dynasty, eventually a rift between rich and poor began to grow again. After nearly a century of Jewish independence, internal power struggles led to the Roman general Pompey being virtually invited to invade Jerusalem to bring some measure of peace and stability (in 63 BC).[2] The cost of the Roman intervention and the internal skirmishes that followed led to a noticeable decline in the wealth of the average Israelite (Bammel 1984: 109).

The first strong and influential client-king in Palestine under Roman rule was Herod the Great (37–4 BC). In many ways, his perspectives

[2] For more details of the various policies and practices of taxation and tribute under the Ptolemies, Seleucids and Hasmoneans, see Mittwoch (1955).

and policies were as ruthless as those of Antiochus Epiphanes, but he proved far more shrewd politically. An Idumean who claimed to have converted to Judaism, Herod engaged in massive building campaigns and numerous public works that genuinely benefited the Jewish people. But the cost was enormous, as taxation and slave labour increased.[3] When Herod died and his kingdom was divided among his sons, Archelaus, who was given Samaria and Judea, proved so oppressive that a Jewish embassy to Rome in AD 6 successfully bid for his ousting. Imagery of that event may lie behind part of Jesus' parable of the pounds in Luke 19:11–27. Between the more than 23.3% of goods that had to be paid in Jewish tithes, the temple tax and other occasional or freewill offerings, and the additional tribute to Rome, the average Jew in the early first century laboured under a tax burden that ranged from roughly 30% to 50% of his total income (cf. Schmidt 1992: 804–807 with Oakman 1986: 57–77).[4]

Although we have no statistics from ancient Rome to reflect the exact economic breakdown of first-century society, sociological studies of ancient empires more generally disclose a pervasive pattern as follows: roughly the top 2% of the population – the emperor and his court, the landed aristocracy and key military and religious rulers – usually controlled from one half to two thirds of the entire wealth of the empire and comprised the truly and enormously rich. Another 5%–7% formed a 'retainer' class of bureaucrats and aides to the ruling class, functionaries who implemented the policies of the elite and who, as long as they retained their positions, were also quite well-to-do. A small 'middle class' of merchants and traders, along with the more successful priests and religious leaders, plus the occasional artisan, could expand the percentage of those whose level of existence brought them above the poverty line to probably no more than 20% of the whole society. At the opposite end of the spectrum, up to 10% were extremely destitute, sick or disabled and formed the 'expendable' class whose lives were at any given time in literal jeopardy. The remaining 70% or so would still be considered quite poor by any contemporary standard. These made up the villagers and farmers that accounted for a majority of the population and whose seasonal welfare depended almost entirely on the success of

---

[3] See Gabba (1990) for details of the finances of King Herod.

[4] In a study of Roman history not biased by an explicit agenda of determining how ripe for revolution first-century Israel had become, Hopkins (1980) determined that Roman taxes were quite low during this period, which he defines as under 10% of one's gross income. This still leaves a lower boundary of roughly 33% as the combined total of the Jewish and Roman take. Still helpful for much of this historical background is Grant (1956).

the harvests or the catches of fish (see especially Herzog 1994b: 53–73; following Kautsky 1982 and Lenski 1966). On the use of the language of lower, middle and upper 'class' in biblical times, Soares-Prabhu's conclusions (1991: 170–171) are balanced and helpful: class distinctions are neither altogether different from nor identical to today's divisions. For example, 'the biblical poor include and transcend Marx's proletariat'. Class struggle is present but 'purged from elements that are not compatible with Jesus' command to universal and non-exclusive love'.

It is anachronistic to speak of capitalism or communism in ancient societies such as these, although elements of both later models were clearly present. Banks at times held large sums of money, and we know of modest investment and interest schemes in the ancient Roman economy. Lending and borrowing had flourished from at least the days of classical Athens (Millett 1991). But the lending of money was strictly limited by cash in hand and was practised exclusively with non-productive purposes in mind, such as lending to the poor so that they might pay their debts (M. Finley 1973: 141).[5] Inflation was negligible until after New Testament times, often as low as 1% (Duncan-Jones 1994: 29). Grant's conclusion of over forty years ago (1956: 114) remains sound: 'Capitalism existed, but again it was a limited operation; there was nothing like modern capitalistic production', and 'none of the industrial revolution's dehumanizing forces leading to Marxian analyses'. So, too, what would probably better be called 'communalism' rather than communism characterized village life, as the honour of individuals demanded a subordination of one's own well-being to that of the community. It has often been argued by sociologists that the ancient world was dominated by the so-called 'theory of limited good'. In a world before Adam Smith or Karl Marx, it was assumed that the enormously wealthy got that way only at the expense of the poor. In other words, the size of the total 'pie' was fixed; the more one individual had, the less by definition was available to others (see esp. Malina 1981: 71–93). There is some evidence that opposite views cropped up at times in ancient Greece and Rome (see esp. Hamel 1990: 98), but the pervasive invective against the majority of rich people as wicked through ill-gotten gains gives the sociological analysis a fair measure of plausibility.

First-century Galilee seems to have been a society in transition. Numerous Jewish families still held and farmed their small ancestral

---

[5] González (1990: 38) believes that rates varied from 12% to 48%!

plots of land, but they might well exist side by side with the large estates owned by absentee landlords (Fiensy 1991: 21–73). And if the climate or the economy proved unfavourable for too long, the peasant farmers who still owned their own property would be unable to pay their taxes, would go deeper into debt, and in extreme cases would be thrown into slavery or debtors' prisons. The three main options for peasants who did not own their own land were to work as tenants paying a fixed rent to their landlords, to pay a predetermined portion of their produce to the owner, or to join on with one of the great latifundia and be functionally equivalent in status to a slave (Fiensy 1991: 75–117). The fishing industry, too, was often controlled by wealthy merchants, so that the fishermen themselves obtained a minimal margin of profit (Freyne 1980: 173–174).

These economic factors, therefore, clearly made first-century Palestine ripe for revolt. The seeds of the Zealot movement began with Judas the Galilean in AD 6 and continued sporadically, even if they did not emerge in any kind of organized form until the unrest and ultimate war with Rome in the mid- to late 60s. Again, that revolt involved a combination of factors, not least the religious element. But we dare not minimize the economic components, either.[6] Even as Galilee remained relatively prosperous, perhaps into the 40s and 50s, Judea, with less of an agricultural basis, became increasingly impoverished, aided, too, by a severe famine in the late 40s. Taxation, indebtedness and latifundism all increased, and the Jewish historian Josephus' account of the events that led up to the Jewish war clearly include socio-economic unrest (see esp. *Jewish War* 2–3). Combine this with the religious conviction that God meant the Jews to live in their land free from foreign oppressors, and one can understand the rebellion that broke out. 'Economic problems had joined hands with spiritual revolt' (Applebaum 1989: 259).

## The literature of the Jews

Although the prevailing view in Judaism seems to be that during the intertestamental period 'prophecy' had ceased (see esp. Sommer 1996), so that there is no evidence that Jews ever considered as canonical any books other than the current Protestant Old Testament, a wide variety of Jewish literature often closely modelled on the genres of the Hebrew

---

[6] See esp. Goodman (1987: 51–75). More broadly, *cf.* Horsley (1987), who emphasizes the late development of the formal Zealot movement, with Hengel (1989), who stresses the earlier seeds of the movement.

Scriptures nevertheless emerged. The bulk of this literature is known as the Apocrypha (roughly a dozen new books, along with additions to a handful of the Hebrew Scriptures, that the Roman Catholic church would later canonize) and the Pseudepigrapha (a larger body of more than sixty items of Jewish literature, often written under the name of great heroes of Old Testament times, that were never canonized by anyone). The more recently discovered Dead Sea Scrolls form another important body of mostly pre-Christian, Jewish writing. Again we can deal only with representative texts on the major themes that emerge from this intertestamental literature. Considerable debate surrounds the dating and milieu of many of these documents, but space prevents us from attempting to set each in its historical context. Nevertheless, where modern consensus suggests a post-Christian date for an entire document, we will not incorporate the material in question. Where there is a significant chance that a document or its traditions may be pre-Christian, or simultaneous with but independent of the rise of the New Testament, we may incorporate some of the material in question.

## Apocrypha and Pseudepigrapha

Because of the foundational role of the Torah for Jewish life and because of the oral nature of the additional laws that developed from Hasmonean times on, we find only a small amount of legal material in the Apocrypha and Pseudepigrapha. Prophecy increasingly gives way to apocalyptic – that branch of literature that sees the only hope for God's people in his miraculous, even cosmic, intervention into the affairs of history. But many of the same themes of justice so characteristic of the prophets pervade apocalyptic literature as well. The closest parallels to biblical genres appear in the wisdom and poetic literature, at times seemingly indistinguishable from their more 'inspired' companions.

The themes of poverty and riches do not dominate this literature, which treats a full range of theological and ethical issues. But from time to time they assume a prominent role.[7] As in the Old Testament, the Apocrypha and Pseudepigrapha recognize the principle of the goodness of wealth. For example, the virtuous heroines Judith and Susanna are both quite well off. But in almost every context in which God's people attain wealth through righteousness, an emphasis on their generosity towards the needy appears as well. The book of Jubilees expands on the wealth and generosity of Abraham (e.g., 13:6; 16:22–25; 21:12),

[7] For an excellent, detailed survey of 'social ideals of the Apocrypha' more broadly, including the advantages and drawbacks of wealth, the woes of the poor, benevolence and its rewards, social justice and world peace, see Cronbach (1944).

as does the Testament of Abraham 1:5 (*cf.* also the Testament of Job 9 – 13 on Job). There is at least a hint of Aseneth's charity in her casting off her luxurious clothing and jewellery, as she also renounces her idols, to become a fit wife for Joseph (Joseph and Aseneth, see esp. 10:11). Pseudo-Phocylides 109 declares, 'When you are rich, do not be sparing; remember that you are mortal.' And the Testament of Benjamin 5:1 reminds those whose minds are set on good that they will make the greedy 'not only abstain from their passion but will give to the oppressed the things which they covetously hold'.[8]

Similarly, Sirach 13:24 acknowledges that riches can be good 'if they are free from sin', while 31:1–11 observes that wealth can be a testing device. On the one hand, it can create anxiety and ruin for those who overly pursue it; on the other hand, one can emerge like gold and fire, purged so that one's prosperity is established and the 'assembly' will relate one's acts of charity.[9] Sirach 44:6 includes among the famous people praised, 'rich men furnished with resources, living peaceably in their habitations', while people of mercy who perform righteous deeds will discover that 'their prosperity will remain with their descendants, and their inheritance to their children's children' (Sir. 44:10–11).

The theme of prosperity as a reward for covenant obedience is made explicit only rarely in this literature, in actual fact (see, *e.g.*, 2 Esdras [= 5 Ezra] 2:18–21, which also notes that the righteous will guard the rights of the dispossessed). But to make any sense of the historical developments, and particularly of the Jewish rebellions against Syria and Rome, this Deuteronomic principle must be presupposed as background to much of the literature of this period. One sees hints of references to obedience and disobedience to the Law in such texts as 1 Esdras 1:58 ('until the land has enjoyed all its sabbaths, it shall keep sabbath all the time of its desolation until the completion of 70 years') and in the theme of giving generously to the Lord in Sirach 35:1–11. More commonly, almsgiving is extolled as a key virtue (see esp. the book of Tobit),[10] and at times is even said

---

[8] In other words, 'Wicked men will change for the better, and behave more positively when meeting a good man' (Hollander 1985: 86).

[9] Skehan and Di Lella (1987: 382) comment: 'The Jewish ideal was a virtuous life together with sufficient wealth to ensure the necessities of life and to enjoy some degree of prosperity.'

[10] Tobit throughout is generous to the poor but also has money he left in a foreign land to draw on when hard times come, to which he trusts the Lord will lead his son despite numerous obstacles. 'To the author of Tobit money and property are useful commodities

to be a means of atonement. Tobit 4:8–11 encourages almsgiving in proportion to what one has; even the person with just a little is encouraged to give. Tobit 12:8–9 reads,

Prayer is good when accompanied by fasting, almsgiving and righteousness. A little with righteousness is better than much with wrongdoing. It is better to give alms than to treasure up gold. For almsgiving delivers from death, and it will purge away every sin. Those who perform deeds of charity and of right-eousness will have fulness of life. (*Cf.* also Sir. 3:30.)

These passages represent the highest level of Jewish piety in the intertestamental period. 'Almsgiving as an act of charity became prized as an unsurpassed meritorious deed' (Pilgrim 1981: 33). The theme would later recur in post-New Testament Christianity (see esp. Garrison 1993). But commentary on the Law is not nearly as pervasive as apocalyptic and wisdom themes.

In apocalyptic literature one can find the motif of detachment from possessions in light of the coming eschaton.[11] 2 Esdras 16:41–48, for example, stresses how buying, selling, building, sowing, marrying and working are all relativized because of the coming judgment and the loss of all possessions in the end times. As part of '6 Ezra', the final form of this text is post-Christian. Has 1 Corinthians 7:29–31 influenced the passage?

In striking contrast, Baruch 1:10–11 expands on Jeremiah 29:7, com-manding the people to sacrifice and pray for the well-being of Nebuchadnezzar (now to be equated with the various Hellenistic rulers). The Testament of Gad 7:1 likewise enjoins one not to be aggrieved at the prosperous but to pray for their complete prosperity, since this would prove advantageous to those who serve them. But verse 6 offers the following consolation: 'The man who is poor but free from envy, who is grateful to the Lord for everything, is richer than all,

---

but not ends in themselves.' They are neither inherently evil nor worth gaining illicitly (Zimmermann 1958: 29).

[11] An important recent challenge to conventional understanding of apocalyptic as God's cataclysmic intervention into human history to recreate the universe appears throughout N. T. Wright (1992) and (1996). Wright denies that Jews envisaged the end of this space-time order but spoke metaphorically of significant social upheavals as this world was substantially transformed and improved. Among various problems with this interpretation (see Allison 1994), is the difficulty in understanding the theme of detachment from possessions if one's property might still remain with one in a continued earthly existence.

because he does not love the foolish things that are a temptation common to mankind.' The Testament of Issachar 6:1–2 retains the increasingly impossible ideal of an exclusively agrarian society, free from the corruption of commerce (on which, *cf.* Safrai 1994: 306).

The Sibylline Oracles repeatedly introduce the theme of the 'great reversal' of Rome and Israel. Oracle 3:350–352 reminds its audience: 'However much wealth Rome received from tribute-bearing Asia, Asia will receive three times that much again from Rome and will repay her deadly arrogance to her.' Lines 531–532 declare that the Romans will see their 'enemies enjoying their private possessions and all their wealth', while line 581 promises that Jews will again inhabit their cities and cultivate their fields 'in prosperity'. Indeed, the theme of the age to come as one of material abundance continues to appear again and again. It is foreshadowed in the blessings of the Maccabean age (1 Macc. 14:4–15) and more specifically enunciated in such texts as 1 Enoch 10:18–19 and Sibylline Oracles 2:320–324; 3:619–623, 783. Characteristic of these passages are the promises of fields that produce crops far beyond anything known in the ancient world, including vineyards producing glorious quantities of wine! 1 Enoch 92 – 105 also contains numerous warnings against the unjust rich, virtually equating the rich and the oppressor (*e.g.*, 94:6–10; 96:4–6, 8; 97:8–10). Much of Enoch's imagery closely parallels the teaching of Jesus in Luke but without Luke's mitigating emphasis on the possibility of salvation for the wealthy (Nickelsburg 1979).

Seemingly aberrant views of material prosperity appear in the Treatise of Shem, which links the Jewish fortunes entirely to the signs of the zodiac, one chapter for each of the twelve signs, a syncretistic combination of religious beliefs that would have been anathema to the average Jew. And the Testament of Asher, in enunciating the principle of the good and evil spirits that pervade all people, seems to reject out of hand good deeds done by people otherwise characterized as evil. For example, 2:5 reads, 'Someone steals, deals unjustly, robs, cheats, but yet he has pity on the poor. This also has two aspects, but is evil as a whole.' The apparent rationale appears in verse 7: 'he kills many, yet has pity on a few'.

When one turns to the wisdom literature, one discovers most of the same themes stressed in the Old Testament material of the same genre (for a brief survey, *cf.* Hengel 1974: 16–19). Perhaps the most dominant of these is how often the rich are wicked or corrupt (see, *e.g.*, Wisd. of Sol. 2:6–11), so that one must not set one's heart on wealth (Sir. 5:1) but must recognize that it comes from the Lord (11:14). Particularly instructive is the attitude expressed in Sirach 11:18–19. Some rich who have toiled diligently and faithfully may say, 'I have found rest and now I shall enjoy my goods.' Yet such people do not know when they may die and leave their goods to others (*cf.* also Sir. 11:21–25 on the possible sudden reversal of fortunes in both directions in this life). One thinks immediately of Jesus' parable of the rich fool in Luke 12:15–21. The Sibylline Oracles 3:235 similarly warn against the 'love of money, which begets innumerable evils' (*cf.* 1 Tim. 6:10). So, too, the Testament of Judah 19:1 reminds us how 'the love of money leads to idolatry'. Of particular interest in this literature is the development of the expression 'dishonest wealth' as a term for *all* money, a concept which will be picked up by Jesus (*cf.* esp. Sir. 5:8, in light of 5:1, with Luke 16:9). Sirach 18:32 and 37:29 also warn God's people against excessive luxury.

Somewhat more consistently than in the canonical wisdom literature, the problem of evil is resolved by the concept of judgment day and a truly just life to come (see esp. Wisd. of Sol. 3 – 5). Nevertheless, much of the Psalms of Solomon still holds out hope for appropriate recompense even in this life (*e.g.*, 10:6; 17:21–34; *cf.* further Hoppe 1987: 140–142). In both strands of thought, interest in personal as well as apocalyptic eschatology increases, in part due to Hellenistic influence (Winston 1979: 25–33).

As in the biblical Proverbs, wisdom and riches are often contrasted (*e.g.*, Wisd. of Sol. 8:5), and we can be encouraged to use the latter to attain the former (*e.g.*, Sir. 51:28: 'Get instruction with a large sum of silver, and you will gain by it much gold').[12] In 4 Maccabees 2:8–9, apparently influenced by Hellenistic philosophy, we learn of the powers of reason, 'Even though [someone] is a lover of money, he is forced to act contrary to his natural ways and to lend without interest to the needy and cancel the debt when the seventh year arrives. If one is greedy, he is ruled by the law through his reason', so that, for example, he will not forget to leave gleanings in his harvest.[13]

Pervasive in the intertestamental literature is God's concern for the dispossessed and therefore the need for his people to care for them (see, *e.g.*, Sir. 4:1–10; Pseudo-Phocylides throughout and esp. line

---

[12] The text can also be translated, 'Acquire but a little instruction: you will win silver and gold through her.' In either event, the apparent monetary reward 'may stand for blessings other than simply material gain' (Rybolt 1986: 110).

[13] In 2:10, the Law 'which in previous verses operated through reason is now silently equated with reason'. One thinks of later, similar developments in Philo (Hadas 1953: 154).

42).[14] The righteous are those 'who give bread to the hungry, and who cover the naked with clothing, and who lift up the fallen, and who help the injured and the orphans, and who walk without a defect before the face of the Lord, and who worship him only' (2 Enoch 9:1b; cf. esp. Jas. 1:27 in the New Testament!). One must provide to all compassionately without discrimination, and if one does not have the physical means, at least one can be sympathetic in spirit, walking and weeping with those in need (Testament of Zebulun 7:1–4). The apocryphal Psalm 154:18 blesses the Lord 'who saves the poor from the hand of strangers; and redeems the innocent ones from the hands of the evil ones'. Sirach 11:12 reminds us that the Lord will exalt the poor, while 14:5–11 adds the interesting twist that people should not be overly stingy with themselves, otherwise how can they be generous to anyone else? Verse 11 concludes the short segment: 'My son, treat yourself well, according to your means, and present worthy offerings to the Lord.' Barry Gordon (1975: 80) notes that economists from Adam Smith to the present have assumed that industriousness and stinginess belong together, while the Old Testament and Apocrypha keep them separate.

Other themes found here and there within the intertestamental wisdom literature include warnings to exercise care in situations of lending and surety (*e.g.* Sir. 8:12–13; 18:33; 29:1–20), injunctions on the value of work and industry (*e.g.* Sir. 10:27) and the observations that time and circumstance prove the great levellers (Sir. 18:19–26). A variety of texts encourages people to strive for moderation in all things (Pseudo-Phocylides 36, 59 – 69; Psalm of Solomon 5:17). J. M. Ford (1980: 44) sums up Sirach's perspective as follows: 'Sirach mingles with the world and enjoys it with prudence and wisdom. He is not oblivious to the poor, but neither is he a social activist on their behalf.' While Sirach is the *one* intertestamental work to devote considerable attention to riches and poverty, this summary could well fit a majority of the Apocrypha and Pseudepigrapha, with appropriate nuancing.

## The Dead Sea Scrolls

When one turns to the Dead Sea Scrolls, one enters the world of sectarian Judaism.

Most scholars still agree that this monastic community on the shores

---

[14] Gordon (1982: 418–419) observes, 'Faced with the seeming contradiction between the commandments and the worldly-wise course, [Sirach] comes down on the side of generosity in lending to a brother or friend,' but less ambiguously than in the New Testament this generosity is limited to the 'deserving' poor (*cf.* 12:7).

of the Dead Sea at the site known as Qumran represented the Essene Jewish sect, even if it differed in a few particulars from those Essenes who still lived in cities (cf. esp. Josephus, *Jewish War* 2.8.2–13; *Antiquities* 18.1.5; Philo, *Quod omnis probus* 12; *Apol. pro Jud.* 11).[15] Best known is the communal arrangement of possessions whereby the would-be initiates surrendered all their property in stages to the common pot of the community. The Manual of Discipline, the foundational ruling document of the community, describes this procedure in the greatest amount of detail. After a one-year trial period the wealth and belongings of the person accepted for admission 'will also be included at the hands of the Inspector of the belongings of the Many' (1QS 6:19b–20a). Yet not until initiates have completed their second year and are accepted are their goods put into the common treasury. In the meanwhile they are merely laid aside (1QS 6:20b–21). Also, 'If one is found among them who has lied knowingly concerning goods, he shall be excluded from the pure food of the Many for a year and shall be sentenced to a quarter of his bread' (6:24b–25). 1QS 7:6–7 adds that if one is negligent with the possessions of the community and suffers a loss, they shall be replaced in full, suggesting that some individuals still had access to other privately held means. 1QS 11:1–2 warns that, among other failings of 'those with a stray spirit', they are 'keen on riches'.

The Damascus Document, reflecting Essene city life, also warns against murdering 'for the sake of riches and gain' or 'taking any of [one's] riches ... except on the advice of the company of Israel' (CD 12:7–8). CD 14:12–16 further explains this communal arrangement:

> And this is the rule of the Many, to provide for all their needs: the salary of two days each month at least. They shall place it in the hand of the Inspector and of the judges. From it they shall give to the orphans and with it they shall strengthen the hand of the needy and the poor, and to the elder who [is dy]ing, and to the vagabond, and to the prisoner of a foreign people, and to the girl who has no protector and to the unma[rried woman] who has no suitor; and for all the works of the company.

CD 4:15–17 reminds us of the Essenes' conviction that both priests and temple in Israel had become corrupt through wealth. Again there are

---

[15] For a complete presentation and translation of all the Greek and Roman sources that discuss the Essenes and the convergence of this data with what we know from Qumran, see Vermes and Goodman (1989).

texts that refer to additional private property still held by individuals (*e.g.*, 9:14; 12:9–11).[16] The term 'wicked wealth' (represented by the Heb. *hôn harāšāʿ*), appears more regularly in the Dead Sea Scrolls than in the Apocrypha or Pseudepigrapha (see, *e.g.*, 1QS 10:19; CD 6:15; 19:17). Here the expression clearly refers to all material possessions outside of the community (Flusser 1992: 179, 182) and thus approximates to 'money' in general (so esp. Kosmala 1964). But the Dead Sea Scrolls can still speak of specifically ill-gotten gain (1QpHab 6:1). Moreover, the wicked priest became conceited, deserted God and betrayed the laws for the sake of riches (8:8–12; *cf.* 12:2–3). Indeed, the Apocryphal Lamentations (B) declare that the entire sons of Israel 'have not placed you before them, but they act the bully against the poor and needy' (4Q501:9). To abstain from the defiling influences of wealth one must refrain from stealing from the poor, from making spoils of widows and from murdering orphans (CD 6:16–17), but must instead 'strengthen the hand of the poor, the needy and the foreigner' (CD 6:21). The founding leader of the Qumran community, known in its literature only as the Teacher of Righteousness, is himself praised in a pesher on Psalm 37:25–26 as one who has compassion and makes loans, and whose offspring is blessed (4Q171 3:17–19). But although it practised communal sharing, there is no indication that the community collectively was particularly impoverished (VanderKam 1994: 82–83). In fact, over forty years ago, Farmer (1955) had already shown considerable evidence for the overall prosperity of Qumran.

As in the Psalms and Isaiah, the Dead Sea literature frequently equates the poor and the pious. In numerous contexts, it is virtually assured that each member of the sect will fall into this category. CD 19:9 declares, 'Those who are faithful to [God] are the poor ones of the flock.' The War Scroll equates 'the anointed', 'the poor', and 'those you saved' (1QM 11:7–9), and later introduces the category of the 'poor in spirit' as equivalent to 'the frail', 'those with broken backs', 'the perfect ones' and 'the remnant of your people' (14:6–8). The Hymn Scroll includes beatitudes blessing the poor: 'Fortunate, the men of truth ... who love compassion, the poor in spirit, those refined by poverty and those purified by ordeal ...' (1QH 6:2–4; *cf.* also 10:32, 34; 13:13, 18). In 1QM 14:7 the term apparently refers to the entire

---

[16] For a good summary of the role of private property among the Essenes both at Qumran and Damascus, see Rabin (1957: 22–36). But Rabin swings the pendulum too far in the opposite direction by denying that the Qumranians practised any 'community of goods' (correctly, Mealand 1975).

Qumran community. It is mistaken to claim that this Essene use of the term 'poor' led to the word being appropriated by early Christians to refer to *all* believers (correctly, Keck 1965; Keck 1966). One of the more recently translated fragments contains a long string of beatitudes, not unlike those found in Jesus' teaching. Again, 'the poor in spirit' appear, in a context that combines religious and socio-economic elements (4Q 525, frag. 2, col. 2; *cf.* Matt. 5:3–12; Luke 6:20–23).[17]

Unlike the Apocrypha and Pseudepigrapha, the Dead Sea literature does contain a significant quantity of exegetical or halakhic writing, which records further commentary and interpretation of the Torah. With respect to economic issues, one finds additional enunciation and explication of the laws on taxes (4Q159, frag. 1, 2:6–14), firstfruits (11QTemple 43:13) and tithing (58:13–14). The Temple Scroll combines the Deuteronomistic theology of blessing for faithfulness with the prophetic theme of social justice in 51:15–16: 'Pursue justice exclusively so that you can live and enter and take possession of the land which I give you as an inheritance for ever.' The severity of this communal group re-emerges in verses 17–18, in which the one who takes bribes and perverts justice is to be executed without qualms![18]

The Hodayoth (hymns) further prioritized truth above wealth (1QH 6:20; 7:27). The recently translated Messianic Apocalypse (4Q521) contains close parallels to the ministry of the servant in Isaiah 61:1, with its proclamation of good news to the poor (frag. 2, 2:7–13; *cf.* 1QH 23:14–15).[19] A certain ideal of moderation occurs again in 4Q416 2.2:14–21 ('Do not stay awake for your riches ... do not glory in your lack'). Various New Jerusalem texts remind us of the literal, material splendour of the anticipated new age (2Q24; 4Q554–555; 5Q15 and 11Q18). Finally, the enigmatic Copper Scroll (3Q15) describes directions to discover the vast hoards of gold, silver and other valuable artifacts buried in the valley of the desert outside the Qumran settlement. Despite the efforts of many archaeologists, no buried treasure has ever been unearthed, and it is difficult to know if the text was even intended to be taken literally.

One obvious conclusion from this survey of intertestamental Jewish literature is that we must be aware of facile generalizations. It is often

---

[17] For discussion see Flusser (1960: 1–13). On the similarities between Qumran's and Jesus' beatitudes, see Brooke (1989); for an emphasis on the differences, Viviano (1993).

[18] On the organizational pattern and the penal code of the Qumran sect, see Weinfeld (1986).

[19] For an analysis of these texts and the entire intertextual tradition of interpretation between Isaiah 61:1 and Luke 4, see J. Sanders (1975).

alleged that the Jews simply equated riches and righteousness because of their covenant arrangement with God. Yet, if anything, however much this theme may be presupposed behind the literature here surveyed, it is not nearly as frequently enunciated as the reverse. Riches are regularly, though not exclusively, seen as ill-gotten. The oppressive nature of the well-to-do, understandable particularly in the decades under Roman occupation, permeates these texts. The poor can at times seem lazy and be commanded to work hard, but more often than not they are seen as the unjust victims of exploitation. And in several important strands of the literature, the poor and the pious become equated, although not at the expense of a certain measure of literal, material poverty. But there is no precedent in Jewish understanding for the godless poor person being somehow inherently favoured by God.

## Other ideological developments prior to the New Testament

### Other Jewish responses

The range of religious responses to economic issues is also organizable by comparing the various Jewish sects. We have just summarized the Essene option and have spoken previously of the Zealots, who ultimately took up arms against Rome. The Sadducees were clearly the wealthiest of the Jewish groups. They were generally priestly, aristocratic and pro-Herodian in outlook, and were largely content with the status quo under Rome because they stood to gain the most by it. Significantly, they proved most prominent in the Gospel narratives towards the end of Jesus' life when he 'cleansed' the temple (Mark 12:15–18 and pars.), and they dominated the Sanhedrin at the time when Jesus was arrested and condemned to die. Despite the antagonism of Pharisees and scribes to Jesus throughout his ministry, it may well have been the Sadducees who were most directly responsible for Jesus' execution. Apparently, some of their enormous wealth and power were recently acquired and their accompanying status was still quite controversial among the rest of the people.[20]

As laymen, the Pharisees in many cases would have occupied a socioeconomic bracket closer to the ʿam hāʾāreṣ, the ordinary 'people of the land', although some may have risen a little higher into the small 'middle class'. The use of 'the poor' in the Psalms of Solomon to refer to the (pharisaically) righteous (e.g., 10:7; 15:2 and 18:3) is thus devoid

---

[20] See further M. Bockmuehl (1994: 109–112), and the literature there cited.

of socio-economic significance. Given the Pharisees' conviction that it was covenant disobedience that led them still to be languishing under foreign domination, and given that they felt that even the generally faithful 'am hā'āreṣ[21] had not sufficiently obeyed God's will, one can understand both the increasing body of oral traditions that arose to explain and clarify the Torah and the friction that emerged when Jesus' teachings clashed with this oral law.[22]

In Judaism, however, the major issue was not one's socio-economic level *per se*, but the amount of honour or shame that accrued to a person. Villagers, particularly in years of poor crops, could be toiling in almost grinding poverty but would not look upon each other with shame. They chipped in, supported one another as best as they could and tried to follow the laws and morals of their traditions. Conversely, the tax collector might well be considerably more self-sufficient and yet be more ostracized because of the shame of working for the oppressive Roman regime.[23] General social stability, connectedness to nuclear and extended families and the close ties within traditional villages all prevented peasants from moving into that bottom class of expendable individuals (see above, p. 89). Thus, a wealthy steward who fell out of favour with his master was actually at greater risk than the average villager, since he could move all the way from the rich retainer class to the expendables and find himself literally in danger of starving to death (*cf.* the fears of the steward in Luke 16:1–9).

Not surprisingly, therefore, at least after AD 70, the Jewish synagogues in most communities had well-organized collections for the poor. The genuinely needy had opportunities to receive either weekly donations of money or daily gifts of food. Clothing was also available. Door-to-door begging, however, was discouraged. Attempts were made to distinguish between genuine and fraudulent claims of need, but later Mishnaic teaching stressed that if people were to err, they should err on the side of charity (Mullin 1983: 30–32). The temple treasury in Jerusalem was also used in part for 'welfare' (Hamel 1990: 216–219). As we recall from the Old Testament, the Torah institutionalized tithes for the poor, almsgiving and community charity. How much of the later synagogue practices

---

[21] On the 'am hā'āreṣ, see esp. Oppenheimer (1977).

[22] On the sociology of Pharisees, scribes and Sadducees, see Saldarini (1988).

[23] But one must also distinguish the publican proper, like Zacchaeus (a 'chief tax collector'), who was clearly wealthy (Luke 19:1–10), and the go-between tax farmer like Levi/Matthew, who may have been little better off than other Jewish peasants (Schottroff & Stegemann 1986: 7–13).

pre-dated the rise of Christianity is more difficult to determine.[24]

## The Greco-Roman world

The Greco-Roman world proves more crucial as background for Paul and the later epistle-writers, but given the inroads of Hellenism into first-century Israel, especially Galilee, we may make brief mention of Greek and Roman developments here as well. In general, Greeks, unlike their Jewish counterparts, saw poverty as an unadulterated evil, shame and disgrace, and often blamed the victims. Other poor were seen as less culpable and more to be pitied, even as the objects of charity, but with the end result that the rich felt their superiority that much more (Rosivach 1991). There was little, if anything, in this state of humanity to be respected, because there was no tradition of God as the protector of the poor.

The Roman Empire generally lacked any organized welfare system, although in times of severe famine or after natural disasters, such as earthquakes, modest relief efforts did emerge. The corn dole established in 58 BC was limited to the city of Rome and to those who were its citizens. The institution of benefaction, however, filled in various gaps that the government left. Wealthy people were generally expected to function as 'patrons' of various poor or unemployed in their community (known as their 'clients'). This was a tit-for-tat relationship in which the patron supplied monetary aid to his clients, in return for which they provided political favours, worked odd jobs and in general offered the patron public acclaim to enhance his honour and esteem. The institution was one by which wealthy people acquired a good reputation among their peers, more than one which was developed out of genuine compassion for the needy.[25] Often such benefaction by the wealthy substituted for their paying Roman taxes, at least in early post-Christian times.

When one turns to the major Greek and Roman philosophers and political theorists, one discovers yet another diverse collection of perspectives on economic issues. Plato in his *Republic* imagined a utopian and communitarian society in which equality prevailed, at least among the well-to-do. Both penury and excessive wealth, he believed,

---

[24] Jeremias (1969: 126–134) thinks they were in place; Seccombe (1978) disputes it.

[25] *Cf.* Saller (1982) and Wallace-Hadrill (1989). Among those who have applied the model to the New Testament, see esp. Winter (1994: esp. 41–60). For a compilation of texts describing ancient civic benefactions, see Danker (1982). Danker also demonstrates the pervasiveness of literal and metaphorical language of benefaction in the New Testament, particularly with reference to God and Jesus.

corrupted the state, the former inciting crime and the latter sloth and luxury (*Laws*, 919b-c).[26] Aristotle, on the other hand, strongly defended private property against various forms of communalism but agreed that the middle class provided the real strength of a city (*Politics*, 1295b). The Stoics put forth an ideal of self-sufficiency but also contentment with that part of life that one could not control. Their founder, Zeno, believed that wealth could prove a hindrance to wisdom. Two centuries later, Cicero would exemplify the Stoic ideal in helping the needy: 'our obligation is not to take upon ourselves bitterness and pain for the sake of others; it is simply, where possible, to relieve others of their pain' (cited in Hands 1968: 82): In other words, the Stoics sought a rational rather than an emotional response. Against the Stoics, the Epicureans were best known for their slogan, 'Eat, drink and be merry, for tomorrow you may die', although this is often misrepresented as reflecting a hedonistic outlook. Epicurus himself, however, was somewhat sickly and more concerned to avoid pain, cultivate pleasure, develop friends, attend cultural activities, and the like. The Cynics preferred a more radical option as they promoted an extremely simple lifestyle, dependent on begging, and viewed the divestment of worldly goods as a virtue. These traits, combined with their itinerant wanderings, have led some scholars to find parallels in the careers of Jesus and his disciples, but the differences outweigh the parallels (see esp. Boyd 1995) and this was the one philosophy that made the fewest inroads into Palestine.

Neo-Pythagoreanism promoted a sectarian form of communalism, but it seems to have had little influence. The Platonic dualism that emerged so prominently in early Gnostic thought easily led to an attitude of either asceticism or indulgence with respect to bodily appetites, but neither approach would have laid great spiritual emphasis on caring for the physically needy. Only Cicero in the first-century BC and Seneca in the first-century AD emerge as well-known Romans who have significant elements in common with both the motives and contents of later Christian thought (Mullin 1983: 15–24).[27]

As far as Roman government was concerned, a policy that generally distinguished it from both Jewish and Greek thought was the absolute freedom of the aristocracy to own property and to use it however they liked, even if that involved what we would we call abuse. From the

---

[26] *Cf.* the historian Thucydides (3.45.4) who spoke of 'poverty which leads to sharing through necessity, and affluence which leads to greed through *hubris* and pride'.

[27] For additional information on most of these Greco-Roman developments, see esp. González (1990: 3–19).

days of Augustus onward, the emperors were known for increasing extravagance in their spending and did not always balance their budgets. Expenditures included laying on lavish banquets for the social elite, sustaining a vast army, remunerating urban employees, caring for the imperial household and providing a variety of gifts and monies for public works, foreign subsidies and debts (Duncan-Jones 1994: 33–45). But the Roman cities' revenue came not so much from taxes or manufacturing as from agricultural trade and rents collected from the farmlands (Jones 1974: 25–31). Free men usually despised the trades or manual labour, which included both carpentry and fishing.

Ironically, in the ancient Roman empire, as so often today in the Two-Thirds World, many villagers and farmers left the stability of rural poverty for the large cities in hopes of improving their lot, but only a handful managed to do so. In many instances they found their circumstances even more appalling, because jobs were unavailable and they had separated themselves from their support networks of family and friends who could care for them during difficult times. Meanwhile, the rich in Rome grew richer, as they bought up large tracts of land and imported vast quantities of luxury items from far-flung corners of the empire. Increasingly, too, the imperial treasury was replenished with larger and larger sums of tribute money from subjugated peoples (Jones 1974: 114–129). Unlike the Jews, the Greeks and Romans apparently never developed a graduated or progressive tax, but typically charged flat amounts or percentages, so that the rich never made the same sacrifice as the poor (Jones 1974: 172–175).

## Conclusions

Comparing Jewish, Greek and Roman thought and practice increases the often bewildering diversity of perspectives on material possessions. Given the interpenetration of Hellenism and Judaism in Israel, and given the combination of Jews and Gentiles in most of the early Christian churches, especially in the diaspora, we will have to beware of assuming any one monolithic background in our interpretation of any given New Testament text. Nevertheless, certain elements will prove more prominent in some contexts than in others. In general, Christianity would share with Judaism a distinctive concern for the poor.

# Information from the Gospels bearing on the socio-economic status of the main characters

There is a long tradition of viewing Jesus and his family as quite poor (cf., e.g., Batey 1972:5–9; Stegemann 1984: 23–26). Luke 2:24 describes Mary and Joseph as having to offer the sacrifice in the temple of 'a pair of doves or two young pigeons', following the provision of Leviticus 12:8 for those who could not afford more expensive animals. The picture of the baby Jesus lying in a manger – a food trough (Luke 2:7) – and among animals has been viewed as proving Jesus' poverty. The statement about Christ becoming poor so that we might become rich in 2 Corinthians 8:9 has also been said to support this interpretation. Nevertheless, the latter verse is clearly a theological, rather than a sociological, statement (see below, p. 193), while the nature of the holy family's accommodations in Bethlehem can be attributed to the crowds present due to the census and do not necessarily reflect the family's normal living circumstances. The sacrifice, nevertheless, does suggest that at least at the time of Jesus' birth Mary and Joseph had very few financial resources.

As with many other people in the history of the world, however, this need not have remained their situation as the boy Jesus grew up. The key details for determining the family's later circumstances are the references to Jesus and Joseph as carpenters (Mark 6:3 and par.). The Greek word is *tektōn*, which could mean a woodworker or stonemason, and there is some evidence that such artisans could have arisen to at least the lower level of what today we would call 'blue-collar workers'. Of course, by any modern Western standards, work conditions would have seemed appalling, but by the standards of first-century Galilee, it may be appropriate to think of Jesus as part of the lower 'middle class'. At any rate, it seems that his family in later days was not subject to the 'grinding, degrading poverty of the day labourer or rural slave' (Meier 1991: 282).[28]

Some have tried to raise Jesus' level of income even higher by pointing to the construction boom in the mid-20s at nearby Sepphoris, an almost exclusively Gentile city that had originally been Herod Antipas's capital in Galilee. Granted that this city was only about five miles from the much smaller Nazareth, there is nevertheless no reference in the Gospels to Sepphoris. The same is true of Tiberias, the other even more prominent Gentile city in Galilee. This information is subject to two quite different interpretations, both of which involve arguments from silence. On the one hand, it could imply that Jesus would have had a good chance to work at Sepphoris and prosper above many of his contemporaries in other parts of the province (Batey 1991:

---

[28] On the problems of identifying Jesus with the poor and marginalized workers of the world, see Draper (1991).

65–82). On the other hand, the fact that he is never described as visiting there during his ministry could suggest the conventional Jewish avoidance of things Gentile and make it more likely that he would have avoided employment related to the construction industry there, even in earlier years (the traditional view). We simply do not have enough data to determine the probability of either thesis (J. Riches 1996: 391).

When we turn to Jesus' disciples, we again know rather little, but can make a few inferences. Fishermen at times were comparable in class to carpenters, though perhaps slightly less well off, inasmuch as their labour required less skill. Zebedee and his sons, John and James, were perhaps better off than many, given the reference to 'hired men' in the plural in Mark 1:20. The possession of one slave was extremely common, even for relatively poor Jewish families, but two or more probably indicated a higher level of prosperity.[29] Levi (or Matthew), as a converted tax collector, may also have been substantially better off, though we must be careful not to exaggerate the wealth that middlemen who were not 'publicans' (like Zacchaeus) would have accrued (recall above, p. 102, n. 23).[30] Levi does at least have the means to throw a party for his many associates, and indeed Jesus himself developed a reputation for enjoying such festivities (Matt. 11:19 and pars.). Matthew 11:19 (= Luke 7:34) also introduces us to the caricature of Jesus as a 'glutton and drunkard' and 'friend of tax collectors and sinners'. While the main point of the core truth behind this exaggeration is Jesus' welcome of the outcasts, Jesus' frequent practice of intimate table-fellowship with such riff-raff indirectly testifies to his anti-ascetic tendencies. He will endorse the expenditure of enough money to enjoy a good meal or party (cf. esp. Kee 1996).

It is a reasonable assumption that the remaining disciples were ordinary peasants, save perhaps Judas. If 'Iscariot' means 'man of Kerioth', a small town in Judea, Judas may have been the only non-Galilean disciple and therefore from a different social background as well. That he was responsible for the disciples' treasury (John 12:6) may indicate some prior experience in working with money. On the other hand, his willingness to betray Jesus for the sum of thirty pieces of silver (Matt. 26:15) may indicate that he was actually not that well off. Still, if these were shekels, the equivalent of four days' wages apiece, Judas would have received 120 days' worth of income, a

---

[29] Cf. Waetjen (1989: 79): 'James and John, who are in partnership with their father, probably enjoy a kind of middle-class prosperity and comfortability.'

[30] On the historical background and setting of tax collectors, see esp. Herrenbrück (1987), who also argues that only the Pharisees strongly stigmatized the tax collectors.

significant sum even to fairly prosperous folk.[31] Ultimately we must admit that we know nothing much at all about Judas' economic standing or his motives for betraying Jesus.[32]

As Jesus and the disciples travel together throughout most of his adult ministry, they clearly adopt an itinerant lifestyle. They depend on the gifts and provisions of others, but there is no indication that they have sold or permanently abandoned what material resources they had at home. In John 21:3, Peter can return to his fishing practice. Throughout the Gospels his family retains a house in Capernaum that becomes Jesus' home-base for later ministry (Mark 1:29–31 and pars.; cf. 2:1; 9:33; Matt. 4:13; 17:24). The group's itinerant lifestyle is temporary and freely chosen; Matthew 8:20 and parallel ('foxes have holes and birds of the air have nests, but the Son of Man has nowhere to lay his head') must be interpreted in this light. The same is all the more true for the short-term missions of the Twelve and the Seventy/Seventy-two (Mark 6:7–13 and pars.; Luke 10:1–24), in which Jesus sends his disciples out to replicate his ministry. Luke 22:35–38 explicitly rescinds many of the provisions for travelling simply, as Jesus anticipates rougher days ahead. Still, in 1 Corinthians 9:14 Paul will refer back to Luke 10:7 when stressing that the labourers are worthy of their wages. An even more explicit quotation of this verse appears in 1 Timothy 5:18. A cross-cultural principle apparently remains in force; one should depend for material support on those among whom one ministers (cf. further below, p. 186).[33]

The miracles of the feeding of the five thousand and four thousand obviously demonstrate Jesus' compassion and concern to feed the hungry masses. But it is interesting that Mark links Jesus' compassion for the five thousand more directly to the fact that the crowds were 'like sheep without a shepherd' (Mark 6:34). Only in the feeding of the four thousand is the danger from the crowd's hunger at all acute (Mark 8:2–3). The primary focus of both feeding miracles is clearly Christological, meant to recall Moses and the Israelites with their manna in the wilderness. John, by appending Jesus' 'Bread of Life' discourse (John 6:35–59), merely makes explicit what is already implicit in the Synoptics, that Jesus is the new and greater Moses (cf. Blomberg 1986).

---

[31] Reiner (1968: 186–190), however, suggests that 'thirty shekels' reflects an idiomatic Sumerian expression for 'a trifling amount'.

[32] For a succinct summary of Christian speculation, see Brown (1994: 1401–1404); and cf. further below, p. 142.

[33] The particulars, however, clearly vary in these and other New Testament and early Christian texts that may allude to Jesus' saying: see Harvey (1982).

The same may be said of Jesus' miracle-working ministry more generally. Again, Christ clearly concentrates on healing or exorcizing the physically needy. But this ministry always also occurs in a context of calling them to faith and discipleship, and he steers his audiences to the claims that in his miracle-working ministry the kingdom has arrived, and therefore the king, the Messiah, has come (see esp. Matt. 12:28 and pars.). The refrain that occurs four times in the Synoptic Gospels, 'your faith has saved you', might better be rendered 'your faith has made you whole'. In three out of the four passages in which this refrain occurs, the individuals addressed have been physically healed and have come to faith in Jesus (Mark 5:34 and pars.; 10:52 and par.; Luke 17:19). It is at least arguable that such holistic salvation is present in the fourth text as well (Luke 7:50; see further Blomberg 1994c: 76–83).

In Luke 7 – 8 one observes the interesting sequence of the story of Jesus anointed by the disreputable woman (7:36–50), followed immediately by a passing reference to women who travelled with Jesus along the road and 'were helping to support them out of their own means' (8:1–3; quotation from v. 3). Presumably, all of these women – Mary Magdalene, Joanna the wife of Chuza, Susanna and the unnamed others – were sufficiently well off to form the core of Jesus' 'support team'. At least Joanna, as the wife of a man identified as 'the manager of Herod's household' (8:3), would surely have fitted into this category.[34] At the end of Jesus' life, Joseph of Arimathea is described both as rich and as a closet disciple (Matt. 27:57; John 19:38; cf. the more nuanced parallels in Mark 15:43 and Luke 23:50–51). He volunteers a presumably costly unused tomb to give Jesus a decent burial following his extremely indecent execution.

# Conclusions

Economic developments in Israel in the centuries leading up to the time of Jesus set the stage for greatly misguided enthusiasm if anyone plausibly claimed to be the Messiah. In the midst of all the diversity of first-century Israel, every Jew could plainly see that Rome governed them, which was not what God had promised in his Word as their

---

[34] On these three verses more generally, see esp. Witherington (1979). Sim (1989) denies that we can demonstrate that any of the other women were wealthy and doubts whether Joanna, married to a non-Christian, could have contributed much, but his study relies heavily on several arguments from silence and a certain circular reasoning that begins from what Jesus 'usually' does elsewhere.

ultimate destiny. With the arrival of the messianic age would come not only political freedom but social prosperity. Religious and economic issues were deeply intertwined. In ways largely uncharacteristic of the Greek and Roman worlds, Judaism had a God who cared passionately about the poor and marginalized and opposed both religious idolatry and social injustice. It is crucial to understand these dominant trends if we are to make sense of the emergence of the New Testament teaching on material possessions in its historical context.

# Chapter Four

# The teaching of Jesus in the Synoptic Gospels

At last we turn to the New Testament itself. In light of the background of Old Testament and intertestamental teaching thus far surveyed, it is clear that a broad spectrum of beliefs and expectations surrounded economic matters, including those related to the time of a coming Messiah. We cannot simply presuppose any one monolithic background when it comes to interpreting New Testament texts. The New Testament itself affords clues as to specific background in the immediate context of a number of its key passages, and we will note these as we proceed. We will follow as best as it can be reconstructed the historical sequence of the developments narrated in the New Testament beginning with the teaching of Jesus in the Synoptic Gospels. I have elsewhere defended on historical grounds the substantial trustworthiness of both the Gospels' record in general and Jesus' teaching on rich and poor more specifically (Blomberg 1987; Blomberg 1994c: 87–93).

This chapter subdivides into two main parts: information gleaned from Jesus' parables, followed by the remaining, non-parabolic teaching of Jesus. There is a certain degree of arbitrariness to this division, but given the distinctive rules necessary for interpreting the parables, and given the fact that even those who are more sceptical of the historicity of the synoptic tradition more generally tend to accept a significant portion of the parables as bedrock, core 'Jesus material' (*cf.* Blomberg 1990), the division is perhaps a logical one. If the themes that emerge from an investigation of the parables are repeated and elaborated in the teaching of Jesus elsewhere in the Synoptics, the criterion of 'coherence' should support the authenticity of that additional material as well. The issues surrounding the Gospel of John are sufficiently distinctive to merit treating the data of the Fourth Gospel separately (see below, pp. 233–236). In each main section of this chapter, we will present individual passages as they appear in the sequence of Aland's synopsis (1982). While we cannot know in detail the exact chronological location of every gospel pericope, the general contours of the life of Christ are plain, and following a standard synopsis is perhaps a reasonable way to proceed and about as close an approximation of actual chronological sequence as we can reconstruct.

# The parables of Jesus

## Introduction

The interpretation of the parables has received an enormous amount of attention throughout church history, not least in the twentieth century. I have devoted numerous works to this topic and will not repeat myself here (see esp. Blomberg 1990; 1994b; 1996).[1] Nevertheless, little here depends on my somewhat distinctive thesis that the central lessons of each parable line up with the central characters of those narratives. Indeed, the two most important dangers to avoid in a survey of the parables for their contribution to a topic such as wealth and poverty are as follows: 1. we must beware of turning a parable into an explicit discourse on economic theory when it was never intended as such, and 2. we must beware of not taking a passage as teaching fairly directly on economic matters simply because we recognize a second or spiritual level to the story. In each case, we must also be alert to the possibility that the local colour in each parable provides us further information about standard economic arrangements in first-century Palestine. At the same time, almost every parable in at least one key place breaks the bounds of realism; this is usually the key to its allegorical or symbolic (*i.e.*, second level of) meaning.[2] Also presupposed in this discussion is some general background information on the kingdom of God. The

---

[1] I have been heartened by the generally positive responses of those who have taken the time to interact with my views. The one recent book-length study particularly compatible with my approach, though with important nuancing, is J. Sider (1995). The only detailed attempt to refute my approach of which I am aware is Parker (1996: esp. 82–87). But his criticism, which begins by challenging my equation of parable and allegory (or more precisely challenging my rejection of the limited definition of 'allegory' widely adopted by modern biblical critics), simply winds up by rejecting the usefulness of my broader definition (which parallels the study of rabbinic parables and literary criticism more generally). Nothing Parker writes actually undermines the *content* of my approach (*i.e.*, apart from debates over terminology or labels), despite his claims to the contrary. Parker's own alternative, that parables were 'painfully clear' from the outset without any element of concealment, like so many other approaches before him, requires jettisoning the Gospels' contexts in which the parables are embedded (92–105, 123–159) without offering any response to the second major objective of my volume, which was to defend the historical trustworthiness of those original contexts.

[2] For all of these points, *cf.* also Lambrecht (1992: 86).

synoptists summarize Jesus' preaching as a call to repentance in light of the imminent arrival of the kingdom (Mark 1:15 and pars.). It is widely agreed that the parables are one of the central devices that Jesus used for communicating about the kingdom, whether the term 'kingdom' itself actually appears in a given narrative or not. Specifically, we will take it as broadly demonstrated that Jesus through his parables teaches that God's dynamic reign has broken into human history through his person and ministry in a new and decisive way and that God intends to create a new community of his people who model, at least in part in the present, what God intends for all humanity and what he will one day perfectly create in a new age (cf. esp. B. Chilton 1996; Beasley-Murray 1986; Ladd 1974b).[3]

## The two debtors (Luke 7:41–43)

This short parable is embedded in the larger context of Jesus' dining at the home of Simon the Pharisee relatively early in his ministry.[4] Jesus is anointed by a disreputable woman from the community, with a lavish outpouring of perfume, to the disgust of Simon himself (Luke 7:36–40, 44–50). Two dimensions of this passage demonstrate immediately that Jesus does not object to using one's wealth for various kinds of celebrations. First, on numerous occasions he accepts invitations, including from Pharisees, to join people for dinner (see esp. Mark 2:15–17 and pars.; Luke 11:37; 14:1–24; 19:5–9; and cf. the generalization of Matt. 11:19 and par.). When these meals were hosted by well-to-do leaders, cultural mores would have dictated the provision of a sumptuous feast. Second, Jesus' refusal to rebuke the woman for 'wasting' the contents of an expensive jar of perfume on his feet further reinforces the conclusion that Jesus approves of at least occasional carefree expenditures as demonstrations of people's lavish love for him.

The major focus of this passage and the parable it contains, however, is on Jesus' surprising identification of the one who loves God more. The description in verse 37 of the woman as one 'who had lived a sinful

---

[3] Other views (e.g., Crossan's 'permanent eschatology' [1973] or Hedrick's dissociation of the parables from the kingdom [1994]) are idiosyncratic and unconvincing and have been adequately refuted elsewhere (see N. T. Wright 1996: 174–182; Blomberg 1996).

[4] Many have argued that all four Gospel accounts of Jesus being anointed by a woman must have been generated from only one original historical incident, but it is far more likely that Matt. 26:6–13, Mark 14:3–9 and John 12:1–8 represent one episode and Luke 7:36–50 a quite different one (cf., e.g., I. H. Marshall 1978b: 305–307; Carson 1991: 425–427).

life' may well be a euphemism for calling her a prostitute. If she was a prostitute, she may have earned enough through her 'profession' to be slightly better off than the average peasant, especially given her possession of expensive ointment.[5] Simon, on the other hand, would have been considered an upstanding member of the community; the Pharisees were by far the most respected and popular of the Jewish sects among the common people of the day. The parable itself uses a typical economic situation to teach a lesson about God's forgiveness. As we have seen (above, p. 91), numerous Jewish peasants would have amassed debts that forced them to borrow money to try to pay off the moneylenders.[6] The one unrealistic element designed to teach about God's lavish forgiveness is that the moneylender decided to cancel both debts when the debtors could not pay him back (7:42; cf. Bock 1994: 699). These material debts are thus used to teach a lesson about spiritual debts. At both levels, clearly the one forgiven the most has the most for which to be grateful (7:43). To the extent that the woman represented the 'have-nots' of her society more generally (and even if she were slightly better off than many, she certainly accrued the shame and disgrace that attached to her lifestyle), Jesus here shows his concern and compassion for the outcasts of his world early on in his ministry.[7]

## The seed among the thorns (Mark 4:18–19 and pars.)

In Jesus' well-known parable of the sower (Mark 4:1–9 and pars.), three kinds of soil ultimately prove fruitless. One of these three is described as full of 'thorns, which grew up and choked the plants, so that they did not bear grain' (4:7). When Jesus identifies the people who correspond to the seed sown among the thorns, he explains that they are those who 'hear the word; but the worries of this life, the deceitfulness of wealth, and the desires for other things come in and choke the word, making it unfruitful' (4:18b–19). Not only would the description of the vagaries of sowing and harvesting have proved lifelike for a first-century Palestinian farmer, but they would have reminded him of how much of

---

[5] Cf. Schottroff & Stegemann (1986: 15), who see this woman as 'a well-groomed "high-class" prostitute who could afford the most expensive perfumed oil' as over against the 'vast majority of prostitutes' who 'were a wretched lot'.

[6] A *denarius* is widely assumed to have been about a day's minimum wage (cf. Tobit 5:14; Matt. 20:2). Excluding Sabbaths and other holy days, we can estimate a 300-day work year for those who had regular employment. The two debtors would therefore have owed approximately twenty months' and two months' wages, respectively.

[7] For more on the implied sociology of the passage and Jesus' inversion of the recipients of honour and shame, see Thibeaux (1993).

his produce was 'unfruitful', going to pay off rent, tax, and the like. The less realistic hundred-fold yield pointed to an eschatological miracle: 'With such surplus, the farmer could not only eat and pay his rent, tithes, and debts, but indeed even purchase the land, and thus end his servitude forever' (Myers 1988: 177).[8]

The key exegetical issues surrounding the unfruitful seeds is whether they stand for some kind of genuine but imperfect discipleship or whether these individuals are not to be treated as true followers of Jesus at all. Given the fact that the farmers are anxious at harvest time to see if plants bear the crop for which they have been cultivated, it is almost certainly the latter that Jesus intends here (*cf.* his words elsewhere: 'by their fruit you will recognize them'; Matt. 7:20).[9] One important obstacle to true discipleship, therefore, is the distraction of material possessions in this life. One must not exaggerate the number of people who fall into this category, as, for example, by assuming that approximately a quarter of the seed fell in each kind of soil. The final stress and climax of the parable is on the good, fruitful soil, and Mark's version of the parable contains some distinctive grammar to suggest that the last category of soil is also the largest.[10] Nevertheless, in light of the larger patterns of Jesus' teaching which we will observe, we dare not underestimate the potential deceitfulness of wealth to keep people out of the kingdom.

## The hidden treasure and the pearl of great price (Matthew 13:44–46)

Roughly half way into his public ministry, Jesus' teaching becomes increasingly pointed and demanding, and the crowds begin to fall away. Matthew 13 offers a chapter of parables in which Jesus discusses this turn of affairs and continues to challenge his would-be followers with the costs of discipleship. Particularly significant in this light are the parables of the hidden treasure and the pearl of great price. These two short parables demonstrate that it is worth sacrificing whatever is required in order to obtain the kingdom of God, even if what it takes is

---

[8] But to see this, with Myers, as the main point, and thus bypass the spiritual lesson of the parable, wholly misunderstands the purpose and nature of Jesus' preaching.

[9] Hooker (1991: 132), comments, 'The existence of four groups of hearers should not conceal the fact that basically there are only two: those whose hearing of the word bears fruit, and those whose hearing proves to be fruitless. The parable conveys the same message as the saying in v. 11: the proclamation of Jesus divides mankind into two camps ...'

[10] He uses the singular form of the words, 'some' and 'other' in 4:4, 5, 7, while in 4:8, the word for 'other' before 'seed' is plural.

all that one has. A few commentators, embarrassed by the language of purchase, have assumed that the individual finding the treasure in each passage is Christ purchasing his people through his death on the cross (*e.g.*, Gibbs 1987), but this is probably to press the imagery too far. A similar rabbinic parable uses the imagery of the Israelites buying the Promised Land, but clearly the Jews did not literally purchase Canaan (*Mek. Beshallach* 2:149–155). Treasures found in fields are the stuff of much ancient lore, and merchants looking for pearls would have been well known in Jesus' time (Crossan 1979). For someone to discover a find so valuable that he would sacrifice all for it is, however, extremely unusual. The point is therefore made incisively. While not everyone necessarily sells his or her goods to become a disciple, all must be prepared to do so if circumstances demand it. Those who would follow Christ must be willing to risk whatever they have if the priorities of the kingdom threaten the security of their earthly existence (*cf.* P. Perkins 1981: 28).

## The unforgiving servant (Matthew 18:23–35)

A little later on, as Jesus teaches his disciples privately on themes of humility and forgiveness, he tells another parable about two starkly contrasting debtors to make a point about spiritual debts and forgiveness. A king forgives a servant an enormous debt, but that servant turns round and refuses to forgive a fellow servant's comparatively paltry debt. The first servant is thus handed to the jailers to be tortured! In this passage, the debts compare to roughly 200,000 years' and three months' wages, respectively.[11] Theologically, the issue debated here deals with the question of the loss of salvation. A straightforward reading of the passage would at first suggest that the king does retract forgiveness already given. But in light of earlier teaching in Jesus' ministry according to Matthew (particularly 6:12, 14–15, in which the true disciple by definition forgives others, and 7:23, in which Jesus says to those whose works do not prove fruitful, 'I never

---

[11] In fact, ten thousand talents looks suspiciously like a large round number for the greatest debt conceivable, since the talent was the largest unit of currency, while ten thousand (literally a 'myriad') was the largest named numeral in the Greek language. P. Perkins (1981: 124) thinks that the amount would have reminded a Jewish audience of the fabled riches of Egyptian and Persian kings, not wholly inconceivable but not within the bounds of their actual experience. Weber (1993) notes the possibility of a Palestinian background. One might imagine a king like Antipas with such wealth to distribute. But he agrees that there is a transparently allegorical dimension to the king and his servants as well. Forgiving such an enormous debt conjures up the background of the Old Testament teaching on the year of Jubilee.

knew you'), we should probably agree with Ridderbos (1987: 346):

> Whoever tries to separate man's forgiveness from God's will no longer be able to count on God's mercy. In so doing he not merely forfeits it, like the servant in the parable. Rather he shows that he never had a part in it. God's mercy is not something cut and dried that is only received once. It is a persistent power that pervades all of life. If it does not become manifest as such a power, then it was never received at all.[12]

Again, Jesus is not limiting his application of forgiveness to those who have material debts, but neither does his story preclude us from applying these principles to financial situations.[13] Another text, which Jesus' disciples would have already heard, was Luke 6:35 on lending, expecting nothing in return (see below, p. 130). Clearly, the servant in this parable demonstrated a diametrically opposite behaviour.

## The good Samaritan (Luke 10:29–37)

Numerous parables appear in Luke's so-called travel narrative (9:51 – 18:34), a loose collection of Jesus' teaching while on the road to Jerusalem under the shadow of the cross. The first one relevant to our theme is the well-known one of the good Samaritan. Whether one looks for one central point or admits three lessons, one per each main character or groups of characters, the message commonly derived from this passage – compassion for the needy – must take second place to the lesson that emerges from understanding the parable as the answer to the question by the lawyer that actually triggered the discussion in the first place: 'Who is my neighbour?' (Luke 10:29). The lawyer is forced to admit that even the Samaritan could prove to be a neighbour (10:37). Given the hostility between Jews and Samaritans at the time, this is tantamount to affirming that even one's enemy is one's neighbour (see esp. Funk 1982: 29–34). Then, as now, in many cultures rich and poor were also virtual enemies, with the former shunning the latter as much as possible. One recent Indian reading of this parable demonstrates how apropos it is to challenging the caste system in Hinduism (Gnanavaram 1993). Oakman (1992) highlights the bad reputation of inns and the

---

[12] Or, more simply, with Hagner (1995: 541), 'The failure to forgive one who is repentant casts doubts on the genuineness of a person's discipleship.'

[13] Herzog (1994b: 131–149) takes the parable purely at the sociological level and thinks it an ironic commentary on the behaviour of first-century despots. But the implausibility of a king forgiving so enormous a debt is the crucial key to its second level of meaning and spiritual application.

'foolish' blank cheque that the Samaritan offers as further evidence for the enormous generosity of God depicted here. If we admit verse 37b as authentic, however,[14] there is clearly a second, exemplary function to the story, which suggests that we must also show compassion to those in acute crises like the man who was robbed, stripped and left for dead (10:30). And, third, the verdict on the behaviour of priest and Levite reminds us that religious duty can never excuse our lovelessness.[15] Tellingly, a barrage of recent psychological studies has demonstrated little observable difference even today between the behaviour of religious people, including religious professionals, and the general populace when they encounter needy persons in places of potential danger.[16]

## Two parables of asking for material assistance (Luke 11:5–8; 18:1–8)

The hospitality demanded of villagers in the Galilee of Jesus' day assures us that the answer to Jesus' rhetorical question that comprises the parable of the friend at midnight is that no-one would refuse to get up and provide bread for the man requesting it, despite the inconvenience of the hour (see esp. m. Peah 8:7). In light of the appended verses (Luke 11:9–13, 'Ask and it will be given to you ...'), and in light of God's willingness to grant the Holy Spirit to those who ask him for it (11:13), it is clear again that a spiritual, rather than a material, application to this parable proves primary. But Matthew's parallel to this verse speaks merely of God giving 'good gifts' (Matt. 7:11), at least some of which are surely material.[17]

The element of social justice is more prominent in the otherwise similar parable of the unjust judge. The primary applications of this story involve the promise of God's vindication of his people and the call for persevering faith (Luke 18:7–8). But as we continue to read more of Jesus' teachings, there will be no question that part of the justice God wants to dispense for his elect includes meeting their basic

[14] On which see esp. Kimball (1994: 119–135), who demonstrates the original unity of all of 10:25–37.

[15] Hedrick (1994: 93–116) sees the parable as a parody of the ideals of righteous living in ancient Judaism.

[16] The classic study was Darley & Batson (1973).

[17] Given Luke's predilection for inserting references to the Holy Spirit, Matthew's version may actually reflect the more literal translation of Jesus' words, whereas Luke may employ synecdoche to refer to the Holy Spirit as the pre-eminent good gift. Of course, if these highly parallel sayings reflect Jesus' re-use of similar teachings in two different contexts, there is no reason why he could not have said both, with each evangelist giving an equally literal rendition of his words.

material needs (*cf.* esp. Herzog 1994b: 215–232). Luke's version of the Lord's Prayer comes in 11:1–4 in the context of the parable of the friend at midnight, just discussed above. Lochman (1990: 98) cites the Latin American prayer that captures some of Jesus' emphasis in both texts: 'O God, to those who have hunger give bread; and to those who have bread the hunger for justice.'

## The rich fool (Luke 12:16–21)

This passage is introduced with the description of an inheritance dispute between two brothers that Jesus refuses to adjudicate (Luke 12:13–14). He knows that the man making the request is interested not in justice but in getting his own way. Jesus did not care to promote the transfer of property from one covetous man to another! Verse 15 makes it plain that Jesus tells the parable to warn people against 'greed', because a person's life does not consist in the abundance of his or her possessions. This observation disproves the allegation that the man in the parable is condemned simply because he is rich. The final word in the story further reminds us that this was an individual who stored up things for himself but was 'not rich towards God' (12:21). For those who divorce the parable proper (12:16–20) from this interpretive framework (12:13–15, 21), there is still the feature of the six-fold repetition of the first-person singular pronoun 'I'.[18] The rich man demonstrates an unrelenting, self-centred focus and an unmitigated accumulation of surplus goods, with no thought for anyone else. But Malherbe (1996) has called attention to the Greco-Roman 'topos' on *pleonexia* ('greed' or 'covetousness'), which points to verses 13–34 as a unity, shot through with classic warnings against the dangers of excessive wealth. It is also worth noting that God's address to the rich man as a 'fool' evokes the frequent Old Testament background of one so labelled as not merely silly or ignorant but also sinful and immoral (*e.g.*, Ps. 107:17; Prov. 14:9; Eccles. 2:14).[19] Thus it is clear that the man is condemned not just for being rich. Still, it is important for professing Christians today to ask themselves how many unused surplus goods, property or investments they accumulate without any thought for the needy of our world. If the parallels become too close, presumably Jesus would say that their professions of faith are vacuous.

---

[18] Kistemaker (1980: 182) calls this the most striking feature of the passage.

[19] Hedrick (1994: 142–163) considers the parable against the backdrop of Ecclesiastes, concluding that it stresses the overall meaninglessness of a life of accumulating goods.

If we hold that true wisdom is to be rich toward God, then work will have a limited place in our lives. We shall work hard enough to provide the necessities; we shall leave the future in God's hands. We will not make work a means of securing our lives against all possible calamities (Purdy 1985: 48–49).

## Inviting the outcast (Luke 14:12–24)

Before he tells the parable of the great supper (Luke 14:16–24), Jesus presents two short metaphors that articulate the theme of the reversal of the roles of powerful and powerless (14:7–14). Again Jesus has accepted an invitation to a Pharisaic banquet, so again we are reminded that he is not against enjoying a gourmet meal. Still, he uses this occasion to rebuke those who seek places of honour (14:8–11) and who invite only those who can invite them back (14:12–14). Even then, Jesus' point is clearly more about motives than about the actual nature of those invited (14:14). The contrast between one's family or fellow rich friends and the 'riff-raff' is not as absolute as it seems. Rather, it reflects the Semitic idiom of expressing a sharp contrast as 'x and not y', meaning 'not so much y as x' (R. Stein 1992: 390; I. H. Marshall 1978b: 583). Nevertheless it is a shocking rebuke in a culture where reciprocal responses of hospitality were deeply embedded in a sociology of honour and shame. Have we improved at all today in inviting 'the poor, the crippled, the lame, the blind' or their contemporary equivalents (14:13)?

The parable of verses 16–24 re-uses this imagery of the outcasts of Jesus' day (14:21) to explain why Jesus' ministry centres on inviting them into the kingdom. Stein summarizes the central lessons succinctly: 'The point is that the kingdom of God has come and that those who would have been expected to receive it (the religious elite) did not do so, whereas the ones least likely to receive it (the publicans, poor, harlots, etc.) have' (R. Stein 1981: 89). The feast, as frequently in Jewish symbolic literature, stands for the messianic banquet in the eschaton. The excuses given for refusing to come (14:18–20) prove remarkably flimsy in the culture of the day (Bailey 1980: 95–99). No-one in those days bought fields or oxen without examining them any more than people today would buy used cars without seeing if they ran. And marriages would have been planned well in advance. How often does our materialism become one of numerous equally flimsy excuses for avoiding the call of the gospel to follow Jesus wholeheartedly?

## Counting the cost (Luke 14:28–33)

Again, we find a pair of short, closely parallel parables, although they do not make the identical point. Rather, the passage seems to build toward a climax. The man who discovers too late that he does not have the money to complete the construction of a tower risks losing his investment and being ridiculed by his community (14:28–30). The king who fails to reckon with an opposing army twice the size of his own risks utter defeat in battle and the loss of many lives (14:31–32).[20] Verse 33 then concludes with an even more absolute statement, 'In the same way, those of you who do not give up everything you have cannot be my disciples.' As is by now emerging as a consistent pattern in the parables, the main point is a spiritual one: beware of any obstacle that hinders total allegiance to Christ. But again, as we have repeatedly seen, the outstanding example of Jesus' spiritual lesson comes in the area of finances. Verse 33 is best understood as calling would-be disciples to renounce their claims to cling tightly to their material possessions, not necessarily to abandon them entirely (see esp. Liu 1992). But as the climactic statement of the three, verse 33 must not be overly diluted. 'Of course not all are called in the same way to the same form of discipleship. But it is equally sure that there is no such thing as a totally middle-class discipleship where there is only preservation of one's heritage and radical renunciation can never flower' (Schweizer 1984: 242).

## The unjust steward (Luke 16:1–13)

This parable is arguably the most perplexing of all that Jesus told and is an exegetical hornets' nest.[21] Perhaps the most central question to be resolved is why the steward is praised. A popular option in recent years has been that he was laudably reducing the portion of the debtors' bills that involved unjust usury, or from which he could have personally skimmed additional profits (cf. Derrett 1961; Fitzmyer 1964). Bailey (1976: 86–110) believes that the steward simply reduced the bills to highlight the master's generosity and assumed the master would not risk losing his newly acquired reputation by countering the order. Others have tried to mitigate the force of Jesus apparently praising injustice by reading his concluding remarks as irony, sarcasm or a rhetorical

---

[20] Derrett (1977) and others again try to see Christ as the tower-builder or warring king, but this interpretation proves unconvincing (see Blomberg 1990: 283).

[21] For a superb guide to the history of interpretation and for sane exegesis of each part of the parable, see Ireland (1992).

question.[22] But the text states explicitly in verse 8 that the master commended the dishonest manager 'because he had acted shrewdly'. No other point of comparison from the steward's behaviour need be in view. Matthew 10:16 then provides an apt and succinct commentary: 'I am sending you out like sheep among wolves. Therefore be as shrewd as snakes and as innocent as doves.' There *is* irony in verse 8b, in Jesus' observation that the unregenerate are often more astute in dealing with their own people than are the people of God. But verse 9a should be taken in a more straightforward sense. 'Worldly wealth', as we have seen from its numerous intertestamental uses, need not mean ill-gotten gain but simply money in general (somewhat equivalent to our expression 'filthy lucre' – see above, p. 99; *cf.* also Molina 1978). Jesus thus commands his followers to use the possessions of this life for kingdom purposes – to gain friends for themselves by making and nurturing disciples and putting God's kingdom principles into practice so that his will is indeed done on earth as in heaven. Then those who have become Jesus' followers as a result and preceded us into the eternal realm will welcome us when we arrive (Luke 16:9b).[23] Stegemann (1984: 63) concisely captures the contemporary application of verse 9: 'We affluent Christians, too, can make friends for ourselves by means of unrighteous mammon. We can become poorer in a purposeful way by giving away part of our wealth to benefit the poorest people of the world.' But we must do so in the name of Jesus as we proclaim a gospel of spiritual as well as physical wholeness.

The appended verses (10–12) then spell out in three ways the relationship between material and spiritual riches. The former is the proving ground for the latter. Material possessions are referred to as 'very little', 'worldly wealth', and 'someone else's property'. By way of contrast, spiritual riches are referred to as 'much', 'true riches', and 'property of your own'. Verse 13 climaxes this segment of Jesus' teaching by stressing one's inability to give ultimate allegiance to two masters at the same time. In this context the two masters being contrasted are God and mammon – that is, material possessions and

---

[22] For the most recent representatives of each of these views, see, respectively, S. Porter (1990); du Plessis (1990); and Parrott (1991). For a rebuttal of each of these and several other recent novel interpretations, see Mathewson (1995). Binder (1995) makes the steward stand for Jesus, but he can do so only after dissecting the passage into authentic and inauthentic portions that are idiosyncratic even by the criteria of standard tradition criticism.

[23] F. Williams (1964) convincingly points to almsgiving as the example of using worldly possessions most relevant to the original historical and literary contexts of this parable.

resources, broadly speaking. In an age when one's 'master' could have absolute power over one's life, verse 13 makes good sense. While verses 14–15 can be taken as the introduction to the rest of the chapter, they follow naturally at this point as well, reminding us that at least some of the Pharisaic leaders had a slightly higher standard of living than the majority of the people, or else aspired to one. But the average person would not have viewed them as loving money. They 'sneer' (16:14), yet Jesus sees into their 'hearts' (16:15). Self-justification or rationalization of one's attachment to material possessions continues to trouble those in every age of human history, including those who, like most Pharisees in Jesus' day, are also generous in giving to charity. Only God knows a person's true motives.

## The rich man and Lazarus (Luke 16:19–31)

As with the story of the rich fool, at first glance it appears that this story condemns all rich people *per se*. But again there are clues, including from within the narrative itself, that this is not the case. Abraham himself had been rich but did not end up in Hades. After the rich man dies and finds himself in torment, he appeals to Abraham for someone to go and warn his brothers who are still alive, so that they can avoid this place of agony (16:27–28). When he repeats his request, the rich man says, 'If someone from the dead goes to them, they will repent' (16:30). All this strongly suggests that the rich man realized that his problem was that he had never truly repented and become right with God. He knew the Old Testament teaching about caring for the needy, yet never lifted a finger to help poor Lazarus right on his doorstep. He could not plead ignorance of the Law or of his need or ability to help (see esp. Seccombe 1983: 176–177).

No information is given about Lazarus' spiritual condition, however. Are we thus to assume that God saves all poor people? No, for Lazarus is the only character in any of Jesus' parables explicitly named, and probably for good reason. His name is the Greek equivalent of Eliezer, Hebrew for 'God helps'. And the most famous Eliezer in the Hebrew Scriptures was Abraham's faithful servant (Gen. 15:2). Given the central role of Abraham in this passage, neither of these features is likely to be coincidental (Jeremias 1972: 185; Cave 1968–69: 323–325). Lazarus is meant to be understood as the proto-type of the pious poor in Israel. Nevertheless, at best this point is implicit and is not as dominant a focus of the passage (Kvalbein 1987: 80–87). It surely does not permit us to limit application of the parable to helping only Christian poor and needy.

## The labourers in the vineyard (Matthew 20:1–16)

Here is a classic example of a parable with considerable economic imagery, yet it does not teach directly on financial management. Various commentators have viewed it as a protest against the poor wages often paid to day-labourers in Jesus' time. Herzog (1994b: 79–97) and Kaylor (1994: 129–137) go so far as to argue that Jesus is encouraging social protest by means of this passage. More likely, he is teaching that God treats his people by grace, not by a wage that is dependent on the amount of work they have done. Would-be economists cannot model their policies on the behaviour of the landlord here, lest all workers rush to come only for the last hour each day! Nevertheless, the broader principles of generosity, fairness and equality will find a variety of applications in the marketplace, especially when echoes of Deuteronomy 15:7–11 are heard in the description of the landowner's gracious treatment of those who had worked even a little (Busse 1996: 71). And to the extent that the parable teaches that God gives grace to the neediest rather than judging strictly according to merit, one may see a precedent here for certain 'affirmative action' plans for classically disenfranchised groups (Rodríguez 1988).[24]

## The pounds and talents (Luke 19:11–27; Matthew 25:14–30)

The last group of parables treated here comes from the final week of Jesus' ministry, when his conflict with the Jewish leaders comes to a head and leads to his arrest and crucifixion. Although usually treated as parallel, these two passages, known as the parables of the pounds and the talents, are presented in entirely different contexts in the two Gospels in which they appear and probably reflect Jesus' use of similar themes on two different occasions (see Blomberg 1984c). The more pointed of the two with respect to economic matters is Luke's parable of the pounds (or *minas* – approximately three months' wages), with its additional details about the hostility against the 'throne claimant'. Again the stewardship of money appears as a metaphor for discipleship in general without excluding the literal use of one's finances as a primary illustration of that discipleship. In both passages, the servants' investments increase their assets, but all the income is turned over to the master. There is at least a tacit endorsement of the rudimentary form of

---

[24] *Cf.* Doyle (1994: 55): the parable 'offers a cameo of what much of the Gospel of Matthew is presenting: concern with the marginalized, open to all, upsetting and overturning worldly wisdom, welcoming the nobodies, treating each, old hand and newcomer, as equal'

capitalism practised by banks and moneylenders in the ancient Greco-Roman world. But this must be kept in the context of our discussion of the last chapter (see above, p. 90) and subordinate to the larger spiritual lesson of imitating the behaviour of the good servants in all areas of discipleship.[25] Clearly, all of our time, talents and treasures are to be used for kingdom purposes. To make the varying details of the two stories teach varying amounts of return or to conclude that God's people are rewarded to different degrees throughout all eternity presses those details beyond what is appropriate.[26] The basic contrast between the good and wicked servants in both parables is between those who attempt to do their master's will and the one who utterly refuses even to try. The latter clearly demonstrates that he is no disciple at all.[27]

## The wicked tenants (Mark 12:1–2 and pars.)

Once again the main point of this passage is not to teach an economic lesson, but the story becomes intelligible only against the backdrop of absentee landlords' brutal treatment of tenants and the occasional peasant revolt in first-century Israel.[28] Attempts to commend the behaviour of the wicked tenants as necessary peasant revolts (Hester 1992) or to see their action as codifying the futility of armed rebellion (Herzog 1994b: 98–113) must disregard the clear applications attributed to Jesus by all three evangelists. C. A. Evans (1996) argues that the wicked tenants would have been viewed as akin to the profit-hungry priests and temple leaders. Given the role of wicked servants elsewhere as symbols for Jewish leaders, this thesis seems plausible. However precisely we identify the various characters in the story, at the spiritual level the upshot is that all of us owe God good stewardship of that which he calls us to manage, and again this includes money, while not being limited to it.

## The sheep and the goats (Matthew 25:31–46)

This passage is not, strictly speaking, a parable, but, given its meta-

---

[25] It is arguable, though less likely, that the master is in essence saying, 'If you thought I was wicked you should have acted wickedly' – *i.e.*, by engaging in unlawful, usurious commerce (*cf.* C. F. Evans 1990: 672).

[26] Carson (1984: 517), however, notes that the differentiation may suggest that 'grace never condones irresponsibility; even those given less are obligated to use and develop what they have'.

[27] To argue that one should follow the Gospel of the Nazarenes, in which the servant who buries his talent is accepted (Fortna 1992), follows faulty textual and historical criticism and misses the distinctive thrust of Jesus' teaching against conventional Jewish reluctance to invest, a convention preserved in this later apocryphal Jewish-Christian tradition. A similar problem attaches to the approach of Rohrbaugh (1993).

[28] For the greatest detail see Snodgrass (1983).

phorical imagery, it is often treated as such. Throughout church history there have been two dominant interpretations. The majority perspective has understood Jesus' 'brothers' in verse 40 to refer to spiritual kin, as the term (*adelphoi*) does elsewhere in Matthew in every instance in which biological siblings are not in view (see 5:22–24, 47; 7:3–5; 12:48–50; 18:15 twice, 21, 35; 23:8; 28:10). The term 'little ones', of which 'the least' (25:40, 45) is the superlative form, also without exception in Matthew refers to disciples (10:42; 18:6, 10, 14; *cf.* also 5:19 and 11:11). This makes the point of Jesus' teaching closely parallel to Matthew 10:42: Jesus' itinerant followers (today we might call them Christian missionaries) must be cared for by those to whom they minister. Affording material help to those who preach in the name of Jesus demonstrates acceptance of the missionaries' message at the spiritual level (*cf.*, *e.g.*, Ladd 1974a; Court 1985; Donahue 1986). This view is almost certainly correct.

Today, however, the prevailing interpretation is that Jesus is teaching about the need to help the dispossessed whether or not they are Christian (*cf.* esp. Gray 1989, who also gives a history of interpretation). This is obviously an important biblical theme, but is far less likely to be the focus of this particular passage, given the consistent meaning of the terms and the larger context of parables focusing on the disciples (24:43 – 25:46). On either interpretation, however, the text must not be taken to teach works-righteousness; the people here act out their faith to demonstrate that they already have a right relationship with God. Nor does this passage teach the 'anonymous Christian' theory of Karl Rahner and many post-Vatican II Catholics (rightly Lambrecht 1992: 282). The righteous are not surprised that they are granted eternal life, as would be the case for people who never claimed to follow Christ; they are simply perplexed as to how they ministered directly to him when he was no longer physically living on earth (25:37–39). The slogan based on this passage, made particularly famous by Mother Theresa, 'seeing Jesus in the face of the poor', irrespective of their religious commitment, therefore at best encapsulates only a partial truth and at worst proves highly misleading.

## Conclusions

The parables always contain a spiritual dimension relating to Christian discipleship, forgiveness of sins, salvation by grace, and the like, as the primary foci of God's kingdom or dynamic reign. But this discipleship will inevitably produce a tangible impact in the area of stewardship of material possessions. Indeed, this area is often the most important test-case of one's profession of discipleship. Such stewardship will include, but is not limited to, giving away one's surplus goods, self-imposed restrictions on the amount one accumulates, and sharing with others, all for the sake of those less well off, particularly fellow believers. There is no indication in any of Jesus' stories that this kind of stewardship can be quantified or that any economic reversals would ever lead to pure egalitarianism. But it is clear that Jesus believes there are extremes of riches and poverty that are intolerable in the circle of his followers. It now remains to be seen how these themes play out in the rest of Jesus' non-parabolic teachings.

## The remaining teachings of Jesus

We return to the outset of Jesus' ministry and again proceed in roughly chronological sequence.

### The temptations of Jesus (Matthew 4:1–11; Luke 4:1–13)

All three temptations of Jesus by the devil at the beginning of his ministry involve material possessions to one degree or another. The clearest is the temptation to turn stones into bread to satisfy Jesus' intense hunger. Quoting Deuteronomy 8:3, Christ replies that 'people do not live on bread alone, but on every word that comes from the mouth of God' (Matt. 4:4). Spiritual sustenance ultimately takes priority over physical sustenance. Jesus also refuses to have the angels save his life in a spectacular show of divine power or to acquire all the kingdoms of the world in return for worshipping the devil. There is a situation-specific nature to these temptations that does not necessarily carry over to all believers. Satan is clearly trying to dissuade Jesus from accepting the way of the cross, which would culminate in his atoning death for the sins of humanity. No disciple can replicate Jesus' atonement. Still, the types of temptations Jesus received reflect the whole gamut of human temptation (cf. 1 John 2:16 with its 'lust of the flesh, lust of the eyes, and pride of life'; cf. also Gen. 3:6 on the triple temptations of Adam and Eve in the garden).[29] And to the extent that Jesus will later make it clear that disciples must be prepared to carry their crosses, too, and even die for him if necessary (see Mark 8:34–35 and pars.), then it becomes clear that all Christians must beware of the

---

[29] 'Each involves a seizure of palpable power.' The Hellenistic reader might think of 'the threefold categories of vice: love of pleasure, love of possessions, love of glory', while the Jew would undoubtedly recall the Israelites' testing in the wilderness (L. Johnson 1991: 76).

lure of possessions and the temptation to protect one's physical existence at the expense of one's eternal destiny.[30]

## The Sermon on the Mount/Plain (Matthew 5 – 7; Luke 6:20–49)

The first major occasion on which Jesus teaches in detail about the attitudes his followers should adopt toward worldly wealth comes in the sermon that both Matthew and Luke place, in different forms, early on in Jesus' ministry. Whether each version is a collection of disparate sayings from different contexts in Jesus' ministry or an abbreviation of a much longer original told on just one occasion, many texts relevant to a study of material possessions emerge. The contexts of Matthew 5:1–2 and Luke 6:17 must be kept in mind throughout, however; Jesus is speaking first of all to those who already are disciples, and he is speaking to them in community. The principles of the Sermon on the Mount/ Plain are meant not as a constitution for governments, or merely as a guideline for individuals, but as a manifesto for those already willing to follow Jesus in the context of 'church' (Cahill 1987; Lischer 1987).

Both versions of the sermon begin with the beatitudes, and the beatitudes commence with Jesus declaring the 'poor' to be blessed. The Greek word *ptōchos* is the term that referred to someone not just below the poverty-line but utterly destitute.[31] In the Septuagint, *ptōchos* often translates the Hebrew *'anāwîm*, which we discussed particularly in conjunction with Isaiah 61:1. The background of often equating pious and poor doubtless explains the difference between Luke's 'you who are poor' (Luke 6:20) and Matthew's 'the poor in spirit' (Matt. 5:3). It is not a matter of Matthew contradicting Luke; each brings out a different emphasis of a term that had both a material and a spiritual dimension to it (Meadors 1985; Jörns 1987). Luke 6:22–23 clearly demonstrates that Luke saw a spiritual as well as a material component to those whom Jesus blesses in his beatitudes:

> 'Blessed are you when people hate you,
> when they exclude you and insult you
> and reject your name as evil,
> *because of the Son of Man.*'

---

[30] *Cf.* esp. Nouwen (1993), who likens these three temptations to the desires Christian leaders perennially face: to be relevant, popular and directive (often at the expense of prayer, true ministry and a willingness to be led by others).

[31] *Cf.* Stegemann (1984: 14): 'They are the desperately poor, wretched creatures who are fighting for their survival.'

So, too, Matthew 5:3 is not appropriately defined if all elements of physical destitution are removed. The rest of the sermon will make clear the economic obligations of those with surplus goods (esp. Luke 6:25–34). As Carson comments, both writers picture 'those who because of sustained economic privation and social stress have confidence only in God' (Carson 1984: 131).[32]

A similar 'both/and' approach to the material and spiritual dimensions of those Jesus considers blessed carries through the remainder of the beatitudes. People may 'mourn' because of spiritual or physical affliction (Matt. 5:4). The third beatitude alludes to Psalm 37:11, where 'the meek' refer originally to the faithful Israelites oppressed by wicked people who seemingly enjoy greater benefits from the land (Matt. 5:5). Those who hunger and thirst for righteousness yearn to see people made right with God, as well as God's holy will performed justly on earth (5:6), and so on (cf. further Crosby 1981). Yet at the same time, the next section of the sermon, dealing with the disciples as salt and light, reminds them that monasticism is not a current option. The countercultural lifestyles commended in the beatitudes must be lived out in full view of the world so that others might glorify God (5:16).[33]

The latter half of Matthew 5 presents various antitheses, as Jesus contrasts his views on key ethical questions with those of Torah (5:21–48). Among these, we read in Matthew 5:42, 'Give to the one who asks you, and do not turn away from the one who wants to borrow from you.' In context, Jesus is forbidding the trading of insults, such as the backhanded slap from a right-handed person to another's right cheek (5:39), and prohibiting retaliation against those who would sue fellow disciples (5:40). In verse 41 he commends going the extra mile with the Roman soldier who would conscript a Jew to carry his goods (cf. esp. Horsley 1986). There is probably equally specific historical background which prevents verse 42 from being taken quite as absolutely as it seems when read in isolation. To the extent that the sabbatical year, if not the Jubilee, was at least occasionally practised, one would be more reluctant to grant a loan the closer one found oneself to the next sabbatical year. Jesus would thus be saying that giving to the needy

[32] See also Bruner (1987: 135): 'If we say that "blessed are the poor in spirit" means "blessed are the rich too, if they act humbly", we have spiritualized the text. On the other hand, if we say "blessed are the poor" means "poor people are happy people", we have secularized the text ... Jesus said something incorporating Matthew's spirituality and Luke's sociality, with the best of each.'

[33] For the structure of the sermon more generally, see esp. Davies & Allison (1988: 88–97).

should not be determined on the basis of the amount they can repay (*cf.* the parallel in Luke 6:30: 'Give to everyone who asks you, and if anyone takes what belongs to you, do not demand it back').[34] And even if we generalize beyond this specific situation, as Augustine pointed out centuries ago, Jesus does not say *what* to give to the one who asks (*De Sermone Domine en Monte* 67; *cf.* also Luke 12:13–15). The context of the final antithesis (Matt. 5:43–48) is one of enemy love, rather than calculating self-interest, and this informs our interpretation of verse 42 as well. The partial parallel in Luke 6:34–35 probably refers to giving loans without interest (Harvey 1990: 94–96), and the word sometimes translated 'beg' in Matthew 5:42 (*e.g.*, NRSV) is more literally just 'ask'. All of this suggests that Jesus was not commanding, either in his day or in ours, that his followers necessarily give all beggars everything they demand. What is best for them is not always what they request. But to the extent that we can determine people's genuine physical or material needs, we should be concerned to point them towards the kind of help that stands a reasonable chance of remedying the situation. At the very least, against the dominant principle of reciprocity in antiquity, Jesus is enjoining his followers to avoid the 'I'll scratch your back if you scratch mine' mentality.[35]

Matthew 6:1–4 proceeds to the question of almsgiving. In this context, Jesus specifically addresses the problems of those who give publicly, tossing their coins noisily into various collection receptacles, for the purpose of receiving human praise (6:1–2). The formal contradiction between 6:1–2 and 5:16 is quickly resolved once we understand the motives concerning who should get the glory in each passage; they are entirely different (people versus God). Jesus insists that his disciples must not parade their piety in public. Matthew 6:3 ('do not let your left hand know what your right hand is doing') does not mandate irresponsible stewardship, failing to keep track of one's giving or resisting financial disclosure. Paul's care in a later collection for the needy in Judea (see esp. 2 Cor. 8 – 9) will demonstrate the need for scrupulous accountability. Rather, Jesus' point is that giving should be so 'secretive' that one is never tempted to do it for any human thanks or favours. Unfortunately, contemporary Christian practice often seems more akin to the approach Jesus condemns here, as generous benefactors of our churches and charities are solicited with the lure of public recognition and, for the largest donations, the

[34] On which parallelism, see esp. Pilgrim (1981: 137).

[35] On the implications of the specifics of the first-century context for contemporary ethics, see esp. Tannehill (1970).

prospect of one's name for ever attached to a building or plaque.[36]
Similar principles pertain to prayer (Matt. 6:6–15). We have already
alluded to the Lord's Prayer in the context of the parable of the friend at
midnight (Luke 11:5–8). Both Luke 11:3 and Matthew 6:12 clearly
include as one of the legitimate requests of Jesus' disciples a prayer for
the bread that they need each day. It is worth noting too, though, that in
both contexts the focus on God and his will precedes petitions for
human needs, and that Matthew 6:11–12, like Luke 11:3–4, balances
material needs (daily bread) with spiritual needs (forgiveness of sins).
In an age of annual and multi-year planning, it is worth being reminded
that Jesus tells us to pray for 'daily' bread.[37] We should ask God to
meet our needs, not our greeds. Among other things, this helps us better
to avoid taking God's provisions for granted. Matthew's version of the
next clause of the Lord's Prayer refers uniquely to the forgiveness of
'debts' (*opheilēmata*, 6:12). Clearly this is a metaphor for the 'sins' that
Luke explicitly mentions (*hamartias*, Luke 11:4) but, as with the
parables discussed above, it reflects a background of Jewish experience
with literal indebtedness. And, in light of Matthew 5:38–48 earlier in
the sermon, we cannot exclude a material dimension to the disciples'
promise to forgive their debtors (*cf.* Overman 1996: 97–98).

Matthew 6:19–34 (*cf.* Luke 11:34–36; 12:22–32, 33–34; 16:13) addresses the theme of treasures on earth versus treasures in heaven at
greater length. As in the parable of the rich fool, the image is one of
unused accumulation – treasures stored up 'where moth and rust[38]
destroy, and where thieves break in and steal' (Matt. 6:19). Jesus is not
teaching that we can never store or safeguard possessions, but we must
scrupulously determine which are really necessary.[39] Verses 22–23 go

---

[36] Contrast Bassler (1991) on 'asking for money in the New Testament'.

[37] The *hapax epiousios* is perhaps best translated 'bread for tomorrow'. This has led to
an eschatological interpretation in which the whole prayer is then taken as a plea for
Christ's return. But this view is less likely, not least because it requires taking *peirasmos*
as 'test' rather than 'temptation', which in turn seems improbable given the parallelism
with the petition for rescue from the devil. Instead, faithful believers pray each day for
enough to sustain them for the day to come (Hemer 1984). Alternatively, *epiousios* may
mean 'what is necessary for existence', given 6:34, which stands in some tension with
our interpretation (Betz 1995: 398–99). Boismard (1995) notes that early Greek and
Latin Fathers typically spiritualized 'daily bread' as either the *logos* or the eucharist, and
he argues for understanding *epiousios* in this context as '*par excellence*'. But neither of
these concepts had yet been introduced when Jesus gave his original prayer and therefore
could not have been part of his original meaning.

[38] Or 'corrosion' or 'vermin'.

[39] Guelich (1982: 373) summarizes, 'Part of the presence of the Kingdom is indeed
material blessings ... we can hardly live under God's reign, receive his blessings, and not
use them to help alleviate the evil of hunger and need elsewhere.'

on to highlight how one's handling of one's finances affects every other area of life. One's motives again prove all-controlling. Thus verse 24 can conclude that one cannot ultimately serve both God and *mammon* ('material possessions'). It is arguable that materialism is the single biggest competitor with authentic Christianity for the hearts and souls of millions in our world today, including many in the visible church.[40]

In striking contrast, verses 25–34 command us not to worry about material needs (*mē merimnate*; not 'take no thought' as in KJV). We must trust in God's sovereign care, because he values humans even more than all the rest of creation, and he knows all our needs. The crucial command in this section comes with verse 33: 'But seek first his kingdom and his righteousness, and all these things will be given to you as well.' Either one must entirely spiritualize this promise or relegate its fulfilment to the eschaton, neither of which fits the immediate context of one who is worrying about *current material* needs; or else we must understand the plurals of verse 33 as addressed to the community of Jesus' followers corporately (as indeed the entire sermon is – recall the comments above). As the community of the redeemed seeks first God's righteous standards, by definition they will help the needy in their midst. The unique juxtaposition of Luke 12:33 to the Lukan parallel (12:31) supports this conclusion: 'Sell your possessions and give to the poor. Provide purses for yourselves that will not wear out ...' We will see a similar concept even more clearly taught in Mark 10:29–30 and parallels below. Serious application of this principle to contemporary churches would require such radical transformation of most Christian fellowships that few seem willing even to begin. But Schmidt (1988: 188) remarks, 'To stand still because the end is so far away is to miss the point of discipleship as a journey.' And against those who fear too radical an application of the text, he adds, 'Most of us could travel a considerable distance on that road before anyone suspected us of extreme obedience.'[41]

Finally, Jesus encourages his followers to ask, seek and knock because they will receive, find and have the door opened to them (Matt. 7:7–8). The so-called prosperity gospel at times applies these verses in ways that suggest that the person with adequate faith can receive

---

[40] Betz (1995: 458) notes that giving materialism a foreign name is equivalent to designating wealth or property, when it takes control of a person's life, as 'magical' and even 'demonic'. 'The relentless pursuit of money and possessions is tantamount to the worship of a pseudo-deity.'

[41] On this whole passage *cf.* further Blomberg (1992c); Wischmeyer (1994).

anything he or she wants in prayer, particularly of a material nature. Yet, as we have already noted above, the Lukan parallel makes clear that at the spiritual level the pre-eminent good gift God promises to give those who ask him is the Holy Spirit (Luke 11:13). And while we live in the age between the 'already' and the 'not yet', so that at times God will indeed grant requests for material resources, the logic of Matthew 7:9–11 is 'from the lesser to the greater'. Jesus is shifting from the exclusively material (7:9–10) to the primarily spiritual (7:11). It is also worth mentioning that the phrase 'it will be given to you' of 7:7 translates a simple third-person-singular passive-voice verb. There is no expressed subject in the Greek corresponding to the 'it'. The passive may well be a divine passive equivalent to 'ask and God will give to you' (Hagner 1993: 174). But that leaves it up to God's sovereign will *what* he chooses to give![42] The body of Jesus' sermon ends with the famous 'Golden Rule' in 7:12. Its application in the economic realm would surely include our being as generous in helping meet others' needs as we would want others to be when we are in need.

## The Nazareth manifesto (Luke 4:16–21)

Despite Luke's programmatic location of this passage early in his Gospel, the parallels in Mark and Matthew make it clear that Jesus' return to Nazareth takes place after a considerable portion of his initial Galilean ministry has elapsed (Mark 6:1–6; Matt. 13:53–58). As he rivets the attention of the Nazareth synagogue-goers, he outlines the same two-pronged approach to God's blessings that we discovered in the beatitudes. Quoting Isaiah 61:1–2a and 58:6 and claiming that they are fulfilled on that very day, Jesus declares,

> 'The Spirit of the Lord is on me,
>     because he has anointed me
>     to preach good news to the poor.
> He has sent me to proclaim freedom for the prisoners
>     and recovery of sight for the blind,
>     to release the oppressed,
>     to proclaim the year of the Lord's favour.'
>                                              (Luke 4:18–19)

As in Isaiah, Jesus understands the poor here to refer to the *ʿnāwîm*. In

---

[42] On the interplay between God's sovereignty and the need for human petitionary prayer for God to grant some of the good gifts he wants to give to his people, see Murray & Meyers (1994).

light of the numerous blind people Jesus heals throughout his ministry, there is unquestionably a literal element to the pronouncement of recovery of sight for those who cannot see. But in light of his equally frequent references to himself and his followers as lights of the world (Matt. 5:16; John 8:12; 9:5), we cannot exclude a spiritual dimension either. The captives and the oppressed must doubtless be treated similarly.[43] The 'year of the Lord's favour' seems to allude to the arrival of the Jubilee, although it is not necessary to argue that Jesus, speaking in AD 26 or 27, said this in a literal Jubilee year (as in Strobel 1972). Rather, as Jesus understands the Sabbath and the other festivals of Judaism fulfilled in his ministry more generally (see esp. Talbert 1992: 80–178), so, too, the liberation promised by the Jubilee can ultimately be achieved only by those who attach themselves to him.

These blessings, then, will be extended to another category of outcast, namely the Gentiles (*cf.* esp. Siker 1992). It is interesting that even after Jesus' remarkable announcement in Luke 4:21, 'All spoke well of him and were amazed at the gracious words that came from his lips' (4:22; although this statement has been interpreted more negatively). It is not until he begins to compare the Nazarenes to Jews in Old Testament times whom God overlooked in favour of granting miracles to the Gentile widow in Zarephath and the Syrian military officer Naaman that 'the people in the synagogue were furious' (4:28). Isaiah 58:6, alluded to earlier, refers to the hungry, the poor and the naked among fellow Israelites. Jesus, however, declares that God's concern for the oppressed extends to those who, at the human level, are Israel's enemies.

## Jesus' response to the messengers from John the Baptist (Matthew 11:5/Luke 7:22)

Matthew 11:5 and Luke 7:22 agree verbatim in reinforcing the link between the materially and spiritually oppressed (the Greek differs only by the addition or omission of the connecting conjunction, *kai,* 'and').[44] Sending messengers from John, who has been languishing in prison, back to him with a cryptic answer to their question as to whether or not he was the Messiah, Jesus instructs them to describe what they have seen and heard: 'The blind receive sight, the lame walk, those who have leprosy are cured, the deaf hear, the dead are raised, and the good news is preached to the poor.' Linked with the literally blind, lame, lepers

[43] In brief, see Klein (1986); in detail, M. Prior (1995).
[44] The clause 'the good news is preached to the poor' stands out as emphatic both because of its climactic position and because of its difference from the other categories of people listed (Bock 1994: 667–668).

and deaf, not to mention the physically dead, the poor in this context must be those who are physically destitute. But given Jesus' consistent holistic ministry of healing, often in response to faith or in order to instil faith in him (see Blomberg 1992a: 300–301), one dare not discount a spiritual dimension to each of these categories as well.

## Various disputes and dialogues (Mark 7:9–13 and pars.; Mark 7:27 and par.; Luke 10:38–42)

Scattered references from the next section of Jesus' ministry may be combined and briefly discussed. When Jesus criticizes the Pharisaic practice of *corban*, he touches on money matters (Mark 7:9–13 and pars.). Money could be pledged to the temple to be paid on one's death. These funds could not be transferred to anyone else, even the needy in one's family, but could still be used for one's own benefit (see esp. Baumgarten 1984–85). 'Against the dominant group boundaries Mark offers a countervision in which a new, morally defined community upholds the radical demands of scriptural tradition, which condemns profiteering and defends the welfare of the weakest members of society' (Myers 1988: 223). The seemingly unkind words of Jesus to the Syrophoenician woman in Mark 7:27 and parallel have sometimes been taken as a rebuke of the Syrians' practice of aggrandizing themselves at the expense of the underprivileged Jews (see esp. Theissen 1991: 61–80). And the famous episode of Jesus with Mary and Martha puts spiritual priorities above the cultural responsibility of providing hospitality, including in the material realm (Luke 10:38–42).[45]

## Give alms and tithes (Luke 11:41–42; Matthew 23:23)

As Jesus' ministry progresses, conflicts with Israel's leadership intensify. In the context of Jesus' berating many of the Jewish leaders for their hypocrisy, he declares, 'But give what is inside [the dish] to the poor, and everything will be clean for you' (Luke 11:41). This verse reads more literally, 'give alms for what is within ...' The context is one of contrasting the external ritual cleansing of cups and dishes, so dear to the Pharisees' agenda, with their internal greed and wickedness (Luke 11:39). The external–internal contrast suggests that to give what is inside the dish is primarily a metaphor for spirituality, referring to the goodness that issues from one's heart. But, as we so often saw with the parables, one prominent way of demonstrating one's spiritual concern is

---

[45] For the debate over whether Luke's portrayal of these two women supports or challenges a feminist agenda (which has implications for women's contemporary roles with respect to finances), see Corley (1993: 133–134).

through material help: in this context, almsgiving. Charity for the poor becomes 'an expression of what is inside', just as 'almsgiving, while being literally intended, becomes at the same time a symbol for single-hearted devotion to God and not to humanly achieved security in this world' (Nolland 1993a: 664, 670).

As Jesus goes on to pronounce a woe on the Pharisees, because they tithe down to the most minute of their herbs and spices but neglect the justice and love of God, he adds, 'You should have practised the latter without leaving the former undone' (Luke 11:42; *cf.* Matt. 23:23). During intertestamental times, tithing of all agricultural produce was increasingly required. In the later Mishnaic tractate *Masa'oth*, even the most unimportant herbs are mentioned (Vischer 1966: 7). This is the only passage in the entire New Testament that could be taken as promoting the tithe. But what is crucial to note in this context is that Jesus is appealing to the 'more important matters of the *law*' (Matt. 23:23), which is still in force until the establishment of God's new covenant at Pentecost, especially for the Jewish leaders who studied it so scrupulously. So long as the Old Testament era remains, tithing is mandatory for God's people. Whether it continues to be required in the era of the new covenant must be determined on the basis of other passages.[46] It seems significant that no other New Testament text explicitly commands it, while the principles of generosity and sacrifice yet to be surveyed will suggest that different people should give varying percentages based on their varying circumstances. Those who are at least reasonably well off should give considerably more than a tenth of their gross income to God's work. 'We must even go a step farther: the demand that the Christian tithe can even become a dangerous thing, for it permits the false conclusion that the problem of Mammon has been met and conquered' (Vischer 1966: 10).

## *What does it profit a person ... ? (Mark 8:36 and pars.)*

We have already alluded to Jesus' warnings that his followers may have to carry their crosses and experience persecution. One key passage which elaborates on this theme is Mark 8:31–38 and parallels, which Jesus delivers as he and the Twelve begin their trek toward the crucifixion. Verse 35 stresses that those who would save their physical

---

[46] Those inclined to see a particularly conservative Jewish-Christian bent to Matthew's and/or Luke's teachings often cite such texts as these without sensitivity to the salvation-historical issues they raise. For a defence of Luke's concern to stress freedom from the Law at the redactional level, see Blomberg (1984a). For a more balanced view of Matthew's redaction throughout his Gospel, see Blomberg (1992b).

lives at the expense of their spiritual well-being will ultimately lose both, but that those who are persecuted and even killed for the sake of the gospel will preserve their lives for eternity. Jesus then immediately adds, 'What good is it for you to gain the whole world, yet forfeit your soul?' (Mark 8:36). As with the temptations of Jesus, there is a clear prioritizing of spiritual above material security in this context. It is interesting also to note the preponderance of language of commercial transactions in verses 36–37: 'profit' (NIV 'good'), 'gain', 'forfeit', and 'in exchange for'. A proper handling of one's finances is not the only way of demonstrating loyal discipleship and standing unashamed on judgment day (8:38), but it is a key test-case. 'The way into the reality of God's rule begins with death, as it did for Jesus himself. And it is as complete a death experience as his was, inclusive of the social, economic, political, cultural, and religious realities of human existence in society ... slow, painful, and ostensibly full of shame' (Waetjen 1989: 146).[47] And even acts of mercy that seem relatively insignificant count greatly in God's eyes (Mark 9:41; Matt. 10:42).

## The temple tax (Matthew 17:24–27)

The sole New Testament allusion to the half-shekel tax of Exodus 30:13 appears in this tantalizingly brief passage. Shortly before the little troupe's final departure for Jerusalem, certain tax collectors ask if Jesus pays the 'two drachma' tax (one *shekel* equaled four *drachma* or *denarii*), a natural question in light of Jesus' critique of so many other Jewish conventions. Peter replies that he does (Matt. 17:24–25a). When Peter returns to Jesus' home in Capernaum, Jesus addresses the topic by asking from whom earthly kings collect their taxes. Peter's reply suggests what Jesus then makes explicit. 'Children', probably to be equated with the kingdom's citizens, are often exempt from the tribute required of other, subjugated peoples (17:25b–26). In one of the most cryptic verses in the entire New Testament, Jesus then instructs Peter to go to the lake, catch a fish and find a coin in its mouth that would cover exactly the four drachma that the two of them together would owe that year. Christ concludes, 'Take it and give it to them [the authorities] for my tax and yours' (17:27). Whatever one makes of this unique method,[48] Jesus is apparently teaching that God's people, in principle,

---

[47] For further elucidation and contemporary application, see Garland (1996: 321–340).

[48] Van Aarde (1993) sees a protest against having to pay with the idolatrous-imaged Tyrian silver shekels and a method that bypasses the potential extortion of the money-changers.

should be free from this previously God-ordained taxation.[49] But because the turn of the ages has not yet come, to avoid unnecessary offence Jesus devises a way of paying the tax that does not take money away from anyone else. Bauckham (1986) has further argued that Jesus and the Twelve were literally so impoverished at this point in time that they could not afford this amount of money. Others have suggested that verse 27 should be taken somewhat more metaphorically.[50] At any rate, the key principle seems to be that God's true children are on the verge of entering an era in which they will no longer contribute compulsorily to his work according to one fixed standard. But abolishing a mandatory religious contribution does not exempt them from *political* taxes (see below, p. 144).[51]

## The rich young ruler and Zacchaeus (Mark 10:17–31 and pars.; Luke 19:1–10)

Jesus and the Twelve are now on the road to Jerusalem, fielding questions from various passers-by. Countless generations of readers have puzzled over Jesus' command to this young man who had great wealth: 'Go, sell everything you have and give to the poor, and you will have treasure in heaven' (Mark 10:21b). Was this somehow a unique command for one solitary individual? Must all Christians do likewise? Or is some mediating application more appropriate?[52] The first point we must observe with respect to the larger context (10:17–31) is to resist the temptation to psychologize that about which we simply have no data. Why does Jesus quote several of the commandments as part of his answer to the man's question of how to inherit eternal life (10:17–19)? One might imagine that he was setting him up for a logic similar to that of the antitheses of the Sermon on the Mount, to show how in fact he has *not* kept all of the commands. But Jesus does not take this tack when the man insists that he has kept these laws since he was young (10:20). Instead Christ declares with love, 'One thing you lack' (10:21a). As so often, Jesus has special insight into the situation of a

---

[49] See esp. Horbury (1984), who also provides important historical background.

[50] For a survey of possibilities see Blomberg (1984b: 433–434).

[51] Cassidy's attempt (1979) to relate this passage to a civil tax is unconvincing, not least for failing to deal adequately with its explicitly stated amount as equivalent to the tax of Exod. 30:13.

[52] The medieval church often applied this and similar passages to the 'higher class' of people in holy orders who took vows of poverty, but contemporary Catholic scholars have recognized that the texts themselves support no two-tiered system of Christian obedience (cf., e.g., Légasse 1977: 53).

particular individual.[53] He knows that this man's wealth is standing in the way of discipleship. The one addition to the portion of the Decalogue quoted in verse 19 is the command, 'Do not defraud', perhaps a clue that the man had sinned with his money (Myers 1988: 272).[54]

Thus, when we come to Mark 10:21b, we must be sure to read all of it. The command to sell everything and give to the poor cannot be separated from the accompanying, climactic command, 'Then come, follow me.' The only charity that counts is what comes as the price of discipleship (Gundry 1993: 554; cf. also 1 Cor. 13:3). The man's distress suggests that at least here the covenant scheme of riches as a reward for obedience may be presupposed. If this synagogue ruler were a respectable person in his community, one can understand why he (and others) might think his wealth a reward for obedience and not something to be surrendered. The disciples' shock at Jesus' reply on how hard it is for the rich to enter the kingdom then follows naturally (10:23–24a). If a godly, rich person cannot be saved, who on earth can? Jesus merely repeats his statement (10:24b) and then adds, 'It is easier for a camel to go through the eye of a needle than for the rich to enter the kingdom of God' (10:25). Furfey (1943) believes that *plousios* ('the rich') here refers to those who are wealthy enough to support themselves by operating with their capital and freed from the routine of daily work. Attempts to refer to a hypothetical narrow gate in the Jerusalem wall, known as 'the Eye of the Needle', or to a textual variant which substitutes 'rope' for 'camel',[55] founder on the subsequent dialogue. As the disciples' incredulity grows (10:26), Jesus replies, 'Humanly, this is impossible, but not with God; all things are possible with God' (10:27). Jesus has indeed described a literal impossibility, humanly speaking, by referring to the largest well-known animal and the smallest common aperture in his world. But with God, human impossibilities become possible.

We must again resist the urge to impute specific motives to Peter's next remark: 'We have left everything to follow you!' (Mark 10:28). Whether genuinely curious or secretly selfish, Peter raises the issue of the disciples' radical itinerancy. What can they expect for their sacrifice? Jesus' answer provides both an assurance and a challenge.

---

[53] Sänger (1992: 187) believes that Jesus realizes that the man does not really understand the consequences of his own claims.

[54] Understandably omitted by B* K W $\Delta$ $\Pi$ $\Psi$ $f^1$ $f^{13}$ and a variety of less important witnesses.

[55] There is no historical evidence for the former from within the first millennium of Christianity, and the textual support for the latter is limited to very weak or very late manuscript evidence (59, lect. 183 and Armenian and Georgian versions).

Anyone who has abandoned family or property for the sake of the gospel (10:29) will not fail 'to receive a hundred times as much in this present age (homes, brothers, sisters, mothers, children and fields ...)' (10:29–30a). Given that Jesus explicitly refers to these possessions as available 'in this present age' in contrast with eternal life 'in the age to come' (10:30b), we must understand the text as unequivocally teaching that Jesus' followers can expect material reward for their sacrifice in this life. But what is this reward and how do they receive it? The innumerable brothers, sisters, mothers and children that they gain are, without question, the spiritual kin they acquire as they become part of the large family of God's people. There is no reason to take the 'homes' and 'fields' any differently. As in the Sermon on the Mount, a new family means a new community of those who share with one another. The new homes and fields are those that God's people share with those in need (see esp. May 1990). No-one considers their possessions their own, and the plight of the poor takes priority over the desires of the affluent. As Via (1985: 142) concludes,

> The existence of a community based on the renunciation of natural family and personal wealth (10:28–29), or, more accurately, the affirmation that there should be such a community, is the social horizon which makes conceivable the imperative to sell all one has and give to the poor (10:17–22). Mark 10:17–22 needs 10:28–29 in order to make sense at the level of social-historical existence.

The story of Zacchaeus' conversion (Luke 19:1–10), following closely after the story of the rich young ruler, contrasts markedly with the previous account. Zacchaeus was a 'chief tax collector', perhaps one of the Roman publicans, who worked directly for the imperial state, rather than functioning as a middleman, as with Levi/Matthew. There was a good chance, therefore, that he was enormously wealthy, but in part at the expense of the ordinary Jewish people and, no doubt, commandeering extortionary profits. Little wonder that the crowd mutters that Jesus has gone to be the guest of a 'sinner' (19:7)! Interestingly, Christ does not command Zacchaeus to give up all and follow him. Indeed, he does not command him to do *anything*. Zacchaeus, nevertheless, stands up and volunteers to give half of his possessions to the poor and to pay back four-fold all those he has cheated (19:8). Pilgrim (1981: 129–130) sees this narrative as a paradigm of the right response of the would-be rich Christian for at least four reasons: 1. it comes right on the heels of 18:18–30 and Luke's version of the account of the rich young ruler with its question of how anyone can be saved (19:26), and not too far removed from 16:9 with its commands to make friends by means of one's wealth; 2. it is the climactic incident in Jesus' public ministry before he enters Jerusalem; 3. it leads to a key Lukan summary of the gospel (19:10); and 4. it is the fullest treatment of the topic of stewardship anywhere in Luke. Restitution thus becomes the sign of true repentance, as also in rabbinic thought, even if the amount is paralleled only in the case of cattle theft (Exod. 22:1). What is more, later rabbis usually forbade one to give away more than 20% of one's assets, lest one become too poor and then be a drain on others (b. Ketub. 50a).

We must not use Zacchaeus' 50% giving to create a new legalism, however, any more than with the 100% demanded of the rich young ruler. But the fact that Zacchaeus goes beyond what any combination of Jewish taxes and tithes required shows that his giving far exceeded mere tokenism (Pilgrim 1981: 133). There is a debate as to whether the present-tense verbs of verse 8 are to be taken as customary (or iterative) and refer instead to Zacchaeus' regular practices, thus vindicating him in the eyes of those who had unjustly viewed him as a sinner (see esp. Mitchell 1990; Ravens 1991). But given the parallels to John the Baptist's teaching in Luke 3:13–14 and to the story of Levi's conversion in 5:27–32, and given the climactic declaration, 'today salvation has come to this house', in verse 9, this view seems much less likely (see esp. Hamm 1991; cf. Nolland 1993b: 906). And it makes little sense for Zacchaeus to promise to restore whatever he has consistently defrauded people of if he has led an exemplary life more generally. Zacchaeus comes to salvation not by his stewardship, but by his encounter with the Son of Man. Notice how Jesus himself takes the initiative in verse 5, although Zacchaeus had been eager to see him in verse 4. Nevertheless, what Zacchaeus does with his money once again proves a prime example of the good works that flow from true repentance.

## Mary's anointing of Jesus in Bethany (Mark 14:3–9 and pars.)

As noted above (p. 113 n. 4), Mark 14:3–9 and parallels bear a significant resemblance to Luke 7:36–50 but probably reflect a different incident six days before Jesus' final Passover (John 12:1). We are now on the eve of 'Palm Sunday'. This incident of Mary anointing Jesus at Bethany has afforded many their classic proof-text for justifying lavish expenditure in the name of Christ. Further support for this interpretation seems to come from Jesus' use of Deuteronomy 15:11, when he declares, 'The poor you will always have with you, and you can help them any time you want. But you will not always have me' (Mark 14:7). But the clause 'you can help them any time you want' surely means that disciples should have an ongoing ministry to the poor. And the second part of Deuteronomy 15:11 proves even more explicit: 'Therefore I command you to be open-handed towards those of your people who are poor and needy in your land.' 'Jesus rebukes the woman's accusers, but not for their concern for the poor; he rebukes them for presumptuously singling out this woman, for self-righteously judging her when the very presence of the poor judges the whole community' (Verhey 1984: 18–19). On the other hand, the fact that Mary 'wasted' more than three hundred denarii (roughly a year's wages for the average worker) reminds us that Jesus is not an ascetic or an advocate of an unrelentingly simple lifestyle. Still, we must note that this lavish gift is given for a non-repeatable event – Jesus' death – and corresponds to the similar expense at someone's funeral that was not considered unseemly in the ancient Jewish world (Bruce 1983: 257). There undoubtedly will be unique, non-recurring opportunities for costly expenditure in the service of Christ today as well – perhaps a few building projects that particularly glorify God through the worship they cultivate. But, as in Jesus' case, these should be the exceptions, not the rule.

Generosity to the poor is the regular mandate in the New Testament as much as it was in the Old. Escobar (1983: 101) is right to insist, therefore, on a hermeneutic of suspicion, as well-to-do Westerners exegete this text and often make it imply, 'The rich you will have with you always'! It is also interesting to note John's unparalleled juxtaposition of comments about Mary and Judas (John 12:4–7). Might they have been the first two to recognize that Jesus really was going to Jerusalem to die, although they reacted in diametrically opposite ways, both of them involving the use of money? Carson (1991: 429) astutely refers to those like Judas whose personal greed 'masquerades as altruism'.

## Clearing the temple (Mark 11:15–17 and pars.; cf. John 2:13–17)

Less than a week before his death, Jesus wreaks havoc with merchandisers and money-changers in the Jerusalem temple. Almost all are agreed that the main point, particularly in the synoptic accounts, is not one of a 'cleansing' but of a prophecy of the temple's impending destruction and a look to the new age that Jesus hopes will emerge beyond.[56] There is no question but that he is upset with the corruption of the money-changers. It is quite possible that Caiaphas and the Sadducees have only recently moved this trafficking from the Kedron Ravine into the temple and that they have grown enormously wealthy on outrageous exchange rates (M. Bockmuehl 1994: 69–71). John's account, which may or may not describe a separate episode, more clearly refers to the problem of commerce replacing worship in the temple (John 2:16). Particularly when this occurred in the Court of the Gentiles, one can understand Jesus' outrage; after all, the prophet Isaiah had stressed that the temple should be a 'house of prayer for all nations' (Mark 11:17a; Is. 56:7). There may be further innuendos, however, in Jesus' use of the phrase 'den of robbers' from Jeremiah 7:11 (in 11:17b) to describe a nationalist stronghold (C. K. Barrett 1978: 17). The ethnocentrism of first-century Judaism has turned the temple into a sanctuary for precisely the exclusive, nationalist spirit that this part of the building was intended to temper. In an age of rampant tribalism worldwide, not to mention confusion between spiritual and financial activities, Jesus' righteous indignation can find numerous contemporary applications. Indeed, seeking financial security is often cloaked in the language of patriotism or 'national interest'.

## Give to Caesar ... (Mark 12:13–17 and pars.)

One day after Jesus' 'temple tantrum' (Witherington 1990: 107), the Herodians and the Pharisees joined forces to try to trap Jesus, even though they would not normally have cooperated with one another. The issue they ask him about goes to the heart of the tension between Israel and Rome. Paying the tax was the consummate sign of allegiance to the occupying imperial force. If Jesus denied the validity of the Roman tax, the Herodians would no doubt report him to the authorities; if he overtly supported it, the Pharisees would be outraged at his disloyalty to God.[57] Either way, there seems to be no escape for him in this 'Catch-22' context. But in fact he finds a way out as he utters the famous words, 'Give to Caesar what is Caesar's and to God what is God's' (Mark 12:17). An increasingly popular interpretation has taken this to mean that because God is sovereign over all, giving to God what is God's potentially removes any claim of Caesar on the Christian (Giblin 1971: 516–526; Owen-Ball 1993). Herzog (1994a: 350) thinks Jesus is

---

[56] See E. P. Sanders (1985: 61–76); with important qualifications and modifications, cf. Witherington (1990: 107–116).

[57] For an excellent survey of the historical background to this impasse, see Bruce (1984).

saying in essence, 'Throw the coins back in Caesar's face. Rid the land of the idolatrous and blasphemous denarii.' This interpretation, however, destroys the delicate balance of Jesus' reply, which causes his audience to be amazed at how he evades the trap set for him by *both* parties (R. Stein: 1992: 496). Romans 13:6–7, in which Paul alludes to this teaching by commanding Christians to pay everyone what is owed them, including taxes and revenue, also counters this one-sided interpretation.

Historically, Jesus' saying became crucial in the Reformation debates about separate kingdoms of church and state, and even more influential in the more recent history of the establishment of the American Constitution and Bill of Rights, which put up a high 'wall of separation' between government and religion. It is virtually impossible that Jesus specifically intended either development in an age of totalitarianism and imperial regimes, which themselves often claimed divine authority, and given the ability of God's people to obey these commands successfully under subsequent centuries of monarchies. That is not to say, however, that these later historical developments cannot be viewed as consistent with the spirit of Jesus' initial teaching. In any event, in the original context, Jesus' saying must be denying the right of rulers to receive worship (see esp. Haacker 1986), and it thus leaves the door open for arguments concerning civil disobedience, including the withholding of taxes, if it can be demonstrated that such payment would force an individual to violate God's moral or theological standards.

## The widow's mites (Mark 12:41–44 and par.)

Just before Jesus leaves the temple for the last time, he sees the crowds contributing to the treasury. Thus unfolds the famous story of the widow and her 'mites' (AV; NIV: 'two very small copper coins', 12:42). The temple treasury comprised tithes and offerings but was funded largely by the rich (*cf.* 12:41). It would have been highly unusual to find a poor woman giving the last of her meagre possessions. What other resources this woman might have had access to, we do not know; but she remains a model which demonstrates that it is the percentage or amount of sacrifice, not the net giving, that counts in God's eyes. A. Wright (1982) has seen here a direct rebuke of the Jewish leadership that fostered such injustice, but his view founders on the fact that the woman gives entirely voluntarily and that we have no evidence that poor people in general frequently contributed to the treasury. On the other hand, the milder version of Kinukawa (1994: 66–77), in which the text at a secondary level may reflect an ironic lament about a system that *allowed* the woman potentially to divest herself of any further resources, may not be too far wide of the mark.

# Conclusions

The good news of the gospel is consistently holistic, according to the teaching of Jesus. Material sustenance without spiritual salvation proves meaningless, but the liberation that God in Christ grants regularly includes a physical or material dimension to it as well. The only way God's people can consistently obey all of his commands is as the entire Christian community worldwide, and any local expression of it, increasingly captures the vision of sharing its resources with the needy in its midst. When believers realize that others will care for them if they unexpectedly find themselves impoverished, they can then be freed to give more generously in times of plenty. A full range of socio-economic conditions emerges among Jesus and his disciples and the people with whom they mingle. Nevertheless, there is a clear emphasis in Jesus' ministry and teaching on meeting the needs of the outcasts and have-nots of his world. Jesus' opponents are not the rich *per se*, but key representatives of the Jewish leadership, many of whom happen to be somewhat more well-to-do than the masses. Jesus is not crucified for his teaching about material possessions, but the controversies with the Jewish leaders that become increasingly pointed include items of stewardship as one prime arena in which they do not please God.[58]

It goes too far to say that one cannot be rich and be a disciple of Jesus, but what never appears in the Gospels are well-to-do followers of Jesus who are not simultaneously generous in almsgiving and in divesting themselves of surplus wealth for the sake of those in need. 'This free attitude to possessions may be expressed in a disposal of private property, though this is not mandatory. It will certainly find expression in an almost reckless generosity, motivated not by a dour sense of obligation but by a warm and unselfish compassion' (France 1979: 18). There is room for the periodic celebration of God's good, material gifts, even at times to a lavish extent. But these celebrations will be the exception, not the norm. The covenant model that assumes material reward for piety never reappears in Jesus' teaching, and is explicitly contradicted throughout. As in Proverbs 30:8–9, Jesus is concerned to moderate extremes. But the main focus of his ministry, the

[58] Schmidt (1987) stresses that the 'hostility to wealth' in the synoptic tradition is independent of any narrowly defined historical circumstances.

road to the cross, and his call to disciples to imitate him in similar self-denying sacrifice rather than basking in glory, suggests the overarching paradigm of generous giving, rather than 'godly materialism', for the one who would faithfully follow Christ.

# Chapter Five

# Earliest Christianity

In this chapter we survey data on the earliest decades of Christian history. In the first half we will look at the epistle of James. Although its date is uncertain, a strong case can be made for viewing it as the earliest extant Christian writing. It was most likely composed by James, the brother of Jesus and chief elder of the church in Jerusalem (Jas. 1:1; *cf.* Acts 15:13 with 15:21–22), writing to communities of Jewish Christians in the Diaspora, but probably limited to the eastern half of the empire, or to Palestine or Syria more specifically. The nature of the relationship between the writings of James and Paul has increasingly suggested to commentators that James penned his letter prior to and independently of Paul, particularly because of his comments on the issue of faith and works, and thus that the epistle should be dated to as early as the mid-40s of the Christian era.[1] Few of the actual exegetical conclusions of this survey, however, depend on such an early dating or on the acceptance of James as the author of this epistle.

The second half of this chapter will deal with material from the book of Acts. A considerable majority of the relevant data in Acts come from the first half and primarily Jewish Christian phase of this work. Hence it is natural to group it together with James in this treatment of earliest Christianity. Chapter 8 will return to both the Gospel of Luke and the Acts in a discussion of the distinctive theologies of each of the synoptic evangelists and will highlight the nature of Luke's redactional concerns. At that point it will become clear that Luke is more interested in addressing later Gentile and increasingly well-to-do Christians. Thus his preservation of the more distinctively Jewish and

---

[1] For representative treatments of these issues and for similar conclusions, see the commentaries by Davids (1982: 2–22); Moo (1985: 19–34); and L. Johnson (1995: 89–123). Geyser (1975) takes the Diaspora language of 1:1 to refer to literally displaced persons, based on the scattering of believers after the stoning of Stephen (Acts 8:1), and sees the consecutive themes of the letter unified by the concerns of a literal refugee community.

even Palestinian-Christian circumstances of the much poorer believers of the first years of this fledgling religion are that much more likely to be historical.[2]

## The epistle of James

Particularly under the influence of the major commentary of Martin Dibelius, an older generation of commentators often found little indication of an organized structure to, coherent theology in or a specific Christian community behind the letter of James. The epistle was viewed as roughly a New Testament equivalent to the book of Proverbs, and its links with other wisdom literature were stressed (Dibelius 1976). This approach in recent years has been abandoned increasingly in favour of one that sees James as a very purposive theologian writing to Christian communities, the nature of which can be fairly explicitly described, even if their location remains uncertain. This approach also generally finds a discernible structure in the epistle (see esp. Davids 1982: 22–28). Davids himself has identified 'wealth and poverty' as one of three main clusters of themes to which the letter repeatedly returns. He sees chapter 1 as identifying these three clusters in two sections: trials/temptations (1:2–4; 1:12–18), wisdom and speech (1:5–8; 1:19–21) and poverty and wealth (1:9–11; 1:22–25), with verses 26–27 as a summary and transition. The body of the epistle then retraces these three themes in reverse sequence, unpacking them in greater detail (2:1–26; 3:1 – 4:12; 4:13 – 5:6) (Davids 1982: 29). It is arguable that this delineation of the beginnings and endings of discrete sections is overly precise, but the identification of the main themes and the sequence in which they appear seem sound.

In fact, it can be argued that all of 1:2–18 deals with the theme of trials and temptations, with the exhortation to seek wisdom and the commands to rich and poor subsumed under that topic. More specifically, for a survey of the theme of wealth and poverty, one may take one's cues from 2:1–7 and 5:1–6 and assume that many in James' audience are poor Christians, facing precisely the socio-economic persecution of wealthy landlords mistreating their 'migrant' farm-hands and the temptation to show favouritism to the rich described in those passages (Davids 1982: 28–34; Tamez 1990: 18–26). This then enables one to read the teaching about trials in chapter 1 as first of all addressed

---

[2] On the historical plausibility of Acts 1 – 12, see esp. Bauckham (1995). The entire five volumes of Winter (1993–96) along with Hemer (1989) provide massive evidence for rehabilitating Luke's reliability as a historian in the book of Acts more generally.

to the socio-economic plight at the forefront of the community's concern, although 1:2 encourages us to apply James' principles very widely by referring to 'trials of many kinds'.

## James 1:9-11

The first section explicitly addressing issues of material possessions appears in 1:9-11. Echoing Matthew 5:3, James begins, 'Believers in humble circumstances ought to take pride in their high position' (1:9). 'Believers' is literally the 'brother' (*adelphos*), James's frequent, generic term for 'Christian' (*cf.* 1:2, 16, 19; 2:1, 5, 14, *etc.*). 'In humble circumstances' translates the Greek adjective *tapeinos*, which in other contexts can refer to an attitude of humility (*e.g.*, Matt. 11:29; 2 Cor. 10:1), but which in a context of contrasts with the materially rich becomes a virtual synonym for the financially impoverished (*ptōchos*; *cf.*, *e.g.*, Luke 1:52; Rom. 12:16). The high position in which such a believer is to take pride, therefore, must refer to the spiritual blessings which he or she can receive in part in this life and to the coming material and spiritual perfection of the eschaton (Moo 1985: 67).

More disputed is the identity of the rich person (*plousios*) in verses 10-11. The parallelism between verse 9 and verses 10-11 makes it natural to assume that this wealthy individual is also a Christian, with the term 'brother' to be supplied from verse 9. Rich Christians, then, should 'take pride in their low position, because they will pass away like a wild flower' (1:10). Recognizing the transience of earthly riches, indeed of earthly life more generally, well-to-do believers exult not in their earthly goods but in their state of spiritual dependence on God (*cf.* esp. Adamson 1976: 62-66; Moo 1985: 68-69).

There are a number of reasons, however, why several recent commentators have challenged this interpretation and taken the rich person in 1:10-11 to be a non-Christian instead (see esp. R. Martin 1988: 25-26; Maynard-Reid 1987: 40-47). First, the omission of 'brother' in verse 10 could be deliberate, designed to stress that the rich person is, in fact, not a Christian. Second, the rest of the epistle has no unambiguous reference to rich people as Christians. Rather, they consistently seem to form part of the wicked class of people oppressing James's audience. Third, verses 10-11 say nothing explicit about any spiritual future for the rich people described here, but refer only to their destruction. Fourth, to be more specific, it is the rich people themselves who 'will pass away like a wild flower' (1:10) and 'will fade away even while they go about their business' (1:11); it is not simply that their riches are dissipated. Fifth, the word translated 'business' in verse 11 is *poreia*, literally a 'going'. But this word is often used quite literally to refer to commercial travel and enterprise, similar to that of the well-to-do in 4:13–17 who are taking no thought for God.[3]

On the other hand, the interpretation that sees the rich person in 1:10–11 as a believer has the weight of Christian history and tradition on its side. Indeed, each of the five points just made can be countered. First, as already noted, the omission of 'brother' in verse 10 is more naturally explained if it is meant to be carried over from verse 9. Second, we will see below that there is reason to believe that rich Christians do appear elsewhere in the letter, both in 2:1–4 and 4:13–17. Third, that only the negative consequences of being rich are mentioned is not surprising, given the antithetical parallelism with verse 9 in which only the positive benefits for the brother 'in humble circumstances' are mentioned. Fourth, the more natural understanding of verses 10 and 11 would not distinguish between the rich and their wealth. Both clearly come to an end, at least in terms of any benefit these people may receive from their present material existence at the end of their lives, and that is the only point being made here. Nothing is mentioned about eternal destruction. Fifth, *poreia* can be used metaphorically and is probably a synonym for *hodos* ('way') in verse 8 (Kistemaker 1986: 45).[4] In verse 8, in which one's activities in general are in view, nothing in the immediate context supports a restriction of the rich person's 'business' to any strictly commercial sense.

In addition, to make verse 10 intelligible as a command to rich non-Christians to 'take pride in their low position' requires us to take this verse as bitter irony. Obviously, a rich unbeliever should lament such a fate, not exult in it. And while it is true that throughout his letter James uses an 'intense, imaginative, rhetorical style of writing' (Stulac [1990: 97], who supports the ironic interpretation), there are no other imperatives in the letter obviously meant to be taken as the direct opposite of their face value. Certainly that is not the way verse 9 is intended. So it would seem that the traditional understanding of verses 10 and 11 as referring to the rich believer should still be preferred. The debate is an important one because there are those who have argued that James does not envision the possibility of someone being both rich and Christian (see esp. Maynard-Reid 1987: 63; Tamez 1990: 48). On the other hand, it is surely the case that 'in the light of [1:9–11] it is difficult to credit that some Christians apparently teach that a person's wealth is a sign of blessing from God and that to possess it is a sign that

---

[3] Its only other New Testament usage (Luke 13:22) gives precisely such a sense.
[4] The NIV's 'in all they do' is more literally 'in all his ways'.

one has been living faithfully and obediently' (Townsend 1994: 15)!

## James 1:27

Whether as a conclusion to all of chapter 1 or simply as part of James's second statement of the theme of riches and poverty, 1:27 offers a unique definition of 'religion'. The word *thrēskeia* refers to the outward manifestation of one's religious system.[5] Here James combines two elements not often kept together (but *cf.* 2 Enoch 9:1, cited above, p. 99): 1. a concern for holiness and spirituality, often characteristic of various separatist movements; and 2. a paradigm of social concern, more commonly found among so-called activists.[6] It is the second of these themes that is most directly germane to our topic: 'to look after orphans and widows in their distress'. Here James clearly echoes the numerous Old Testament and intertestamental Jewish references to the woman who has lost her husband and the child without parents as classic examples of those in need of compassion and justice.

## James 2:1–7

All of chapter 2 at one level proceeds to unpack this concern. The theme of the paragraph is stated in verse 1: 'don't show favouritism'. The illustration of verses 2–4 then describes a striking contrast between two kinds of people who enter the believers' assembly. The two obviously represent extremes of wealth and poverty. The perennial temptation, as here, is to treat the rich person with great honour and the poor person shabbily, in this case as indicated by the seating arrangements. Verses 1–4 could reflect a merely hypothetical situation, but their historical verisimilitude and the subsequent indicatives of verses 5–7 make it more probable that they represent an actual occurrence in James's churches (R. Martin 1988: 60; Laws 1980: 98).

Verses 5–7 proceed to enunciate the primary problem with such favouritism. God has 'chosen those who are poor in the eyes of the world to be rich in faith and to inherit the kingdom he promised those who love him' (2:5). Conversely, the rich are typically those who exploit Christians, dragging the believers into court and blaspheming the name of Christ (2:6–7). Several expressions in this paragraph

---

[5] Louw & Nida (1988: 2:531) define the term as 'appropriate beliefs and devout practice of obligations relating to supernatural persons and powers – "religion, piety"' On p. 532, they add, 'one may always speak of this phase of culture by some phrase such as "how to act toward God" ...'

[6] So difficult was this combination for one early Christian scribe that $p^{74}$ replaces *aspilon heauton tērein* ('to keep onesself from being polluted') with *hyperaspizein autous* ('to protect them' – *i.e.*, the widows).

require closer attention. The 'poor in the eyes of the world' renders the Greek phrase *ptōchous tō kosmō*. How is the dative case with the noun 'world' (*kosmō*) being used in this context? Some have tried to deny a reference to literal material poverty here (*e.g.*, Dibelius 1976: 137– 138), while Maynard-Reid (1987: 62) has gone so far as to take the dative as a simple locative of place (the poor 'in the world'). More likely the dative is one of reference or respect and should be translated as in the NIV, in the sense of 'those whom the world can see only as materially destitute' (Ropes 1916: 193; Kistemaker 1986: 80). This best explains the contrast with the next clause. From a Christian perspective, such people can be 'rich in faith' (another dative expression, this time as part of the explicit prepositional phrase *en pistei,* 'in faith'). W. Baker (1990: 50) calls verse 5 'an observation of reality: the poor are more inclined toward God than are the rich'.

From this verse has emerged the famous slogan of liberation theology, 'God's preferential option for the poor'. But this slogan is often applied indiscriminately to Christian and non-Christian poor alike. In this context James is quite explicit that the poor who are rich in faith and inherit the kingdom are also 'those who love him [*i.e.*, God]' .[7] While the materially impoverished of our world should provoke Christian compassion, irrespective of their world-view or religious allegiance, James 2:5 is not teaching anything about automatic religious superiority based on low socio-economic standing, even if it is often the case that the materially poor more quickly recognize their dependence on God than the materially rich. In context, James has in mind the majority of the members of the Jewish-Christian communities to which he is writing, many of whom are day labourers on the large farms owned by rich absentee landlords (see above, p. 148; *cf.* the discussion of 5:1–6 below, p. 157).[8] As we have observed in previous chapters, the frequent inability of such small share-croppers to pay off their increasingly large debts often led to virtual slavery, and even penury consignment to debtors' prison. The behaviour of the rich Roman or Jewish landlords, neither of whom would have honoured the name of Christ, best accounts for the references to the legal and verbal behaviour of the rich in verses 6–7.

[7] The *ʿanāwîm* background and the echo of the beatitudes are both clear. See, *e.g.*, Hartin 1991: 149–151.

[8] James 'stops short of an unqualified idealisation of poverty as the distinguishing mark of membership' in the community. It is 'faith that is the mark' (Laws 1980: 103). *Cf.* Wall (1997: 115): 'the poor of James are those without financial security, who have come to depend upon God with their future'.

If we then return to verses 1–4, we can easily understand why Christians might try to curry favour with rich believers if they were ever to visit their assemblies. But to kowtow to those who normally oppress them is to insult the poor who are oppressed, including many from their own midst (2:6). It is possible that this passage contains a strong rebuke of the typical patron–client relationships of the ancient world (Vyhmeister 1995). But it is not clear to what degree the patronage system had made inroads into what may have been a more exclusively Jewish milieu. At any rate, 'the problem of discrimination is a perennial one for Christians because it is a tendency of basic human nature to favour those we serve to profit from the most' (Polhill 1986: 398).

There is a quite different interpretation of 2:1–4, however, which merits attention as well (see esp. Ward 1969). The unparalleled term *synagōgē* in 2:2 for the Christian assembly literally means 'synagogue'. This may be a carry-over from these Christians' Jewish background, but it may also refer to a more specific type of meeting than the church gathered for worship. The command not to show favouritism employs a Semitism (Gk., *prosōpolēmpsia*; *cf.* Heb. *nāśā' pānîm*) that was common in legal contexts (*cf.* Faber 1995). The language of verse 4 ('have you not discriminated among yourselves and become judges with evil thoughts?') could be metaphorical but could also suggest the context of a courtroom. Verse 6 also describes the practice of the wicked rich in the legal arena. Given that several rabbinic passages refer to the synagogue functioning as the equivalent of a courtroom for Jews to settle legal disputes among themselves, especially related to property matters, the view that understands James's community to be functioning as a Jewish-Christian courtroom has much to commend it. Several of these parallels even refer to preferential seating arrangements (*Sifra, Kid. Per.* 4.4; ARN 1.10) or to differences in dress according to wealth (Deut. R. 5.6; b. Sheb. 31a). But if this is the Christian community settling its legal disputes internally (as Paul would later wish the Corinthians would do, 1 Cor. 6:1–6), then 'the natural assumption would be that both men are members of the community' (Ward 1969: 94).[9] This hypothesis then provides for us a second

---

[9] Maynard-Reid (1987: 57, 63–65) opts for this understanding of the *synagōgē*, too, but inexplicably concludes that the rich man is not a Christian. Wall (1997: 104–105) follows Maynard-Reid but suggests two possible scenarios: the rich Jewish landlord appeals to the 'synagogue/courtroom' for justice in collecting from a poor Christian debtor, or the poor Christian worker sues the rich Jew for unpaid wages. But Wall gives no historical evidence to suggest that either scenario was probable. The letter of James itself suggests that a rich non-Christian would typically resort to more

passage in James that admits the presence of a rich person who is also a believer. But because so many other rich people have mistreated Christians, one must not tempt the rich Christians to act immorally themselves by showing favouritism toward them.

## James 2:14–17

The second major part of James 2 is best known for its discussion of faith and works (2:18–26) and the apparent contradictions with Paul's teaching on the same topic (*e.g.*, Rom. 3:28; Gal. 3:11). What is often missed is that this discussion is actually a subordinate part of the larger treatment of the right use of riches begun already in verse 1 and continuing with verses 14–17. The latter passage again is couched as a hypothetical situation but may well refer to the very real scenario of a believer in great physical need who receives no material help from a fellow Christian (2:15–16).[10] This tragedy leads James to speak of a workless faith as dead (2:17).

Verses 14 and 17 frame this paragraph with an inclusio which stresses that faith without deeds cannot save a person. The rhetorical question of verse 14b uses the Greek adverb *mē*, intended to elicit a negative answer. 'Faith' without deeds cannot save an individual. Attempts to take the verb 'save' (*sōzō*) as referring to anything other than eternal and eschatological salvation founder on the consistent use of the term in James (*cf.* 1:21; 4:12; 5:20; the lone exception is 5:15) and on the immediate context of this passage (the merciless judgment of the unmerciful in verse 14 and the discussion of justification in verses 18–26, rightly MacArthur 1990 and Heide 1992). That Paul and James do not actually contradict each other has been demonstrated repeatedly elsewhere (*e.g.*, Jeremias 1954; Davids 1982: 50–51; L. Johnson 1995: 249–250) and need not detain us here. Both writers believe that saving faith necessarily leads to transformed living. What is crucial for our purposes is to notice how the empty words of wishing someone well, warm and filled with food, without offering any help, classically illustrate a vacuous profession of Christian faith (2:15–16). It is interesting, too, to note in this context that the Greek noun *adelphē* ('sister') is explicitly included in James's text (2:15), even though

---

severe, punitive measures, while poor people almost never sued the rich, not even in the Greco-Roman world.

[10] D. Watson (1993) correctly notes that the diatribe style which pervades James 2 leaves the question of the reality behind James's several rhetorical questions quite uncertain. But he agrees that some similar problems in the community, even if exaggerated in these examples, must have triggered James's remarks.

'brother' would have adequately covered both men and women, as indeed it does throughout the rest of the letter. James goes out of his way here to call attention to the dispossessed sister. Perhaps it is precisely that widows who fail to come under the protection and provision of any men are still prominently in view, as in 1:27. The situation described was so extreme that it would have shocked many pagans, let alone those familiar with the Jewish prophetic writings and laws of charity. As L. Johnson (1995: 238) reminds us, such situations in the Jewish world led to the creation of the pauper's dish, eventually available in every local synagogue, for similar emergency needs (*e.g.*, m. Peah 5:4, 8:7; m. Demai 3:1).

So, too, professing Christians today who have surplus income (*i.e.*, a considerable majority of believers in the Western world), who are aware of the desperate human needs locally and globally, not least within the Christian community (a situation almost impossible to be unaware of, given our barrage of media coverage), and who give none of their income, either through church or other Christian organizations, to help the materially destitute of the world, ought to ask themselves whether any claims of faith they might make could stand up before God's bar of judgment. This is not salvation by works any more than the examples of Abraham and Rahab in James 2:20–25, but it is the demonstration of a changed life, a heart begun to be transformed by the indwelling Spirit of God, which thereby produces an outpouring of compassion for those so much less well off than oneself.

## James 4:1–3, 13–17

Scattered references throughout James 3 – 4 are helpfully illuminated when one reads the entire epistle with the socio-economic plight of the majority in James's audience in the background (see esp. Geyser 1975). Ralph Martin (1988: lxii–lxxvii) has plausibly argued for a date for James in the 60s in the context of the rise of the Zealot movement, and reads 4:1–3 particularly in this light (144–148). This enables the references to battles and murder in these verses to be taken literally. But the killing may also be metaphorical, and the principles about fighting and quarrelling, replete with improper desires and motives, are sufficiently timeless that they need not be linked to any specific situation. On the other hand, if we read these verses in light of the broader background of socio-economic persecution, they can be seen as a classic example of what psychologists call 'displacement' or 'projection'. When oppressors are not present for the oppressed to attack, internal quarrels within the community of the victims often ensue (cf. Moo 1985: 170). James 4:3 also reminds us that one reason prayers go unanswered is that God's people ask so that they might spend what they get on their own self-centred desires (Gk., *hēdonai*). Nevertheless, it is not until we come to 4:13–17 that we find another explicit teaching passage about material possessions.[11] Here we are introduced to the merchants who probably formed part of the small middle class of the ancient world. They are sufficiently well-to-do to go on business trips and to spend a year in a foreign city (4:13). Some have tried to identify this group with the rich oppressors of 5:1–6, particularly on the basis of the parallel introductory exhortations ('Now listen') in 4:13 and 5:1.[12] But verse 15, in providing the antidote for planning without considering the unpredictability of life (4:14), commands these traders to say, 'If it is the Lord's will, we will live and do this or that.' Presumably, James would not expect the non-Christian to make room for God's will in his or her plans, without that person first of all becoming a believer. So it is likely that there are at least a handful of relatively prosperous Christians in James's communities to whom these verses are addressed. Their attitudes, however, do not fit their ultimate commitments, as they live out a 'practical atheism' (Adamson 1976: 180). In our age of sophisticated long-term strategic planning in the business world, often imitated in churches and Christian organizations, how often do we fall prey to the identical temptation to plan without leaving room for God's sovereign will? The transience of life described here recalls the language of 1:10–11 and supports a connection between these people and the rich portrayed in chapter 1. But as we noted in that context, these parallels simply make it more likely that both 1:10–11 and 4:13–17 describe rich believers, even if they are not at the moment behaving as they ought. Verses 16–17 conclude the latter passage, not by condemning these business persons outright but by stressing the sinful nature of their behaviour. By acknowledging God's will in their process of planning, they can repent of this sin.[13]

## James 5:1–6

With this paragraph, we come to the harshest and most pointed teaching

[11] Wall (1997: 199) plausibly labels 4:4–10 as 'the crisis of materialism', but at most this is one key application of a much more generally worded exhortation.

[12] Maynard-Reid (1987: 69–71) believes that the rich in 2:1–7, 4:13–17 and 5:1–6 are all the same individuals, simply viewed from the differing perspectives of their varying roles.

[13] *Cf.* Townsend (1994: 87): 'The point of the rebuke is not that commerce is somehow unethical in itself, but that the assumptions on which these plans are based are thoroughly secular, both as regards their timing and their content.'

of James against the non-Christian rich who are oppressing his audience. Rhetorically addressing them in verse 1 does not imply that they are present in James's church. This is a classic example of the literary device known as 'apostrophe'. If their oppressive behaviour, described in verses 4–6, continues without repentance,[14] it will lead to eschatological condemnation, described as a great 'misery', worthy of weeping and wailing (5:1). The perfect tenses of verse 2 are often taken as prophetic, but the rarity of this grammatical form, particularly in standard *koinē* Greek, which James has well mastered, makes the more common past-tense use more likely here. The problem is not that these individuals have amassed wealth *per se*, but rather that they have accumulated unused riches, which therefore have simply rotted and been moth-eaten and corroded (5:2–3a; recall Matt. 6:19–21 and par.). Verse 3b would seem to confirm this conclusion. Their problem is that they 'have hoarded' their riches, rather than sharing them with the needy (see esp. Mayordomo-Marín 1992). As already noted, these wealthy people could be either Greco-Roman or Jewish; if the latter, then as landowners they were most likely Herodians or Sadducees (Adamson 1989: 244–245).

Verses 4–6a then enumerate more specific sins against the Christian field-hands that their landlords have committed. First, they have failed to pay certain wages (5:4). This could refer to the lack of an adequate wage, the withholding of a timely wage or the simple failure to pay altogether. Second, and in striking contrast, they 'have lived on earth in luxury and self-indulgence' (5:5a). Louw and Nida (1988: 1:769) define the two key Greek verbs here (*tryphaō* and *spatalaō*) as 'to live a life of luxury, usually associated with intemperate feasting and drinking' and 'to indulge oneself excessively in satisfying one's own appetites and desires'. James recognizes that as the Christian era signals the beginning of the 'last days' (5:3), these wicked rich are fattening themselves in a period that will culminate in their slaughter.[15] Third, these rich 'have condemned and murdered innocent people'. Particularly if a date in the 60s in the throes of the Zealot rebellion is adopted, one could again see this murder as literal. But, with most commentators, it is more natural to take it as judicial

---

[14] Wall (1997: 227) muses whether the weeping and wailing could be 'a prelude to repentance and restoration', but at best this is implicit and probably not the reaction of a majority.

[15] It is also possible that the evil behaviour against James's community is partially in view with the term 'slaughter' here. Less probably one could translate verse 5b as 'You have fattened yourselves as in a day of feasting' (NIV mg.).

murder. Condemning the innocent involves taking away their livelihood and consigning them to slavery, destitution or debtors' prison, and in extreme cases leaving them there until they die. Verse 6b is susceptible of two quite different interpretations. It is normally understood as continuing a description of the innocent people 'who were not opposing you'. There is no relative pronoun or any other connective particle in the Greek, however, leading some to translate these three words (*ouk antitassetai hymin*) as a question. Schökel (1973), for example, proposes understanding the subject of the verb as God and translates the sentence as, 'Does God not oppose you?' This rendering would fit contextually, but without the explanatory inclusion of 'God' in the sentence one would more normally take the antecedent as the nearest singular noun in the sentence, namely, *dikaios*, the 'innocent' person of verse 6a. The asyndeton may simply be a device to create emphasis, even pathos, given the contrast between the oppressive behaviour of the wicked rich and the lack of opposition by the innocent poor.

In light of the numerous Two-Thirds World countries today, not least in Latin America, in which vast tracts of land are owned by a handful of wealthy people or, in many instances, large multi-national corporations that fail to pay decent wages to their labourers, would-be Christians need to reflect long and hard on this passage in James. To what extent do we tacitly endorse such injustice by our purchases from such companies, often without even being aware of their practices, or by supporting politicians who promise tax cuts for the upper and middle classes, when programmes helping the needy at home and abroad are slashed in the process and not likely to be replaced by private-sector equivalents?[16] To what extent do the well-to-do Christians in the West and North live lives little different from those described in 5:1–6 (*cf.* esp. Hanks 1983: 43–45), even if we plead innocent of the more blatant forms of oppression described in this text? Verses 7–11, while not explicitly about material possessions, commend a quite different response to the tragedies of verses 1–6.

## James 5:7–11

Many have read James as simply encouraging the oppressed in his

---

[16] Townsend (1994: 95) is even-handed in his agreement: 'Appropriate responses to James' charges will be a matter of individual conscience, but at the very least ought to involve a concern for fair world trade and political liberty. If that involves rich Christians in paying higher prices for some of the goods they consume, as well as higher taxes in order to help inter-governmental aid to become realistic, it is a fair price to pay. In the light of James' words, charity is not enough.'

community to be patient because the Lord would soon vindicate them against their oppressors when he returns (5:7–9). This theme is clearly present. No amount of social action or concern, however well balanced or properly motivated, can ever create utopia on earth, short of the eschaton. But verses 10–11 suggest that there is more that concerned Christians could and should do in this present age. James encourages us to take as an example of patience in the face of suffering first the prophets and then Job. But these are two curious examples of patience, if simple passive waiting is all that James has in mind. Tamez (1990: 52–56) rightly speaks of a 'militant patience'. It is prophetic *speech* which is specifically highlighted in verse 10 ('the prophets who spoke in the name of the Lord'), and prophetic speech was notorious for its denunciatory rhetoric against the unjust and their injustice, even among the community of those claiming to be part of God's people. Job's perseverance, too, was hardly silent. What stands out more than anything, in even a cursory reading of the biblical narrative of his sufferings, is his complaint, his indignation at the seeming injustice of it all, as he brings his laments before the Lord and decries the inadequacy of the conventional explanations of his suffering offered by his friends.[17] One may speak of James, like Jesus before him,[18] choosing a 'prophetic option' and rejecting both the violent rebellion of the Zealots and the quietistic separatism of the Essenes (*cf.* Adamson 1989: 257). Together, these two examples in verses 10–11 strongly suggest that Christians today should besiege God with complaints about injustice, particularly among the oppressed poor of our lands, and plead before God's people for a greater measure of compassion, generosity and sacrifice. They should also speak out in public to any others who will listen, explaining how God's standards differ radically from the typical practices of Western democracies or capitalistic economics little influenced by a Christian ethic of compassion.

## Conclusions

It goes too far to claim that James knows no-one who is both rich and Christian. But clearly those whom he addresses within the community as rich must behave in certain ways, recognizing the utter transience of their wealth, not seeking or receiving favouritism in any way, and leaving room for God's sovereign will to override any economic plans they might make. The majority of James's community, however, seems

---

[17] Fine (1955: 28) concludes that 'honesty, not patience, is the real virtue of Job'.

[18] James's ethical teaching is particularly indebted at numerous points to the Sermon on the Mount.

to be relatively impoverished and at times even exploited and oppressed. Those who retain their trust in God and wait for his vindication can be said to be among his chosen on whom he lavishes special concern. The entire community is called to look out for the most dispossessed within its midst: the orphan, the widow or the person without adequate clothes or daily food. Those who have even a modest surplus of goods with which they could help the destitute, but who refuse to do so, prove thereby that they are not truly Christian, regardless of any profession they may make. Social injustice must always be denounced, even if its ultimate abolition awaits Christ's return.

## The book of Acts

In our survey of Jesus' teaching on material possessions, we have already noted a preponderance of passages from the Gospel of Luke (chapter 4). When we return to focus on the distinctive contributions of the synoptic evangelists to our topic, we will see that Luke is a particular advocate for the poor (chapter 7). Yet the most plausible reconstruction of the Christian community he was addressing allows for at least a significant minority in his church to have been well-to-do Christians. And by the time Luke wrote, the gospel had spread throughout the Roman empire to all classes of people, and Christian communities were responding to socio-economic needs with diverse models of help. It is interesting, therefore, to note that most of the data relevant to our theme in Luke's second volume, the Acts of the Apostles, comes in the first half of the book when he is describing the earliest years of Christianity while it was still a largely Jewish phenomenon and more or less limited to the eastern end of the Mediterranean. It is arguable, therefore, that while Luke's redactional interests lie with the spread of the gospel to all people groups and with the incorporation of the full range of socio-economic strata of individuals into the church,[19] he has preserved historically accurate information about the poorer nature of the earliest church and about the way the first Christians responded to economic concerns. Simply put, most of the bits and pieces of information from Acts that we will survey in this half-chapter cut against the grain of Luke's redactional emphases and therefore are particularly likely to be firmly rooted in the history of the early church. Thus, we accept that these data provide a window into the events of the first two decades of primarily Jewish Christianity just

[19] See esp. the survey of 'Acts and the Urban Élites' by Gill (1994).

as we postulated with the book of James. It is almost universally agreed that the Apostolic Council of Acts 15:1–29 is to be dated to AD 48 or 49; hence, all but the very last few references in this survey deal with events prior to that date, beginning with the formation of the church in AD 30 or 33.[20]

## The earliest Christian community (Acts 2:42–47)

Immediately after Peter's first recorded sermon on the day of Pentecost, the book of Acts provides us with our earliest glimpse of patterns of Christian community. Verse 42 identifies four features of the most primitive church gathering: 1. the apostles' teaching; 2. fellowship; 3. the breaking of bread; and 4. prayer.[21] In that Peter ended his sermon with a call to repentance and baptism, promising forgiveness of sins and the gift of the Holy Spirit (2:38), it is natural to assume that this combination of elements was also understood to be a central part of the ministry of the Holy Spirit in the earliest church. It is the second of these four elements in verse 42 that interests us here. 'Fellowship' translates the Greek *koinōnia*, which has a broad semantic range, but which in this context is at least partially unpacked by verses 44–45: 'All the believers were together and had everything in common. Selling their possessions and goods, they gave to anyone who had need.' Krodel (1986: 95) quite clearly perceives the link between the gift of the Spirit in verse 38, the *koinōnia* of verse 42 and the material arrangements of verses 44–45: 'What we do or do not do with our material possessions is an indicator of the Spirit's presence or absence.' Other elements of this *koinōnia* discernible from the immediate context include regularly worshipping and living in physical proximity to one another (Acts 2:44a, 46a), a strong emphasis on joy and praise to God, and evangelistic growth (2:46b, 47b). As throughout the early chapters of Acts, there is a powerful sense of Christian unity permeating these verses (*cf.* 1:14; 4:24; 5:12).[22]

But what specifically would have led to the 'common purse' and its distribution described in verses 44b–45? The initial concept may very well be a carry-over from the days in which the disciples spent considerable portions of their time in itinerant ministry with Jesus, themselves apparently sharing the same supply of money (John 12:6; *cf.*

[20] For the chronology, *cf.* now esp. Riesner (1998: 35–58, 280–281).

[21] 'The periphrastic *ēsan proskarterountes* could be translated "persevered in." In such summaries, Luke wants to show continuing and consistent patterns of behavior' (L. Johnson 1992: 58).

[22] A theme that has stood out to interpreters across the ages, despite disagreements over almost all other major interpretive issues. See McGee (1990).

Thurston 1993: 23). Jerusalem, moreover, itself had a very tenuous economy, being primarily a centre for religious and political elites who were not economically productive. Frequent social unrest and drought in that part of the ancient Mediterranean world could compound the problem. Initially many of the Pentecostal pilgrims who would have otherwise returned to their homes in the Diaspora may have stayed as part of this fledgling Christian community, creating a mass of 'refugees'. Finally, even those local Jerusalemites who joined the first church and who themselves were already impoverished probably cut themselves off from the standard Jewish sources of charity. Needless to say, not all of these elements are present in every subsequent Christian community, so the mechanisms for meeting needs may vary too.

The phrase 'everything in common' (*hapanta koina*) in verse 44 is a generalization which is immediately qualified by verses 45–46. Just as Luke could write that 'all the believers were together' and yet make it clear that they continued to live and meet in their own homes (Acts 2: 44a, 46b), so also having everything in common is explained as 'selling their possessions and goods, they gave to anyone who [lit., 'as he (or she)'] had need' (2:45). Verses 43–47 are dominated by highly marked imperfect tense verbs, whereas one normally expects aorists in historical narrative. There is no once-for-all divestiture of property in view here, but periodic acts of charity as needs arose.[23] Interestingly, the clause in the latter half of verse 45, 'to anyone [as he (or she)] had need' formed half of Karl Marx's communist manifesto (the other half will appear in Acts 11:29)! But Marx, of course, attempted to create by legislation, by a totalitarian regime, and by a crusade against religion, what arguably could have been accomplished only in a voluntary religious community such as is described in the book of Acts.[24] What is more, it is only consumption and not also production that is shared in Acts' model.

There are commentators who have argued, no doubt in part fearing the spectre of Marxism, that this early Christian experiment was in fact a mistake (*e.g.*, Criswell 1978: 113–119). Some have gone so far as to claim that the inability of the Judean church to cope with the famine prophesied in Acts 11:27–30 came about because the Christians there had divested themselves of all their capital![25] Others more cautiously

[23] Dupont (1977: 32–34). *Cf.* also C. K. Barrett (1994: 169): 'Luke is describing a state which persisted for some time.'

[24] *Cf.* also Bruce (1988: 74): 'This pooling of property could be maintained voluntarily only when their sense of spiritual unity was exceptionally active.'

[25] Harrison (1986: 98–99) assumes that 'eventually the resources of the more affluent members would be drained, and the common fund would have to be replenished from

claim that one simply cannot draw normative commands from narrative literature.[26] It is certainly true that everything the Bible says *happened* is not necessarily a timeless, positive example to be emulated. But as part of inspired Scripture, narrative is as much a database for theology as any other genre (2 Tim. 3:16). Still, one must read it with lenses appropriate to its literary form. The narrator will often give clues by his introductions, conclusions, comparisons and contrasts with other episodes as to whether he believes certain events were exemplary, counterproductive or simply neutral.[27] Commentators have frequently compared Acts 2:43–47 and 4:32–35 with Greco-Roman idealizations of communalism. Most recently, Sterling (1994) finds in these passages a *topos* shared by a variety of Hellenistic texts intended to commend a given community as exemplary and honourable. Larkin's conclusions (1995: 83) are worth citing at length:

> We must understand, however, that the structure Luke points to is not a coercive communism that dispenses with private property through once-for-all expropriation to a common fund. Luke never presents the system as a failure but rather sees all churches as living out not only their responsibility for the poor (Acts 20:5) but also their interdependence through caring for one another ... Seen in this light, what Luke calls for is fully normative. With a mindset of unity we will view our economic resources as available to meet others' needs. We will voluntarily, periodically supply our local assembly's common fund for the poor.

There is no exegetical or historical support for understanding early Christian communalism as an improper or failed experiment.[28] The various factors mentioned on the previous page, combined with the severe famine of the late 40s, are adequate enough explanation for the subsequent poverty of the Jerusalem church.

---

other sources or be abandoned.' But this assumes what Acts never states – that the well-to-do sold so much that they had too little left to invest for future needs.

[26] Thus even the otherwise excellent handbook of Fee & Stuart (1982: 97).

[27] See esp. Liefeld (1995: 49–59), esp. with reference to the Ananias and Sapphira narrative; *cf.* Ryken (1987: 77–87).

[28] Talbert (1997: 64) believes that 'the values espoused by Acts continued in the church', and cites Lucian's *Peregrinus* 13 about how Christians helped an imprisoned rogue who became a believer, because 'they despise all worldly goods alike, regarding them merely as common property'.

## Peter and John respond to the temple beggar (Acts 3:6)

The very next passage in Acts describes Peter healing the crippled beggar at the temple gate called 'Beautiful' (3:1–10). The relevant verse for our topic is verse 6, in which Peter tells the beggar, 'Silver or gold I do not have, but what I have I give to you. In the name of Jesus Christ of Nazareth, walk.' Interestingly, we know from the previous text (2:42–47) that Peter and John did in fact have silver and gold, even though their participation in the 'common pot' meant that they did not consider it exclusively theirs. Nevertheless, they clearly could have accessed this treasury to supply the man with money. Rather, they want to go to the root of his problem, the illness which has prevented him from working for himself. Still, the miracle they work is one of physical healing, so this is scarcely a protest against social concern.[29] As with the healings of Jesus in the Gospels, the miracles performed by the disciples in Acts preserve God's holistic concern for body and soul. Cassidy (1987: 25), commenting on this passage in conjunction with 1:15–20 and 8:18–20, concludes also that there is 'a certain skepticism about the purposes for which silver and gold might be useful'.[30]

## More on early Christian communalism, both good and bad (Acts 4:32 – 5:11)

A second summary paragraph describes and elaborates the financial koinōnia of the Jerusalem church (4:32–35). Again the passage begins with a reminder of the strong unity of the fellowship. Verse 32 continues by clarifying that individuals retained private property but did not cling to their possessions as if they belonged exclusively to themselves. From their unity flowed a willingness to share, encapsulated by our slogan, 'What's mine is yours' (Guinan 1977: 67). Similarly Aristotle (Politics 1263a) and Cicero (De officiis 1.16) held that the ideal was to own private property but to put it at the disposal of one's friends.[31] Verse 33 discloses another clue to the narrator's approval of

---

[29] For each of these points in the last four sentences, see I. H. Marshall (1980: 88).

[30] Cf. also Hamm (1986: 314–315) who recalls the stereotyped use of 'silver' and 'gold' in association with idolatry in the Old Testament (e.g., Exod. 20:23; Deut. 7:25; Hos. 8:4; etc.), suggesting that Luke sees the passage about wanting to turn the man away from anything that would deflect him from worshipping the true, risen Lord.

[31] But these writers limited this practice to 'friends', and the sharing of goods actually led to never-ending obligations of reciprocity among those friends. Luke applies the concept radically to the entire church, across socio-economic lines, and encourages people to give without thought of return (recall Luke 6:34–35; 14:12–14). Cf. further Mitchell (1992: 262–266).

this scheme: their fellowship combined with powerful testimony to the resurrected Christ in a grace-full witness.

Acts 4:34a then declares flatly, 'There were no needy persons among them.' The term translated 'needy' (*endeēs*) appears only here in the New Testament. In other Greek literature it can be a synonym for *ptōchos*, but it often focuses more on a person who lacks certain needed resources while not in a state of utter destitution (Louw & Nida 1988: 2:564). Interestingly, *ptōchos*, so common in Luke, never appears once in Acts. Perhaps Luke means that the church saw to it not only that its members were no longer left destitute but also that they lived above a reasonable poverty line.[32] Verses 34b–35 continue, 'For from time to time those who owned lands or houses sold them, brought the money from the sales and put it at the apostles' feet, and it was distributed to anyone who had need.' Again we have a rash of imperfect tense verbs here, this time explicitly reflected in the NIV's 'from time to time'. The periodic selling of property confirms our interpretation of Acts 2:44 above. This was not a one-time divestiture of all one's possessions. The theme of 'according to need' reappears, too. Interestingly, what does not appear in this paragraph is any statement of complete equality among believers. Presumably, there was quite a spectrum, ranging from those who still held property which they had not sold (*cf.* the reference to the home of John Mark in Acts 12:12) all the way to those who were still living at a very basic level.[33] But the church was committed to taking the principle of Deuteronomy 15:4 very seriously: 'there should be no poor among you' (F. Martin 1972: 46).

Acts 2:36–37 proceed to give a specific, positive example of the sale and distribution of property. Here we are introduced for the first time to 'Barnabas', who will become crucial in the formative Christian development of Paul later in the book (9:27; 11:25–26; 13:2–3). This nickname for Joseph, meaning 'Son of Encouragement' (4:36), may, however, have been given initially because of his exemplary compassion for the poor in the church. At least, this is the context in which the explanation of his name appears, as he sells a field he owned and brings the money to the apostles who are in charge of disbursing it. Dunn (1996a: 59) speculates that Barnabas is singled out for attention, too, because he may have been the first person of 'substantial wealth and position' to contribute a large gift to the common fund.

Acts 5:1–11, however, balances Barnabas' positive example with the negative example of Ananias and Sapphira, which is narrated

---

[32] The term also alludes to the *endeēs* of Deut. 15:4, LXX (L. Johnson 1992: 34).
[33] Thus persuasively Fiensy (1995).

in considerably greater detail. The story begins as if it will closely parallel the Barnabas incident. Ananias and Sapphira also 'sold a piece of property' (5:1) and brought a part of the money to be disbursed by the apostles (5:2b). But in between we read, 'With his wife's full knowledge[34] he kept back part of the money for himself' (5:2a).[35] The verb 'kept back' actually reflects a rare use of the very specific term *nosphizō*, meaning 'to swindle' or 'to embezzle'. In the New Testament it occurs elsewhere only in Titus 2:10. Its only occurrence in the Septuagint, apart from the Apocrypha, is in Joshua 7:1 in conjunction with Achan's sin.[36] Haenchen (1971: 237, n. 4) notes that in Hellenism the term always implied '(a) that the theft was secret, (b) its object was part of a larger sum, (c) which was the property of a community'. Undoubtedly, Luke intends us to see a parallel with the Achan narrative. In each case a serious sin in the opening phases of the community of God's people, following the giving of a new covenant, is punished by death, seemingly out of proportion to the crime, precisely to persuade God's people of the seriousness with which he takes sin. There are also parallels with Jesus' temptations (Luke 4:1–13); both Jesus and the early church must win a decisive battle against Satan's lies at the beginning of their ministries.[37] Verses 3 and 8 make it clear that Peter understands that the sin was not in failing to give all but in lying about the amount given and, hence, the price paid for the land. What is more, this lying is not simply to humans but to the Holy Spirit (5:3), who is equal to God (5:4). Verse 4 further stresses how voluntary the donations were and how there was private ownership of both the

---

[34] This phrase sets the stage for the close parallelism between the fates of Ananias and Sapphira in Acts 5:3–6 and 7–10. It is worth noting in passing that Sapphira is treated as a fully independent and accountable individual. There is no biblical justification for the notion that a wife must submit to ungodly demands from her husband; indeed this passage flatly contradicts that notion.

[35] Derrett (1971: 156) speculates that this sum might have been the *ketubah* or dowry given by the wife to her husband and kept by him intact in the event of any subsequent divorce, in which case it had to be repaid to her. Today we might speak of someone's 'nest egg'.

[36] *Cf.* Longenecker (1981: 314): 'Like the act of Achan, this episode was pivotal in the life and mission of God's people, for the whole enterprise was threatened at its start. And while we may be thankful that judgement upon deceit in the church is not now so swift and drastic, this incident stands as an indelible warning regarding the heinousness in God's sight of deception in spiritual and personal matters.' Recall also the seriousness of 1QS 6:25–65.

[37] O'Toole (1995), who also presents and discusses other possible parallels inside and outside Luke-Acts in the context of a wide-ranging literary and theological analysis of Acts 5:1–11. Marguerat (1993) offers a survey of recent approaches to the passage and defends the theory of close parallels with Gen. 3.

field and the proceeds of the sale, even after the transaction.

Although most commentators have stressed the differences between this voluntary arrangement and the mandatory initiation proceedings of the Essene communities, Capper (1995: 338–340) makes a plausible case for drawing the parallels more closely. It could be that a certain level of funds was mandated to be put in a common pot and that 5:4 reflects a procedure similar to 1QS 6 with its instructions for the stages of the surrender of an initiate's property (1QS 6:18–27), complete with the requisite punishment for lying about one's goods (1QS 6:24–25). In other words, Ananias' and Sapphira's donation may have corresponded to that phase of Essene initiation in which would-be members gave their property but could still reclaim it if either party after another year opted out of the process that would otherwise have culminated in full membership.[38] Capper (1983) also suggests that the ceremony of laying the proceeds at the feet of the apostles indicated that they were claiming to give all the monies from the sale of their property and demonstrating subjection to apostolic authority. Whichever interpretation be accepted, the resulting fear which seizes the church and all who hear about God's judgment of Ananias and Sapphira (Acts 5:11) also leads to high regard for the apostles (along with an understandable caution about getting too close to them; 5:13!). Verse 14, however, indicates Luke's approval as the narrator of the events that have transpired: 'Nevertheless, more and more men and women believed in the Lord and were added to their number.'

## Helping the Hellenistic widows (Acts 6:1–4)

We never hear explicitly of these early Christian communal arrangements again. But the situation described at the beginning of Acts 6 presupposes their continuation, in the absence of any indication to the contrary. The 'Grecian' Jews begin to complain against the 'Hebraic Jews' 'because their widows were being overlooked in the daily distribution of food' (Acts 6:1). Introduced as if the reader already knows about it, 'the daily distribution' is presumably tied in with the disbursement of the common treasury described in 2:44–45 and 4:32 – 5:11.[39]

Much debate has gone into trying to determine what distinguished

---

[38] S. Johnson (1954) had already argued that Ananias and Sapphira may have taken a vow to enter an inner circle of the community which required giving up all possessions, while no regular rule required such sacrifice of all Christians.

[39] Dunn (1996a: 81) notes that with the rapid growth of the early church, any attempts to support the poor 'must quickly have made almost impossible demands upon the common fund'.

these two groups of Jews (see esp. Hengel 1983 vs. Hill 1992). At the very least there was a linguistic difference. Grecian Jews would have come primarily from the Diaspora and have spoken Greek as their native language. Hebraic Jews, whether from the Diaspora or from Israel, would have retained Hebrew or Aramaic as their primary language. But it is not improbable that various cultural differences exacerbated the conflict. With the twelve apostles all representing the Hebraic Jewish wing of the fledgling church, it is understandable that the needy in the more Hellenized wing would be the first to be overlooked, particularly if finances were tight or responsibilities heavy. In addition to the factors already noted causing so much poverty among the Jerusalem Christians, many pious Jews 'retired' to Jerusalem to be buried in or near their holy city. If the widows referred to in 6:1 included the wives of such individuals, we can understand why they may have been plentiful in number (Haenchen 1971: 261). To their credit, the apostles recognized the need to redress this injustice (recall Jas. 1:27), but not at the expense of the ministry to which they were primarily called (Acts 6:2a).

If the later rabbinic practices or some predecessors of them were already in place (see above, p. 102), one may view the apostles' solution here as modelled on a combination of the elements of existing Jewish charity. Instead of a weekly dole of money for members within the community (the *quppah*) and a daily delivery of food to the neediest non-residents (the *tamhuy*), we read here of a daily distribution of food to those within the community. This communal sharing has again suggested that one should understand the model of Qumran as an important precedent. It is also significant that the Twelve in no way minimize the authority of the seven who are chosen to alleviate the plight of the widows. In fact, 'this physical/social ministry has equal validity with the apostles' evangelism/edification ministry' – the term *diakonia* is used for them both (6:1, 4) (Larkin 1995: 100).

In verse 2b, the apostles refer to the ministry that is being neglected as waiting 'on tables'. The tables in question could be for dining and, hence, refer to the distribution of food; or for banking, and refer to the distribution of money. The NIV assumes that food is in view by describing the daily distribution in verse 1b in precisely these terms, but nothing in the Greek explicitly corresponds to the phrase 'of food'. Nevertheless, this was probably the more common of the two possible kinds of distribution and more probably what is in view here. The verb translated 'wait on' in verse 2 renders the Greek *diakoneō*, which, like *diakonia*, is cognate to the noun *diakonos*, the name for one of the two main offices in early church polity (*cf.* our English 'deacon'). Two extreme conclusions must be avoided: on the one hand, one cannot directly appeal to 6:1–6 for the origin of the later Christian diaconate, particularly since the noun 'deacon' (*diakonos*) does not even occur in this passage. On the other hand, one cannot ignore this passage as irrelevant. By Luke's time, Christians probably recognized a precedent in these verses for the later development of the office (*cf.* C. K. Barrett 1994: 314 with Coppens 1979: 421).

In any event, the call for the Hellenistic Jewish-Christian community to choose leaders from among themselves to meet their own needs demonstrates wisdom in supporting indigenous leadership for a neglected group. The subsequent ministries of at least two of the seven (the only ones we hear anything more about in Acts) demonstrate that their roles were every bit as 'spiritual' as 'practical'. Stephen and Philip, in fact, are known more for their bold witness in the rest of Acts 6 – 8 than for any administration of charity. It is interesting, too, that the choice of seven followed a standard Jewish procedure for creating an *ad hoc* board or committee to meet a specific need (I. H. Marshall 1980: 126). It is not a little ironic that various other biblical criteria for the diaconate have often been taken as timeless without the necessary supporting hermeneutical reflection.[40]

## The problem of simony (Acts 8:18–23)

The next reference to material possessions in Acts comes in chapter 8 in the context of the apparent conversion of Simon the Magician. For the third consecutive time, a passage about money in Acts demonstrates the grave problems that its mistreatment can generate. The gospel has for the first time since Pentecost moved beyond explicitly Jewish and Judean settings and come to Samaria. This chapter raises numerous theological problems – about the timing of the arrival of the Holy Spirit or the presence and nature of charismatic gifts – which this study need not resolve.[41] What is relevant is that Simon sees some manifestation of the Spirit when the apostles Peter and John arrive in Samaria and lay their hands on the new believers there (Acts 8:18a). As one who perhaps viewed this power as a greater 'magic' than that which he had previously employed, Simon adopts a common pagan assumption that the gods can be bought off and offers the apostles money for the ability to confer the Holy Spirit on those on whom he, too, would lay hands

---

[40] On the need for flexibility in applying Acts 6:1–6, see esp. Longenecker (1981: 331).

[41] For particularly helpful perspectives, see Dunn (1970: 55–72).

(8:19). Peter rebukes him for this extremely non-Christian notion: 'May your money perish with you, because you thought you could buy the gift of God with money!' (8:20). J. B. Phillips' 'paraphrase' is actually more literal at this point: 'To hell [Gk. *apōleia*] with you and your money!' The larger context of verses 21–23, combined with later church tradition, suggests that Simon is not saved at this point, nor does he repent later. What is condemned in the immediate context is 'any attempt to manipulate God for personal gain' (Polhill 1992: 220). Although the term 'simony' in English would later come to be used for attempts to bribe or purchase ecclesiastical office, the original context of the offence is clearly broader.

## People praised for giving to the poor

Three scattered references in the first, primarily Jewish half of the book of Acts (chs. 1 – 12) continue the theme (which by now has dominated our survey of the biblical material) of the need to provide material help for the poor, especially within the community of God's people. In 9:36 the recently deceased Dorcas is praised as one 'who was always doing good and helping the poor'. The term 'doing good' may include, or even be equivalent to, early Christian benefaction – as a replacement for the standard Greco-Roman patron–client relationships requiring reciprocity (see Winter 1994: 25–40; *cf.* below, pp. 180–181). Helping the poor almost certainly includes almsgiving, along with other acts of charity. Spencer (1994) sees 9:36–43 as providing some closure that 6:1–7 does not, in terms of completing Peter's concern for the dispossessed. His view requires understanding Peter's solution in chapter 6 as deficient, because Peter does not acknowledge the ministry of the new 'deacons' as on a par with his. As already observed, that conclusion does not follow. Nevertheless, it makes good sense, with Spencer, to read Acts 9 as completing a series of references to widows in Luke's two-volume work and as recognizing the priority status that widows are given.

In 10:2, 4 and 31, Cornelius, too, is described as a model almsgiver. This is one of the reasons he is portrayed as particularly deserving of hearing the gospel from Peter, despite his Gentile background. Classic Jewish language, reminiscent of the theology of Tobit (see above, p. 94), echoes in the words of the angel, 'Your prayers and gifts to the poor have come up as a memorial offering before God' (10:4). Almsgiving virtually substitutes for sacrifice. It is not necessary, with Berger (1977), however, to see this as the Christian equivalent to the Jewish belief that almsgiving was a literal means of atonement for

Gentiles. Clearly the point of Cornelius' story is that his piety was just the beginning of his journey to full-fledged Christian faith. Cornelius becomes a true believer only in 10:44, while Peter is preaching to him.

Thirdly, in 11:27–30, Agabus comes to the church in Antioch and predicts the subsequent famine in Judea. As already noted, here appears the other half of Marx's manifesto: from 'each according to his ability' (11:29). In response to Agabus' prediction of the coming famine, the disciples decide to provide help for their co-religionists in Judea by sending gifts to the Jerusalem elders through Barnabas and Saul (11:29–30). The famine described is almost certainly the same as the one Josephus mentions, which hit Judea particularly severely in AD 45–47 (*Antiquities* 20.2.5).[42] The model of relief presupposed in this passage clearly varies from that of the earliest chapters in Acts.[43] There is no indication of a communal treasury; each believer simply has his or her own sources of income, with varying levels of wealth or prosperity. Still, all are concerned to help according to their ability. Here appears also the first mention of 'elders' in Jerusalem, who will apparently oversee the distribution of the gift. With the persecution of Stephen, all but the twelve apostles scattered, leaving Jerusalem (Acts 8:1), so presumably a new group emerged to replace the first 'deacons' in that role in the capital city. Later we see the elders replacing many or all of the apostles themselves, as the leaders in the Jerusalem church, when the apostles were no longer permanently based in Judea (*cf.* 12:17 with 15:2, 6).[44]

## Christians of considerable means in Acts

From the earliest stages of Christianity, the most common and natural meeting place for believers was in private homes (Acts 2:46; see esp. Blue 1994). Some of these would undoubtedly have been quite modest, but the gathering of the 120 in one place at Pentecost (2:1 – referring to the same upper room of 1:13?) would have required a larger meeting area. When 'a large number of priests became obedient to the faith' (6:7), they could very easily have opened their larger villas to Christian congregations.[45] Later characters in Acts who would probably have been prosperous include Cornelius, in his role as a Roman centurion

---

[42] *Cf.* also the references to frequent droughts in that area during the reign of Claudius in Suetonius, *Life of Claudius* 18; Tacitus, *Annals* 12.43.

[43] For further background to the famine and for helpful comments on Christianity's transformation of the convention of benefaction, see Winter (1994: 59–78, esp. 76).

[44] See esp. Bauckham (1995: 427–441).

[45] On the self-definition, prestige and status of Jewish priests towards the end of the Second Temple period, see Maier (1993).

(10:1); the family of John Mark, who hosted many Christians in its home (12:12); Sergius Paulus, the Cypriot proconsul (13:6–12); Lydia, a businesswoman and head of her household (16:14–15); the Philippian jailer, another Roman official (16:31–34); Jason, who housed Paul and his travelling companions, perhaps as part of a regular ministry of offering Christian hospitality, but who at least had money enough for bail so as to be released from arrest (17:5–9); many prominent Greek women in Thessalonica (17:12); a few members of the Areopagus, along with Damaris, presumably a female visitor of some status invited to this otherwise all-male assembly (17:34); Aquila and Priscilla, fellow tent-makers with Paul who had money to travel around quite a bit (18:2–3); Titius Justus, a God-fearer who could accommodate gatherings to hear Paul preach (18:7); and Mnason, who provided hospitality for Paul and numerous travelling companions in Caesarea (21:16). Nothing requires this list to reflect the status of a majority of early church members, but it places a sizeable question mark in front of any hypothesis that sees virtually all of them as impoverished.[46] Tellingly, most of these references come from the later years of Christian expansion narrated in Acts and reflect the growth of a Christian middle, or even upper, class.

## The interaction of Christianity with the pagan economies around it

Additional scattered references relevant to a survey of a theology of material possessions in Acts all come from its second major section (Acts 13 – 28), in which Luke is focusing primarily on the ministry of Paul and the rapid growth of Gentile Christianity. Chronologically, these references, like several in our last subsection, belong with our survey of the epistles of Paul in the next chapter, but, for the sake of keeping them with the rest of the book of Acts and providing a transition to the epistolary literature, we may briefly note them here.

First, in 16:17–24 Paul delivers a Philippian slave girl from her demonic possession. As a result, he is mobbed and arrested because her owner's hope of income from her 'prophesying' spirit has dried up. Larkin (1995: 241) sees here an example of Christian concern for the temporal or physical needs of non-Christians; once again there is holistic salvation.

Second, as noted above, 17:12 refers to 'a number of prominent Greek women' in Berea who believed. These no doubt came from the

---

[46] Or, as with Stegemann (1984: 32–44), as no better than 'middle class'.

small class of wealthy Greco-Romans and probably included some with considerable education. These individuals would seem to be Acts' counterpart to the women of Luke 8:1–3 and the source of some of the Macedonians' later financial support for Paul (see below, p. 192).[47]

Third, in 18:3 we read of how Paul's tent-making ministry supplied his own needs while in Corinth. We will discuss this practice more in conjunction with the details of the Corinthian correspondence below (p. 186). We may note here, however, that verse 5 combines with verse 3 to replicate the pattern that we will see from Paul's own writings: he recognizes the need to have his own source of income – either by working or by receiving gifts from outside – so that he is not dependent for support on the local congregations he is currently serving and so that his integrity is not compromised in any way. This frees him to preach exactly what God tells him, however unpopular the message may be.

Fourth, a riot breaks out in Ephesus because the silversmiths are losing too much money as people abandon idolatry and the purchase of silver idols in favour of Christian discipleship (19:23–41). Although Demetrius appeals to national patriotism and religious allegiance to whip up the crowds (19:26b, 27b), it is clear that economic concerns lie at the foundation of his complaint (19:25b, 27a). 'Any Christianity worth its salt will be a challenge to the pocketbook, the flag and the shrine' (Larkin 1995: 283). Similarly, Luke tells us in Acts 19:19 that when the Ephesian Christians burned their magical papyrus scrolls (of which many from a slightly later date have survived and can be read today [see esp. Betz 1986]), the value was the equivalent of 50,000 days' wages (19:19).[48] Would that Christian witness could have similar effect on industries such as pornography in our own age!

Fifth, Acts 20:33–35 excerpts a portion of Paul's farewell address to the Ephesian elders at Miletus. In these verses Paul declares, 'I have not coveted anyone's silver or gold or clothing. You yourselves know that these hands of mine have supplied my own needs and the needs of my companions. In everything I did, I showed you that by this kind of hard work we must help the weak, remembering the words the Lord Jesus himself said: "It is more blessed to give than to receive." ' These verses again corroborate the principles that will become clearer in 1 Corinthians 9 and add a salutary focus on 'those in need of social

---

[47] Corley (1993: 111) speaks of the women of Luke 8:1–3 as 'cast instead as Greco-Roman "patronesses"', the explicit function of these women in Acts here.

[48] 'Seemingly Paul was accomplishing such a shift in popular attitudes that the continued viability of an entire industry was being called into question' (Cassidy 1987: 57).

assistance' (Lövestam 1987: 7). They also introduce to us a rare *agraphon* (a saying of Jesus not found in the four Gospels). Out of context, this saying can be misunderstood and turned into a self-serving concept, no less than the view it is intended to combat. In context, what Paul understands Jesus to be saying is that 'It is better for a person who can do so to give help to others rather than to amass further wealth for himself' (I. H. Marshall 1980: 33b).[49]

Finally, Acts 24:17 alludes to the collection that dominated a decade or so of Paul's attention (see below, pp. 191–199). Further discussion of the collection must await our next chapter, but this reference seems to confirm that the individuals mentioned in 20:4 who accompany Paul from Greece to Jerusalem on his final trip there probably correspond to the independent witnesses by whom Paul is concerned that the successful delivery of the gift be confirmed (2 Cor. 8:16–24). Acts 24:17 also belies the claim that Acts makes no reference to the collection, but without additional background information, 'the reader of Acts can scarcely understand the allusion here; it is clear that Luke knows more than he says' (Conzelmann 1987: 199).

## Conclusions

It is true that nowhere else in the rest of Acts or in the New Testament more generally is anything heard of the communitarian model of 2:42–47 and 4:32 – 5:11. But a line of continuity can be drawn from those chapters through the establishment of the informal 'diaconate' in Acts 6:1–6 and the famine-relief effort in Acts 11:27–30 to the later more formal establishment of the office of deacons in Philippians 1:1 and 1 Timothy 3:8–13 (see esp. Thurston 1989). A middle class and even an upper class in Christianity developed (as the next chapters will elaborate), as the gospel spread into more well-to-do Greco-Roman circles, although those classes still remained a minority in the church. But concern for the poor, especially via almsgiving, recurs throughout Acts, as Christians are committed to reducing the gap between the 'haves' and the 'have-nots' in their congregations.

In subsequent Christian history, one can draw a second line from a number of these early charitable practices in Acts to the monastic movement, which unfortunately in emergent Catholicism developed a two-tiered mentality. Those called to vows of poverty showed exemplary compassion for the poor in divesting themselves of their own property, but the average rank-and-file layperson rarely imitated these

---

[49] For a more detailed study of the role of 20:35 in Paul's sermon to the Ephesian elders, see O'Toole (1994).

models. On Protestant presuppositions, all Christians should be committed to modelling patterns of generous benefaction without the expectation of reciprocity. The various particulars will change from situation to situation, but generous giving rather than selfish hoarding, accompanied by compassionate commitment to doing what will most help the genuinely needy, must remain a priority for God's people.

# Chapter Six

# The life and teaching of Paul

From his autobiographical remarks in the epistles and from the data of Acts, we learn that Paul's own socio-economic background seems to have been relatively prosperous, at least by ancient standards. Tutored in Jerusalem under the rabbi Gamaliel (Acts 22:3), after a probable elementary-school education in Tarsus, a centre of Greek culture, Paul would have been among the top few percent in his society in terms of level of education.[1] He also had training in leather-working, of which tent-making was one common application (Acts 18:3).[2] As one who inherited Roman citizenship from his father, he also would have been among just a handful of non-Romans in the empire with this privilege (Acts 22:28). Gillian Clark (1985: 111) concludes, 'The chances are that Paul, though prepared for the sake of the gospel to identify himself with the artisans, was at home in more prosperous levels of society.' Nils Dahl (1977: 35) concurs, adding that Paul probably came from a rather well-to-do family.

In his evangelistic ministry Paul focuses on the major urban centres of the Greco-Roman empire, with only a handful of exceptions. This also suggests that he would have encountered and come to be at home in the whole socio-economic spectrum. He both experienced and contributed to that period of Christianity which began to see at least some noticeable improvement in the overall socio-economic standing of its converts (see esp. Judge 1960: 49–61; *cf.* W. Meeks 1983: 73). In this chapter we will survey in chronological order, as best as we can determine it, the teaching in Paul's epistles relevant to a theology of

---

[1] Jewish boys who trained under rabbis usually began this post-elementary-school education at the age of twelve or thirteen. On the general historicity of Paul's pre-Christian career according to Acts, see Légasse (1995).

[2] This occupation in and of itself would not have distinguished Paul from other 'despised' manual labourers in Greco-Roman society. But rabbis were supposed to have a trade (recall above, p. 76), and Paul's qualification of his Jewish legacy on this matter (see below on 1 Cor. 9) makes it clear that his 'abasement' is strictly voluntary. On the nature and status of a *skēnopoios*, *cf.* further Szesnat (1993). In addition to leather, Paul may have worked with linen and/or goat hair.

material possessions. Clearly, the most extensive teaching passage on the topic is 2 Corinthians 8 – 9, as Paul gives detailed instructions for the collection for the saints in Judea. So we will stop and take a particularly close look at these two chapters when we arrive at that stage in Paul's ministry.

## Galatians

Although many still date Galatians after the Apostolic Council of Acts 15, and therefore usually after 1 and 2 Thessalonians, conservative commentators have put forward well-founded arguments for correlating the visit to Jerusalem described in Galatians 2:1–10 with Acts 11:27–30 (cf., e.g., Longenecker 1990: 61; Bruce 1982: 126). This makes it probable that Galatians 2:11–14 corresponds to Acts 15:1 and that Galatians was written in haste as Paul had just heard of a Judaizing faction plaguing Galatia similar to that at Antioch, while he was preparing to head for Jerusalem. If the Apostolic Council took place in 48 or 49, then Galatians should probably be dated to these same years.[3] It is thus significant that Paul in probably his earliest letter, as he was still fashioning his relationship with the original apostles in Jerusalem, notes that all easily agreed 'that we should continue to remember the poor, the very thing I was eager to do' (Gal. 2:10). While theology and territory for ministry were still being hashed out, no debate centred around the need to help the poor.[4] If this passage is correlated with Acts 11:27–30, then clearly it refers to the famine Agabus predicted in Judea, to which reference has already been made (see above, p. 171). And it reminds us that a key concern of early Jewish Christianity, as we saw in our survey of James and the first part of Acts, was also a point that Paul eagerly endorsed. Indeed, it seems that he would spend the better part of the coming decade organizing a large collection of funds from throughout the Greco-Roman cities he evangelized to be sent back to Jerusalem.[5]

[3] For details see especially Riesner (1998: 286–291).

[4] Lührmann (1992: 41–42) observes: 'In Jerusalem and all the more now in his own new mission area around the Aegean, Paul could have played his trumps: rapidly growing mission areas and no doubt also an economic superiority in the new churches. But he does not do so because what matters is the gospel.'

[5] There is no reason to assume that Paul's preoccupation with the collection of 1 and 2 Corinthians and Romans in the mid-50s implies that nothing had previously been delivered at the height of the famine in the late 40s. In fact, Acts 11:29–30, without explicitly saying so, implies the opposite. This calls into serious question the major premise underlying Hurtado (1979), which leads to his conclusion that the data of the later Pauline epistles demonstrate the collection to have been a point of contention already at the time of the meeting of the apostles in Gal. 2:1–10.

The other reference in Galatians to what believers should do with their money appears in 6:6. Many commentators have seen this verse as an isolated command in a loose series of miscellaneous closing exhortations: 'Those who receive instruction in the word must share all good things with their instructor.' Even so, C. K. Barrett (1985: 82) is almost certainly right in observing that this 'may be the earliest reference to any kind of paid Christian ministry'. Paul hints at what will become more explicit and detailed in 1 Corinthians 9, namely, full-time Christian ministers' right to earn their living by the gospel. This command sets Paul off from conventional Judaism, in which rabbis were expected to have a trade to practise so that they did not have to rely on financial support from others for their ministry. It agrees with Greco-Roman wisdom, but Paul will later stress the numerous situations in which he finds it important to forgo his rights. Nevertheless, far from being an isolated exhortation, Galatians 6:6 probably forms one significant application of the broader principle of verses 1–5 of believers bearing one another's burdens. Similarly, while verses 7–10 generalize about people reaping as they sow and encourage Christians to 'do good to all people, especially to those who belong to the family of believers' (6:10), it is probable that Paul is thinking primarily of the *financial* principle of reaping as one sows and of doing good to fellow believers with one's *money* (see esp. Fung 1988: 292–299; *cf.* Matera 1992: 222–223).[6]

# 1 and 2 Thessalonians

Most scholars date 1 and 2 Thessalonians to approximately AD 50–51, as Paul writes from Corinth to a community he has quite recently evangelized. 1 Thessalonians 4:11–12 hints at a problem in Thessalonica that Paul will develop in greater detail in his second letter. He encourages the Christians there 'to lead a quiet life, to mind your own business and to work with your hands, just as we told you, so that your daily life may win the respect of outsiders and so that you will not be dependent on anybody'. In 5:14 he urges them to 'warn those who are idle'. By way of contrast in 1 Thessalonians 2:6, 9, he has stressed how hard he and his companions worked night and day not to burden the Thessalonians while they ministered among them. In other words, Paul made his own living while staying in Thessalonica. Apparently there

---

[6] Whether or not a special allusion to the Galatians' contributing toward the needs of the Jerusalem Christians is in view (thus Hurtado 1979: 53–57) is more difficult to determine.

was a problem in that city with some who were not working and therefore were inappropriately dependent on the generosity of others to care for them. Paul's rhetoric becomes more pointed in 2 Thessalonians 3:6–15 as he warns the Christians 'to keep away from every brother who is idle' and disregards his teaching (3:6). Paul again reminds them of his example of working hard and not eating anyone's food without paying for it (3:7–8). He clarifies that he actually had the right to receive such help but refrained from demanding his rights as an example worth imitating (3:9). Paul then proclaims, 'For even when we were with you, we gave you this rule: "Anyone who will not work shall not eat" ' (3:10). The subsequent verses explain that the idle were not busy but 'busybodies', and that they should 'settle down and earn the bread they eat' (3:11–12). Meanwhile all the Christians in Thessalonica should not tire of doing good (*kalopoiountes*; 3:13). The dissociation from believers who ignore these mandates should not be understood as full-fledged excommunication ('do not regard him as an enemy') but as a stern warning (3:14–15).

Traditionally, the problem that seemingly permeates all of these verses has been assumed to stem from theological roots. Much of Paul's eschatological teaching in 2 Thessalonians makes it clear that some people are thinking that the parousia is extremely imminent or has actually passed (see esp. 2 Thess. 2:2). Not working is then related to the assumption that this life or present world-order is on the verge of vanishing.[7] But increasingly, scholars are agreeing that a sociological problem is more likely in view here.[8] Paul never explicitly connects the Thessalonians' idleness with his teaching about the parousia, but there is much in the Greco-Roman practice of patronage and benefaction that could have led to the problems described here.[9] If a significant number of the Thessalonians before converting to Christ had been clients who worked only sporadically and relied on the gifts of their wealthy patrons (see above, p. 103), then it is understandable that they might have expected well-to-do leaders in the Christian community to treat them in a similar fashion (Wanamaker 1990: 279–290).[10] But Paul will consistently challenge the conventional system of patronage

---

[7] For a vigorous recent restatement of this view, see Menken (1992).

[8] Of course, one may not have to choose between these two views. If there was a fundamental problem with the unemployed, it may have been exacerbated by beliefs that the end was extremely near. See Richard (1995); D. Williams (1992).

[9] On the specific networks and patterns of benefactor–client interaction in Thessalonica, but without direct reference to 1 and 2 Thessalonians, see Hendrix (1991).

[10] Less plausibly, Thurston (1995: 191, 193), following Malherbe (1987), sees an Epicurean and Cynic background.

throughout his epistles. 'The secular client must now become a private Christian benefactor' so as 'to wean such persons away from the welfare syndrome' (Winter 1994: 42, 53; *cf.* also all of 41–60). 'Doing good' (NIV 'doing what is right') in verse 13 may have charitable benefaction especially in mind. In this larger context, 2 Thessalonians 3:10 is clearly directed at those who are 'not willing' to work, not at those who are unable to work or to find work. The Greek makes this clearer than the English, with its use of the separate verb *thelō*, meaning 'to will' or 'to be willing'.[11]

But given the general impossibility of enforcing such a rule if all believers simply ate in their private dwelling places, Jewett (1994: 73–86) may well be correct in suggesting that Christians in Thessalonica continued to share daily communal meals. Archaeologists have determined that a significant percentage of the poorer sections of first-century Thessalonica were made up of multi-story 'tenement dwellings'. Christians there may well have preserved the model of Acts 2:46 of believers eating with one another daily, not least as a way for the poorer members of the community to pool their resources, buy in bulk and eat more cheaply. If this reconstruction is accurate, then what Paul is insisting on in 2 Thessalonians 3:10 is that those who will not do their best to find work so as to donate a portion of their income to the common 'pot' should not be allowed to participate in the common meal. This would also explain what Paul meant by dissociation without excommunication in verses 14–15.

Thus, 1 Thessalonians 4:12 reminds us of Paul's two-fold objective in all these commands: first, not to burden or become dependent on others within the Christian community; and second, to gain the respect of those outside the Christian community, as they see previous recipients of 'welfare' turning into industrious and productive citizens (*cf.* further Russell 1988). Given the rampant abuse and increasing demands of reciprocity in the ancient system of patronage, successful implementation of these objectives would have caused Christians to stand out considerably from their society. Although one cannot move directly from these texts to determine in detail what modern welfare reform should look like, one can find certain precedents here, namely:

[11] Menken (1994: 136) observes the heavy influence of this verse, often misinterpreted, in the history of Christian thought on labour. It has led to monks being required to perform manual labour, and it even entered the Soviet Constitution of 1936 in mutilated form. With respect to the idea that it suggests the development of laws 'saying that to have an income to live on is a right for the economically useful and a favour granted to others', Menken notes that 'early Christians in fact thought quite differently (see, *e.g.*, Matt. 25.31–46; Eph. 4.28)'.

1. the Christian community taking great pains to ensure that the genuinely needy in their midst do not suffer because of the lack of an adequate government programme for them; and 2. a concern to put as many to work as possible, even in conditions of higher unemployment than in most First World countries today.[12]

# 1 Corinthians

We proceed to the mid-50s. Paul has evangelized Corinth at greater length than any previous city in which he has ministered (Acts 18:11). But the church, no doubt due to the rampant immorality of the city, has matured little. Paul's first letter to the Corinthians has generated a flurry of recent scholarly interest, as the sociology of Corinth and the Christian community there is discerned from a variety of comments Paul makes in his letter (see esp. Theissen 1982; *cf.* Gill 1993; Horrell 1996). 1 Corinthians 1:26–29 reminds us that the majority of the Christians in Corinth by human standards were not wise, influential or of noble birth. Nevertheless, Paul's statement that 'not many of you' fell into each of these categories implies that a few apparently did. There is substantial evidence that many, if not all, of the problems Paul has to address throughout this letter were caused by conflicts emanating from the handful of well-to-do Christians (see esp. Clarke 1993; Chow 1992). Incidental evidence again points to well-to-do individuals as we saw in Acts.[13]

We may begin with 1:11–12. The explanation of the factions described in these verses may again prove more sociological than theological. Given that even the most elaborate villas excavated in Corinth could hold no more than fifty to seventy-five people, the church there probably met in individual house congregations, although they may occasionally have come together in larger public assemblies. Each 'house church' would then have been hosted by one of the minority of the well-off Christians, who could easily have been viewed (or who could have viewed themselves) as Christian 'patrons'. This would explain the problem of the man living in incest in 5:1–13 whom the

---

[12] *Cf.* Mott (1975: 72): 'poverty programs must be conceived with the goal of increasing the recipients' economic, political and social ability to reciprocate so that their response to society is a reality and is power'.

[13] Stephanas, Fortunatus and Achaicus (1 Cor. 16:17) may or may not be the same individuals as those of Chloe's household who have met up with Paul (1 Cor. 1:11), but the arrival of travellers from Corinth in Ephesus is perhaps best explained if these men are on a business trip. Crispus (1:14) may be the converted synagogue ruler of Acts 18:8 and be similarly well off.

church was unwilling to judge. Such a flagrant abuse of even conventional Greco-Roman morality (5:1) seems explicable only on the assumption that the offending man was one of the powerful patrons of the church. The problem of lawsuits among believers (6:1–11) was almost certainly limited to the wealthy, since only they sued one another in the ancient Greco-Roman empire, and then not so much to accrue financial holdings as to increase their honour and to shame their rivals.[14] The warnings against gluttony and prostitution in 6:12–20 may stem from the custom of lavish feasting followed by sexual merriment with hired courtesans practised by elite men in Rome, particularly just after their social coming of age at eighteen (Winter 1997a). The problems with celebrating the Lord's Supper in 11:17–34 are likewise clarified by a sociological model. The well-to-do who did not have to work long hours at manual labour could arrive for the Christian gathering early, bring excess food and drink, and consume too much of both. The poorer members, arriving later with fewer provisions, were unable to enjoy an equal share of what was intended to be a communal meal or 'love feast'. In all of these instances, then, people are trusting and perhaps even boasting in their economic prosperity, rather than exulting solely in the Lord Jesus (1:30–31).[15]

Turning to Paul's explicit teaching in 1 Corinthians about material possessions, we must begin with 4:8–13. Here Paul ironically contrasts the lifestyles of the Christian leaders in Corinth with his own desperate and despicable circumstances as an itinerant apostle. In 4:8 he employs scathing sarcasm to contrast the triumphalism of the Corinthian leaders with his personal plight ('Already you have all you want! Already you have become rich! You have begun to reign – and that without us!'). Although there is clear hyperbole in the verses that follow (*e.g.*, 'We have been made a spectacle to the whole universe' – 4:9), the lament of verse 11 should not be muted: 'To this very hour we go hungry and thirsty, we are in rags, we are brutally treated, we are homeless.' Verse 12 begins by reminding the Corinthians that Paul and his travelling companions worked hard with their own hands. 2 Corinthians 4:3–12; 6:3–10 and 11:23–29 will catalogue Paul's sufferings and hardships in poignant detail (on which, see esp. Savage 1996; Harvey 1996). In his world, Paul believed that tribulation was the expected lot of one who

---

[14] Winter (1994: 105–121); *contra* Mitchell (1993), who imagines the upper class suing the lower class (at this point based more on modern studies of the sociology of law than on ancient Roman sources).

[15] For elaboration and other relevant secondary literature, see Blomberg (1994a *ad loc.*); and Dunn (1995: 46–68).

faithfully preached for Christ. He did not endorse the ease in which some of the Corinthian Christians could live. Of course, some of Paul's hardships stemmed simply from the difficulties of travel in the ancient world, and some from his choices about how to provide for himself, but a good number came from overt persecution for his faith. Whatever its origin, Paul understands the material disparity between himself and the house-church leaders in Corinth as a sign of his legitimacy and of their illegitimacy, particularly in view of their numerous misuses of their wealth and power (cf. P. Marshall 1987: 209).

In 1 Corinthians 5, as Paul deals with the incestuous offender, he explains that it is the church's business to deal appropriately with flagrantly sinning members in their own midst, rather than to try to judge those outside the church (5:9–13). In this context, Paul refers to the 'immoral', including at the head of his list 'the greedy and swindlers' (5:10). Both terms reappear again in verse 11 and in 6:10. Ephesians 5:5 and Colossians 3:5 will later condemn greed in vice lists that include other seemingly more flagrant and idolatrous sins.[16] The term translated 'greedy' in 1 Corinthians 5:10–11 (*pleonektēs*) comes from the same root as words often translated 'covet' or 'covetousness'. What is at stake here is nothing less than the tenth commandment of the Decalogue (Exod. 20:17). It is a sign of our modern Western culture that these terms stand out as seemingly different from grosser forms of idolatry or sexual immorality. Paul would not have considered greed or covetousness in his world as any better! The implication for Western Christians whose lifestyles differ little from their surrounding culture in the accumulation of unneeded possessions and material luxuries is staggering. In 1 Corinthians 6:10 Paul proclaims that such people, if in fact this is their characteristic lifestyle rather than merely an occasional lapse,[17] simply will not inherit the kingdom of God!

Whether or not belief in the imminent parousia accounted for the behaviour of the idle in 1 and 2 Thessalonians, it surely lies behind Paul's next statements in 1 Corinthians on the theme of material possessions. In 7:25–35, Paul is addressing the topic of marriage and divorce, specifically with respect to those who have never previously been married. In verse 26 he writes, 'Because of the present crisis, I think that it is good for you to remain as you are' (*i.e.*, single). Corinth

---

[16] And Col. 3:5 equates greed itself with idolatry. O'Brien (1982: 183–184) explains, 'Since a man can serve only one master, God or mammon, but not both (Matt 6:24), then if he sets his heart on wealth, he adores false gods and abandons the one true God.'

[17] This is the force of the collection of nouns in 6:9–10 that become appropriate labels for individuals only after persistent sin in particular areas (cf. D. Prior 1985: 89).

at this time was apparently as prosperous as any Greco-Roman city in the first century (Engels 1990: 61–65; *contra* Winter 1989). Most probably, verse 29a explains Paul's words in verse 26: 'What I mean, brothers and sisters, is that the time is short' (see esp. C. K. Barrett 1968: 174–178).[18] Thus in 7:29b–31, Paul encourages believers who have family to live as if they had none and 'those who buy something, as if it were not theirs to keep; those who use the things of the world, as if not engrossed in them. For this world in its present form is passing away.' Paul is adopting the stance of what Wimbush (1987) has called a 'worldly ascetic'. He is calling not for renunciation of material possessions, but for people who own or acquire them to 'sit very loose' with respect to them.

The problem of eating food sacrificed to idols in 8:1 – 11:1 is again best explained by socio-economic factors. One reason many of the 'weak' Christians' consciences did not permit them to eat idol meat probably stems from their poverty. The poor would not have eaten meat (or good quality meat) regularly, and the context in which they would have enjoyed it most would have been in conjunction with pagan festivals. Much more so than the rich, many of these poor Christians could not dissociate meat-eating from their past pagan idolatry (see esp. Theissen 1982: 121–143; *cf.* Fisk 1989).[19] Similar problems may lie behind Paul's parallel discussion in Romans 14:1 – 15:3, although a better case can be made there for the weak/strong distinction to reflect Jew–Gentile debate over the dietary laws.[20]

In 9:1–18 we come to Paul's first extensive explanation of his philosophy of asking for or accepting financial support for his itinerant ministry. Clearly, two key, contrasting principles are balanced in these verses. On the one hand, in verses 1–12a and 13–14 Paul takes pains to stress that he and his travelling companions have as much right to material support for their ministry as anyone else in the ancient Greco-Roman world, including the Jerusalem apostles themselves (see esp. 9:5). Paul will later indicate his repeated reliance on the Philippian Christians for precisely such gifts (see below, pp. 205–206). On the other hand, in verse 12b and verses 15–18 Paul stresses that in Corinth, he relinquishes these rights, particularly when he believes his

---

[18] *Cf.* also Deming (1995: 177–197) who stresses the necessary tribulations preceding the end in similar apocalyptic references.

[19] Meggitt (1994) thinks Theissen misread the actual evidence (and promises in a later study to overthrow his views altogether!), but thus far has shown only that the lack of access of the poor to meat has perhaps been slightly exaggerated.

[20] For the options and for this conclusion, see Moo (1996: 826–833).

missionary purposes will be advanced.[21] We have already noted that rabbis were required to practise a trade and were rarely allowed to accept money for ministry. In the Hellenistic world, itinerant rhetoricians and philosophers frequently required payment for their services. More specifically, they could gain a living in four possible ways: 1. by becoming the formal clients of wealthy patrons; 2. by charging their audiences direct fees for their public speaking; 3. as so often among the Cynics, by resorting to begging; or 4. by working in a trade and thus supporting their own ministries themselves. Interestingly, the fourth of these options was viewed as the least honourable because it involved the minister or speaker in no direct ties of friendship with anyone else who was a financial supporter (see esp. Hock 1980: 59–62). Working with a trade was also the most demeaning in the eyes of well-to-do Greeks and Romans because of their low view of manual labour (see above, p. 105).[22] Nevertheless, Paul consistently chose this option. It left him with fewest strings attached. In a world in which friendship implied reciprocity, a 'give and take' or 'tit for tat' relationship, Paul wanted to make it clear that he was bound to no-one but God in the preaching of the gospel. He could therefore remain faithful to God's Word in saying whatever needed to be said, however pointed or unpleasant it might be for precisely those people who might otherwise have expected favours in return for their support.[23]

Because of this choice, however, Paul repeatedly has to explain himself to those who think less of him for his practice. Thus in 1 Thessalonians 2:5, Paul has already insisted that he never used flattery, or 'put on a mask to cover up greed'. Similarly, in 2 Corinthians 2:17, a verse Witherington (1995a: 371–374) takes as the *propositio* for the entire epistle, Paul insists, 'Unlike so many, we do not peddle the word of God for profit.' Rather, Paul does whatever he can to prevent the gospel from falling into disrespect through charges either of ministry for the wrong motives or of the misuse of funds received.[24]

---

[21] For all of the points in this paragraph thus far, *cf.* Pratscher (1979).

[22] This low view did not necessarily characterize all the elite and was usually not extended to agricultural labour, *i.e.*, farming (Balme 1984).

[23] Horrell (1996: 210–216) also stresses the tie-in with 9:19–23. Paul identifies with the 'weak' Christian by working at manual labour (and thus accepting social degradation) precisely to 'win' the weak, even if it creates a stumbling-block at times for the 'strong'/rich.

[24] See P. Marshall (1987: 282–340), for a detailed reconstruction of the charges against Paul in Corinth.

Contemporary application of these principles should lead congregations to seek to compensate generously those who lead them in Christian ministry. Pastors and leaders themselves should take care never to demand their rights to be paid, or to be paid at any particular level. As Carson (1987: 125) comments on Matthew 10:10, a text which may well lie behind Paul's practices in Corinth, 'The church does not *pay* its ministers; rather, it provides them with resources so that they are able to serve freely.' And if there is serious likelihood that a particular culture or subculture will view their receiving of material remuneration as so inappropriate that it hinders the reception of the gospel, or if a local community is simply too poor to support its leaders, then they should forgo their rights altogether. Bivocational ministry is the norm out of necessity in many parts of the Two-Thirds World. More affluent Westerners ought more frequently to consider in what other contexts it might prove strategic, as our increasingly anti-Christian public is more and more repulsed by the Christian media's constant appeals for money.

When one understands the sociological factors at work behind the Corinthians' abuse of the Lord's Supper, well-known verses in chapter 11 appear quite different (see esp. Theissen 1982: 145–174).[25] The Corinthians who eat the bread or drink the cup of the Lord 'in an unworthy manner' (1 Cor. 11:27) are not those who are particularly aware of their sinfulness or who feel unworthy to partake. The word translated 'in an unworthy manner' is the adverb *anaxiōs* ('unworthily'). Those who should refrain from the bread and wine lest they profane the eucharist are not those with a profound sense of their own inadequacy, but those who are actually eating and drinking in an unworthy fashion. And verse 21 explicitly recounts what that unworthy fashion involves: 'each of you goes ahead without waiting for anybody else. One remains hungry, another gets drunk.'[26] Obviously, few if any contemporary worship services have this exact problem with the Lord's table. But once one understands that the gluttony and drunkenness described take place during a larger communal meal at the expense of the needy Christians in their midst, then 'eating and drinking unworthily' applies in our modern culture to any who continue glibly to partake of the Lord's Supper, yet who have no track-record in their own lives of giving from their surplus possessions to the poor. The question of who

[25] This is not to say that Theissen's larger interpretive framework of Christianity as 'love patriarchalism' stands without challenge. See esp. Engberg-Pedersen (1987).

[26] Blue (1991) argues for translating *prolambanō* as 'devour' and *ekdechetai* as 'welcome', and believes those neglected to be Christians who did not belong to a secure household.

should and should not take the Lord's Supper in any given church could be revolutionized if we began to obey Paul's words and apply them as they were intended in their original context. In this context, too, verse 29 probably takes on a significance different from that which it is often given. 'For those who eat and drink without recognising the body of the Lord' in its original context could not possibly have had anything to do with later debates about transubstantiation or consubstantiation, the actual change of the elements into Christ's body and blood or his real presence 'in, with and under' the bread and wine (so classically Roman Catholicism and Lutheranism, respectively). It is possible that 'recognising the body of the Lord' refers to recognizing the symbolism of this meal as a memorial to Christ's broken body and shed blood in his crucifixion. But even more probable is the view that 'the body of the Lord' is a synonym for Paul's frequent expression 'the body of Christ' – that is, a metaphor for the church. Those who eat and drink without concern for the needs of the poorer members do not recognize the nature of the church – a refuge for refugees, in which all must care for one another (see esp. Fee 1987: 563–564).

In his famous love chapter (1 Cor. 13), nestled in the midst of his discussion of spiritual gifts (chs. 12 – 14), Paul writes, 'If I give all I possess to the poor and surrender my body to the flames, but have not love, I gain nothing' (13:3). This declaration balances some of his previous teaching. As committed as he is to philanthropy and humanitarian aid for the needy, Paul recognizes that altruism in and of itself accomplishes nothing, at least for the giver, unless it is motivated by genuine Christian love (*agapē*). The NIV marginal reading ('my body that I may boast') may actually reflect Paul's original text at this point (Petzer 1989). It is certainly the harder reading and somewhat better attested ($\mathfrak{p}^{46}$ א A B *etc.* versus K Ψ Byz *etc.*). Either way, giving up everything without Christ's love for others profits one nothing.

The last passage relating directly to the theme of material possessions in 1 Corinthians comes in 16:1–4. Here Paul makes his first explicit mention of 'the collection for God's people' (16:1) which will occupy his sustained attention throughout 2 Corinthians 8 – 9. In addition to the previously noted causes of famine in Judea, along with the generally destabilizing economic trends in the area (above, p. 162), it may well be that by this time the church in Jerusalem had to provide hospitality for large numbers of visiting Christians. Whatever the exact combination of factors, clearly the church in and around Jerusalem remained considerably impoverished even into the mid-50s. Paul's primary motivation would then have been simply to alleviate this human need in keeping with the principles of compassion that permeate God's Word. But his allusion back to this effort later in Romans 15:27 suggests a second motivating factor – the unity of the church and the recognition that Gentile Christianity owed its origin to the 'mother' Jewish-Christian congregation in Jerusalem. As Georgi (1992: 55) explains, 'Paul was eager to show that his mission had resulted, not in the establishment of some disintegrated clubs, but in genuine communities willing to remember in gratitude their origin and, hence, were bound to the church as an ecumenical body ... giving material proof of their individual responsibility.' Nickle (1966: 129–142) and Munck (1959: 282–308) have also speculated that Paul saw this collection as one means of fulfilling Romans 11:11–32: Gentile Christians provoking non-Christian Jews to jealousy so that many of them would respond with faith in Christ. This more speculative suggestion finds no explicit support in the text but is by no means improbable.[27]

Paul's brief words regarding the collection in 1 Corinthians 16:1–4 provide the oldest known reference to a weekly Sunday collection of money, although it is not clear if Paul implies that this is to be taken when the congregation gathers for worship. Verse 2a, 'each one of you should set aside a sum of money ... saving it up', in verse 2a reads more literally, 'let each of you place by himself ... treasuring', leading to the possibility that each person stored his or her contributions at home. Verse 2b's 'in keeping with your income' reads somewhat more literally, 'however one has prospered', and could imply (but does not demand) what Paul will make more explicit in 2 Corinthians 8:13–15: the concept of a 'graduated tithe' (see esp. R. Sider 1997: 193–196). In addition, the collection is systematically planned to avoid last-minute frenzy or embarrassment at not having adequate funds available (1 Cor. 16:2b). That individuals in the church need to save on a weekly basis may also suggest that the majority were not well off and had to set aside small sums carefully (cf. Murphy-O'Connor 1991: 77). Verses 3–4 refer to issues of accountability with respect to overseeing the delivery of the collection, on which Paul will also elaborate in his next epistle. He will determine when he sees the size of the gift whether or not he will accompany it. He does not want to be embarrassed by a paltry sum, or go along if the integrity of the collection will in any way be compromised.

---

[27] Nickle's further claim (1966: 87–93), however, that the collection was a Christian equivalent to the Jewish temple tax seems belied by his own list of the considerable differences between the two, following an enumeration of their similarities.

# 2 Corinthians

Whereas 1 Corinthians comprises a series of instructions on a remarkably diverse set of problems in a very immature church, 2 Corinthians 1 – 7 is largely congratulatory in tone and suggests that the Corinthians had made major strides in obedience and growth. Chapters 8 – 9, however, return to the theme of the collection in great detail and make plain that much work has yet to be done in Corinth on this matter. In chapters 10 – 13, Paul unleashes a bitter invective against Judaizers who may have just recently begun troubling the church.

We have already alluded to 2:17 above, as Paul is at pains to distinguish his ministry from the money-grabbing practices of many of his Hellenistic counterparts (not least in the Sophist movement).[28] We have also alluded to his catalogues of sufferings; it is worth adding that 6:10 refers specifically to Paul's material poverty as a result of his freely chosen style of ministry. His gospel must be offered free of charge to unbelievers. In 7:2 we find another of Paul's disclaimers that he has wronged, corrupted or exploited no-one, as he has refused to accept money for ministry from the Corinthians (*cf.* also 12:14–18). And in 11:7–12, he responds to his critics who devalue his ministry, precisely because it has been offered freely, by stressing that he simply wanted to avoid burdening anyone or allowing anyone else to boast in the ways in which they have helped him (*cf.* further N. Watson 1993: 118–120). Verse 9 alludes to the fact that Paul did accept money from Macedonia, probably referring especially to the Philippian congregation, and the principles behind this practice will be unpacked in our discussion below (pp. 192–193). Apart from these references, however, the major section of 2 Corinthians that deals with financial matters is chapters 8 – 9, which therefore merits substantially closer attention.

Of all of Paul's letters, 2 Corinthians has given rise to more theories of partitioning than any other. Several of these are irrelevant for our concerns in chapters 8 – 9; others prove more significant. There are those who have taken these two chapters together, or each chapter singly, as separate pieces of correspondence from Paul to the church at Corinth (see esp. Betz 1985). A considerable number of scholars, however, agrees that chapters 1 – 9 should be taken as a unity.[29]

---

[28] On which, see esp. Winter (1997b).

[29] If chs. 10 – 13 are taken as an intermediate letter in between 1 Cor. and 2 Cor. 1 – 9, allusions in 11:7–12 and 12:14–18 can be seen as signs that things got worse in Corinth before they got better. Until recently even most conservative scholars were largely convinced that chs. 10 – 13 were either a later letter or a piece of writing that Paul resumed after an interval in his dictation upon the arrival of fresh news from Corinth.

2 Corinthians 9:1 ('There is no need for me to write to you about this service to the saints') is the stumbling-block which has led some to separate this chapter off from its predecessor. It seems to introduce the topic of the collection *de novo* and to repeat much of the information of the previous chapter. But the verse can also be interpreted as resuming Paul's train of thought after 8:16–24 and implying, 'It is superfluous for me to go on writing to you like this' (C. K. Barrett 1973: 233), while the repetition of themes can be explained by Paul's 'embarrassment which he constantly showed about gifts' (Wiles 1974: 237).

2 Corinthians 9:3–5 would be largely unintelligible without the background information of 8:16–24. So our discussion will proceed by assuming the unity of chapters 8 and 9.

So many principles for Christian giving can be derived from these chapters that we must proceed extremely slowly through this text, at times even verse by verse or clause by clause. 2 Corinthians 8:1 and 9:14–15 create an inclusio around these two chapters on the theme of the collection as a gift or manifestation of God's grace (a further argument, incidentally, for their unity). Indeed, these verses apply a rich diversity of terms to the collection: 'fellowship' or 'sharing' (*koinōnia*, 8:4; 9:13), in an 'act of grace' (8:6), 'grace of giving' (8:7), and 'offering' (8:19) – all translating the Greek *charis*; a 'liberal' or 'generous gift' (*eulogia*, 8:20; 9:5); and a 'service' (*diakonia*, 8:4, 9:1; *leitourgia*, 9:12, 13). All this justifies Barnett's conclusion (1997: 388–389) that grace is the central theme of this entire two-chapter section. Christian giving is a gift from the grace of God, which he enables Christians to exercise.

Paul begins by telling the Corinthians of the exemplary participation of their Macedonian counterparts (the churches in the northern half of Greece) in this collection. Their generosity proves all the more striking because they gave out of a 'most severe trial' and 'their extreme poverty' (2 Cor. 8:2). Although some have argued for an inherent poverty in the Macedonian churches, what we know of that province in the mid-50s in general suggests that they were relatively prosperous, even if not quite so much so as the city of Corinth or the province of

---

In this case the arrival of false teachers could have exacerbated the problem of attitudes to finances that might have previously begun to improve. The latest three evangelical commentaries on this epistle, nevertheless, argue fairly persuasively for the unity of the entire letter (Witherington 1995a; Belleville 1996; Barnett 1997), in which case financial matters remain the one unresolved issue that Paul knows all along he will have to address in both chs. 8 – 9 in detail and 10 – 13 in passing, despite the largely conciliatory tone of 2 Cor. 1 – 7 on other matters.

Achaia (the southern half of Greece). The churches' 'severe trial', therefore, probably refers primarily to religious persecution (as in Acts 17:1–15), leading to socio-economic hardship (C. K. Barrett 1973: 219). This conclusion especially fits our sociological analysis of the Thessalonians' plight (above, pp. 180–181). Precisely because of this hardship, the Macedonians could empathize with the suffering church in Judea and gave more than anyone had a right to expect. The word translated 'generosity' (*haplotēs*) in verse 2 could also be rendered 'single-mindedness', but in this context financial liberality is more probably in view. The Macedonian giving was simultaneously sacrificial and voluntary (8:3). As Hughes (1962: 288) remarks, 'The most genuine liberality is frequently displayed by those who have least to give.' These churches even took the initiative in requesting the privilege of participating in this endeavour. Precisely because of their poverty, Paul may have originally felt that it was unfair to involve them in his undertaking. But they recognize this opportunity as a chance for fellowship (8:4). The phrase translated in the NIV as 'sharing in this service' (*koinōnia tēs diakonias*) could contain either an objective or a subjective genitive; that is, the Macedonians may have wanted, as the NIV takes it, to *contribute to* the collection or to experience the fellowship with the Judean Christians *produced by* the collection. Ralph Martin (1986: 254) plausibly incorporates elements of both interpretations and adds, 'Normally we think of the fund-raiser as "begging" the would-be donors. Here it is the donors, who could least afford it, who entreated Paul for the favor of having a part in this enterprise' (256).

Nor was the Macedonians' concern to give worked out in isolation from larger spiritual commitments. Verse 5 proceeds to speak of them giving themselves 'first to the Lord'. Their gift forms part of their larger and more fundamental consecration of themselves to God in Christ. The second half of this verse ('and then to us in keeping with God's will') may imply that they recognized Paul's apostolic authority in the process (R. P. Martin 1986: 255). With verse 6, Paul begins to make the comparison between the situations in Macedonia and Corinth. As was often done in the ancient Hellenistic world, though not always as tactfully, the apostle appeals to a spirit of competition to enjoin virtuous behaviour. If Macedonia could prove so generous under substantially more difficult circumstances than in Corinth, Paul could surely send Titus to encourage the Corinthians to complete their part in this 'gift' (*cf.* NIV 'act of grace', 8:6). The Corinthians have already demonstrated substantial improvement in many of the areas that required pointed exhortation in Paul's first epistle (8:7a). Now he wants them to finish acting on their good intentions in 'this grace of giving' as well (8:7b). The unusual grammar of the last clause of this verse (literally, 'in order that you must also abound in this grace' – *i.e.*, a *hina* [purpose] clause with an imperative-mood verb) is deliberately striking. Putting both halves of the verse together, Paul's point is 'to make the Corinthians see that participation in the collection was the consequence of all the gifts of grace (*charismata*) they had previously been granted' (Georgi 1992: 82). Witherington (1995a: 412) thinks that the flow of thought suggests that money matters remain the single most serious obstacle to reconciliation between Paul and the Corinthians.

In 2 Corinthians 8:8, Paul employs psychologically sophisticated rhetoric in insisting that he is not commanding them, even though the entire two-chapter segment makes Paul's desires quite clear. But in this verse his point is that he wants to test the 'genuineness' (perhaps a slightly better translation of *gnēsios* in this context than 'sincerity')[30] of their love. Yet the ultimate object of comparison is not the Macedonians' generosity or any other human action but the incredible condescension of Jesus Christ in his incarnation. Hence, verse 9 continues, 'For you know the grace of our Lord Jesus Christ, that though he was rich, yet for your sakes he became poor, so that you through his poverty might become rich.' *Contra* some liberation theology, this statement probably does not refer to the material or socio-economic circumstances of Jesus throughout his earthly life. Rather, it offers a far more profound theological summary of all that he gave up in leaving his heavenly home for the constrictions of earthly existence and the ultimate ignominy of crucifixion. Philippians 2:6–11 forms Paul's most poignant commentary on this condescension (*cf.* esp. Craddock 1968). But if Christ could sacrifice so much for us, how dare we refuse to give generously to the needy! 'Mercy and money belong closer to each other than we usually think' (Brändle 1985: 269).

With verse 10, Paul starts to spell out in detail his 'advice'. The Corinthians began to respond to Paul's initial appeal with the correct attitude and action. Now they must fulfill their pledge (8:10–11a). 'No matter how strong the intentions or desires, they are fruitless unless they are expressed in action' (Kruse 1987: 156). *Epiteleisate* ('finish', 8:11a) is the imperative form of a verb often used in the Greco-Roman world for the completion of a religious duty, and the Corinthians may well have understood it as such (Ascough 1996). In verses 11b–12, Paul

---

[30] Louw & Nida (1988, vol. 2: 675): 'pertaining to possessing purported good character or quality – "genuine, real"'.

does not encourage them to sacrifice as much as the Macedonians have done, but merely to give according to their means, that is, 'according to what one has, not according to what one does not have'. 'No one will be criticised if his modest means do not allow exceptional sacrifices' (Héring 1967: 61). Even small gifts are acceptable when accompanied by the right attitudes.

We reach the heart of Paul's argument in 2 Corinthians 8:13–15, in which he invokes the precedent of God's supplying manna in the wilderness (Exod. 16:18). Paul makes it clear that he is not looking for a role reversal of rich and poor but only for a *relative* 'equality' (8:13). In fact, the term used here (*isotēs*) is better translated as that which is 'equitable' or 'fair' (Belleville 1996: 223). Just as we pointed out that the Israelites would have both gathered and consumed varying amounts in the wilderness according to their needs, so, too, Paul is not enunciating the ideal of some fully egalitarian communism. But he does recognize that there are extremes of wealth and poverty which are intolerable in the Christian community. If those who are better off will simply provide from their surplus, all of the most basic human needs of the more impoverished will be met (*cf.* Furnish 1984: 419; Thomas 1994: 291). The theological rationale for this compassion appears in verse 14. The tables may one day be reversed, and the Corinthian Christians would certainly hope for help from Judea. Given the improbability of Corinth and Judea exchanging socio-economic roles, at least in Paul's lifetime, it may well be that verse 14 has in mind spiritual blessings which Corinth can receive from Judea, even as Judea receives material gifts from Corinth (*cf.* again Rom. 15:27). It is also possible that there are some eschatological overtones here, namely, that the beneficiaries of Christian giving in this life will welcome one another with material and spiritual blessings in the life to come. But given that little else in the immediate context points to the end of the age, at best these overtones are muted and secondary.[31]

In applying these verses to Christian stewardship in any age, the concept of a graduated tithe proves helpful. The more money one makes, the higher percentage he or she gives. As Belleville (1996: 220) points out, 'Whereas a fixed 10 percent would most likely be negligible

[31] Stott (1990: 143) helpfully sums up five principles he deduces from this text: 1. 'God has provided enough for everybody's need'; 2. 'any great disparity between ... wealth and poverty, is unacceptable to him'; 3. such a situation 'ought to be corrected by an adjustment'; 4. 'the Christian motive for desiring such "justice" is "grace"'; and 5. we are to follow Christ's example in becoming 'poor' in order to show 'the genuineness of our love'.

for someone with an income of $100,000, it could well cripple a person with an income of $10,000.' For a successful and equitable implementation of the model of 8:13–15, what is needed is 'not a fixed percentage but relative proportion'. While it is true that the equality envisioned here does not imply rigid uniformity, it nevertheless clearly involves closing the gap between rich and poor in the body of Christ so that no-one lacks.

> Theologically, Paul teaches the importance of mutual sharing as part of God's 'manna economy'. In a manna economy, daily sustenance needs were met, making hoarding futile, all in a spirit of trust for God's provision (Gornik 1991: 23).

Paul's insistence on the right of all to a fair share has never been more timely than it is today, when in every respect – economically, socially, culturally and educationally – the rich are getting richer and the poor poorer (N. Watson 1993: 92).

Verses 16–24 proceed to delineate the accountability factors that Paul is building into this fund-raising project. Titus is coming to oversee the collection as one who has much concern and enthusiasm for the effort and is voluntarily taking the initiative Paul hopes all Christians will imitate (8:16–17). Paul also stays at an appropriate distance from the collection until he is assured of a proper response. Verses 18–21 speak of a second, unnamed, Christian 'brother' who is praised and well respected 'by all the churches' (presumably in Macedonia) and whom they chose to help oversee the delivery of a substantial sum of money. Hence, the potential damage, if funds were to be mismanaged, looms all the larger. Whereas Titus is Paul's handpicked emissary, this unnamed brother was chosen by the churches independently of Paul, thus adding further checks and balances and ensuring the integrity of the administration of the collection. Verses 22–24 then refer to a third individual who is simply called 'our brother', one who is zealous and now has great confidence in the Corinthians. This may well be one of the three Macedonians who appear by name in Acts 20:4 – Sopater, Aristarchus and Secundus. Both Paul and the churches clearly trust this third person; thus, if any dispute should ensue between Paul and the churches involved in the collection, each side will have someone to represent them, and a third party who is trusted by both. One could hardly imagine greater parity.[32] Commentators frequently quote Cicero (*De*

---

[32] *Cf.* Betz (1985: 78), who also notes that, from Paul's perspective, at least two out of the three are people he trusts.

*officiis* 2.21[75]): 'But the chief thing in all public administration and public service is to avoid even the slightest suspicion of self-seeking.' In verse 21, Paul makes it clear that it is important not only to maintain financial integrity before God but to be perceived as doing so by others. Verse 24 reminds us that a proper response to Paul's appeal will not only demonstrate the genuineness of the Corinthians' love, but also vindicate Paul's previous claims about them, again in both instances in public view of the other churches. Christians in all times and places should know what other believers are doing with their finances in ways that help to hold them accountable for good stewardship.

Acts 9:1–5 resumes Paul's comparison between the Macedonians and the Corinthians. This paragraph repeats a number of the points made in 8:1–3 and verses 10–12, with the added observation that it was the Corinthians' initial enthusiasm that had stirred most of the Macedonians into action (9:2). Hence, it would be all the more incongruous and embarrassing for all parties concerned if the Corinthians failed to make good their initial pledge (8:3–5a). The ancient culture of honour and shame clearly shines through here. Verse 5b literally reads, 'Then it will be as a blessing and not as a covetousness.' The NIV, though paraphrastic, catches the sense with its contrast between a generous and a grudging gift.[33]

In 2 Corinthians 9:6–11, Paul returns to the theme introduced briefly in Galatians 6:6. One harvests in proportion to one's sowing: 'whoever sows generously will also reap generously'. Wealth is portrayed as a good, particularly if it leads to generosity (Betz 1985: 116). But *contra* 'prosperity theology', Paul's primary referent cannot lie in the material realm. Those who give generously of their surplus income know from experience that in the vast majority of instances they do not recoup that money from other sources. Rather, as verse 8 explains, 'God is able to make all grace abound to you, so that in all things at all times, having all that you need, you will abound in every good work.' The Greek word for 'all' appears four times in this verse with a staccato effect that is hard to reproduce in translation. 'All grace', 'all things', 'all that you need', and 'every good work' are expressions that cannot be limited to the financial realm. Indeed, Barnett (1988: 154) describes Paul as spiritualizing the Old Testament prosperity theme. One might add that he is also spiritualizing the reciprocity obligations of the Greco-Roman world. 'Having all that you need' actually translates the clause *echontes autarkeian*. *Autarkeia* was a frequent Stoic term for self-sufficiency, but

---

[33] R. P. Martin (1986: 285) renders the contrast as 'a blessing, not as a species of "avarice"'.

in this context Paul is referring to a 'God-sufficiency'. Nevertheless, if the model outlined in 8:13–15 is being practised, 9:6–11 must include financial care, even if the spiritual blessings described are considerably broader than mere monetary possessions. We are reminded of the applications of Matthew 6:33 and Mark 10:29 discussed above (pp. 132, 140).[34] Talbert (1987: 187) aptly sums up: 'Here God's financial blessings are a gift ('blessing', RSV), not a payment for services rendered, that enables one to provide for others.' What is more, God's ideal is that each gives 'not reluctantly or under compulsion, for God loves a cheerful giver' (9:7b). 'Various faulty motives may inspire us to give generously, but only a real appreciation of God's grace to us can prompt us to give "cheerfully" ' (Barnett 1988: 153). Verse 10 confirms that we are not speaking merely of material blessing, with its use of the phrase 'the harvest of your righteousness'. Verse 11, however, balances this spiritual dimension by reminding us that we will be enriched sufficiently to 'be generous on every occasion'. Verse 11 also introduces the theme that will dominate the closing paragraph of this section (9:12–15): people will thank God because of Christians' generosity.

At the very least, the remainder of 2 Corinthians 9 alludes to the praise, thanksgiving, prayers and concern that those helped by the collection will offer, not to mention the similar reactions of other Christians in the communities to which the gift is sent. The ultimate purpose of the collection is that God might be glorified. But the 'many expressions of thanks to God' (9:12) may come not only from fellow Christians, depending in part on how broadly one interprets the phrase 'with everyone else' at the end of verse 13. Nickle (1966: 137–138) thinks of an evangelistic function here: unbelieving Jews in and around Jerusalem will come to faith in Christ when they see how generously the Gentile Christians share with their Jewish brothers and sisters. Whether or not this broader reference is intended, it is at least clear that Paul does not envisage the principles behind this collection as limited in any way to this one specific act of sharing. As Barnett (1997: 447) observes, the 'everyone else' gives expression to Paul's 'belief in a worldwide covenant fraternity, for which the constituent members had obligations of reciprocity. Paul is not narrowly congregationalist nor individualistic in his outlook.' It is also interesting that Paul uses the phrase 'the service of this service' in verse 12 (NIV,

---

[34] Murphy-O'Connor (1991: 93) employs the identical logic here. We can give generously because we trust others to care for us, if it turns out we have given away too much to continue to meet our own needs.

'This service that you perform'). The second word for 'service' in this phrase is the Greek *leitourgia*, often used of Greco-Roman civic obligations (Witherington 1995a: 428). While rejecting the formal patron–client relationship that created so many problems in the Hellenistic world, Paul seems to imagine a kind of benefaction within the Christian community. The beneficiaries may never return material gifts (although they should be prepared to do so if the tables are turned; recall 8:14), but at the very least they will be led to pray for their benefactors with a longing affection (9:14). Paul then closes this portion of his letter with his own thanks to God for an indescribable gift (9:15), doubtless referring primarily to the gift of Jesus and the salvation he wrought.

As we reflect back over these two detailed chapters on Christian stewardship, at least four points stand out. First, Paul has changed from the simple commands of 1 Corinthians 16:1–4 to much more elaborate rhetorical and psychological appeals. It is arguable that this change stemmed in part from Paul's lack of success with the simpler exhortation in his previous letter.[35] Second, Paul appears to differ little from James (or Jesus or the early church in Acts) in his concern that genuine Christianity should lead to obedience, particularly in the area of financial stewardship. Georgi (1992: 98) speaks of these chapters as comprising 'Paul's own doctrine of justification, spelled out now in its concrete dimensions.'[36] Joubert (1992: 111) notes that if any 'refuse to get involved in the collection, their religious maturity and integrity will automatically be brought into question'. Third, Paul's principles, like the Old Testament material on which he draws, cut right across all current economic models. Absent here is all language of a market economy. Instead, jubilary and utopian themes prevail (Georgi 1992: 154–158): 'It is giving instead of gaining, thanks instead of interest, confidence instead of credit, trust instead of security, community instead of market, spiritual worship instead of temple cult, charisma instead of property' (160). But neither is the morality depicted here legislated in any formal way, as in socialist models. This leads us to our fourth and final observation, namely, the complete absence of any reference to a tithe. We have already seen how a 'flat tax' of 10% for all churchgoers would lead to great inequality between the very rich and the very poor. The standard Paul exhorts us to follow is actually a more

---

[35] For extensive detail on Paul's strategies and leadership styles in both letters, see Verbrugge (1992).

[36] *Cf.* also his 'Afterword: Is There Justification in Money? A Historical and Theological Meditation on the Financial Aspects of Justification by Christ' (141–165).

stringent one than the traditional tithe. If most affluent Western Christians were to be honest about the extent of their surplus, they would give considerably higher than 10% to Christian causes. And given the paltry percentages of most church budgets that help the materially needy, locally or globally, they would make sure that a substantial percentage of their giving went directly to individuals and organizations that offer holistic salvation of body and spirit to the desperately poor throughout the world.

## Romans

Although written closely on the heels of Paul's two letters to the Corinthians (c. AD 56–57), the epistle to the Romans at first glance appears to be entirely different in nature. It is far less situation-specific and seems to have little to do with our theme of material possessions. On the other hand, the Greek term *dikaiosynē* and its cognates refer not only to 'justification' in a legal sense but also to 'righteousness' in a moral sense. The potential implications of Paul's letter to the Romans for issues of social justice, not least those of Christian stewardship and sharing of material possessions, become clear if one substitutes expressions like 'justice' or 'to secure justice' for 'righteousness', 'justification', and 'justify' (see esp. Tamez 1993). Thus, for example, Romans 3:22 could be rendered, 'The justice of God comes through faith in Jesus Christ to all who believe.' All whose lives are transformed by being declared just in God's sight will work to ensure justice for others. Nevertheless, this is not the dominant point of Paul's theological chapters (Rom. 1 – 11); we must turn to the final section of his letter for more directly relevant material.

In the exhortational part of his epistle (Rom. 12:1 – 15:13), Paul refers to 'contributing to the needs of others' as one kind of spiritual gift. Those who possess this gift must 'give generously' (12:8). This does not excuse others from *not* giving generously, any more than those who lack the spiritual gift of faith are permitted to exercise no faith. But it does suggest that some may be enabled to give particularly sacri-ficially.[37] By way of example Paul supplies one very pointed command that Christians often have been loath to obey: believers must leave vengeance to God. On the contrary,

---

[37] Byrne (1996: 370) suggests that all three of the gifts mentioned in 12:8bcd 'seem to be concerned in some way with the exercise of charity'. *Ho proistamenos* could refer to a patron; and *ho eleōn* to one who brings (financial) relief to the unfortunate.

'If your enemies are hungry, feed them;
   if they are thirsty, give them something to drink.'
         (Rom. 12:20, quoting Prov. 25:21)[38]

In the paragraph on submitting to the governing authorities (13:1–7), the rather bland statement in most English translations that the government is 'God's servant to do you good' (13:4) could in fact refer to the standard role of the Roman government to praise and commend those who were generous benefactors.[39] This would explain the language at the end of verse 3 as well: 'do what is right and [the one in authority] will commend you'.

In 13:7–8, Paul alludes to Mark 12:17 and parallels (M. Thompson 1991: 111–120). Paying tax and tribute is part of the Christian's task of submitting to God-ordained authorities. Of course, submission is not the same as blind obedience, and there are times when the demands of the government conflict with demands of God, at which point Christians must obey God (Acts 4:19; 5:29, and recall our comments above, pp. 143–144).[40] But there appears to be no support in either Testament for God's people to refuse to pay taxes simply because they disagree with the way their government spends that money. Particularly if part of Paul's purpose in penning these words was to respond to civil unrest in the late 50s 'centering upon abuses in the collection of taxes' (Byrne 1996: 386), it must be God's will that Christians render financial tribute to the government even when the authorities spend some of that money in ways that displease God. Otherwise it would have been impossible for Paul to commend paying any taxes to a pagan, totalitarian regime that ultimately came to deify itself.[41]

Romans 13:8 reflects the devastating effects of debt in the ancient Roman empire (on which see above, p. 91), one of the afflictions that most cripple the average Westerner's ability to follow Christian principles of stewardship today as well. 'This commandment does not

---

[38] The 'burning coals' this response heaps on the enemy's head are likely to be pangs of shame or remorse, not punishment. Cf., e.g., Dunn (1988: 751).

[39] See esp. Winter (1994: 25–40), who stresses the frequency of language about 'doing good' or 'right' in contexts of civic benefaction.

[40] Cf., e.g., Cranfield (1979: 662). L. Johnson (1997: 191) sees this implied also by the phrase 'for conscience's sake' in Rom. 13:5.

[41] On the broader issues of civil disobedience, one must beware of absolutizing either the view that government is divine (Rom. 13) or the notion that it is demonic (Rev. 13), despite numerous attempts throughout Christian history to make one of these themes normative at the expense of the other. Légasse (1994) reviews a variety of proposals for seeing Romans 13:1–7 as at least in part determined by distinctive historical circumstances.

forbid a Christian from ever incurring a debt (*e.g.*, to buy a house or a car); it rather demands that Christians repay any debts they do incur promptly and in accordance with the terms of the contract' (Moo 1996: 812). Prompt payment of debts, however, simply forms a transition to the main theme of love that the second half of verse 8 stresses. And in 16:1–2 Paul commends his spiritual sister Phoebe, a Cenchrean deacon who 'has been a great help to many people, including me'. The Greek literally calls her a *prostatis*, most naturally translated in this context as 'patron'. Phoebe was most likely one of the prominent women who generously contributed to Paul and other early Christians in financially supporting their ministries (*cf.* Keener 1992: 240). Gaius, too, had hosted Paul and the whole Corinthian church (Rom. 16:23a), and so must have been quite well off.

In addition to these scattered references, Romans 15:24–27 refers back to the collection with which the Corinthian correspondence was so concerned and outlines Paul's travel plans and desires, which apparently include the desire that the Roman church should provide some financial assistance for his further missionary travels. Verse 24 describes his plans finally to come to Rome in person *en route* to new ministry among unreached peoples in Spain. *Propempein* (NIV, 'assist me on my journey') is seemingly a technical term for missionary support (Moo 1996: 901). Here we have our second hint, which will be fleshed out in Philippians, that Paul is not above accepting or asking for financial help from churches to which he is not currently ministering. Apparently he does not sense the same danger of compromising strings attached. Because of his subsequent arrest in Jerusalem and various imprisonments, no canonical text ever confirms that Paul actually made it to Spain. But, of course, he does arrive in Rome, even if under house arrest (Acts 28:17–31).

Romans 15:25–27 demonstrates that the collection among the churches in Macedonia and Achaia ultimately proved successful.[42] Corinth apparently chipped in an adequate amount, and after penning this epistle Paul would set sail for Jerusalem with the emissaries from the other churches to assist in delivering the funds.[43] Here, too, is where the theme of the Gentiles' tribute to their 'mother church' enters in.

[42] Peterman (1994) argues against most scholars that the *koinōnia* of verse 26 should be translated 'fellowship' rather than 'contribution'. Nevertheless, establishing fellowship with the saints in Jerusalem would still have involved their financial support.

[43] The view that 'the poor among the saints' in Jerusalem (15:26) is to be taken as involving an appositional genitive ('the poor who are the saints'), thus equating the poor with Jerusalem Christians as a spiritual rather than a socio-economic label, was decisively refuted by Keck (1965; 1966).

Verse 31 suggests that Paul is not entirely sure how the Christians in Jerusalem will accept this offering and fears trouble or persecution from the non-Christian Jewish community as well. Acts 21 demonstrates that both of these fears are well founded. The church itself receives Paul warmly enough (Acts 21:17), and the local leadership is appropriately gracious (21:18–20). But it also reports to Paul about the reputation he has acquired among the Palestinian Jews for teaching Diaspora Jews to turn from their ancestral traditions, most notably circumcision. The plan they concoct to refute this mistaken report finds Paul paying for the sacrifices of some fellow Jews who are completing a vow. The project disastrously backfires, so that Paul has to be arrested by Roman soldiers to protect him from the Jewish mob (21:21–36). Luke will nevertheless make it clear that this is all part of God's sovereign plan to get Paul to Rome (*cf.* 23:11 with 25:11–12).

The final relevant reference in Romans to the theme of material possessions comes in Paul's closing words in 16:23b. He writes, 'Erastus, who is the city's *director of public works*, and our brother Quartus send you their greetings.' The Greek expression for the italicized phrase calls Erastus simply the *oikonomos* ('steward') of the city, but this could well be a rough Greek equivalent of the technical term in Latin, *aedile*. Interestingly, an inscription in Corinth, from where Paul was writing the letter to the Romans, refers to an Erastus the *aedile*, strongly suggesting[44] that these two references have the identical person in view. In this case, further evidence emerges for a Christian in the Corinthian congregation who would have been a quite well-to-do, prominent public official (see esp. Gill 1989: 293–301). The *aedile* would have been responsible for the upkeep of city property, for judging commercial and financial litigation and for the oversight of public games (Winter 1994: 184).

## The Prison Epistles

It is difficult to determine the exact chronology of the four letters that have traditionally been understood as Paul's correspondence during a first imprisonment in Rome in AD 60–62. There is some reason for dating Philippians a little further along in this period of house arrest (*cf.* Acts 28:17–31) because of its somewhat more sombre tone, especially when speaking of Paul's possible death (*e.g.*, Phil. 1:21–26; 2:17). Paul may have sent Philemon, Ephesians and Colossians all with the same

[44] For the problems with definitively concluding that these two references refer to the same individual, see Meggitt (1996).

letter-carrier at the same time (*cf.* Phm. 23–24; Eph. 6:21; and Col. 4:7–14). We will treat brief references from Philemon and Ephesians in that order without making any assumptions about their chronological sequence. Then we will proceed to the more detailed information on material possessions that emerges from Paul's epistle to the Philippians.[45]

## Philemon

The traditional understanding of the circumstances surrounding the writing of this short letter is that Philemon's runaway slave, Onesimus, has become a Christian after coming into contact with Paul in prison in Rome and is now being sent back to his master. Paul does not want Philemon to punish Onesimus but to welcome him back as a Christian brother and possibly even volunteer to send him back to serve Paul.[46] In verses 18–19, Paul explicitly tells Philemon, 'If he [Onesimus] has done you any wrong or owes you anything, charge it to me. I, Paul, am writing this with my own hand. I will pay it back – not to mention that you owe me your very self.' Runaway slaves often stole property in order to provide for themselves as they fled. So it is natural to assume that Onesimus may have done likewise. Even if he did not, Philemon would have lost the man-hours in labour during the time of Onesimus' absence. The language that Paul uses in these two verses is laden with financial terminology – 'charging it' to Paul's account and repaying his 'debt'. Paul hopes that Onesimus may receive a fresh start now that he is a Christian. Nevertheless, Paul also wants to let Philemon know that he is prepared to compensate him for what he has lost, although the rhetoric of the entire epistle suggests that Paul would prefer Philemon to recognize the spiritual debts he owed Paul and not accept his financial offer.[47] If Philemon was well enough off to host one of the Colossian house churches (verse 2), he probably had many slaves and would not have suffered great loss from just this one.

[45] For alternative reconstructions and for details of the position adopted here, see, *e.g.*, Guthrie (1990: 489–495, 545–555). *Cf.* the introductions in the standard commentaries on the prison epistles.

[46] There have been variations on this traditional interpretation, but a good defence of it in light of recent challenges appears in Nordling (1991: 97–119).

[47] To be able to pay the amount of money potentially at stake here may have been impossible for Paul, especially as a prisoner under house arrest in Rome. This is a remarkable promise that must be based on the assumption that if Philemon takes him up on his offer, Paul will have to ask some of his wealthy friends to help him pay what he has promised (Dunn 1996b: 339).

## Ephesians

Only one verse in this famous epistle proves directly relevant to our topic (though recall our reference to 5:5 above, p. 184), but it is an important text nevertheless. In 4:28 Paul writes, 'Those who have been stealing must steal no longer, but must work, doing something useful with their own hands, that they may have something to share with those in need.' Paul appeals here to the Old Testament principle of restitution. Not only must the thief give up his or her previous lifestyle as part of becoming a Christian (*cf.* the context of vv. 22–27), but the very instruments used to commit the crimes – one's hands – instead must perform a useful service. Even the robber must share with those in need. Given that ancient thieves were often poor people simply trying to find a way to survive, the about-face implied by this verse is remarkable. And as Lincoln (1990: 304) observes, 'The motive for work is not individual profit but communal well-being.' The later commands in Ephesians to slave-owning masters (Eph. 6:9) parallel the similar commands to the Colossians (Col. 4:1), and provide a further indirect reminder that most Christian communities had at least a few members with considerable means.[48]

## Philippians

What we may deduce from Acts, Paul's letters and extra-biblical information suggests that the church in Philippi consisted of a broad cross-section of socio-economic groups (Peterlin 1995: 135–170). At one level, the entire epistle to the Philippians was occasioned by Paul's need to write a 'thank-you' note for the financial assistance he had received from that congregation. Philippians 2:25 refers to Epaphroditus, 'whom you sent to take care of my needs'. Most commentators recognize this as an allusion to his delivering funds from Philippi.[49] But

---

[48] The letters in which these commands appear are often alleged to be post-Pauline. But no difference in social context between Ephesians or Colossians and the indisputably Pauline corpus can be sustained from the commands regarding slavery, especially given Philemon's inclusion among the authentic epistles. The larger claim that the later Pauline (or pseudonymous) epistles betray a more bourgeois Christianity is belied by the evidence we have found for influential well-to-do believers in every stage of the Pauline churches.

[49] Many unanswerable questions surround the nature of the risk Epaphroditus took in delivering the funds, the illness from which he almost died, and the reason the Philippians were previously unable to give additional help (2:26–29; *cf.* 4:16 – '*at last* you have renewed your concern for me. Indeed, you have been concerned, but you had no opportunity to show it'). To conclude, with Buchanan (1964), that Paul always refused gifts in principle or that Paul's ministry had been under attack among the Macedonian Christians far outruns the actual evidence of the text.

it is 4:10–20 that unpacks in more detail Paul's response to their gift. Here Paul walks a fine line between seeming ungrateful and saying anything that would make him bound by the ancient conventions of friendship and reciprocity (directly alluded to in the phrase, 'in the matter of giving and receiving', 4:15).[50] The entire eleven-verse section unfolds without any formal 'thank you' ever being expressed, but this was a standard convention in the Greco-Roman world among intimate friends when the writer wanted to make clear that he was not binding himself to some reciprocal financial obligation. This section of the letter has been aptly termed a 'thankless thank-you' (Peterman 1991; *contra* Reumann 1993: 440).[51]

On the one hand, Paul really did need the Philippians' support. Ancient prisoners depended on friends or family from the outside to take care of their daily necessities of life; prison rations could be so poor as to put one's life in peril (Rapske 1994: 209–216). That the Philippians had not provided for Paul for some time could have called their friendship into question. But Paul acknowledges that he understands that they were previously unable to help.[52] On the other hand, Paul articulates a principle of contentment in Christ in whatever circumstances he finds himself (4:11–13). The sufficiency (*autarkēs*, 4:11) which Paul experiences in Jesus enables his friendship with the Philippians to be of the highest kind – for virtue's sake rather than for utility or pleasure (Berry 1996: 112–117; Fitzgerald 1996).[53] Here again we see the theme that has become so familiar to us from Proverbs 30:7–9 of seeking neither poverty nor riches, although we should say that what Paul is stressing here is his ability to be content with *either* poverty *or* riches. Verse 13 must not be divorced from this context. There are plenty of things Christians are physically, intellectually or even spiritually unable to do, even in Christ, but the 'everything' we can do through him who gives us strength involves modelling Paul's contentment in all of life's socio-economic circumstances. As Fee (1995: 436) elaborates, 'Those in "want" learn patience and trust in

---

[50] For comprehensive detail on 4:10–20 against the background of Greco-Roman patron–client relationships, see Bormann (1995: 136–224).

[51] Reumann (1996) provides an excellent survey of recent scholarship on the possibilities of understanding Philippians, and esp. ch. 4, as a letter of 'friendship'.

[52] Is this to be related to the impoverishment of the Macedonian churches more generally, as in 2 Cor. 8:1–2 (see O'Brien [1991: 519] for this and other possibilities)? Peterlin (1995) rejects all attempts to excuse the Philippians' behaviour, suggesting a divided church and stronger animosity against Paul than is usually perceived, but his conclusions often outrun the explicit data.

[53] Malherbe (1996) ably demonstrates that the self-sufficiency Paul models differs greatly from the Stoic ideal.

suffering; those in "wealth" learn humility and dependence in prospering, not to mention the joy of giving without strings attached!' Philippians 4:14–16 nevertheless makes it plain that Paul is genuinely grateful for the help which alleviated his misery and for the past relationship of support from the Macedonians while he was ministering in other places.[54] Verses 17–18a immediately qualify this expression of gratefulness with language that keeps Paul from being financially indebted to the Philippians ('not that I am looking for a gift ... I have received full payment'). Verse 18a, with its use of *apechō*, suggests that Paul is giving a verbal 'receipt' for the gift. But the language need not be technical and may simply suggest that the Philippians have paid whatever 'debt' they may have felt they accrued in not having been able to support Paul for some time (*cf.* further Peterman 1997: 142–144). Verses 18b–20, especially with their cultic language of the gift as an acceptable offering or sacrifice, round out the discussion by placing finances in the theological context of worship to God.[55]

## The Pastoral Epistles

Critical scholarship, of course, has regularly doubted the Pauline authorship of the Pastoral Epistles. This perspective is often bound up with their being located in second-generation Christianity as representatives of a *christliche Bürgerlichkeit*, a sort of bourgeois religion. Several recent major commentaries, however, are vigorously arguing afresh for the traditional claims of authorship and for a setting within Paul's life (G. W. Knight 1992; *cf.* Mounce [Word Biblical Commentary]; Towner [New International Commentary]; both forthcoming). More specific studies of the community in Ephesus to which 1 Timothy is addressed have concluded that this church's socio-economic spectrum differs little from Corinth in the mid-50s (see esp. Kidd 1990). There was an emerging 'middle class' and a handful of wealthy people who often created a large part of the problems that Paul had to

[54] Capper (1993), following Sampley (1980: 51–77), goes further and argues from the potentially commercial language of the passage (esp. *koinoō* in 4:15 and *apechō* in 4:18) that Paul actually contracted with the Philippians to preach full time with their financial support, but that the Philippians had not consistently carried through with their end of the bargain. Yet the whole conciliatory tone of the letter and the broad semantic range of the various terms thought to support this thesis call it into significant question.

[55] For a study of the entire letter and of 4:10–20 in particular from the perspective of 'friendship and finances in Philippi', see Witherington (1994a), and note esp. his excursus on pp. 123–124. For helpful applications to the area of Christian giving, see I. H. Marshall (1991: 123).

address. There is nothing from the historical background or from the letters themselves that requires a post-Pauline date or context (see also Wainwright 1993). We will therefore include the Pastoral Epistles in our survey of Paul's teaching.

In 1 Timothy 2:9, Paul wants 'women to dress modestly, with decency and propriety, not with braided hair or gold or pearls or expensive clothes'. This 'dress code' is a sign that the wealthy women at Ephesus were the primary offenders addressed. They alone would have been able to afford the elaborate hair-dos described. In fact, the Greek text reads more literally, 'not with braided hair *and* gold or pearls ...' There was nothing wrong with braided hair as such, but the ornate coiffure in which jewels were interwoven into the braids, as one way of holding a woman's hair together, involved hours of attention to one's external appearance and was often accompanied by lavish, costly attire (see esp. Hurley 1981: 199). So there is a timeless principle, even in these seemingly very occasional remarks, that women (and presumably men too) should not preoccupy themselves with overly expensive or fancy dress, jewellery and the like. One wonders how many Christian worshippers today violate Paul's principle every Sunday.[56]

In 1 Timothy 3:3, 8, under the criteria for church leaders, we read that an overseer must 'not be a lover of money' and a deacon not 'pursuing dishonest gain'. The former expression translates *aphilargyros*, with an etymology that leads very literally to the NIV translation. The latter expression renders *aischrokerdēs*, which could also refer to 'shameful' or 'disgraceful' gain. In light of the close parallels between the numerous criteria for the two offices of Christian leadership, the terms are likely to be synonyms. In neither case is money for ministry condemned, or even the expectation of a reasonable amount of remuneration. But when desire for material recompense develops into an allegiance that can be described as 'love', it becomes shameful or disgraceful. G. W. Knight (1992: 169) sees the terms as roughly equivalent to 'greedy'. Thus it is not surprising that the false teachers of Titus 1:11 are explicitly described as seeking 'dishonest gain' (*aischros kerdos*). And in 2 Timothy 3:2, 4, the terrible people that will arise in the last days are said to be *philargyroi* ('lovers of money') and *philēdonoi* ('lovers of pleasure') rather than 'lovers of God'. Titus 2:14 and 3:8 both enjoin

---

[56] To the extent that women were behind the promulgation of the false teaching in Ephesus, even perhaps from positions of leadership in the church (highly debated issues that need not detain us here), they would have been almost certainly been limited to these elite circles that had access to power in an otherwise highly patriarchal Greco-Roman culture (see esp. Padgett 1987).

Christians to be eager to do 'what is good'. One wonders if the Hellenistic language of benefaction that we have seen elsewhere may lie behind these seemingly more general statements as well.[57]

At any rate, in 1 Timothy 5:3–16, benefaction is clearly in view. This is a passage, at first glance, with little contemporary application, as it deals with widows in Ephesus who should be enrolled on the list of those worthy of material help from the church (5:3, 5).[58] In short, Paul encourages the congregation to support only those who have no-one else to provide for them and who are too old to work. If there are children or grandchildren, they should follow their cultural obligations, widely recognized in Judaism and Hellenism, and take care of their aged relatives (5:4). This is the context for understanding the often abused verse 8, 'Anyone who does not provide for relatives, and especially for immediate family members,[59] has denied the faith and is worse than an unbeliever.' This verse says nothing about a man being the primary 'breadwinner' for a family; the language is completely generic in the Greek.[60] Instead, it says everything about working-age adults, explicitly including women (5:16, assuming the reading *piste*), having the responsibility to care for their elderly relatives. In the modern world, this of course does not dictate exactly how that care should be provided, whether in one's home, in a nursing home or via numerous other mediating alternatives. But it does suggest that a family has financial responsibility to its own members before the church (or any other community) should be burdened. This indeed was an ideal throughout antiquity (Spicq 1969: 531–532). How disgraceful, therefore, if Christians behaved worse than the pagans among whom they lived (hence the language of verse 8b)!

[57] Verner (1983: 151) sees the language of benevolence behind 1 Tim. 3:1: the person desiring the office of overseer aspires to a 'good work' (*kalon ergon*).

[58] Verner (1983: 161–166) discusses arguments for and against taking the widows of 1 Tim. 5:3–8, 16 (real widows) as different from the widows of 5:9–15 (official widows), but his distinctions do not affect the discussion at hand.

[59] The Greek reads literally, 'but if anyone does not take care of his *own*, that is, his *household* ...' Campbell (1995) thinks that 'household' should be translated as in Gal. 6:10 and Eph. 2:19 to refer to fellow Christians, so that the verse equates the individual's relatives with believers. He correctly recognizes that *malista* (NIV 'especially') in its five occurrences in the Pastorals probably means 'that is', but the unqualified use of 'household' makes it unlikely that only believers are in view. A better translation than either the NIV or Campbell's would be, 'If anyone does not provide for his own people, that is, his household, ' understanding 'household', to refer to whatever extended family (including slaves or servants) lived together in one domicile.

[60] In fact, there is no word for 'man' in the Greek of this passage at all, only the pronoun *tis*, the form of which was identical in both masculine and feminine genders and meant simply 'someone' or 'anyone'.

The requirement in 1 Timothy 5:9 that a widow qualifying for aid should be at least sixty years old probably reflects the maximum age in antiquity at which individuals could reasonably be expected to work and provide for themselves (Towner 1994: 116). Even then, for a widow to qualify for church assistance, she has to have been 'faithful to her husband' and well-known for good deeds (5:9–10). Here the list of those deeds clearly includes benefactions, as well as other conventional motherly roles in the ancient world – rearing children; providing hospitality, which included washing the feet of guests; and helping those in trouble. Paul then encourages younger widows to remarry (5:14). In addition to the obvious problems of controlling unfulfilled sexual desire and becoming an annoyance to their neighbours, problems to which single adult women in those days could easily fall prey (5:6, 11–13, 15), this command provides one further method by which no-one else's financial resources need to be depleted for the widows' care. Winter (1994: 64–66) points out that widows would normally have had their dowries returned to them, so that, in addition to the possibilities of children caring for their parents, and younger women continuing to work, and/or their remarrying, there was yet this additional financial means that should have limited the number of individuals the church had to support in any substantial way.

It is interesting to trace the later Christian development of this category of duly enrolled widow. While it did not develop in the same sense as the 'offices' of overseer and deacon outlined in 1 Timothy 3, the order of widows persisted well into the fourth century. But increasingly common in various parts of early Greek and Latin Christianity was the office of deaconess, in part as an outgrowth of 5:3–10. Women leaders were thought to be particularly well suited for ministries of prayer and practical service, including those in which it would not have been appropriate for men to be involved – especially counselling, visiting, catechizing or baptizing other women (S. Clark 1980: 117–123). Eventually the order of widows gave way altogether to the monastic movement, and women's roles in church leadership became restricted to nuns and their abbeys.[61]

In 1 Timothy 5:17–18, financial considerations may well recur in the context of giving 'double honour' to those who direct the affairs of the church well, 'especially those whose work is preaching and teaching'.[62]

---

[61] For a thorough study of widows and their successors in the early church, see Thurston (1989).

[62] Schöllgen (1989) nevertheless points out several reasons why 'double honour' may not refer to money in this context. The reference may indeed be more general.

Again, given the use of *malista* (NIV, 'especially') in the Pastoral Epistles as a virtual equivalent for 'namely' (see also Skeat 1979: 173–177), no support is offered here for the Presbyterian distinction between teaching elder and ruling elder. The sole category of 'elder', which is to be equated with the office of overseer in 3:1–7, distinguishes itself from the second office of 'deacon' by its joint teaching and ruling function in the church (3:2; 5:17).[63] Based on Deuteronomy 25:4 and Luke 10:7, Paul once again encourages adequate financial compensation for Christian leaders who perform their tasks well (recall 1 Cor. 9:9, 14). So, too, in 2 Timothy 2:6 he writes, 'The hard-working farmer should be the first to receive a share of the crops.'

The penultimate passage in 1 Timothy directly relevant to our topic appears in 6:3–10. Here Paul refers in greater detail to the dangers of the love of money. Godliness must not be seen as a means to financial gain (6:5b). Rather, godliness with contentment in whatever circumstances one finds oneself is viewed as great spiritual gain (6:6). This contentment need not depend on more than the basic necessities of life (6:7–8).[64] Obviously, 'some people in the church, whom the writer associates with the heretical opposition, thought that godliness led to monetary gains. A desire to be rich animated some of the congregation' (I. H. Marshall 1990: 89). Verse 7, reminiscent of Job 1:21, explains why Paul can encourage such contentment: 'For we brought nothing into the world, and we can take nothing out of it.' The danger of riches involves both heteropraxy and heterodoxy (6:9, 10b): 'Those who want to get rich fall into temptation and a trap and into many foolish and harmful desires that plunge people into ruin and destruction.' Furthermore, 'Some people, eager for money, have wandered from the faith and pierced themselves with many griefs.' In between these two statements appears one of the most famous verses in Scripture on our theme: 'For the love of money is a root of all kinds of evil' (6:10a). The NIV gets both the translation and the interpretation correct at two key points that are often missed elsewhere. First, there is no article in the

---

Schöllgen's own interpretation of extra portions in the early Christian love feast is, however, less persuasive.

[63] *Cf.* Acts 20 in which Paul refers to the Ephesian elders (20:17) as 'overseers' (20:28); and Phil. 1:1, which distinguishes 'overseers' and 'deacons.' The term 'pastor' is used nowhere in the New Testament as the title for an office holder, but it is an explicit function of the elder/overseer (Acts 20:28) and a spiritual gift of many Christians (Eph. 4:11).

[64] As elsewhere in Paul, *autarkeia* ('contentment') recalls Stoic and other Hellenistic philosophical notions of self-sufficiency. But in Paul's context it depicts a God-centred reality (*cf.* Brenk 1990).

Greek before 'root'. It would be difficult to demonstrate that the love of money is *the* most foundational cause of all kinds of evil, but it certainly is *an* important one. Second, no scripture ever declares *money* as the root of all kinds of evil, but rather the *love* of, allegiance to or attachment to money in the fashion that led Jesus to declare, 'You cannot serve both God and Money' (Matt. 6:24; Luke 16:13).[65]

Finally we come to 1 Timothy 6:17–20. Verse 17 obviously envisions the possibility of a rich person being a Christian ('those who are rich in this present world' must put their hope 'in God'). Paul also readily acknowledges how wealth can be a blessing. God 'richly provides us with everything for our enjoyment' (6:17b). We may enjoy the fleeting pleasures that wealth can provide for a short time in this life, but we dare not put our trust in material possessions. Instead, we must lay up treasures in heaven (recall Matt. 6:19 and par.), 'as a firm foundation for the coming age'. In this way, Christians of all socio-economic circumstances 'may take hold of the life that is truly life', that is, the eternal state in the age to come. Again Paul is challenging the conventional Hellenistic system of patronage and reciprocity. He is telling those who have this world's goods not to count on being able to buy the favours of others in return. But one way in which he does draw on convention is to command rich people to be generous benefactors themselves (6:18). 'Paul's desire that the rich use their possessions this way can scarcely be stated more emphatically' (L. Johnson 1996: 207). There are four terms in verse 18 that all reinforce the same command: 'to do good', 'to be rich in good deeds', 'to be generous', and to be 'willing to share' their material possessions.

## Summary and conclusions

Right from the outset of his letter-writing career, Paul is eager to remember the poor (Galatians). The Thessalonian Christians may have been more impoverished than many of the Pauline churches, but that gives them no right to be idle and depend solely on 'welfare' from others (1 and 2 Thessalonians). The church at Corinth is torn apart by wealthy house-church leaders who expect their riches to buy them all the privilege and influence it did when they were pagans

---

[65] On the indirect relationship of both 1 Tim. 6:6–10 and 17–19 to the Jesus tradition, see Dschulnigg (1993). In fact, he claims these passages are the purest reflections of Jesus' teaching on wealth and poverty anywhere in the New Testament (77). The similarities seem far too close to allow for theories of the development of a *christliche Bürgerlichkeit*, foreign to the original Jesus movement, in the Pastoral Epistles (69–71).

(1 Corinthians). Instead Paul calls on them to give as generously as less well-to-do believers have already done to meet the needs of the acutely poor in Jerusalem (2 Corinthians). It seems the Corinthians and others eventually agree and give generously (Romans). Christian freedom should produce liberating relationships and accountability structures (Philemon and Ephesians). Christian workers should be grateful for financial support from fellow believers but not depend on it (Philippians). And ultimately, the Christians with material possessions must recognize their seduction and avoid their snare by giving generous quantities of them away (the Pastorals).

Although Paul is not regularly thought of as devoting as much attention as James or Jesus to the works that flow from faith, particularly in the financial realm, the detailed survey of this chapter creates a quite different impression.[66] There is no tension on this topic between Paul and his predecessors. All the primary New Testament witnesses agree that grace through faith justifies but inevitably produces good deeds and works of compassion, particularly by means of financial stewardship, especially in the household of faith. We may perceive some increase in the numbers and influence of well-to-do Christians, especially those who may have related as patrons to their clients at one time, though many no doubt remained relatively poor, even in Paul's churches. But with whatever growing urbanization and standard of living may be detected with the shift from Jewish to Hellenistic Christianity, problems associated with wealth and the wealthy also emerge. Paul may not issue any of Jesus' wide-ranging or radical calls to abandon everything, although we have already argued that none of those calls was intended to be normative for all believers in the first place. But he does insist that Hellenistic Christians be equally counter-cultural in rejecting the systems of patronage and reciprocity so endemic in their culture. And he calls all believers to act as generous benefactors regardless of their net worth and with no thought of any material reward in this life. Should they fall into acute need, they should be able to count on their fellow believers to minister to them, even as they are expected to give from their surplus at the moment. In short, Paul commands generosity simply because it honours God; the only guaranteed reward awaits in the life to come. Paul as much as Jesus recognizes the danger of mammon as an idol and its potentially damning effects. Christ must be served rather than money.

---

[66] *E.g.*, Paul uses the word 'poor' (*ptōchos*) only four times and 'rich' (*plousios*) only three times. But word-counts, of course, cannot determine the frequency of *themes*.

Chapter Seven

# The rest of the New Testament

This final exegetical chapter falls into two main parts. First we will return to the synoptic evangelists, but this time to focus primarily on the distinctive redactional contributions of the three authors rather than on the teaching of Jesus *per se*. The earliest plausible datings for Mark, Matthew and Luke are from the late 50s to early 60s; the latest, some time between AD 70 and 100 (*cf.* further Blomberg 1997: 121–123, 133–135, 150–152). Either way, they betray no knowledge of or dependence on the Pauline epistles and therefore are best treated as a discrete group, separate from, if not also subsequent to, Paul's letters. Second, we will review the New Testament writings not yet surveyed: the epistles of Hebrews, 1 and 2 Peter and Jude, and the writings traditionally attributed to John – the Fourth Gospel, 1, 2 and 3 John, and the Revelation. Again, dates vary widely, in part dependent on whether or not one accepts the traditional ascriptions of authorship in each case. These dates vary from the 60s to the end of the first century, but the better arguments support dates for Hebrews, 1 and 2 Peter and Jude in the 60s (with Jude arguably even earlier) and the Johannine literature in the 80s or 90s.[1] But in general it seems justifiable to treat all this material as part of the latest stages in the development of New Testament theology.

## The synoptic evangelists

### Methodological options

We have already dealt in chapter 4 with the teachings of Jesus in some detail, surveying them roughly in chronological sequence as his ministry unfolded and basing our comments on assumptions about their general historical trustworthiness. But with multiple examples of the gospel genre in the New Testament, we have a unique opportunity to discover redactional emphases of the individual evangelists, even if we

---

[1] *Cf.*, *e.g.*, Guthrie (1990); Carson, Moo & Morris (1992); both *ad loc.*

reject the substantial dichotomy between history and theology that has often plagued gospel criticism.[2]

One approach to arranging the synoptic material is largely source-critical, following the consensus that identifies Mark and Q (the material shared by Matthew and Luke but not found in Mark) as the two earliest Gospels or gospel-like documents. Following Streeter's classic four-source hypothesis, some would still add M and L as additional gospel sources from which Matthew and Luke derived much or all of their unparalleled material (cf. Blomberg 1997: 86–93). When one looks at the Gospel of Mark as the foundational synoptic document, one may observe the following pericopae dealing with material possessions in the so-called triple tradition (material shared by Mark, Matthew and Luke) or double tradition (of either Mark and Matthew or Mark and Luke): Jesus as a carpenter or carpenter's son (Mark 6:3; Matt. 13:55); the call of the first disciples to leave their fishing profession (Mark 1:16–20 and par.); the call of Levi and Jesus' celebration with tax collectors (Mark 2:13–17 and pars.); Jesus' charge to the disciples to travel light (Mark 6:8–11 and pars.); the seed among the thorns as the person who hears the word but is choked by the riches and pleasures of this world (Mark 4:18–19 and pars.); Jesus' compassion for the hungry at the feedings of the five thousand and four thousand (Mark 6:32–44 and pars.; Mark 8:1–10 and par.); the controversy over Pharisaic corban practices (Mark 7:9–13 and par.); the repartee between Jesus and the Syro-Phoenician, with its possible socio-economic background (Mark 7:24–30 and par.); the teaching about losing one's life in order to save it (Mark 8:36 and pars.); Jesus' encounter with the rich young ruler (Mark 10:17–22 and pars.); his follow-up dialogue with the disciples about the difficulty the rich have in entering the kingdom and about the reward that will be received by those who have left possessions to follow him (Mark 10:23–31 and pars.); Jesus' clearing the temple (Mark 11:15–17 and pars.); the saying about paying taxes (Mark 12:13–17 and pars.); Jesus' praise for the widow and her sacrificial giving (Mark 12:41–44 and par.); the anointing at Bethany (Mark 14:3–9 and pars.); and Judas betraying Jesus for money (Mark 14:10–11 and pars.).

These doubly or triply attested Markan passages form a representative cross-section of the teachings of Jesus already surveyed, along with information from the broader historical portrait of Jesus and his followers that the synoptics paint (recall ch. 4, pp. 105–109). The only

---

[2] Particularly helpful in overcoming this false dichotomy are the contributions to the introduction and theology of each of the four Gospels by France (1989); R. P. Martin (1972); I. H. Marshall (1988[3]) ; and Smalley (1978), respectively.

major form of Jesus' teaching not abundantly represented is the parabolic instruction surveyed in the first part of chapter 5 above. It is difficult to discern any patterns in this collection of passages distinctive from those broader surveys, which further supports the general trustworthiness of the core of the synoptic tradition on this topic.

Q-material relevant to the theme of riches and poverty includes Jesus' temptations (Matt. 4:1–11; Luke 4:1–13); the beatitudes and woes (Matt. 5:3–12; Luke 6:20–26); giving to those who want to take from you (Matt. 5:40, 42; Luke 6:29–30); the request in the Lord's Prayer for bread one day at a time (Matt. 6:11; Luke 11:3); the prohibition against laying up earthly treasures and warnings about anxiety for basic material needs (Matt. 6:19–34; Luke 12:22–34); the saying about not being able to serve both God and mammon (Matt. 6:24; Luke 16:13); the invitation to ask of God because he wants to give his children good things (Matt. 7:7–11; Luke 11:9–13); the 'Golden Rule' (Matt. 7:12; Luke 6:31); Jesus' radical itinerant discipleship (Matt. 8:18–22; Luke 9:57–62); the good news that Jesus preaches to the poor as a sign of who he is (Matt. 11:5; Luke 7:22); the accusation that Jesus is a glutton and a drunkard, showing at least that he is not averse to occasional feasting (Matt. 11:19; Luke 7:34); and the commands about tithing (Matt. 23:23; Luke 11:42).

A huge literature debating the nature of the hypothetical Q source has attempted to lay out a coherent theology of this putative document and even to reconstruct the early Christian community in which it may have emerged.[3] Q is often seen as including some of Jesus' most stringent teachings on divesting oneself of wealth, particularly with its commands to the Twelve when they are sent out on their own missionary travels (e.g., Schottroff & Stegemann 1986: 38–66). Theissen's thesis (1978) has become popular: that behind Q lay two groups of Christians – wandering 'charismatic' preachers and sympathizers in local villages who supported them. But Horsley (1989) has placed a significant question mark in front of major portions of this proposal. In addition, a sizeable percentage of the references given above come from Matthew's Sermon on the Mount and its various parallels scattered about the Gospel of Luke, so that if it were to turn out that each writer was abbreviating a much longer sermon of Jesus, and that Luke was interspersing similar teaching that Jesus repeated on other occasions in his ministry (thus, e.g., Kennedy 1984: 67–69), the remaining material distinctive to Q would not seem nearly so considerable or unidirectional

---

[3] For recent summaries contrast Tuckett (1996) with Vaage (1994).

in emphasis. If Q was indeed a connected written document, it is not implausible to see it as a source derived from, or a handbook intended for, early itinerant Christian ministers. But so many speculative hypotheses must be combined, one on top of another, that however plausible each may be in its own right, many of the more detailed conclusions of Q research have a rather low overall probability. The same is all the more true for hypotheses about the contents, origins and communities of M and L. Particularly since the data that emerge from the unparalleled material in Matthew and Luke, at least with respect to riches and poverty, fit in so well with the redactional emphases of each gospel writer, it is not clear that it is worth our time here to list them separately. A more helpful and common approach to the Synoptic Gospels, therefore, is to focus on what is *distinctively* Markan, Matthean and Lukan, *both* in terms of these evangelists' redaction of material paralleled elsewhere in the Synoptics *and* of the main themes of their otherwise unparalleled material. One can also make some suggestions with a bit more profit about the communities to which the Gospels of Matthew, Mark and Luke may have been addressed.

## The Gospel of Mark

Mark, in general, is the hardest Gospel on which to perform redaction criticism following the standard two-source hypothesis, because we simply do not have access to any written sources on which he may have relied, and the amount of distinctively Markan material is quite small.[4] On the theme of riches and poverty, there are *no* uniquely Markan pericopae. Among paralleled pericopae, one may identify several uniquely Markan touches, or at least information omitted by the parallels in Matthew and/or Luke. Only Mark refers to hired servants (*i.e.*, in the plural) that the sons of Zebedee left behind (Mark 1:20). Only Mark has Jesus give permission to the disciples to take a staff or sandals with them on the road as they embark on their initial missionary activity within Israel (Mark 6:8). Mark 6:34 is unique in having Jesus, on the occasion of the feeding of the five thousand, refer to the crowds as like 'sheep without a shepherd'. Mark 10:30 alone adds the phrase 'in this present age' to Jesus' promise that those who had left family or property for him would be recompensed a hundred-fold. In the temple

---

[4] The most generous estimate of the amount of this material of which I am aware computes it at 21.02% of the Gospel: 347 words (3.09%) in wholly unparalleled passages and 2,013 words (17.93%) comprising additional minor details in Mark not found in Matthew and Luke in otherwise paralleled passages (Linnemann 1992: 107).

clearing, Mark distinctively adds that Jesus would not allow anyone to carry anything through the temple (Mark 11:16). In Mark's account of the widow's mites, he uniquely observes how many rich people 'threw in large amounts' (12:41). Finally, in 14:7 Mark alone includes Jesus' words regarding the poor that 'you can help them any time you want'.

Again, it is difficult to find a common thread running through these various references. Some seem to soften the most radical statements of Jesus found in other Gospels, while others make Jesus' teaching and practice in caring for the poor or abandoning one's wealth that much more emphatic. It is not surprising, therefore, that the standard surveys of Mark's major theological emphases and redactional distinctives do not include treatment of the themes of wealth and poverty. Yet certainly the major theme of 'power through powerlessness' in Mark (*e.g.*, Lee-Pollard 1987) suggests that he would not have promoted Christians trying to amass the wealth of this world. One study of the cross-section of society reflected in the episodes of Mark's Gospel engages in 'mirror readings' to suggest that Mark's audience is largely a peasant community with typical ancient rural Mediterranean social interaction (Rohrbaugh 1993; *cf.* also in part Kee 1977: 77–105). But the cross-section of characters in the Gospel account need have no necessary correlation with the community Mark was addressing. Certainly, there is nothing distinctive enough in Mark's Gospel to overthrow the early church's tradition that Mark was addressed to Christians in Rome (see esp. Irenaeus, *Against Heresies* 3.1.2; Eusebius, *Church History* 6.14.6–7), where one could expect a broad cross-section of socio-economic backgrounds corresponding to that which we have seen behind several of the epistles of Paul.[5]

## The Gospel of Matthew

Matthew holds out slightly more promise for detecting redactional distinctives. In Matthew's infancy narratives (chs. 1 – 2), nothing explicit about the theme of riches or poverty appears, save for the lavish gifts of the Gentile magi (Matt. 2:11) – gifts fit for a king and in keeping with Matthew's royal Christology. Nevertheless, there is a striking contrast, particularly in chapter 2, between the emphasis on the well-to-do and powerful Jews bound up with the religious establishment in Jerusalem, who are terrified and fight against the arrival of the Messiah (see esp. Matt. 2:3), and the theme of Jesus' coming to save

---

[5] Belo (1981) and Clévenot (1985) have developed 'materialist' readings of the Gospel of Mark, but these deal more with questions of power and revolution than with strictly economic matters.

the powerless and outcast (the category into which the magi would have fallen as Gentile astrologers, irrespective of their actual financial assets).[6] In 6:1–4 Jesus presupposes that his followers will give alms, but insists on their doing so in 'secret', rather than from the desire for human praise. That the giving of a cup of cold water to a 'little one' will be rewarded (Matt. 10:42) teaches Jesus' disciples that the least significant Christian has great spiritual value in God's eyes and deserves at least the basic material provisions of life. The parables of the hidden treasure and pearl of great price stress that it is worth sacrificing all to acquire the kingdom (13:44–46). And the little pericope about the temple tax reminds Christ's followers of their freedom from the Law (17:24–27). Three additional parables are all relevant to our topic: the unforgiving servant, on the need to forgive literal and spiritual debts (18:23–35); the labourers in the vineyard, from which we learn that God treats his people by grace and does not pay them a wage (20:1–16); and the so-called parable of the sheep and the goats, stressing the need for people to respond to Christian missionaries with material aid as well as spiritual receptivity (25:31–46). Finally, only Matthew includes the story of the 'repentance' of Judas, as he returns the money to the priests who refuse to let him off the hook, and the narration of their subsequent use of that money to buy a cemetery (27:3–10).

Werner Marx (1979) thinks he discerns an emphasis on 'money matters' in Matthew with its six passages referring to tax collectors (as against one in Mark and five in Luke), its total number of references to money (forty-four as against six in Mark and twenty-two in Luke), and its use of terms for specific coins or units of currency, such as *lepton*, *kodrantēs*, *chrysos*, *chalkos*, *argyrion* and *talanton*. Matthew is also allegedly fond of the terms *kēnsos*, *didrachma*, and *nomisma*. If Matthew was written by Levi/Matthew, the tax collector, all this would make sense, but it scarcely adds up to a *theological* emphasis of any kind. And the statistics are a bit skewed. Fourteen of Matthew's forty-four references to money involve the word 'talent' (*talanton*), which dominates two of the parables unique to Matthew (Matt. 20:1–16 and 25:14–30; the latter has a parallel of sorts in Luke 19:11–27 but involving *minas*). And the other terms for coinage and currency are all too infrequent to substantiate any emphasis.

What we know about Matthew's community gives us only slightly further help. His Gospel was most probably written to a Jewish-Christian congregation in the eastern part of the empire, still fresh from

---

[6] See further Blomberg (1991).

breaking away from the local synagogue and still in considerable tension with its non-Christian Jewish neighbours (see esp. Stanton 1984). Rowland (1994), on the one hand, discerns in Matthew's redaction a concern for the relatively impoverished, which could fit our assessment of the one other New Testament document addressed to a distinctively Jewish-Christian audience – the epistle of James. On the other hand, nothing in Matthew suggests a rural audience or the problem of migrant farm workers, as we saw in James. Instead it is usually assumed that Matthew's audience is urban (Antioch and Jerusalem are the two most common suggestions, both modern and ancient), and Matthew's predilection for parables featuring kings and other wealthy people has suggested to some a slightly greater urban and even upper-class focus (see, *e.g.*, Goulder 1968; R. H. Smith 1980: 265–271). Certainly the sums that are used in the parables involving talents are enormous. And to the extent that a motif may be discerned by combining the passages on treating Jesus' messengers as if one were treating Jesus himself, the seemingly more 'spiritual' emphasis of the beatitudes and other portions of the Sermon on the Mount could suggest that Matthew's portrayal of Jesus is slightly less 'one-sided' or radically concerned for the socially marginalized than Luke's. But, again, the data are not abundant or clear enough to make any of these pronouncements with high levels of confidence.

## The Gospel of Luke

All of this changes when we turn to the third and final Synoptic Gospel, the Gospel of Luke. Here we have an enormous amount of data and scholarship with which to reckon. When liberation theology first came to the fore in the 1970s, Luke was regularly and understandably perceived as the radical evangelist who sided with the poor, who promoted God's preferential option for the disenfranchised of this world and who was the theologian of social justice *par excellence* in the New Testament.[7] The interest generated by the theologians spawned several important studies from biblical scholars, which all insisted on nuancing Luke's portrait more than the liberationist writers had thus far done. By the end of the 1970s, treatments of Luke's dominant interest in wealth and poverty could be categorized under three main headings.

*Scholarly options*
*1. A theology of non-violent protest.* Richard Cassidy (1978) focused on

---

[7] Most recently from a feminist-liberationist perspective; see Ringe (1995).

Jesus' special, though not exclusive, concern for the poor, the infirm, women and Gentiles, but stressed that the most striking feature of Luke's Gospel was his universalism. Riches create real problems for those who possess them, but Luke does not condemn them outright. He does not blame the rich for the problems of the poor, but calls on them to use their possessions to benefit the poor, so that poor and rich alike may help each other to participate fully in the life of the Christian community. But Jesus' counter-cultural admonitions against accumulating surplus possessions, and in favour of servanthood and humility, combined with his prophetic denunciations of the abuses of power in his society to create a genuine, albeit non-violent, challenge to the empire of his day. Cassidy saw the struggles of Mohandas Gandhi in the Indian movement for independence as a helpful modern parallel to Jesus' approach.[8]

2. *The proclaimer of the year of the Lord's favour.* R. B. Sloan (1977) focused on Jesus' proclamation of the arrival of the year of Jubilee.[9] Luke's use of such words as *euangelizō* ('preach good news'), *aphēsis* ('forgiveness'), and *ptōchoi* (the 'poor') and concepts such as the eschatological reversal of fortunes and the resulting ethical demands of the present must all be read in light of Jesus' programmatic sermon with its jubilary significance (Luke 4:16–21). The idea of Jubilee is both socio-economic and cultic; the two may not be divorced from each other. Christians today must seek to meet people's physical needs, while at the same time helping them understand that ultimately only God can release them from their oppression, and then fully only in the coming eschaton. In this respect Sloan differed significantly from others who studied jubilary theology and saw Jesus as attempting more literally to reinstate the Deuteronomic law or focusing more exclusively on socio-economic change in this life (*cf.* also Ringe 1985).

3. *An editor of traditions in conflict.* David Mealand (1980) embarked on a tradition-historical study of the Gospel of Luke, believing that Jesus' original teachings called his disciples to make a radical break from their past, including their previous attitudes to possessions, even though he tolerated a certain diversity of practice in the application of this teaching. Pre-Lukan (including some Q) traditions indicate that a time of great deprivation came upon the early church, causing it to take

[8] Similarly Osborne (1978), while rejecting liberation theology's one-sided appropriation of Luke, saw him as a theologian of social concern, calling Christians to constructive, peaceful involvement with the physically needy of our world.

[9] *Cf.* Yoder (1972: 34–40, 64–77), who thought this coincided with a literal year of Jubilee.

a more rigid stance in favour of the poor and against the rich (probably to be related to the time of the famine of Acts 11:27–30). By the time Luke himself compiled his Gospel, the harshness of these attitudes had begun to wane and, in some cases, previous commands by Jesus were abolished altogether in favour of new ones (see esp. Luke 22:36). Contemporary application based on Jesus' original teaching must not absolutize any one particular system, either for economic reform or for personal discipleship. R. J. Karris (1978) found even less of Luke to reflect the historical Jesus, and saw the tension between commands like Luke 9:3 and 22:36 to imply not two different stages of tradition history but two different situations of application within Luke's day, the former applying in peacetime, the latter in times of persecution.[10]

*Defining the poor*
In the 1980s, attention increasingly began to turn to the question of just who the *ptōchoi* ('poor') in Luke were. Against a general consensus that Luke was primarily focusing on the materially destitute, a variety of alternatives began to emerge. David Seccombe (1983) perceived a balanced focus in Luke between the poor and the well-to-do as those who gained Jesus' favour. Seccombe read the references to the *ptōchoi* against the *ᶜnāwîm* background of Old Testament prophecy and saw a close equation between Luke's 'poor' and the nation of *Israel*. He played down the absolute nature of the various passages in Luke that call people to renounce possessions, stressing rather that Christians should help the needy and attempt to create diverse structures and relationships that embody Christian values.

Walter Pilgrim (1981) stressed more the need for radical sharing by the rich, offering the poor both dignity and daily bread within the Christian community and fighting against the oppressive structures in society that thwarted this. But he, too, recognized the diversity of Lukan teaching and put forward *Zacchaeus* as a kind of paradigm or golden mean for the behaviour of the rich Christian. As for the *ptōchoi*, they are those who belong to the bottom socio-economic rung of society who discover that God sides with them. But the ultimate reversal of all unjust situations must await the eschaton. Nevertheless, the church, here and now, can create a substantially better model of equality and justice within its own ranks both locally and globally.

Luke Johnson (1981) recognized the potential for 'the poor' to refer

---

[10] *Cf.* also the two-tiered mentality of Degenhardt (1965) that distinguishes between commands for the *laos* (equivalent to all Christians) and those for the *mathētēs* (equivalent to the later Christian leader or office holder).

to the literally impoverished, but stressed Luke's use of the term as metaphorical and *symbolic* of the proper spiritual life and human relationships. Thus those who reject or oppress the 'poor' often oppose them on religious rather than socio-economic grounds. So also those whom God accepts, even though they may be impoverished or socially outcast, are first of all those whose hearts are right with God. As for behaviour that rich Christians can practise to alleviate the plight of their literally poor brothers or sisters, almsgiving takes pride of place.

More recently Halvor Moxnes (1988) has evaluated Luke's treatment of rich and poor against a sociological background of the culture of honour and shame in the ancient Mediterranean. He determines that, irrespective of their actual socio-economic condition, the poor are those who are *outcast* within Israel. Luke, through his various teachings and emphases, directly challenges the Greco-Roman scheme of benefaction and reciprocity and calls on a community which probably contains more urban elites than are found in any of the other Gospels' audiences (and therefore more akin to some of the communities which Paul addressed) to share with the larger, less well-to-do majority that comprised their church. Recent article-length studies by Heard (1988) and Green (1994) have stressed, respectively, the ties between the poor in Luke and the *righteous remnant* within Israel, and the poor as corresponding to the '*have-nots*' (who could include the wealthy tax collectors, still despised according to the cultural standards of Judaism). Despite their differences, all three of these works seem to be creating a new consensus on which we can build in our survey of the relevant Lukan passages that follow: *the poor are those who are both pious and disenfranchised.*

### A survey of texts

In Luke's birth narratives (Luke 1 – 2), among his substantial percentage of unparalleled material, appear several poems or hymns of praise to God by the various recipients of the angelic announcements of the coming births of John the Baptist and Jesus. Mary's 'Magnificat' (Luke 1:46–55) clearly connects the poor to the righteous remnant of Israel (see esp. 1:54). Yet there is an obvious socio-economic reversal implied in Mary's praise as well (1:52–53). It is the poor who are also spiritually humble who are exalted over against the rich and arrogant. When Mary refers to her own 'humble state' (*tapeinōsis*, 1:48), there is no reason to assume that she is anything other than fairly poor, materially speaking (recall our discussion of 2:24 above, pp. 105–106). But she is also God's servant and recognizes that 'his mercy extends to those who fear him' (1:50). In verses 52 and 53, the rulers who are brought down from their thrones are set in synonymous parallelism with the rich who are sent away empty, while the humble who are lifted up correspond to the hungry who are filled with good things. Spirituality and socially humble circumstances are inseparably linked in these verses, as are riches and arrogance (cf. 1:51 – 'those who are proud in their inmost thoughts').[11] Texts like the Magnificat, when taken as Luke's own creation, can lead to the view that his redaction emphasizes particularly Jewish concerns. But we must proceed and read texts like 7:9 and 13:28–30, in which the faith of those outside Israel proves greater than anything Jewish. There we find pointers to Luke's universalism – his true redactional emphasis – that will permeate his second volume, the Acts of the Apostles.[12]

We have already commented on Mary's and Joseph's relative impoverishment at the time of Jesus' birth, as well as on the ignominy of the entire manger scene. Whether inside a cave or stable, or in the bottom of a split-level house with the guest room up above, Jesus and Mary still remain crowded together with animals in what is not intended to reflect a pastoral or idyllic setting. We may also add here that the shepherds (see 2:8) were often considered outcasts because of a reputation, apparently at least partially deserved, for pilfering property or grazing their flocks on other people's lands as part of their nomadic lifestyle (cf. Talbert 1982: 33).

Unique to Luke's account of the ministry of John the Baptist is an additional paragraph about his ethical teaching (3:10–14). John commands the crowd to share the extra clothing and food that they have, tells the tax collectors to restrict themselves scrupulously to what they must collect, and warns the soldiers against extortion, violence and robbing others, encouraging them instead to be content with their wages. All of this clearly fits Luke's emphasis on economics and social justice. It is all drastically counter-cultural, but it is also part of the outworking of John the Baptist's overarching call to repentance (3:3; cf. further Scheffler 1990).

Further passages distinctive to Luke on which comment has already been made may be noted briefly. The Nazareth manifesto, in Luke 4:16–21, appeals to Isaiah's equation of the poor and pious but stresses real social liberation for the disenfranchised. The socio-economic

---

[11] Cf. Brown (1993: 350–365), who goes on more speculatively to assign an origin for these Lukan canticles in a specifically Jewish-Christian community that saw itself as the current manifestation of the Old Testament *ʿanāwîm*.

[12] That he preserves distinctively Jewish concerns against the grain of this universalism speaks all the more strongly for their authenticity. Cf. further Farris (1985).

emphasis in the Sermon on the Plain (Lk. 6:20–26) not only leads to a more straightforward blessing of the economically marginalized (6:20–22) than in the Matthean beatitudes but also causes Luke uniquely to include four woes against the rich, the well-fed, those who laugh and those whom everyone praises (6:24–26a). The context again makes it apparent that these attributes are tied in with the oppression of God's messengers (6:26b), but the contrast with Matthew remains striking. Verses 27–35 are largely paralleled in Matthew, but Luke's text emphasizes more the responsibility to lend to the needy without expecting anything in return (6:30, 34, 35; and recall the possible Jubilee background for these verses).[13] Luke 7:22 once again alludes to Isaiah 61:1 and answers the question of John the Baptist's followers concerning Christ's identity by calling their attention to his miracle-working ministry and also to the fact that 'the good news is preached to the poor'.

The parables of the rich fool (12:13–21) and the rich man and Lazarus (16:19–31) obviously warn against the greedy and indulgent lifestyles that wealth can often spawn. The parables about counting the cost (14:28–33) challenge would-be disciples with the need to renounce ownership of their wealth, at least in principle. The parable of the unjust steward (16:1–13)[14] and the story of Zacchaeus' conversion (19:1–10) demonstrate how almsgiving plays a central role in that renunciation. And the uniquely Lukan creation of a triad of models of giving – a demand to surrender all (Luke 18:22–25), a voluntary giving up of half (19:1–10) and an investment of everything (19:11–27) – demonstrates the diversity of application.

We previously noted, too, that Jesus is not averse to eating with the wealthy, even with the Jewish leaders. Yet in the three main instances unique to Luke in which this takes place, the initially festive occasions serve primarily as a springboard for Jesus to criticize his hosts severely. Luke 7:36–50 presents the story of Jesus at the home of Simon the Pharisee, but the hero in the story, as in the short parable of 7:41–43, reverses conventional expectation. The woman who is a 'sinner' demonstrates by her love that her sins have been forgiven. In 11:37–54, Jesus unleashes a string of denunciations of the Pharisees and scribes. Likewise in 14:1–24 Jesus takes the initiative to 'cause trouble' by criticizing the seating arrangement chosen by the guests and the selection of guests chosen by the host. Again, Jesus' concern is not

---

[13] Betz (1995: 608) speaks of not confusing benevolence with business investments.

[14] Luke 16:14–15 also includes a unique reference to Pharisees as lovers of money. See Moxnes (1988: 146–148) for how this passage fits in with other Lukan emphases.

primarily to condemn the rich, but to warn against the self-centred lifestyles that they so frequently displayed.[15]

A survey of Luke's emphasis on the poor would be incomplete without noting the other outcasts, those who were 'shamed' or without honour, who permeate his gospel. These included tax collectors, the one category of people who were not 'down and out' but 'up and out'. But the stigma that attached to their occupation explains their otherwise strange linkage with 'sinners' in, for example, 7:34 and 15:1.[16] The key parable of the Pharisee and tax collector (18:10–14) furthers Luke's theme of the great reversal. And we have already commented on the potentially paradigmatic role of the story of the conversion of one chief tax collector, Zacchaeus (19:1–10).

The second category of outcasts includes the sick. Jesus heals many such individuals in all four Gospels, but Luke shows a particular interest in the most unclean and ostracized of all, the lepers, particularly with his unparalleled story of the cleansing of the ten lepers (17:11–19). This passage, in fact, introduces a third category of outcast, the Samaritans, with its description of the solitary leper cured both spiritually as well as physically. Other unparalleled texts in the Gospel of Luke dealing with Samaritans include Jesus' refusal to call down fire from heaven to punish them, as in the time of Elijah (9:52–55), and the parable of the good Samaritan (10:25–37) discussed above (pp. 117–118).

Fourth on our list of outcasts are women. Luke has a particular interest in presenting them in a favourable light.[17] All of the following are unique to Luke's Gospel: the raising of the son of the widow of Nain (7:11–17); the wealthy women who made up Jesus' 'support team' (8:1–3); the episode of Mary and Martha (10:38–42); the parable of the lost coin, in which the character who in some sense stands for God is a woman (15:8–10); the parable of the importunate widow (18:1–8); and the prominence of Elizabeth, Mary, and the prophetess Anna in the birth narratives (chs. 1 – 2).

Still other needy people appear in distinctively Lukan texts: the friend at midnight (11:5–8); the prodigal son (15:11–32); and the 'thief' on the cross (23:43), whose repentance and acceptance by Jesus exemplify

---

[15] Luke is plausibly credited with arranging these scenes after the model of the Greco-Roman table symposia. See esp. de Meeus (1961). More recently, Braun (1995) has discerned an anti-symposium, Cynic-like parody of the form akin to those found in Lucian's satirical dialogues.

[16] For the theology of 'sinners' in the Gospel of Luke, see esp. Neale (1991); for historicity, Moritz (1996).

[17] Of a huge literature, see esp. Beavis (1994) and Kopas (1986).

the forgiveness for his enemies for which he has already prayed (23:34).[18] We have already discussed the sending of the Twelve (9:1–6), to which may be added the ministry of the Seventy or Seventy-two (10:1–24). In both cases Jesus commands the disciples to travel as lightly as possible and to depend on others' hospitality. In 22:35–38, however, Jesus rescinds these orders, anticipating a time of greater self-dependence due to greater persecution. Each set of commands makes complete sense in its historical context; neither needs to be assigned to conflicting sources or stages of tradition history. The key to understanding Jesus' words in 22:38 ('That is enough') is to recognize them as his cry of exasperation, not as a straightforward reply that two swords are the appropriate number for Peter to take with him into the garden (rightly, I. H. Marshall 1978: 827).

*Final observations*

It is important to compare these various distinctives of Luke with the book of Acts. As much as Luke emphasizes concern for the *ptōchoi*, the term never recurs in Acts at all (although recall the one passage in which *endēs* appeared in reference to the 'needy' in Jerusalem – Acts 4:34)! Conversely, references to the well-to-do increase throughout the book of Acts (see Gill 1994), often in a favourable light, among descriptions of those who have converted to Christianity.[19] It is also important to note a variety of interesting differences in the amount of data on our topic between both the first and second 'halves' of the book of Acts itself. Almost all of the explicit instruction on dealing with riches and poverty comes by the end of Acts 11. The period surveyed by this first main part of Acts is that in which Christianity is still primarily Jewish and even Palestinian in nature. During the rest of the book, which is dominated by the Pauline mission, Luke surveys the developments in early Christianity in which the gospel takes root in a much broader cross-section of socio-economic and ethnic groups. Most studies surmise that Luke, as a Greek writing to a predominantly Greco-Roman Christian community, was the most Hellenistic and 'middle-

---

[18] On reconciliation and forgiveness in Luke's Gospel more generally, see esp. Ford (1984).

[19] It is possible to exaggerate the difference between Luke and Acts by focusing solely on the frequency of certain key words – *e.g.*, 'poor' or 'blind', in which case Acts seems to have no interest in the outcast. On the other hand, there is a genuine difference between Luke's two volumes, given that Jesus' ministry to the needy of his day occurs in part to demonstrate that he is the Messiah, particularly in fulfilment of Is. 35. Thus it is not appropriate for stereotypical formulae, like Luke 4:18–19 or 7:22, to recur in the later life of the church when Jesus is not physically present. *Cf.* further Roth (1997).

class' writer of all the evangelists and that Luke's congregation was the most Hellenistic and 'middle-class' audience of the various communities to which gospels were addressed. As more and more people of some means became Christians, there was greater need for a gospel writer to stress the importance of divesting themselves of enough of their resources to help the needy in their midst. At the same time, Luke recognized the spiritual dimension in which the church was reconstituting the remnant of Israel. Only in this way could the purity of Jesus' radical vision be kept alive and not be domesticated. Thus Luke teaches not so much God's preferential option for the poor as God's having compassion for the outcast to the extent that they are willing to respond to his overtures with faith (*cf.* also Neyrey 1991).

In a number of key areas, then, it is crucial to distinguish themes that are important for Luke in his two-volume work as key aspects of the life of Jesus and of the history of the early Palestinian-Christian movement, even when his theological and redactional interests lie elsewhere, namely, in the multi-ethnic, predominantly Gentile world religion that Christianity had become by the time Paul arrived in Rome and Luke's narrative comes to a close (Acts 28). Thus, even as some have argued that Luke is particularly interested in the disciples who first keep the Law, and indeed in Jewish Christianity more generally (see esp. Jervell 1972), a stronger case can be made for Luke wanting to describe how Christianity moved beyond these initial stages and became a Law-free movement uniting Jew and Gentile alike (see, *e.g.*, Blomberg 1984a; Seifrid 1987). The same is true about Luke's interest in the poor and outcast. Luke in no way idealizes poverty. Indeed, he encourages Christians with means to help others to overcome it. But Luke preserves so much material in his Gospel and in the first half of Acts about the largely egalitarian nature of the Jesus movement and the earliest church, because it is both historical and important in order to understand what the church later became and what, in Luke's mind, it still needed to become. But since Luke's actual community and ultimate redactional focus are somewhat different, these earlier emphases are that much more likely to be historical.[20] And throughout his survey of both early and later periods of the nascent Christian movement, Luke calls for a break in conventional patron–client relationships, insisting that all believers give to others generously without expecting anything in return.

[20] *Cf.* Kraybill & Sweetland (1983), although their neat periodization overly simplifies complex data. For details of Luke's community, *cf.* Moxnes (1994); Esler (1987: 164–200); Gérard (1995).

# The rest of the New Testament

## Hebrews

Although most of the epistle to the Hebrews is a highly theological presentation of the supremacy of Jesus over the heroes and rituals of Judaism, and although the major exhortational sections deal with warnings against committing apostasy, there are at least three passages that bear on a theology of material possessions. In 10:34 the author reminds his audience: 'You sympathised with those in prison and joyfully accepted the confiscation of your property, because you knew that you yourselves had better and lasting possessions.' If the letter to the Hebrews is to be dated to the early 60s just before the Neronic persecution in Rome (so, e.g., Lane 1991a: lx-lxvi; Ellingworth 1993: 29–33; Bruce 1990b: 20–22), then this verse probably refers back to the expulsion of the Jews, including Jewish Christians, from Rome by the emperor Claudius in AD 49. Abandoned properties would have reverted back to state ownership and would not always have been reclaimable when many of the Jews returned after Claudius' death in 54 (Ellingworth 1993: 31). The priority of spiritual over earthly treasures in the mind of the writer of this epistle is clear.

Chapter 11 provides a long litany of the 'heroes of the faith' in Old Testament times as a further encouragement to the Christian recipients of this epistle to hold fast as persecution is on the verge of increasing. This detailed and poignant chapter concludes in verses 39–40 with a reminder that none of these Old Testament saints had received in this life all that God had promised them. The author then explains the reason for the delay in the fulfilment of God's promises: 'God had planned something better for us so that only together with us would they be made perfect'; 11:40). The overall theology of Hebrews makes it clear that the age of the new covenant is the time of a greater fulfilment of God's promises, but that we still live between the 'already' and the 'not yet' (see esp. 4:1–11 with respect to the theme of God's rest, and cf. Ladd 1993: 617–633). So again, Christians are taught not to consider amassing wealth in this age as the be-all and end-all of the Christian life.

Finally, in the closing exhortations of Hebrews, 13:5a declares explicitly, 'Keep your lives free from the love of money and be content with what you have', because God has promised that his presence will be adequate (13:5b–6). Interestingly, this verse comes immediately after a warning to keep the marriage bed pure, and after a reminder of God's judgment on the adulterer and the sexually immoral. Here, as in the

Pastorals,[21] concerns over sexual and financial ethics go hand in hand, possibly influenced by the sequence of the seventh and eighth commandments in the Decalogue. At any rate, selfishness lies behind both kinds of sins. In the case of accumulating financial assets, it may also be that some in Hebrews' community believed that money could protect them from coming persecution (Lane 1991b: 518).

## 1 Peter

1 Peter may well have been written at roughly the same time as Hebrews. But whereas Hebrews seems to have addressed primarily or exclusively Jewish-Christian house churches in Rome (cf. Heb. 13:24), 1 Peter's Asian-Christian addressees (1:1) are more Gentile than Jewish (see esp. 4:3–4). A popular current reconstruction of the circumstances in which 1 Peter was written goes back to the ground-breaking work of Elliott (1981). He has taken the references in 1:1 and elsewhere to Peter's audience as 'strangers', 'aliens', and 'scattered' as literal terms suggesting religious and economic refugees in the first-century world. But given Peter's propensity in this epistle for redefining standard Jewish terminology in 'spiritualized' Christian language and given the broad semantic range of the terms themselves, it is doubtful whether we can limit these words to their purely literal interpretations.[22] Peter also suggests in his first letter that these Christians have found themselves less socially acceptable due to their recently acquired faith in Jesus, which implies that they were originally better integrated and perhaps reasonably prosperous members of their communities (Achtemeier 1996: 56).

The specific passages in 1 Peter dealing with wealth and poverty seem to corroborate these conclusions. In 3:3–4, wives, even those of unbelieving husbands, are told that their beauty 'should not come from outward adornment, such as braided hair and the wearing of gold jewellery and fine clothes. Instead, it should be that of your inner self, the unfading beauty of a gentle and quiet spirit, which is of great worth in God's sight.' As with the instructions to women in 1 Timothy 2:9, these commands fit most naturally into a context of at least a handful of

---

[21] Attridge (1989: 388) notes that 'this particular term [the love of money] appears only in the later stages of early Christian literature, when there were more Christians from comfortable social strata'. Among early post-New Testament sources, cf. Didache 15.1, and Polycarp, To the Philippians 5.2. Shepherd of Hermas, Vision 3.9.6, warns against 'rejoicing' in one's wealth.

[22] Cf. esp. the combination of 'aliens' and 'strangers' in 2:11 in a context of abstaining from sinful desires, and note the use of 'as' to indicate the presence of a metaphor in this passage. Contra Elliott, see esp. Chin (1991).

quite well-to-do women who are dressing lavishly and ostentatiously. Michaels (1988: 161) notes that *polytelēs* ('of great worth') means 'extravagant' and was often used in Hellenistic critiques of outward wealth. Peter is not forbidding such dress altogether, but is stressing that external adornment should not be the source of a woman's beauty (Grudem 1988: 140). But to the extent that obvious differences in clothing exacerbated class distinctions, Peter would undoubtedly want the women to dress much more simply. This would also free up their money for better use in the service of God's kingdom (*cf.* Davids 1990: 117–118).

Passages like 2:14–15 and 3:13–17 again speak of the need for Christians to do good in the public arena, and they remind us of the statements in Romans 13:3–4 about the role of government in rewarding those who do good but punishing those who do wrong. To the extent that benefaction may be one primary example of doing good in these contexts (Winter 1994: 11–40), the Christian responsibility to 'seek the welfare of the city' is reinforced. Language familiar from our survey of the Pastoral Epistles is echoed in 1 Peter 5:2, as the elders or overseers of Peter's churches are commanded to serve in a way that shows them to be not 'greedy for money'. The word here is *aischrokerdōs*, which more literally means '[seeking] foolish gain'. Peter is not thinking explicitly of any illegal use of money but of that which is inappropriate or counter-productive from a Christian perspective.[23] At the very least, this implies that Christian leaders should not be motivated to minister by the thought of remuneration or any particular level of payment. Peter's words may also imply that these elders were in charge of a community treasury of funds to be disbursed to the needy, much as we have seen in earlier stages of the New Testament (Goppelt 1993: 346), and therefore should scrupulously ensure that all of that money does indeed go to those who are in genuine need.

## 2 Peter and Jude

The literary relationship between these two letters continues to be debated, but it is frequently agreed that Jude is the earlier epistle, with 2 Peter depending on it (J. Knight 1995: 20–22). At any rate, both letters give brief references to false teachers who, in addition to idolatry and sexual immorality, have serious problems with material possessions or the desire for them. Peter's second epistle (2:3) predicts that these false teachers 'in their greed' will 'exploit you with stories they have made

---

[23] Davids (1990: 179, n. 15) describes the use as 'illegitimate'.

up'. And again 2 Peter 2:14 combines references to sexual and economic sins: 'With eyes full of adultery, they never stop sinning; they seduce the unstable; they are experts in greed – an accursed brood!' Here they are likened to the people seduced by Balaam, a reference to the narrative of Numbers. Balaam was originally offered money by Balak to curse Israel. Although he resisted this temptation, it was only as a result of supernatural intervention (Num. 22 – 24), and the subsequent Moabite seduction of Israel to idolatry and immorality (Num. 25) is later ascribed in part to Balaam himself (31:16). In context, then, 2 Peter 2:14–15 unpacks verse 3 by describing how the hearts of these false teachers were, literally, 'well trained in covetousness'. We know little about the actual philosophy or sectarian identification of these false teachers, although Neyrey (1993) has recently made out a plausible case for taking them as Epicurean. Jude 11 similarly alludes to false teachers who have 'rushed for profit into Balaam's error'. But Bauckham's summary comments (1983: 243) could be applied widely to a variety of those masquerading as God's people in ancient and modern times alike: 'In their greed they will exploit you with fabricated arguments' implies 'that the false teachers make a good financial profit out of their followers, who are taken in by their teaching and contribute to their support'.

## The Gospel of John

Finally, we come to the five New Testament books ascribed to the apostle John. Whether or not the direct product of the apostle, there is widespread agreement that these documents reflect Christianity at the end of the first century in and around Ephesus, as traditionally affirmed by the Church Fathers. Again, a healthy cross-section of socio-economic backgrounds may be posited among the addressees of the Johannine literature, who are suffering divisions from within and persecutions from without.[24] The Fourth Gospel adds only a little to the themes we have already examined in detail in the Synoptics. Jesus' first miracle, turning water into wine at Cana, replenishes an astonishing quantity of beverage to enable the feast-goers to continue celebrating (John 2:1–11). Again it is clear that Jesus is no ascetic, and that he is not against the occasional elaborate feast. But the point of the miracle does not lie in this direction. Rather, like the parable of new wine in new wineskins, the miracle at Cana highlights the joy of the presence of

---

[24] Perhaps the best-known and most influential contemporary reconstruction of these circumstances is that of Brown (1979). Many of the necessary modifications and nuancing of his portrait have been made recently in Witherington (1995b: 27–41).

the new age in Jesus' ministry (see Blomberg 1986).[25] The account of the temple cleansing in 2:13–22 may or may not reflect the same episode as the 'synoptic clearing' at the end of Jesus' life (for debates for and against, see Blomberg 1987). But in this context, John's version does focus somewhat more on the commercial corruption of the sellers and money-changers in the temple courts (see esp. 2:16). Nevertheless, again John's climactic emphasis is a Christological one, with his unparalleled reference to Jesus' statement about his ability to rebuild the temple that was his body (2:19–22; *cf.* further Mathews 1988).

Perhaps the most significant episode unique to John's Gospel and relevant to our theme is the account of Jesus and the Samaritan woman in 4:1–42. As in so many stories in the Synoptics, Jesus clearly affirms an individual here who is among the most outcast of her society. She has 'three strikes' against her: she is a Samaritan, a woman and of disreputable marital background (although the text stops short of allowing us to infer with confidence that she was the one at fault for the last of these three factors).[26] 'The author, then, has created a stereotype of the ultimate *outsider* and quintessential deviant, only to have the stereotype broken, but basically in the direction of the inclusivity of *outsiders* and *deviants*' (Neyrey 1994: 89). Coming on the heels of the equally lengthy dialogue between Jesus and Nicodemus in 3:1–21, the remarkably positive interchange between the Samaritan woman and Christ stands out in sharp contrast to the increasing confusion of Nicodemus in the earlier text. Not only is Jesus successfully reaching the triply outcast, but the upstanding, privileged, Jewish male leader fails to understand and is rejected (see further Blomberg 1995; *contra* Munro 1995).

The only miracle found in all four Gospels is the feeding of the five thousand (John 6:1–15), and the points that attached to our previous discussion of that miracle may be carried over here. Jesus certainly demonstrates compassion for the physically needy and hungry. But John more than any of the Synoptics demonstrates the primary Christological intent of the miracle by appending Jesus' subsequent 'Bread of Life' discourse in the Capernaum synagogue (6:25–29).[27] The same kind of comments apply to a uniquely Johannine miracle like the healing of the

[25] Vandana (1991) offers a balanced, contextualized view of God's 'extravaganza' at both physical and spiritual levels in the miracle story.

[26] See esp. Schneiders (1991: 180–199). *Cf.* further Blomberg (1995: 12–13), and the other literature there cited.

[27] Karris (1990: 30–31), however, thinks that the unique phraseology of Jesus' 'testing' of Philip in 6:5–7 contrasts 'the business manager's answer with "trust" in Jesus'.

blind beggar in John 9:1–12. Obviously, Jesus shows compassion for a man highly marginalized from birth (9:1). But the subsequent debate about Jesus' identity (9:13–41) overshadows the miracle. Literal blindness and sight become the springboard for focusing more emphatically on spiritual blindness and sight.[28] We have also already dealt with Jesus' anointing at Bethany, of which John's version (12:1–8) makes somewhat more explicit Judas' role as the keeper of the disciples' common treasury and also the one who apparently often stole from that bag (John 12:6). John directly declares that Judas did not care for the poor (12:6), making his objection to Mary's 'waste' (12:5) a hypocritical sham. On Judas' seeming indignation at Mary's act (12:5), Carson (1991: 429) comments, 'If self-righteous piety sometimes snuffs out genuine compassion, it must also be admitted, with shame, that social activism, even that which meets real needs, sometimes masks a spirit that knows nothing of worship and adoration.' John 13:29 confirms that 'Judas had charge of the money.' The fact that some thought he might be leaving the upper room on this last night of Jesus' life 'to give something to the poor' shows that even Jesus and his itinerant troupe in their self-imposed simple lifestyle found ways to give some of their resources as alms for those in even greater need. It also shows that at this stage Judas had been successful in hiding his hypocrisy from his fellow disciples.

Ironically, the one who dies in utter agony via an execution otherwise reserved for criminals or slaves receives a rich man's burial. Joseph of Arimathea and Nicodemus request the body in order to place it in Joseph's grave. An unused tomb owned by a wealthy man would have been both spacious and a great honour. In addition, the amount of spices used for the embalming of the corpse is paralleled elsewhere in antiquity only in royal burials, and it suggests that Jesus is being laid to rest in a fashion fit for a king (19:38–42; cf. further Witherington 1995b: 312). After his resurrection, Jesus appears to his disciples in the context of providing a miraculous catch of 153 fish (John 21:1–14). Clearly, he supplies material resources for them in abundance, but his primary emphasis in the miracle is to hark back to the initial catch of fish which accompanied his original call of several of his followers (Luke 5:1–11). Now he is 'recalling' them, most notably Peter, who needs a three-fold reinstatement after his three-fold denial just days earlier (John 21:15–19; cf. Talbert 1992: 261).

---

[28] Karris (1990: 48) focuses on the issue of the man's marginalization as a corrective to past, purely spiritual treatments, but he seems to swing the pendulum too far in the opposite direction.

All of this material in John, however, scarcely adds up to a major theme or even a consistent motif, but it does remind us of the balanced portrait of Jesus clearly perceivable from the Synoptics. He does not oppose wealth, even its occasional lavish use in the service of ordinary human needs and ceremonies. But he is concerned to meet the needs of others, materially and spiritually, and is aware of the grave threat of riches to prevent his followers from ministering in this holistic fashion.

## The epistles of John

Issues of material possessions are no more dominant in the epistles of John than in his Gospel, but the three major references which do appear prove quite significant. In 1 John 2:15–17, John warns against loving the 'world' – used here to mean the fallen world order – or anything in it, lest the love of the Father not be in such a person (2:15). Verse 16 then epitomizes the three major categories of temptations to sin that humans experience: 'the cravings of sinful people, the lust of their eyes and the boasting of what they have and do' (cf. New Living Translation: 'the lust for physical pleasure, the lust for everything we see, and pride in our possessions'). The more familiar and literal Greek, 'lust of the flesh, lust of the eyes and pride of life', forms yet a third way of phrasing these striking summaries of the three major kinds of temptations that Adam and Eve, as well as Jesus himself, faced (cf. Gen. 3:6 with Matt. 4:1–11 and par.). There is nothing inherently evil in flesh, eyes or life; 'they become evil and objectionable only when they excite evil impulses in human beings' (Schnackenburg 1992: 121). The 'lust of the flesh' can lead particularly to sexual sin; the 'lust of the eyes' was regularly associated with covetousness; and the 'pride of life' focuses particularly on income, property or wealth. Together these three seductions depict the situation of a person 'having a self-sufficiency to survive but completely incapable of moving toward heaven and God' (Brown 1982: 326).

In addition to avoiding being seduced by the possessions of this world which can only pass away (1 John 2:17), 3:17–18 focuses the problem more pointedly: 'If anyone of you has material possessions and sees a brother or sister in need but has no pity on them, how can the love of God be in you? Dear children, let us not love with words or tongue but with actions and in truth.' One is reminded of both the contents and form of James 2:14–17. The answer to the rhetorical question is clearly that the love of God cannot be in a person who has the ability to help and is aware of desperate human need, particularly within the Christian community, but refuses to act in any way whatsoever. Professions of faith from such a person, however earnest, prove utterly vacuous. Here it is clear, too, that 'John is not saying that the wealthy alone are required to share their possessions with others' but that '*every* Christian who is in a position to help others materially is required' to do so (Smalley 1984: 196). Or as Burge (1996: 169) phrases it, 'One measure of love is the degree to which people blessed with material wealth distribute that wealth within the community.' But the point is that 'someone with wealth' does not mean simply a rich person but someone with *any* surplus possessions whatever.

Finally, 3 John 5–8 commends Gaius for his hospitality towards itinerant Christian missionaries. This little glimpse into early Christian travel reminds us of a commonplace in the Greco-Roman world more generally: the paucity of adequate public facilities to house travellers and the need to rely on friends, or those whom friends recommended, for overnight accommodation.[29] In fact, until quite recently, Christian ministers, often supplied with church-owned parsonages, have been expected to extend hospitality to Christian guests visiting their communities. Here is one significant way to apply the principle of 1 John 3:17–18. In the original context of 3 John, the hospitality commended would have included some measure of financial assistance and support for the missionaries. 'Support "worthy of God" and supplies for the journey are the way those who cannot literally follow Jesus' missionary command make their contribution' (Schnackenburg 1992: 296). What is more, 'It was a signal feature of Gaius' hospitality that he was prepared to extend it to people who were otherwise unknown to him, and had no claims on him except that they formed part of the company of those who like him had come to know the truth (*cf.* 2 Jn. 1)' (I. H. Marshall 1978a: 85).[30]

## The Revelation

Finally, we come to the book of Revelation. Kraybill's detailed study (1996) shows how economic hardship was inextricably intertwined with any late first-century Christian attempt to resist the idolatrous influences of the Roman empire. To the extent that the Apocalypse draws on conditions of John's day in the mid-90s under Domitianic persecution in describing end-time horrors,[31] the economic implications

---

[29] Koenig's survey (1985) offers important background and notes the pervasiveness of the theme of hospitality elsewhere in the New Testament.

[30] On the sociology of ancient hospitality more generally, see esp. Malina (1986).

[31] This traditional date and provenance have been increasingly questioned by modern scholars, with AD 68 or 69, just after Nero's death, emerging as the next mostly likely

for the would-be 'overcomer' (a favourite word of John's for the faithful Christian) prove inescapable. In the letters to the seven churches, Smyrna and Laodicea stand in sharp contrast. Smyrna is materially poor yet spiritually rich (2:9), whereas Laodicea had acquired much wealth and thought its needs were met. Yet from a spiritual perspective the community was wretched, pitiful and poor (3:17). Asia Minor, in general, was one of the wealthier parts of the empire at the end of the first century, and the emerging mercantile class was especially privileged in not having to pay tax on goods sent to Rome or used for religious purposes. But almost all shippers and traders were required to be members of one of the civic guilds, which included a religious dimension that most Christians believed was idolatrous or blasphemous (deSilva 1992: 291). John's Christians were called on to withdraw from syncretistic influences, despite the high economic price, in order that they might 'buy' from Jesus true spiritual 'gold refined in the fire', so that they could become rich from a spiritual perspective (3:18).

Economic imagery reappears in the first set of judgments, known as the seven seals (6:1–17). The famine described by the third seal creates inflationary prices so that an entire day's wage is needed to buy a quart of wheat or three quarts of barley, staples of any family's diet. Ironically, oil and wine, at times more luxury items, were not damaged (6:6). The picture is one of the rich retaining adequate resources to fuel their luxurious lifestyles while the poor scraped by, spending all of their money on basic foodstuffs. The background for this imagery may well be Domitian's edict in AD 92 ordering that the vineyards in all of the provinces be halved, 'but the landed aristocracy – especially in Asia – raised such a protest that Domitian was forced to rescind his edict. The result was rising prices for grain and increased famine among the populace' (González & González 1997: 49; cf. Hemer 1986: 158–159). In 6:15 all four major categories of the social order of the Roman Empire are listed – kings and emperors, the other small percentage of well-to-do and powerful, the remaining free-persons and freed slaves, and those who are still slaves. But such socio-economic distinctions will prove utterly meaningless when God unleashes his judgments on the world. All will try to hide among caves and the rocks of the mountains, preferring to be destroyed by an avalanche so that they might not endure 'the wrath of the Lamb' (Rev. 6:15–16).

---

possibility. See, e.g., Smalley (1994: 40–49). But a date in the time of Domitian still seems best. See, e.g., Collins (1984: 54–83). L. Thompson (1990) accepts this date but warns against overestimating the extent of *imperial* persecution or economic 'crisis'.

The enigmatic mark of the beast (Rev. 13:16–18) also contains economic implications. The Antichrist will force anyone who wishes to buy or sell to receive some kind of mark 'on their right hands or on their foreheads'. This imagery probably reflects the ubiquity of the imperial cults at the end of the first century, not least in Asia. Although no exact parallels to this practice have emerged, the mark could well have referred to an idolatrous imperial image on a coin or have corresponded in function to stamps on deeds of sale from the first-century world (Kraybill 1996: 138–139).[32] At any rate, the theme of Christian self-sufficiency (probably to be understood more communally than individually) which has emerged here and there throughout the New Testament will come especially to the fore in such an end-time context if it is impossible for Christians to participate in the economics of the unregenerate marketplace.

Most dramatically of all, the laments for a blasphemous worldwide empire which persecutes Christians just before Jesus' return (Rev. 17 – 18) has a horrifying economic dimension to it as well. Here again idolatrous religion and excessive luxury are clearly combined. Chapter 18 focuses primarily on the latter and describes those who lament the loss of all their affluence (18:3, 7 and 11–24). The list of all the cargoes which no-one any longer buys reads like a bill of sale for the vast trade in luxury items that the elite in Rome benefited from at the expense of the subjugated peoples throughout their empire (18:11–13; see esp. Bauckham 1991). But the list ends with the staples of olive oil, flour and wheat, and it strikingly appends a reference to 'slaves – human beings!' (literally, 'bodies and souls of people'), a clear allusion to the slave trade. And all of these cargoes find Old Testament parallels, particularly in Ezekiel 27, in the context of prophecies against Tyre. It is not trade *per se*, but commerce in the service of idolatry that is condemned (*cf.* esp. Provan 1996). As the woes of Revelation 18 continue, not only has everything rich and splendid vanished, 'never to be recovered' (18:14), but even the ordinary joys of daily life – music, craftsmanship, the preparation of food, light, and the joy of weddings – have all disappeared (18:21–23). What went wrong? John's answer outlines the emergence of an unholy alliance of a powerful political empire with blasphemous, idolatrous religion, creating huge disparities between the 'haves' and the 'have-nots'. To the extent that Christians were tempted to engage in the mercantilism that would have caught

---

[32] Judge (1991: 160) suspects that the first readers would have thought of 'those who entered the market of Ephesus having first to make their sacrifice, and then receiving their mark in ink on wrist or forehead, just as in Ezekiel 9:2–6'.

them up in this combination of sins, John warns them in no uncertain terms to separate themselves and come out from the evil empire (see esp. 18:4).

Numerous popular works attempting to equate current events with the signs of the end-times have tried to identify this evil empire. A survey of the history of Christian speculation about the Antichrist more generally (McGinn 1994) should warn anyone against such equations, given the 100% failure rate of previous attempts. It is interesting, however, to note that popular recent candidates, such as the former Soviet Union, Saddam Hussein's Iraq or even the European Union, have never wielded the commercial clout of North America, with its many multi-national corporations and its politics of national interest that lead to the impoverishment of countless millions around the world with scarcely a tear shed.[33] Given the growing atheism and paganism of the supposedly once Christian West, given the downfall of communism and the resurgence of worldwide capitalism, and given the increasing exclusion of Christians and Christian morality from the public arena, one need look no further afield than the prevailing mind-set and world-view of most of the public powers in the United States to find frightening contemporary equivalents to the evil empire of Revelation 17 – 18.[34]

Ironically, the very economic paradise that so many are trying to create in our modern West apart from the Christian world-view is precisely what the Bible concludes by offering people in an unlimited and eternal context, but always on God's terms (Rev. 21 – 22). Revelation, and thus Scripture in its entirety, concludes not with the pictures of disembodied immortality and an ethereal heaven, which seem to be the concepts of so many moderns, including not a few in our churches. Rather, the Apocalypse climaxes with the very earthy picture of a perfectly recreated community of God's people living in a new heavens and a new earth, replete with all the wealth of the nations and all the luxuries that anyone could ever imagine (21:10–21, 24, 26). But these will be available only for those who have persevered and remained faithful to Christ and who have demonstrated their faithfulness through proper stewardship and attitudes towards wealth in this life, even when

[33] Rowland (1993: 140) stresses: 'reading the signs of the times and seeking to understand the political dimension of Christian mission is not to be neglected because of its near impossibility'. But it 'will demand a wider perspective for those biblical themes like reconciliation, justice and peace than the narrowly individualistic or ecclesiastical focus that Christians have so often given them'.

[34] Julia Esquivel's powerful poem 'Thanksgiving Day in the United States' (1982: 78–91) crystallizes the issues dramatically. More prosaically, cf. Harrington (1993: 184).

it has led to inconvenience, persecution or even martyrdom. Or as deSilva (1992: 296) concludes,

> The churches cannot be allowed to believe the *societas'* definition of what constitutes desirable wealth. Only if they accept John's attribution of true wealth to the faithful who suffer economic hardships and social ostracism for the sake of the 'testimony of Jesus' will the churches survive the economic pressures that will rise along with the political pressures in the decades to come.

They must create alternative models of *communitas* and demonstrate to the watching world how different is the attitude of redeemed people toward the wealth that cannot survive the end of this age.

## Summary and conclusions

When one focuses on the distinctives of the four evangelists with respect to material possessions, Mark and John have the least to contribute – Mark because he simply offers a fair cross-section of Jesus' teaching and behaviour common to the synoptic tradition more generally, and John because it is not a major theme for him. The fourth evangelist is more concerned with the 'spiritual' and Christological dimensions of the gospel. Matthew shows some noticeable interest in 'money matters', but Luke is the predominant theologian of social concern among the evangelists.[35] Yet a comparison of Luke with Acts and of the early part of Acts with the later part of that same book, as well as a comparison between previous tradition and Lukan redaction more generally, suggests that Luke wants to address well-to-do Christians about their need to be generous to the poor, particularly within the church. His is by no means a wholly impoverished community, and his message is not one of idealizing the poor but rather of encouraging his audience to help alleviate their plight. None of the remaining non-Pauline epistles (Hebrews, 1 and 2 Peter, 1, 2 and 3 John, and Jude) is preoccupied with the theme of material possessions, yet each makes passing references to reinforce principles we have seen

---

[35] 'There is no repentance in Luke that does not practice sympathy toward the poor and outcast, no welcoming the saving act of God in Jesus Christ that does not do justice and kindness, no waiting for his return that does not expect and anticipate God's vindication of the humble poor, no participation in his community that does not give alms or share one's goods or practice hospitality' (Verhey 1984: 95).

earlier. Economic issues come particularly to the fore again, however, with the closing piece of canonical literature, the book of Revelation. As previewed in the days of Domitian, God's people must be prepared in the future for situations of economic persecution, climaxed in the hostility of an idolatrous but extremely affluent end-time 'empire'. Those who remain faithful and resist its seduction can look forward to a glorious millennium and then to a new universe, both of which will be filled with purified 'earthly delights'.

## Chapter Eight

# Summary, conclusions and applications

This chapter will briefly rehearse the major findings of this study, draw some additional conclusions about commonalities among the biblical corpora and introduce various possibilities for contemporary application in a 'post-Christian' world on the threshold of a new millennium.

## Summary

Any attempt to summarize the dominant emphases in any large swathe of biblical material inevitably oversimplifies. So, too, our comments here do not adequately encompass the wealth of detail discussed above. Still, it is useful to note some pervasive impressions that remain. In the historical portions of the Pentateuch, the major contribution to our theme was the goodness of wealth and God's desire to bless his people with material possessions, especially the land of Canaan and its bounty, through which they could in turn bless all the peoples of the earth. The legal portions of these same books prepared the Israelites so that they could obey God and thereby enjoy his blessings. But the major features of the Law with respect to material resources were the restrictions it placed on the use and accumulation of property, precisely so that people would remember that God owns it all and wants all people to be able to enjoy some of it. The remaining historical books of the Old Testament narrate the fluctuating cycles of Israelite obedience and disobedience to God's laws and the consequences that followed from their behaviour.

With the rise of the monarchy, whatever measure of 'freedom and justice for all' that may have been achieved in previous generations was increasingly eroded. The gaps between the 'haves' and 'have-nots' grew, and fewer and fewer people fell into the former category. Wealth was increasingly concentrated in the hands of royalty and their clientele, including a handful of rich landowners who gobbled up larger portions of the countryside. It is difficult to determine exactly to what extent this spread within Old Testament times, but intertestamental developments would greatly exacerbate the inequities of property ownership. Not surprisingly, such economic injustice is a major theme of the Prophets and a significant part of the rationale for exile and lack of full post-exilic restoration or prolonged independence. Israel's economic sins were never unrelated, however, to their idolatry; worshipping false gods led to selfish attitudes with respect to money.

The wisdom and poetry of the Old Testament held in a certain tension two contrasting themes: wealth as a reward for faithfulness and industry, along with warnings against the wicked rich and ill-gotten gain. Job and Ecclesiastes, in particular, protested against human claims to have achieved any consistent justice in this life. These two books, along with the Psalms and Daniel, would sow the seeds for a doctrine that would become clearer in the intertestamental period – judgment day and a life to come are the only true and equitable solutions to this world's injustice. Jewish, Greek and Roman perspectives in the centuries immediately preceding the New Testament era would otherwise exhibit an almost bewildering diversity of views. Yet overall, Jewish thought valued the poor and stressed God's care for their plight more than did any Greco-Roman ideologies. Of the Apocrypha and Pseudepigrapha, only Sirach would make material possessions a dominant theme, and it would reflect the same diversity of perspectives as its canonical predecessor of the same genre, the book of Proverbs. The Essenes at Qumran cultivated a monastic and communal ideal, while maintaining a certain amount of private property.

The New Testament carried forward the major principles of the Old Testament and intertestamental Judaism with one conspicuous omission: never was material wealth promised as a guaranteed reward for either spiritual obedience or simple hard work. This omission flows directly from the fact that the people of God are no longer defined as one ethnic group living in one divinely granted piece of geography. This does not mean that Old Testament promises are entirely spiritualized. God's people from both Old and New Testament ages will one day enjoy all the literal blessings of the land, extended to encompass the entire earth and eventually a redeemed cosmos. But in this age, before the coming of Christ, no predictions can be made as to the level of material prosperity God will grant any individual believer. All Christians, however, should have access to houses and fields 'one hundred times as much in this present age', thanks to the generosity of Christians who share with each other (recall Mark 10:29–30).

Thus, the Bible never views material poverty as good. God wills his people, the church, to distribute their wealth more equitably. Jesus identifies God and mammon as rival masters; ultimately a person can serve only one of them. The kingdom of God contains a noticeable financial component, centred around almsgiving. Jesus and his disciples voluntarily limited their incomes for the sake of ministry, and the early church in Acts took their principle of a common purse and created the temporary mechanism of communal sharing in Jerusalem that modelled more timeless principles of concern for the poor. Within the book of Acts itself these principles would later lead to the more ongoing institutions of a 'deacons' fund' for the local poor and to collections for needy believers outside of one's immediate community.

At first glance, James and Paul seem as different as night and day, not least with respect to 'poverty and riches'. The terms themselves are rare in Paul, while denunciation of the sins of the unjust rich occupies a major portion of James' teaching. But a more careful survey of Paul's epistles discloses that money matters form an important part of his concerns as well. Paul is particularly eager to undermine conventional Hellenistic expectations of reciprocity and standard patron–client relationships. Instead, all Christians should become benefactors, however modestly. The collection for the poor in Jerusalem gives Paul the opportunity to enunciate these and related principles in considerable detail (esp. in 2 Cor. 8 – 9).

The writings of Paul and Luke are the best places to turn to see a growing middle-class and even upper-class minority of Christians in the emerging church. Neither writer calls upon well-off believers to change places with the poor; they are merely to give from their surplus, but also to be honest in acknowledging how much *is* surplus. The remaining New Testament epistles and the Gospel of John add no distinctively new motifs. but repeat previously noted ones, largely in passing. The book of Revelation, however, closes the canon by pointing out extreme instances in which the fallen world-order may be so corrupt that faithful discipleship will require a sectarian kind of separation from the rest of humanity's economic systems and practices.

## Additional conclusions

It is important for biblical theology to capture both the diversity and the unity of the scriptural witness on any given theme. The previous section has highlighted some of the distinctives of the various biblical corpora with respect to material possessions; now we must note some unifying motifs (for both method and content, *cf.* Stackhouse 1987).

1. *Material possessions are a good gift from God meant for his people to enjoy.* This is made plain from God's creation of the material

world as good, from his desire that all have access to at least a modicum of property, and from the fact that material possessions within God's covenant with Israel are a blessing for their obedience. Throughout the Old Testament, Job, Abraham, David, Solomon and a variety of other figures demonstrate that riches and godliness can coexist, at least for a time. The proverbial literature offers riches as a reward for wholesome work. The New Testament likewise recognizes an increasing number of well-to-do Christians throughout the early history of Christianity who host churches in their homes, make business trips and fund itinerant ministers (including Jesus and his original troupe). The community of disciples shares its material resources with one another, not so that all will be equally impoverished, but so that there will be 'no needy persons among them' (Acts 4:34). Even in the harshest of scenarios, the very luxuries that can lead to the demonic (Rev. 17 – 18) will be available for all of God's redeemed people in a very material age to come (Rev. 21 – 22).

2. *Material possessions are simultaneously one of the primary means of turning human hearts away from God.* Adam and Eve coveted the attractive but forbidden fruit of the garden, and everything was corrupted or cursed quickly thereafter. Possession of, or desire for, too many material goods leads to rejection of God, interpersonal hostility and exploitation or neglect of the poor. Thus most of the property laws of the Torah set limits on the amounts to be accumulated. The enormous wealth of the monarchy fuelled social injustice and prophetic critique. And the Prophets and Poets alike warned repeatedly of the many wicked rich. For Jesus, mammon was God's rival. In the undisputed Pauline epistles, it came with strings attached and often hindered ministry. The Pastorals declared, 'The love of money is the root of all kinds of evil' (1 Tim. 6:10). In James's community rich unbelievers judicially murdered the poor Christians, while in Revelation global economics became so skewed as to reflect the direct activity of the demonic. Throughout the New Testament the wealthy included the Jewish and Roman leaders who crucified Jesus, and early Christian leaders who divided the church, wanted to abolish gender roles, and engaged in sexual immorality and spiritual apostasy.

3. *A necessary sign of a life in the process of being redeemed is that of transformation in the area of stewardship.* Ultimately, one's entire life should be dedicated to God, but a particularly telling area for determining one's religious commitment involves one's finances. The wealthy but godly patriarchs and kings of the Old Testament are, without exception, said to have shared generously with the poor and

needy. Old Testament laws mandated tithes and taxes to support 'full-time religious workers' as well as to aid the otherwise destitute. One of the most frequent refrains of Torah, Psalms and Prophets is God's concern for the 'widow, fatherless, alien and poor', a concern which should lead his people ruthlessly to avoid every form of exploitation and to seek ways to meet the genuine needs of the marginalized and to address the causes of their misery. In the New Testament, Luke and Paul enjoin generous almsgiving, while Jesus simply presupposes the practice, most notably in the Sermon on the Mount (Matt. 6:1–4). James and John agree that someone who is aware of his Christian brothers' or sisters' material needs, is in a position to help, and fails utterly to do anything, cannot be saved (Jas. 2:14–17; 1 John 3:17–18). Peter and Paul are particularly consistent in their challenges to the Greco-Roman system of tit-for-tat reciprocity in the giving and receiving of gifts. Both build on Jesus' own command rooted in Old Testament jubilary theology to lend (or give), 'without expecting to get anything back' (Luke 6:35).

4. *There are certain extremes of wealth and poverty which are in and of themselves intolerable.* These extremes cannot be quantified, and they will vary widely under different economic systems and depend on personal attitudes. But sooner or later every economic system leads to certain people accumulating material possessions above and beyond what they can possibly need or even use just for themselves. It is one thing to generate income which is then channelled into kingdom purposes (Luke 16:9; 19:11–27); it is quite another to accumulate and hoard resources which are likely to be destroyed or disappear before being put to good use (Luke 16:19–31; Jas. 5:1–6). In the latter case, by definition, such a surplus prevents others from having a better opportunity for a reasonably decent standard of living. Such hoarding or accumulation is sin, and if left unchecked proves damning (Luke 12:13–21; 16:19–31).

A particularly clear example of the principle of moderation comes with God's provision of manna for the Israelites in the wilderness (Exod. 16:18), an episode cited by Paul as he encouraged the Corinthians to greater generosity in their giving (2 Cor. 8:15). The principle of moderation lies behind the redistribution of property in sabbatical and Jubilee years and behind the prophetic critique of life under the monarchy and aristocracy of Israel. Its reduction of disparity between 'haves' and 'have-nots' variously inspired Qumran, early Christian communalism in Acts, and ongoing collections for the poor throughout the New Testament. The principle of moderation explains

Jesus' and Paul's concerns to live simply, particularly while engaged in ministry, so as to afford no unnecessary cause for bringing the gospel into disrepute. And it summarizes a large swathe of wisdom literature, particularly as epitomized in Proverbs 30:8: 'Give me neither poverty nor riches.'

5. Above all, *the Bible's teaching about material possessions is inextricably intertwined with more 'spiritual' matters.* No ungodly poor people are ever exalted as models for emulation. No godly rich people, who are generous and compassionate in the use of their wealth, are ever condemned. But in a remarkable number of instances throughout history, poverty and piety have been found hand in hand, as have wealth and godlessness. There is no inherent connection between the items in either pair, just recurring trends. The rich are not necessarily wicked, but frequently surplus goods have led people to imagine that their material resources can secure their futures so that they ignore God, from whom alone comes any true security. That was certainly a recurring trend in ancient Israel. Conversely, when the Jews found themselves in desperate circumstances, they more often than not turned back to God. It has not always been so in the history of humanity, but it frequently has been.

None of these observations is intended to idealize poverty; if the poor turn to God, the church is responsible to help them improve their material lot. Christians ought to care in some way for all the needy of the world, but they have a particular obligation to care for their own. The substantial majority of the passages we have surveyed deal with the Israelites' relationships with fellow Israelites or with Christians ministering to the needs of brothers or sisters in the Lord. Still, the recurring obligation of Israel to the alien in the Old Testament, God's judgment against the 'nations' for their mistreatment of the poor, and the distinctively Christian commands to the church in the New Testament to love its enemies all remind us that our obligation does not stop with those who are our spiritual kin. In short, we dare not elevate a theology of material possessions to as central a role in Scripture as salvation itself. God's foremost desire for his fallen world is reconciliation: humans reconciled first of all to God, then to each other and ultimately to the entire cosmos. Thus God is in the process of fashioning what the Bible regularly calls a new creation. But biblical salvation is always holistic – involving body and soul, material and spiritual dimensions. And a major component of the material dimension is transformation in the way God's people utilize 'mammon' – material possessions. To the extent that the kingdom has been inaugurated from the cross of Christ onward, Christians individually and corporately are called to model that transformation, however imperfectly, as a foretaste of the perfect redemption that must ultimately await the age to come.

## Applications

A number of applications to contemporary Christian living have been scattered throughout previous chapters already. Space prohibits all but a cursory treatment of these and additional themes here. One area of application that lies almost entirely outside of our scope is the appropriate role of Christian involvement in the state or in international systems of economics. We have already commented on the fact that the New Testament does not for the most part directly encourage structural change to remedy structural evil (see above, p. 159).[1] So here I want to focus primarily on the levels of individual and ecclesiastical action. We may begin by reviewing and applying the five summarizing themes of the previous section.

First, if wealth is an inherent good, Christians should try to gain it. If some of us succeed more than the majority, our understanding of it as God's gift for all will lead us to want to share with the needy, particularly those who are largely victims of circumstances outside their control. Second, if wealth is seductive, giving away some of our surplus is a good strategy for resisting the temptation to overvalue it. Third, if stewardship is a sign of a redeemed life, then Christians will, by their new natures, want to give. Over time, compassionate and generous use of their resources will become an integral part of their Christian lives. Fourth, if certain extremes of wealth and poverty are inherently intolerable, those of us with excess income (*i.e.*, most readers of this book!) will work hard to help at least a few of the desperately needy in our world. Fifth, if holistic salvation represents the ultimate good God wants all to receive, then our charitable giving should be directed to individuals, churches or organizations who minister holistically, caring for people's bodies as well as their souls, addressing their physical as well as their spiritual circumstances.[2]

There is a danger of speaking too autobiographically in a context such as this, but lest my own motives be misinterpreted, or lest people simply wonder what kind of lifestyle I myself lead, I think it is important to

---

[1] In this respect, Schneider (1994) seems more on target than R. Sider (1997).

[2] *Cf.* Murchie (1978: 343): 'From the NT perspective, Christians may serve only as conduits by which God's gracious material provision is equitably distributed to the world.'

share at least a few of my personal circumstances. In a culture that has been taught not to speak much, particularly in church, about personal finances, we need leaders who humbly but forthrightly explain and model biblical values.

I was challenged early in my adult life by two different pastors, one in the US and one in the UK, who each gave 25% of their total income back to the Lord's work and let that fact be known, not in any arrogant way, but simply to encourage others that it could be done. While I have never followed Sider's actual charts or tables, I have become convinced that the concept of a graduated tithe is both biblical and foundational for contemporary Christian stewardship (R. Sider 1997: 193–196). When we were first married more than eighteen years ago, my wife and I committed to begin with a tithe, based on the very modest income we had while I was a graduate student, and then to increase that percentage if God increased his annual provisions for us. Over the years God has blessed us richly and the percentage of our giving has grown. On our last income-tax returns, we reported in the spring of 1998 our highest combined family income ever (a combination of my salary as a seminary professor, income from my wife's half-time church position, and miscellaneous royalties, interests and dividends). Our overall total put us $4,000 below the average household income for our affluent suburban community. Nevertheless, we were able to give over 30% of our income to our church and to para-church organizations and individuals involved in Christian ministry. This was our fifth consecutive year of topping 30% percent, following the principle of the graduated tithe.

At the same time, I must quickly confess that we live in a large, comfortable, suburban home. It is true that our neighbours, for the most part, are working class or retired, rather than professional, and that our suburb is surrounded by considerably more affluent ones, to which most of my once professional neighbours have moved. Still, our neighbourhood has an excellent safety record and our town has a good school district. And there are many personal priorities that I believe it is completely appropriate to spend money on, including (but not limited to) health care, higher education, and travel – especially when combined with further education and/or ministry. We are happy to give nice gifts to our children so as to make them feel not too different from their peers socio-economically, and to enjoy recreational activities, cultural and sporting events, a meal out from time to time, and so on, although compared to most of our suburban friends we do these latter things considerably less frequently. Nor is anything I have written meant to suggest that I believe savings, investments, insurance or pension schemes are wrong. I have all of these and hope their earnings continue to grow. While I know of others who, for a variety of ministry-related reasons, have adopted a much more radically simple lifestyle, and while I admire and approve of their approaches (see esp. R. Sider 1994), God has not yet led me to follow them, even after considerable discussion, prayer and soul-searching. In short, I feel I have a very rewarding life, materially speaking, and am not a particularly exemplary model of sacrificial giving.

I must also quickly admit that there are some unique features of the American tax structure that particularly benefit ordained ministers and that I have received some generous gifts from my family at birthdays, anniversaries and Christmas, which have enabled us to give as much as we have as easily as we have. I do not assume that others making the same amount as our family would in general be able to give as much away. But when the American Christian average of total giving per family is below 3% of per capita income, surely we can do considerably better! I am convinced that a substantial majority of American Christians, and probably most in other parts of the First World, could at least tithe if they made it a priority. And I am confident that many of my suburban friends could do even better than that. One may debate the appropriateness of doing more than giving to charity, to address structural evil, but one dare not do less (cf. esp. Graham 1990).

So how does one do it? Obviously, by not spending money on the things so many Westerners do. We must remind ourselves and our children regularly of the lies, half-truths and pagan values on which is based the advertising that bombards us daily. With relatively minor hardships, our family has freed up considerable funds by doing with less of many items most Westerners routinely take for granted. We have refused to go into debt for anything except property and education, bought cars only that we could afford to pay cash for, bought other goods in bulk, at discounts, at garage sales and at thrift shops. We have not assumed that we needed the size or quality of lavish 'entertainment centre' items (television, video, stereo, CD player ...) that most of our friends have. We have not heated or cooled our home quite to the extent that most North Americans do, or amassed the number or nature of clothes most Westerners seem compelled to accumulate. Even as simple a decision as not to eat out with the astonishing frequency of so many of our acquaintances has freed up enormous amounts of money.[3] Various

---

[3] On four different occasions in well-to-do suburban Denver churches, I have invited large, adult, Sunday-school classes to answer anonymously on note cards the following question: 'If you knew you would have 20% less income next year, what area of your

works which appeared nearly twenty years ago contain numerous additional suggestions for simplifying one's lifestyle that remain timely today (see esp. Longacre 1980; R. Sider 1980).

In addition to freeing up money for giving, Christians need to consider to whom they should give. We try to contribute generously to our local church and to make sure we belong to a church that shares at least some of the values articulated here. But no church in our area that we know of gives enough of its budget towards meeting the needs of the poor at home and abroad for us to stop with merely church giving. We also support a variety of missionaries and para-church organizations which explicitly target the poor; for example, we sponsor three young girls in the Two-Thirds World through a monthly child-support scheme and give additional monies to promote development in their communities. We support friends who pastor churches or teach in theological colleges overseas but who also help by dealing with community development. We support various ministries in Denver, including our own seminary, which address the spiritual and material needs of the inner city, and at times we have given gifts outright to friends in crisis, even when they could not be tax deductible.

What is true for individuals should be true for churches. We have belonged in the past to congregations which have given up to 50% of their annual budgets for holistic missions. Our current congregation gives slightly less than half that amount but is committed to a series of annual increases in the future and is part of a cooperative venture of suburban and inner-city churches having a significant impact on the needy in Denver. It also manages an active 'deacons' fund' and home and health ministries for an increasing number of suburban needy. The possibilities for church budget realignments could be radical but are seldom explored. One mountain community congregation not far from us employs no paid clergy but utilizes two seminary-trained laymen as their primary preacher-teachers, organizes itself as a collection of house churches, and has at times given up to 90% of its annual offerings to missions. Tom Sine tells the story of a church in Seattle that decided to raise funds so that young first-time home buyers could pay cash outright for their property. These Christians then contracted to pay back to the church what their mortgage payments would have been to fund further ministry and create more home-buying opportunities for other church

---

current budget would be most affected?' The most common answer each time was 'Money for eating out'. I then raise the question, 'Why not voluntarily cut back, without being forced to, for the sake of Christian giving?'

members (Sine 1991: 274–276). When one considers that the average Westerner spends more on repaying a home mortgage (principal plus interest) than on any other single lifetime expenditure, it is tragic that more Christians are not seeking to replicate this model.

When we do give money to missions, we need to calculate the cost of sending short-term or long-term Westerners with what generally approximates to a Western lifestyle versus supporting and training indigenous leadership in areas that already have some kind of Christian work. Choosing the latter option would also help us to channel more missionary effort toward completely or largely unreached people groups. When we do travel abroad, we must ask what kind of lifestyle we will adopt and what messages we will send as we go, oblivious as we may be to the hegemonic cultural signals that we often communicate (*cf.* esp. Bonk 1989). North American Christian colleges and seminaries must ask if they are helping to exacerbate the 'brain drain' as they try to attract the best international students and scholars to come to their institutions. Or are we truly becoming globalized and helping to fund and be a partner to the already numerous Two-Thirds World schools whose material resources and libraries are extremely meagre in comparison?[4]

The danger of reflections as autobiographical as these, of course, is that some will be intimidated by an ideal they do not think they could possibly reach, while others will be outraged at how poorly we have done ourselves. And any who succeeded in exactly imitating us might think they had done what was right when in fact God was calling them to a quite different pattern of stewardship. Further, we have barely even scratched the surface of possible applications in a more public or secular arena. For example, are we prepared to be involved in our workplaces, challenging the enormous amounts of waste of recyclable products, or in our communities to challenge the enormous amounts of waste of food, especially in restaurants?[5] As we become involved in the public arena, will we do so in a balanced way? If the Disney Corporation is worthy of being boycotted because of its policies on homosexuality (as the Southern Baptist Convention has championed), is not Nike even more worthy of such a boycott, given the fact that it has paid Michael Jordan as much money in one year for advertising its products as it has paid its entire 18,000-member Indonesian workforce

---

[4] As, *e.g.*, in one of the few truly partnering ventures of this kind of which I know, between Denver Seminary and Donetsk Christian University, Ukraine.

[5] R. Sider (1997: 89) notes that 'the dollar value of the food North Americans throw in the garbage each year equals about one-fifth of the total annual income of all the Christians in Africa'.

(R. Sider 1997: 144)? For the Christian, public policies at home and abroad can never be based primarily on what is in one's 'national interest', as the rhetoric of most politicians regularly alleges. Rather, we must ask what is in the interest of *all* humanity, materially and spiritually? For those of us who work for national or multi-national corporations, are we prepared to work within the system positively to promote limitations on profit-taking for the sake of more humane policies for the workforce, for trade partners and for a better earth? Still, there are limits to how much we can expect Christian values to take root in non-Christian structures. We should be spending the largest amount of our efforts on remoulding the church into a counter-cultural community. We may debate the best way to help the poor through economic and governmental policies, but the needy and marginalized in our world should have no doubts as to *our* compassion and concern.

The bottom line is surely one of attitude. Does a discussion of issues like these threaten us, leading to counter-charges about guilt manipulation or to rationalizing our greeds as if they were our needs? Or are we convicted in a healthy way that leads us to ask what more we can do to divest ourselves of our unused or unnecessary possessions, to make budgets to see where our money is really going, to exercise self-control and delayed gratification out of thanksgiving for all that God has blessed us with that we never deserved? Are we eager to help others, especially fellow Christians, however undeserving they seem to be?[6] Are we concerned to expose ourselves widely to news of the world, including news from a distinctively Christian perspective, to have the plight of the impoverished millions not paralyse us but periodically re-animate our commitment to do better and to do more? We may disagree on models of involvement, on to whom to give and on how much to give, but will we agree to continue to explore possibilities compatible with our economic philosophies and try to determine what really will do the most short-term and long-term good for the most needy?

Ronsvalle and Ronsvalle (1992: 45) have demonstrated that the amounts of money theoretically needed to eradicate world poverty could be amassed simply if all American Christians would tithe; every other existing Christian ministry could still continue to be funded at its current level. Obviously this does not take into account corrupt politicians, broken-down infrastructures and international obstacles to getting the money into the hands of the most needy in ways that will help them over the long haul. But it does remind us that there is so

---

[6] On the difficulty of labelling any as truly 'worthy poor', see Lupton (1989: 60–61).

much more that we could do without ever coming close to reversing positions with the poor.[7]

God may call a few to radical abandonment. He may not call most of us to do more than to give from our surplus. But how little we do even that, and then it often does not go to the best outlet! Ours is the age that has lost the long-standing Western and Christian tradition of stewardship.[8] If the plight of others is insufficient to motivate us, perhaps a more self-serving scenario is this: unless 'baby boomers' and younger generations reverse the currently deteriorating trends, many churches and Christian organizations that *we* are part of will close their doors in the years to come. And as anti-welfare and anti-state-interventionist trends increasingly diminish public spending, churches and Christians will be asked to bear an enormously larger burden of helping the needy in their own communities, one few seem currently prepared to accept. The greatest transfer of wealth in human history has begun, from the post-war generation of the West to its heirs, and it will continue in the next decade or two. Will the heirs' newly acquired money go merely to fuel the greatest round of consumer spending ever or simply to pay off the massive indebtedness that has already been accrued, or will we recover a biblical perspective on stewardship of material possessions?[9] 'Give me neither poverty nor riches,' prayed the writer of the proverb; but, since most of us already have riches, we need to be praying more often, 'and help me to be generous and wise in giving more of those riches away.'[10]

---

[7] *Cf.* also Hay (1989).

[8] For a dramatic up-to-date survey of attitudes among the richest 1% of Americans, see Todd (1997).

[9] *Cf.* Mouw (1989: 158): 'These are days in which it is urgent that Christians function as a community of *economic* memory. We must keep alive the older perspectives whereby people had a clear understanding – the understanding that is rapidly becoming a scarce resource in our time – of their mandate from God to serve as stewards in the human household. This could be one of the most important services that we can perform in the contemporary economic *milieu*: to remind our fellow humans about whose creatures they really are and about what best contributes to our true profit.'

[10] *Cf.* Santa Ana (1977: 66), quoting Ambrose: 'In a word, the priest's generosity must lie exactly half way between thoughtless prodigality and meanness.' For Protestants, who believe that all Christians are priests, this is wise counsel for believers across the board.

# Bibliography

van Aarde, A. G. (1993), 'A Silver Coin in the Mouth of a Fish (Matthew 17: 24–27) – A Miracle of Nature, Ecology, Economy and the Politics of Holiness', *Neot* 27: 1–25.

Achtemeier, Paul J. (1996), *1 Peter*, Minneapolis: Fortress.

Adamson, James B. (1976), *The Epistle of James*, Grand Rapids: Eerdmans.

——(1989), *James: The Man and His Message*, Grand Rapids: Eerdmans.

Ahlström, Gosta W. (1993), *The History of Ancient Palestine from the Paleolithic Period to Alexander's Conquest*, Sheffield: JSOT.

Aitken, Kenneth T. (1986), *Proverbs*, Edinburgh: Saint Andrew; Philadephia: Westminster.

Aland, Kurt (1982), *Synopsis of the Four Gospels*, New York: United Bible Societies.

Alden, Robert L. (1993), *Job*, Nashville: Broadman and Holman.

Alexander, T. Desmond (1987), 'The Psalms and the Afterlife', *IBS* 9: 2–17.

Allen, Leslie C. (1990), *Ezekiel 20 – 48*, Dallas: Word.

Allen, Ronald B. (1990), 'Numbers', in Frank E. Gaebelein (ed.), *Expositor's Bible Commentary* 2: 657–1008, Grand Rapids: Zondervan.

Allison, Dale C., Jr (1994), 'A Plea for Thoroughgoing Eschatology', *JBL* 113: 651–668.

Andersen, Francis I., & David N. Freedman (1989), *Amos*, New York and London: Doubleday.

Applebaum, Shimon (1989), 'Josephus and the Economic Causes of the Jewish War', in L. Feldman and G. Hata (eds.), *Josephus, the Bible, and History*, 237–264, Leiden: Brill.

Ascough, R. S. (1996), 'The Completion of a Religious Duty: The Background of 2 Cor 8.1–15', *NTS* 42: 584–599.

Ashley, Timothy R. (1993), *The Book of Numbers*, Grand Rapids: Eerdmans.

Attridge, Harold W. (1989), *The Epistle to the Hebrews*, Philadelphia: Fortress.

Bailey, Kenneth E. (1976), *Poet and Peasant: A Literary-Cultural Approach to the Parables in Luke*, Grand Rapids: Eerdmans.

——(1979), 'The Manger and the Inn: The Cultural Background of Luke 2:7', *NESTTR* 2: 33–44.

——(1980), *Through Peasant Eyes: More Lucan Parables*, Grand Rapids: Eerdmans.

Baker, David W. (1988), *Nahum, Habakkuk, Zephaniah*, Leicester and Downers Grove: IVP.

Baker, William R. (1990), 'James', in William R. Baker and Paul K. Carter, *James – Jude*, 9–111, Cincinnati: Standard.

Baldwin, Joyce G. (1972), *Haggai, Zechariah, Malachi*, Leicester and Downers Grove: IVP.

——(1988), *1 and 2 Samuel*, Leicester and Downers Grove: IVP.

Ballard, Bruce (1994), 'On the Sin of Usury: A Biblical Economic Ethic', *CSR* 24: 210–228.

Balme, Maurice (1984), 'Attitudes to Work and Leisure in Ancient Greece', *Greece and Rome* 31: 140–152.

Bammel, Ernst (1984), 'The Poor and the Zealots', in Ernst Bammel and C. F. D. Moule (eds.), *Jesus and the Politics of His Day*, 109–128, Cambridge: Cambridge University Press.

Barnett, Paul W. (1988), *The Message of 2 Corinthians: Power in Weakness*, Leicester and Downers Grove: IVP.

——(1997), *The Second Epistle to the Corinthians*, Grand Rapids and Cambridge: Eerdmans.

Barrett, C. K. (1968), *A Commentary on the First Epistle to the Corinthians*, London: Black; New York: Harper.

——(1973), *A Commentary on the Second Epistle to the Corinthians*, London: Black; New York: Harper.

——(1978), 'The House of Prayer and the Den of Thieves', in E. E. Ellis and Erich Grässer (eds.), *Jesus und Paulus*, 13–20, Göttingen: Vandenhoek.

——(1985), *Freedom and Obligation: A Study of the Epistle of Galatians*, Philadelphia: Westminster.

——(1994), *A Critical and Exegetical Commentary on the Acts of the Apostles* 1, Edinburgh: T. & T. Clark.

Barrett, David (1982), *World Christian Encyclopedia*, New York and London: Macmillan.

Barron, Bruce (1987), *The Health and Wealth Gospel*, Downers Grove: IVP.

Bassler, Jouette M. (1991), *God and Mammon: Asking for Money in the New Testament*, Nashville and London: Abingdon.

Batey, Richard A. (1972), *Jesus and the Poor*, New York: Harper and Row.

——(1991), *Jesus and the Forgotten City: New Light on Sepphoris and the Urban World of Jesus*, Grand Rapids: Baker.

Bauckham, Richard J. (1983), *2 Peter, Jude*, Waco: Word.

——(1986), 'The Coin in the Fish's Mouth', in David Wenham and Craig L. Blomberg (eds.), *Gospel Perspectives*, vol. 6: 219–252, Sheffield: JSOT.

——(1991), 'The Economic Critique of Rome in Revelation 18', in Loveday Alexander (ed.), *Images of Empire*, 47–90, Sheffield: JSOT.

——(1995), 'James and the Jerusalem Church', in Richard J. Bauckham (ed.), *The Book of Acts in its Palestinian Setting*, 415–480, Carlisle: Paternoster; Grand Rapids: Eerdmans.

Baumgarten, Albert I. (1984–85), '*Korban* and the Pharisaic *Paradosis*', *JANES* 16–17: 5–17.

Beasley-Murray, George R. (1986), *Jesus and the Kingdom of God*, Grand Rapids: Eerdmans; Exeter: Paternoster.

Beavis, Mary Ann (1994), '"Expecting Nothing in Return": Luke's Picture of the Marginalized', *Int* 48: 357–368.

Beisner, E. Calvin (1988), *Prosperity and Poverty*, Westchester: Crossway.

Belleville, Linda L. (1996), *2 Corinthians*, Leicester and Downers Grove: IVP.

Belo, Fernando (1981), *A Materialist Reading of the Gospel of Mark*, Maryknoll: Orbis.

Berger, Klaus (1977), 'Almosen für Israel', *NTS* 23: 180–204.

Berry, Ken L. (1996), 'The Function of Friendship Language in Philippians', in John T. Fitzgerald (ed.), *Friendship, Flattery and Frankness of Speech*, 107–124, Leiden: Brill.

Betz, Hans Dieter (1985), *2 Corinthians 8 and 9*, Philadephia: Fortress.

——(ed.) (1986), *The Greek Magical Papyri in Translation*, Chicago and London: University of Chicago Press.

——(1995), *The Sermon on the Mount*, Minneapolis: Fortress.

Binder, Herrmann (1995), 'Missdeutbar oder eindeutig? Gedanken zu einem Gleichnis Jesu', *TZ* 51: 41–49.

Blomberg, Craig L. (1984a), 'The Law in Luke-Acts', *JSNT* 22: 53–80.

——(1984b), 'The New Testament Miracles and Higher Criticism: Climbing Up the Slippery Slope?' *JETS* 27: 425–438.

——(1984c), 'When Is a Parallel Really a Parallel? A Test Case: The Lucan Parables', *WTJ* 46: 78–103.

——(1986), 'The Miracles as Parables', in David Wenham and Craig L. Blomberg (eds.), *Gospel Perspectives* 6: 327–359, Sheffield: JSOT.

——(1987), *The Historical Reliability of the Gospels*, Downers Grove and Leicester: IVP.

——(1990), *Interpreting the Parables*, Downers Grove and Leicester: IVP.

——(1991), 'The Liberation of Illegitimacy: Women and Rulers in Matthew 1 – 2', *BTB* 21: 145–150.

——(1992a), 'Healing', in Joel B. Green, Scot McKnight and I. Howard Marshall (eds.), *Dictionary of Jesus and the Gospels*, 299–307, Downers Grove and Leicester: IVP.

——(1992b), *Matthew*, Nashville: Broadman.

——(1992c), 'On Wealth and Worry: Matt. 6:19–34 – Meaning and Significance', *CTR* 6: 73–89.

——(1994a), *1 Corinthians*, Grand Rapids: Zondervan.

——(1994b), 'The Parables of Jesus: Current Trends and Needs in Research', in Bruce Chilton and Craig A. Evans (eds.), *Studying the Historical Jesus*, 231–254, Leiden: Brill.

——(1994c), '"Your Faith Has Made You Whole": The Evangelical Liberation Theology of Jesus', in Joel B. Green and Max Turner (eds.), *Jesus of Nazareth: Lord and Christ*, 75–93, Carlisle: Paternoster; Grand Rapids: Eerdmans.

——(1995), 'The Globalization of Biblical Interpretation – A Test Case: John 3 – 4', *BBR* 5: 1–15.

——(1996), 'Poetic Fiction, Subversive Speech, and Proportional Analogy in the Parables', *HBT* 18: 115–132.

——(1997), *Jesus and the Gospels: An Introduction and Survey*, Nashville: Broadman and Holman; Leicester: IVP.

Blue, Bradley B. (1991), 'The House Church at Corinth and the Lord's Supper: Famine, Food Supply, and the Present Distress', *CTR* 5: 221–239.

——(1994), 'Acts and the House Church', in David W. J. Gill and Conrad Gempf (eds.), *The Book of Acts in Its Graeco-Roman Setting*, 119–222, Carlisle: Paternoster; Grand Rapids: Eerdmans.

Bock, Darrell L. (1994), *Luke 1:1 – 9:50*, Grand Rapids: Baker.

Bockmuehl, Klaus (1980), *The Challenge of Marxism*, Leicester: IVP.

Bockmuehl, Markus (1994), *This Jesus: Martyr, Lord, Messiah*, Edinburgh: T. & T. Clark, 1994; Downers Grove: IVP, 1996.

Boff, Leonardo, & Clodovis Boff (1987), *Introducing Liberation Theology*, Maryknoll: Orbis, 1987; Tunbridge Wells: Burns and Oates, 1989.

Boismard, M.-E. (1995), '"Notre pain quotidien" (Mt 6, 11)', *RB* 102: 371–378.

Bonk, Jonathan J. (1989), 'Missions and Mammon: Six Theses', *IBMR* 13: 174–181.

Bormann, Lukas (1995), *Philippi: Stadt und Christengemeinde zur Zeit des Paulus*, Leiden: Brill.

Boyd, Gregory A. (1995), *Cynic, Sage or Son of God?* Wheaton: Victor.

Brändle, Rudolf (1985), 'Geld und Gnade (zu II Kor 8, 9)', *TZ* 41: 264–271.

Braun, Willi (1995), *Feasting and Social Rhetoric in Luke 14*, Cambridge: Cambridge University Press.

Brenk, Frederick E. (1990), 'Old Wineskins Recycled: *Autarkeia* in 1 Timothy 6.5–10', *FN* 3: 39–51.

Brin, Gershon (1994), *Studies in Biblical Law: From the Hebrew Bible to the Dead Sea Scrolls*, Sheffield: JSOT.

Brooke, George J. (1989), 'The Wisdom of Matthew's Beatitudes (4QBeat and Mt. 5:3–12)', *ScripBull* 19: 35–41.

Brown, Francis, S. R. Driver, & Charles A. Briggs (1953), *A Hebrew and English Lexicon of the Old Testament*, Oxford: Clarendon.

Brown, Raymond E. (1979), *The Community of the Beloved Disciple*, New York: Paulist.

—— (1982), *The Epistles of John*, Garden City: Doubleday.

—— (1993), *The Birth of the Messiah*, rev. ed., New York and London: Doubleday.

—— (1994), *The Death of the Messiah*, 2 vols., New York: Doubleday; London: Chapman.

Brownlee, William H. (1986), *Ezekiel 1 – 19*, Waco: Word.

Bruce, F. F. (1982), *The Epistle to the Galatians*, Exeter: Paternoster; Grand Rapids: Eerdmans.

—— (1983), *The Gospel of John*, Basingstoke: Pickering and Inglis; Grand Rapids: Eerdmans.

—— (1984), 'Render to Caesar', in Ernst Bammel and C. F. D. Moule (eds.), *Jesus and the Politics of His Day*, 249–263, Cambridge: Cambridge University Press.

—— (1988), *The Book of the Acts*, rev. ed., Grand Rapids: Eerdmans.

—— (1990a), *The Acts of the Apostles: The Greek Text with Introduction and Commentary*, rev. ed., Leicester: IVP; Grand Rapids: Eerdmans.

——(1990b), *The Epistle to the Hebrews*, rev. ed., Grand Rapids: Eerdmans.

Brueggemann, Walter (1975), 'Reflections on Biblical Understandings of Property', *IRM* 64: 354–361.

——(1977), *The Land: Place as Gift, Promise and Challenge in Biblical Faith*, Philadelphia: Fortress.

——(1991), *To Build, To Plant: A Commentary on Jeremiah 26 – 52*, Grand Rapids: Eerdmans; Edinburgh: Handsel.

Bruner, Frederick D. (1987), *The Christbook: Matthew 1 – 12*, Waco: Word.

Buchanan, Colin O. (1964), 'Epaphroditus' Sickness and the Letter to the Philippians', *EQ* 36: 157–166.

Burge, Gary M. (1996), *The Letters of John*, Grand Rapids: Zondervan.

Busse, Ulrich (1996), 'In Souveränität-anders: Verarbeitete Gotteserfahrung in Mt 20, 1–16', *BZ* 40: 61–72.

Butler, Trent C. (1983), *Joshua*, Waco: Word.

Byrne, Brendan (1996), *Romans*, Collegeville: Liturgical.

Cahill, Lisa S. (1987), 'The Ethical Implications of the Sermon on the Mount', *Int* 41: 144–156.

Campbell, R. A. (1995), 'ΚΑΙ ΜΑΛΙΣΤΑ ΟΙΚΕΙΩΝ: A New Look at 1 Tim 5.8', *NTS* 41: 157–60.

Campolo, Tony (1997), 'Is There Anything Wrong with Capitalism?' *Prism* 4.3: 23.

Capper, Brian J. (1983), 'The Interpretation of Acts 5:4', *JSNT* 19: 117–131.

——(1993), 'Paul's Dispute with Philippi: Understanding Paul's Argument in Phil 1–2 from His Thanks in 4.10–20', *TZ* 49: 193–214.

——(1995), 'The Palestinian Cultural Context of Earliest Christian Community of Goods', in Richard J. Bauckham (ed.), *The Book of Acts in its Palestinian Setting*, 323–356, Carlisle: Paternoster; Grand Rapids: Eerdmans.

Carroll R., M. Daniel (1992), *Contexts for Amos: Prophetic Poetics in Latin American Perspective*, Sheffield: JSOT.

Carson, D. A. (ed.) (1982), *From Sabbath to Lord's Day*, Grand Rapids: Zondervan.

——(1984), 'Matthew', in Frank E. Gaebelein (ed.), *Expositor's Bible Commentary* 8: 1–599, Grand Rapids: Zondervan.

——(1987), *When Jesus Confronts the World: An Exposition of Matthew 8 – 10*, Grand Rapids: Baker; Leicester: IVP.

——(1991), *The Gospel According to John*, Grand Rapids: Eerdmans; Leicester: IVP.

——(1995), 'Current Issues in Biblical Theology: A New Testament Perspective', *BBR* 5: 17–41.

——(1996), *The Gagging of God: Christianity Confronts Pluralism*, Grand Rapids: Zondervan; Leicester: Apollos.

Carson, D. A., Douglas J. Moo, & Leon Morris (1992), *An Introduction to the New Testament*, Grand Rapids: Zondervan; Leicester: IVP.

Cassidy, Richard J. (1978), *Jesus, Politics, and Society: A Study of Luke's Gospel*, Maryknoll: Orbis.

——(1979), 'Matthew 17:24–27: A Word on Civil Taxes', *CBQ* 41: 571–580.

——(1987), *Society and Politics in the Acts of the Apostles*, Maryknoll: Orbis.

Cassuto, Umberto (1967), *A Commentary on the Book of Exodus*, Jerusalem: Magnes.

Catherwood, Frederick, *et al.* (1987), 'Christian Faith and Economics', *Transformation* 4.3–4: 1–84.

Cave, C. H. (1968–69), 'Lazarus and the Lukan Deuteronomy', *NTS* 15: 319–325.

Childs, Brevard S. (1992), *Biblical Theology of the Old and New Testaments*, Minneapolis: Fortress; London: SCM.

Chilton, Bruce (1996), *Pure Kingdom: Jesus' Vision of God*, Grand Rapids: Eerdmans; London: SPCK.

Chilton, David (1981), *Productive Christians in an Age of Guilt-Manipulators: A Biblical Response to Ronald J. Sider*, Tyler, Texas: Institute for Christian Economics.

Chin, Moses (1991), 'A Heavenly Home for the Homeless: Aliens and Strangers in 1 Peter', *TB* 42: 96–112.

Chirichigno, Gregory C. (1993), *Debt-Slavery in Israel and the Ancient Near East*, Sheffield: JSOT.

Chow, John K. (1992), *Patronage and Power: A Study of Social Networks in Corinth*, Sheffield: JSOT.

Chutter, Gordon A. (1982), '"Riches and Poverty" in the Book of Proverbs', *Crux* 18.2: 23–28.

Clark, Gillian (1985), 'The Social Status of Paul', *ET* 96: 110–111.

Clark, Stephen B. (1980), *Man and Woman in Christ*, Ann Arbor: Servant.

Clarke, Andrew D. (1993), *Secular and Christian Leadership in Corinth: A Socio-Historical and Exegetical Study of 1 Corinthians 1–6*, Leiden: Brill.

Clévenot, Michel (1985), *Materialist Approaches to the Bible*, Maryknoll: Orbis.

Clines, David J. A. (1978), *The Theme of the Pentateuch*, Sheffield: JSOT.

—— (1984), *Ezra, Nehemiah, Esther*, Grand Rapids: Eerdmans; London: Marshall, Morgan and Scott.

—— (1989), *Job 1 – 20*, Dallas: Word.

Clouse, Robert G. (1984), *Wealth and Poverty: Four Christian Views of Economics*, Downers Grove: IVP.

Coggins, Richard J. (1987), 'The Old Testament and the Poor', *ET* 99: 11–14.

Cole, R. Alan (1973), *Exodus*, London: Tyndale, 1973; Downers Grove: IVP, 1974.

Collins, Adela Y. (1984), *Crisis and Catharsis: The Power of the Apocalypse*, Philadelphia: Westminster.

Conzelmann, Hans (1987), *Acts of the Apostles*, Philadelphia: Fortress.

Cooper, Lamar E., Sr (1994), *Ezekiel*, Nashville: Broadman and Holman.

Coppens, Joseph (1979), 'L'imposition des mains dans les Actes des Apôtres', in Jacob Kremer (ed.), *Les Actes des Apôtres: Traditions, rédaction, théologie*, 405–438, Leuven: Leuven University Press.

Corley, Kathleen (1993), *Private Women, Public Meals: Social Conflict in the Synoptic Tradition*, Peabody: Hendrickson.

Countryman, L. William (1980), *The Rich Christian in the Church of the Early Empire: Contradictions and Accommodations*, New York and Toronto: Mellen.

Court, John M. (1985), 'Right and Left: The Implications for Matthew 25.31–46', *NTS* 31: 223–233.

Craddock, Fred B. (1968), 'Poverty of Christ: An Investigation of 2 Corinthians 8:9', *Int* 22: 158–170.

Craigie, Peter C. (1976), *The Book of Deuteronomy*, Grand Rapids: Eerdmans.

Craigie, Peter C., Paige H. Kelley, & Joel F. Drinkard, Jr (1991), *Jeremiah 1 – 25*, Dallas: Word.

Cranfield, C. E. B. (1975, 1979), *A Critical and Exegetical Commentary on the Epistle to the Romans*, 2 vols., Edinburgh: T. & T. Clark.

Criswell, W. A. (1978), *Acts: An Exposition*, Grand Rapids: Zondervan.

Croatto, J. Severino (1981), *Exodus: A Hermeneutics of Freedom*, Maryknoll: Orbis.

Cronbach, A. (1944), 'The Social Ideals of the Apocrypha and the Pseudepigrapha', *HUCA* 18: 119–156.

Crosby, Michael H. (1981), *Spirituality of the Beatitudes: Matthew's Challenge for First-World Christians*, Maryknoll: Orbis.

Crossan, John D. (1973), *In Parables: The Challenge of the Historical Jesus*, New York: Harper and Row.

——(1979), *Finding Is the First Act: Trove Folktales and Jesus' Treasure Parables*, Missoula: Scholars.

Dahl, Nils A. (1977), *Studies in Paul*, Minneapolis: Augsburg.

Danker, Frederick W. (1982), *Benefactor*, St Louis: Clayton.

Darley, John M., & C. Daniel Batson (1973), 'From Jerusalem to Jericho: A Study of Situational and Dispositional Variables in Helping Behavior', *Journal of Personal and Social Psychology* 27: 100–108.

Davids, Peter H. (1982), *The Epistle of James*, Exeter: Paternoster; Grand Rapids: Eerdmans.

——(1990), *The First Epistle of Peter*, Grand Rapids: Eerdmans.

Davies, W. D. (1974), *The Gospel and the Land*, Berkeley: University of California Press.

Davies, W. D., & Dale C. Allison, Jr (1988, 1991, 1997), *A Critical and Exegetical Commentary on the Gospel According to Saint Matthew*, 3 vols. Edinburgh: T. & T. Clark.

Dearman, John A. (1988), *Property Rights in the Eighth-Century Prophets: The Conflict and Its Background*, Atlanta: Scholars.

Degenhardt, H.-J. (1965), *Lukas: Evangelist der Armen*, Stuttgart: KBW.

Delitzch, F. (1983), *Ezekiel*, repr., Grand Rapids: Eerdmans.

Deming, Will (1995), *Paul on Marriage and Celibacy: The Hellenistic Background of 1 Corinthians 7*, Cambridge: Cambridge University Press.

Derrett, J. Duncan M. (1961), 'Fresh Light on St. Luke xvi: I. The Parable of the Unjust Steward', *NTS* 7: 198–219.

——(1971), 'Ananias, Sapphira, and the Right of Property', *DownRev* 89: 225–232.

——(1977), 'Nisi Dominus Aedificaverit Domum: Towers and Wars (Lk XIV 28–32)', *NovT* 19: 241–268.

deSilva, David A. (1992), 'The Social Setting of The Revelation to John: Conflicts Within, Fears Without', *WTJ* 54: 273–302.

DeVries, Simon J. (1985), *1 Kings*, Waco: Word.

Dibelius, Martin (1976), *James*, rev. by H. Greeven, ET Philadelphia: Fortress (German original 1921).

Dillard, Raymond B., & Tremper Longman III (1994), *An Introduction to the Old Testament*, Grand Rapids: Zondervan; Leicester: IVP.

Donahue, John R. (1986), 'The "Parable" of the Sheep and the Goats: A Challenge to Christian Ethics', *TS* 47: 3–31.

——(1989), 'Two Decades of Research on the Rich and the Poor in Luke-Acts', in D. A. Knight and P. J. Paris (eds.), *Justice and the*

*Holy: Essays in Honor of Walter Harrelson*, 129–144, Atlanta: Scholars.

Doyle, B. Rod (1994), 'The Place of the Parable of the Labourers in the Vineyard in Matthew 20:1–16', *ABR* 42: 39–58.

Draper, Jonathan A. (1991), 'Christ the Worker: Fact or Fiction?' in James R. Cochrane and Gerald O. West (eds.), *The Three-Fold Cord*, 121–141, Hilton, South Africa: Cluster Publications.

Dschulnigg, Peter (1993), 'Warnung von Reichtum und Ermahnung der Reichen: 1 Tim 6, 6–10. 17. 19 im Rahmen des Schlussteils 6, 3–21', *BZ* 37: 60–77.

Du Plessis, I. J. (1990), 'Philanthropy or Sarcasm? – Another Look at the Parable of the Dishonest Manager (Luke 16:1–13)', *Neot* 24: 1–20.

Duncan-Jones, Richard (1994), *Money and Government in the Roman Empire*, Cambridge: Cambridge University Press.

Dunn, James D. G. (1970), *Baptism in the Holy Spirit*, London: SCM; Philadelphia: Westminster.

—— (1988), *Romans*, 2 vols., Dallas: Word.

—— (1995), *1 Corinthians*, Sheffield: Sheffield Academic Press.

—— (1996a), *The Acts of the Apostles*, London: Epworth.

—— (1996b), *The Epistles to the Colossians and to Philemon*, Carlisle: Paternoster; Grand Rapids: Eerdmans.

Dupont, Jacques (1977), 'The Poor and Poverty in the Gospels and Acts', in *Gospel Poverty: Essays in Biblical Poverty*, 25–52 (trans. Michael D. Guinan), Chicago: Franciscan.

Durham, John I. (1987), *Exodus*, Waco: Word.

Eaton, Michael A. (1983), *Ecclesiastes*, Leicester and Downers Grove: IVP.

Ellingworth, Paul (1993), *The Epistle to the Hebrews*, Carlisle: Paternoster; Grand Rapids: Eerdmans.

Elliott, John H. (1981), *A Home for the Homeless: A Sociological Exegesis of 1 Peter, Its Situation and Strategy*, Philadelphia: Fortress, 1981; London: SCM, 1982.

Ellis, Robert R. (1995), 'Divine Gift and Human Response: An Old Testament Model for Stewardship', *SWJT* 37: 4–14.

Ellul, Jacques (1984), *Money and Power*, Downers Grove: IVP, 1984; Basingstoke: Marshall Pickering, 1986.

Engberg-Pedersen, T. (1987), 'The Gospel and Social Practice According to 1 Corinthians', *NTS* 33: 557–584.

Engels, Donald (1990), *Roman Corinth*, Chicago and London: University of Chicago Press.

Escobar, Samuel (1983), 'The Gospel and the Poor', in Vinay Samuel and Chris Sugden (eds.), *Evangelism and the Poor: A Third World Study Guide*, 97–106, rev. ed., Oxford: Regnum.

Esler, Philip F. (1987), *Community and Gospel in Luke-Acts*, Cambridge: Cambridge University Press.

Esquivel, Julia (1982), *Threatened with Resurrection*, Elgin: Brethren.

Evans, C. F. (1990), *Saint Luke*, London: SCM; Philadelphia: TPI.

Evans, Craig A. (1996), 'Jesus' Parable of the Tenant Farmers in Light of Lease Agreements in Antiquity', *JSP* 14: 65–83.

Everson, A. Joseph (1978), 'Isaiah 61:1–6', *Int* 32: 69–73.

Faber, Riemer A. (1995), 'The Juridical Nuance in the New Testament Use of ΠΡΟΣΩΠΟΛΗΜΨΙΑ', *WTJ* 57: 299–309.

Fager, Jeffrey A. (1993), *Land Tenure and the Biblical Jubilee*, Sheffield: JSOT.

Farmer, William R. (1955), 'The Economic Basis of the Qumran Community', *TZ* 11: 295–308.

Farris, Stephen (1985), *The Hymns of Luke's Infancy Narratives*, Sheffield: JSOT.

Fee, Gordon D. (1987), *The First Epistle to the Corinthians*, Grand Rapids: Eerdmans.

——(1995), *Paul's Letter to the Philippians*, Grand Rapids: Eerdmans.

Fee, Gordon D., & Douglas Stuart (1982), *How to Read the Bible for All Its Worth*, Grand Rapids: Zondervan.

Fensham, F. C. (1982), *The Books of Ezra and Nehemiah*, Grand Rapids: Eerdmans.

Fiensy, David A. (1991), *The Social History of Palestine in the Herodian Period*, Lewiston and Lampeter: Mellen.

——(1995), 'The Composition of the Jerusalem Church', in Richard J. Bauckham (ed.), *The Book of Acts in Its Palestinian Setting*, 213–236, Carlisle: Paternoster; Grand Rapids: Eerdmans.

Fine, Hillel A. (1955), 'The Tradition of a Patient Job', *JBL* 74: 28–32.

Finley, Moses I. (1973), *The Ancient Economy*, Berkeley: University of California Press.

Finley, Thomas J. (1985), 'An Evangelical Response to the Preaching of Amos', *JETS* 28: 411–420.

Fisk, Bruce N. (1989), 'Eating Meat Offered to Idols: Corinthian Behavior and Pauline Response in 1 Corinthians 8 – 10', *TrinJ* 10: 49–70.

Fitzgerald, John T. (1996), 'Philippians in the Light of Some Ancient Discussions of Friendship', in John T. Fitzgerald (ed.), *Friendship, Flattery and Frankness of Speech*, 141–160, Leiden: Brill.

Fitzmyer, Joseph A. (1964), 'The Story of the Dishonest Manager (Lk. 16:1–13)', *TS* 25: 23–42.

Fleming, D. E. (1995), 'More Help from Syria: Introducing Emar to Biblical Study', *BA* 58: 139–147.

Flusser, David (1960), 'Blessed Are the Poor in Spirit …', *IEJ* 10: 1–13.

——(1992), 'The Parable of the Unjust Steward: Jesus' Criticism of the Essenes', in James H. Charlesworth (ed.), *Jesus and the Dead Sea Scrolls*, 176–197, New York and London: Doubleday.

Ford, J. M. (1980), 'Three Ancient Jewish Attitudes Toward Poverty', in W. Klassen (ed.), *The New Way of Jesus*, 39–55, Newton: Faith and Life Press.

——(1984), *My Enemy Is My Guest: Jesus and Violence in Luke*, Maryknoll: Orbis.

Fortna, Robert T. (1992), 'Reading Jesus' Parable of the Talents Through Underclass Eyes: Matt. 25:14–30', *Forum* 8: 211–228.

Foster, Richard J. (1989), *The Challenge of the Disciplined Life: Christian Reflection on Money, Sex and Power*, San Francisco: Harper and Row.

France, R. T. (1979), 'God and Mammon', *EQ* 51: 3–21.

——(1989), *Matthew: Evangelist and Interpreter*, Exeter: Paternoster; Grand Rapids: Zondervan.

Freyne, Sean (1980), *Galilee from Alexander the Great to Hadrian*, Wilmington: Glazier; Notre Dame: University of Notre Dame Press.

Fung, R. Y. K. (1988), *The Epistle to the Galatians*, Grand Rapids: Eerdmans.

Funk, Robert W. (1982), *Parables and Presence*, Philadelphia: Fortress.

Furfey, Paul H. (1943), 'ΠΛΟΥΣΙΟΣ and Cognates in the New Testament', *CBQ* 5: 243–263.

Furnish, Victor P. (1984), *II Corinthians*, New York and London: Doubleday.

Gabba, Emilio (1990), 'The Finances of King Herod', in A. Kadrey, U. Rappaport and G. Fuks (eds.), *Greece and Rome in Eretz Israel*, Jerusalem: Israel Exploration Society.

Gamoran, Hillel (1971), 'The Biblical Law Against Loans on Interest', *JNES* 30: 127–134.

Garland, David E. (1993), *Reading Matthew*, New York: Crossroad.

——(1996), *Mark*, Grand Rapids: Zondervan.

Garrett, Duane A. (1991), *Rethinking Genesis*, Grand Rapids: Baker.

——(1993), *Proverbs, Ecclesiastes, Song of Songs*, Nashville: Broadman.

Garrison, Roman (1993), *Redemptive Almsgiving in Early Christianity*, Sheffield: JSOT.

Gay, Craig (1991), *With Liberty and Justice for Whom? The Recent Evangelical Debate over Capitalism*, Grand Rapids: Eerdmans.

Geiger, Linwood T. (1995), 'Market Activity and Poverty: An Analysis of the Impact of the Market Economy on Poverty in Developing Countries', *Transformation* 12.3: 19–29.

George, Augustin (1977), 'Poverty in the Old Testament', in *Gospel Poverty: Essays in Biblical Theology*, 3–24 (trans. Michael D. Guinan), Chicago: Franciscan, 1977; rev. ed. New York: Paulist, 1981.

Georgi, Dieter (1992), *Remembering the Poor: The History of Paul's Collection for Jerusalem*, ET Nashville: Abingdon (German original 1965).

Gérard, Jean-Pierre (1995), 'Les riches dans la communauté lucanienne', *ETL* 71: 71–106.

Gerstenberger, Erhard S. (1996), *Leviticus*, Louisville: Westminster John Knox.

Getz, Gene A. (1990a), *A Biblical Theology of Material Possessions*, Chicago: Moody.

——(1990b), *Real Prosperity: Biblical Principles of Material Possessions*, Chicago: Moody.

Geyser, A. S. (1975), 'The Letter of James and the Social Condition of his Addressees', *Neot* 9: 25–33.

Gibbs, Jeffrey A. (1987), 'Parables of Atonement and Assurance: Matthew 13:44–46', *CTQ* 51: 19–43.

Giblin, Charles H. (1971), '"The Things of God" in the Question Concerning Tribute to Caesar (Lk 20:25; Mk 12:17; Mt 22:21)', *CBQ* 33: 510–527.

Giese, Ronald L., Jr (1992), 'Qualifying Wealth in the Septuagint of Proverbs', *JBL* 111: 409–425.

Gill, David W. J. (1989), 'Erastus the Aedile', *TB* 40: 293–301.

——(1993), 'In Search of the Social Elite in the Corinthian Church', *TB* 44: 323–337.

——(1994), 'Acts and the Urban Élites', in David W. J. Gill and Conrad Gempf (eds.), *The Book of Acts in Its Graeco-Roman Setting*, 105–118, Carlisle: Paternoster; Grand Rapids: Eerdmans.

Gillingham, Sue (1988), 'The Poor in the Psalms', *ET* 100: 15–19.

Gitlin, Emmanuel M. (1963), 'The Tithe in Deuteronomy', *Religion in Life* 32: 574–585.

Gnanavaram, M. (1993), '"Dalit Theology" and the Parable of the Good Samaritan', *JSNT* 50: 59–83.

Gnuse, Robert G. (1985), *You Shall Not Steal: Community and Property in the Biblical Tradition*, Maryknoll: Orbis.

González, Catherine G., & Justo L. González (1997), *Revelation*, Louisville: Westminster John Knox.

González, Justo L. (1990), *Faith and Wealth*, San Francisco and London: Harper and Row.

Goodman, Martin (1987), *The Ruling Class of Judaea: The Origins of the Jewish Revolt Against Rome AD 66–70*, Cambridge: Cambridge University Press.

Goppelt, Leonhard (1993), *A Commentary on 1 Peter*, Grand Rapids: Eerdmans.

Gordon, Barry (1975), *Economic Analysis Before Adam Smith*, London: Macmillan.

——(1982), 'Lending and Interest: Some Jewish, Greek, and Christian Approaches, 800 BC – AD 100', *History of Political Economy* 14: 406–426.

——(1989), *The Economic Problem in Biblical and Patristic Thought*, Leiden: Brill.

Gornik, Mark R. (1991), 'The Rich and the Poor in Pauline Theology', *Urban Mission* 9: 15–26.

Gossai, Hemchand (1993), *Justice, Righteousness and the Social Critique of the Eighth-Century Prophets*, New York: Peter Lang.

Gottwald, Norman K. (1979), *The Tribes of Yahweh*, Maryknoll: Orbis.

——(1985), *The Hebrew Bible: A Socio-Literary Introduction*, Philadelphia: Fortress.

Goudzwaard, Bob (1979), *Capitalism and Progress*, repr., Exeter: Paternoster, 1997.

Goudzwaard, Bob and Harry de Lange (1995), *Beyond Poverty and Affluence: Toward an Economy of Care*, Grand Rapids: Eerdmans.

Goulder, Michael D. (1968), 'Characteristics of the Parables in the Several Gospels', *JTS* 19: 51–69.

Gowan, Donald E. (1987), 'Wealth and Poverty in the Old Testament: The Case of the Widow, the Orphan, and the Sojourner', *Int* 41: 341–353.

Graham, Gordon (1990), *The Idea of Christian Charity*, Notre Dame: University of Notre Dame Press; London: Collins.

Granberg-Michaelsen, Wesley (ed.) (1987), *Tending the Garden: Essays on the Gospel and the Earth*, Grand Rapids: Eerdmans.

Grant, F. C. (1956), *The Economic Background of the Gospels*, rev. ed., Oxford: Oxford University Press.

Gray, Sherman W. (1989), *The Least of My Brothers: Matthew 25:31–46 – A History of Interpretation*, Atlanta: Scholars.

Green, Joel B. (1994), 'Good News to Whom? Jesus and the "Poor" in the Gospel of Luke', in Joel B. Green and Max Turner (eds.), *Jesus of Nazareth: Lord and Christ*, 59–74, Carlisle: Paternoster; Grand Rapids: Eerdmans.

Grigg, David (1993), *The World Food Problem*, rev. ed., Oxford: Blackwell.

Grudem, Wayne (1988), *The First Epistle of Peter*, Leicester: IVP; Grand Rapids: Eerdmans.

Guelich, Robert A. (1982), *The Sermon on the Mount*, Waco: Word.

Guinan, Michael D. (trans.) (1977), *Gospel Poverty: Essays in Biblical Theology*, Chicago: Franciscan; rev. ed., New York: Paulist.

Gundry, Robert H. (1993), *Mark: A Commentary on His Apology for the Cross*, Grand Rapids: Eerdmans.

Guthrie, Donald (1990), *New Testament Introduction*, Leicester and Downers Grove: IVP.

Gutiérrez, Gustavo (1968), *A Theology of Liberation*, rev. ed., Maryknoll: Orbis, 1988.

Haacker, Klaus (1986), 'Kaisertribut und Gottesdienst (Eine Auslegung von Markus 12, 13–17)', *ThBeitr* 17: 285–292.

Habel, Norman C. (1995), *The Land is Mine: Six Biblical Ideologies*, Minneapolis: Fortress.

Hadas, Moses (1953), *The Third and Fourth Books of Maccabees*, New York: Harper and Brothers.

Haenchen, Ernst (1971), *The Acts of the Apostles*, Oxford: Blackwell; Philadelphia: Westminster.

Hagner, Donald A. (1993, 1995), *Matthew*, 2 vols., Dallas: Word.

Halteman, James (1995), *The Clashing Worlds of Economics and Faith*, Scottdale and Waterloo: Herald.

Hamel, Gildas (1990), *Poverty and Charity in Roman Palestine, First Three Centuries C.E.*, Berkeley and Oxford: University of California Press.

Hamilton, Jeffries M. (1992), *Social Justice and Deuteronomy: The Case of Deuteronomy 15*, Atlanta: Scholars.

Hamilton, Victor P. (1990, 1995), *The Book of Genesis*, 2 vols., Grand Rapids: Eerdmans.

Hamm, Dennis (1986), 'Acts 3, 1–10: The Healing of the Temple Beggar as Lucan Theology', *Bib* 67: 305–319.

—— (1991), 'Zacchaeus Revisited Once More: A Story of Vindication or Conversion?' *Bib* 72: 249–252.

Hands, A. R. (1968), *Charities and Social Aid in Greece and Rome*, Ithaca: Cornell University Press.

Hanks, Thomas D. (1983), *God So Loved the Third World*, Maryknoll: Orbis.

Harrington, Wilfrid J. (1993), *Revelation*, Collegeville: Liturgical.

Harrison, Everett F. (1986), *Interpreting Acts: The Expanding Church*, Grand Rapids: Zondervan.

Hartin, Patrick J. (1991), *James and the 'Q' Sayings of Jesus*, Sheffield: JSOT.

Hartley, John E. (1988), *The Book of Job*, Grand Rapids: Eerdmans.

——(1992), *Leviticus*, Dallas: Word.

Harvey, A. E. (1982), '"The Workman Is Worthy of His Hire": Fortunes of a Proverb in the Early Church', *NovT* 24: 209–221.

——(1990), *Strenuous Commands: The Ethic of Jesus*, London: SCM; Philadelphia: TPI.

——(1996), *Renewal Through Suffering: A Study of Second Corinthians*, Edinburgh: T. & T. Clark.

Hasel, Gerhard F. (1995), 'Recent Models of Biblical Theology: Three Major Perspectives', *AUSS* 33: 55–75.

——(1996), 'Proposals for a Canonical Biblical Theology', *AUSS* 34: 23–33.

Hauerwas, Stanley, & William H. Willimon (1989), *Resident Aliens: Life in the Christian Colony*, Nashville: Abingdon.

Hay, Donald (1989), *Economics Today: A Christian Critique*, Leicester: IVP; Grand Rapids: Eerdmans.

Hays, Richard B. (1996), *The Moral Vision of the New Testament*, New York: Harper Collins, 1996; Edinburgh: T. & T. Clark, 1997.

Heard, Warren (1988), 'Luke's Attitude Toward the Rich and the Poor', *TrinJ* 9: 47–80.

Hedrick, Charles W. (1994), *Parables as Poetic Fictions*, Peabody: Hendrickson.

Heide, Gale Z. (1992), 'The Soteriology of James 2:14', *GTJ* 12: 69–97.

Hemer, Colin J. (1984), 'ἐπιούσιος', *JSNT* 22: 81–94.

——(1986), *The Letters to the Seven Churches of Asia in Their Local Setting*, Sheffield: JSOT.

——(1989), *The Book of Acts in the Setting of Hellenistic History*, Tübingen: Mohr.

Hendrix, Holland (1991), 'Benefactor/Patron Networks in the Urban Environment: Evidence From Thessalonica', *Semeia* 56: 39–58.

Hengel, Martin (1974), *Property and Riches in the Early Church*, Philadelphia: Fortress; London: SCM.

——(1983), *Between Jesus and Paul*, London: SCM; Philadelphia: Fortress.

—— (1989), *The Zealots*, Edinburgh: T. & T. Clark.

Héring, Jean (1967), *The Second Epistle of Saint Paul to the Corinthians*, London: Epworth.

Herrenbrück, Fritz (1987), 'Zum Vorwurf der Kollaboration des Zöllners mit Rom', *ZNW* 78: 186–199.

Herzog, William R., II (1994a), 'Dissembling, A Weapon of the Weak: The Case of Christ and Caesar in Mark 12:13–17 and Romans 13:1–7', *PRS* 21: 339–360.

—— (1994b), *Parables as Subversive Speech*, Louisville: Westminster John Knox.

Hess, Richard S., Philip E. Satterthwaite, & Gordon J. Wenham (eds.) (1993), *He Swore an Oath: Biblical Themes from Genesis 12 – 50*, Cambridge: Tyndale House.

Hester, James D. (1992), 'Socio-Rhetorical Criticism and the Parable of the Tenants', *JSNT* 45: 27–57.

Hill, Craig C. (1992), *Hellenists and Hebrews*, Minneapolis: Fortress.

Hock, Ronald F. (1980), *The Social Context of Paul's Ministry*, Philadelphia: Fortress.

Hoenig, Sidney B. (1969), 'Sabbatical Years and the Year of Jubilee', *JQR* 59: 222–236.

Hollander, Harm W. (1985), 'The Testaments of the Twelve Patriarchs', in M. de Jonge (ed.), *Outside the Old Testament*, 71–91, Cambridge: Cambridge University Press.

Hooker, Morna D. (1991), *The Gospel According to Saint Mark*, London: Black; Peabody: Hendrickson.

Hopkins, Keith (1980), 'Taxes and Trade in the Roman Empire (200 BC – AD 400)', *JRS* 70: 101–125.

Hoppe, L. J. (1987), *Being Poor*, Wilmington: Glazier.

Horbury, William (1984), 'The Temple Tax', in Ernst Bammel and C. F. D. Moule (eds.), *Jesus and the Politics of His Day*, 265–286, Cambridge: Cambridge University Press.

Horrell, David G. (1996), *The Social Ethos of the Corinthian Correspondence*, Edinburgh: T. & T. Clark.

Horsley, Richard A. (1986), 'Ethics and Exegesis: "Love Your Enemies" and the Doctrine of Non-Violence', *JAAR* 54: 3–31.

—— (1987), *Jesus and the Spiral of Violence*, San Francisco: Harper and Row.

—— (1989), *Sociology and the Jesus Movement*, New York: Crossroad.

House, Paul R. (1995), *1, 2 Kings*, Nashville: Broadman and Holman.

Houston, Walter (1995), '"You Shall Open Your Hand to Your Needy Brother": Ideology and Moral Formation in Deut. 15.1–18', in John

W. Rogerson *et al.* (eds.), *The Bible in Ethics: The Second Sheffield Colloquium*, 296–314, Sheffield: Sheffield Academic Press.

van Houten, Christiana (1991), *The Alien in Israelite Law*, Sheffield: JSOT.

Hubbard, David A. (1989), *Joel and Amos*, Leicester and Downers Grove: IVP.

Hubbard, Robert L., Jr (1988), *The Book of Ruth*, Grand Rapids: Eerdmans.

Hughes, Philip E. (1962), *Paul's Second Epistle to the Corinthians*, Grand Rapids: Eerdmans.

Hurley, James D. (1981), *Man and Woman in Biblical Perspective*, Leicester: IVP; Grand Rapids: Zondervan.

Hurtado, Larry (1979), 'The Jerusalem Collection and the Book of Galatians', *JSNT* 5: 46–62.

Ireland, Dennis J. (1992), *Stewardship and the Kingdom of God*, Leiden: Brill.

Jagersma, Henk (1985), *A History of Israel from Alexander the Great to Bar Kochba*, London: SCM, 1985; Philadelphia: Fortress, 1986.

Japhet, Sara (1986), 'The Relationship Between the Legal Corpora in the Pentateuch in Light of Manumission Laws', in Sara Japhet (ed.), *Scripta Hierosolymitana*, vol. 31: 63–89, Jerusalem: Magnes.

Jeremias, Joachim (1954–55), 'Paul and James', *ET* 66: 368–371.

——(1969), *Jerusalem in the Time of Jesus*, London: SCM; Philadelphia: Fortress.

——(1972), *The Parables of Jesus*, rev. ed., London: SCM; Philadelphia: Westminster.

Jervell, Jacob (1972), *Luke and the People of God*, Minneapolis: Augsburg.

Jewett, Robert (1994), *Paul: The Apostle to America*, Louisville: Westminster John Knox.

Johnson, Luke T. (1981), *Sharing Possessions*, Philadelphia: Fortress.

——(1991), *The Gospel of Luke*, Collegeville: Liturgical.

——(1992), *The Acts of the Apostles*, Collegeville: Liturgical.

——(1995), *The Letter of James*, New York and London: Doubleday.

——(1996), *Letters to Paul's Delegates: 1 Timothy, 2 Timothy, Titus*, Valley Forge: TPI.

——(1997), *Reading Romans*, New York: Crossroad.

Johnson, Sherman E. (1954), 'The Dead Sea Manual of Discipline and the Jerusalem Church of Acts', *ZAW* 66: 106–120.

Jones, A. H. M. (1974), *The Roman Economy*, Oxford: Blackwell.

Jörns, Klaus-Peter (1987), 'Armut, zu der Geist hilft (Mt 5, 3) als *nota ecclesiae*', *TZ* 43: 59–70.

Joubert, S. J. (1992), 'Behind the Mask of Rhetoric: 2 Corinthians 8 and the Intra-Textual Relation Between Paul and the Corinthians', *Neot* 26: 101–112.

Judge, Edwin A. (1960), *The Social Pattern of Christian Groups in the First Century*, London: Tyndale.

—— (1991), 'The Mark of the Beast, Revelation 13:16', *TB* 42: 158–160.

Kaiser, Walter C., Jr (1979), *Ecclesiastes: Total Life*, Chicago: Moody.

—— (1988), 'The Old Testament Promise of Material Blessings and the Contemporary Believer', *TrinJ* 9: 151–170.

Karris, Robert J. (1978), 'Poor and Rich: The Lukan Sitz im Leben', in Charles H. Talbert (ed.), *Perspectives in Luke-Acts*, 112–125, Danville: AABPR; Edinburgh: T. & T. Clark.

—— (1990), *Jesus and the Marginalized in John's Gospel*, Collegeville: Liturgical.

Kautsky, John H. (1982), *The Politics of Aristocratic Empires*, Chapel Hill: University of North Carolina Press.

Kaylor, L. David (1994), *Jesus the Prophet*, Louisville: Westminster John Knox.

Keck, Leander E. (1965), 'The Poor among the Saints in the New Testament', *ZNW* 56: 100–129.

—— (1966), 'The Poor among the Saints in Jewish Christianity and Qumran', *ZNW* 57: 54–78.

Kee, Howard C. (1977), *Community of the New Age: Studies in Mark's Gospel*, Philadelphia: Westminster; London: SCM.

—— (1996), 'Jesus: A Glutton and a Drunkard', *NTS* 42: 374–393.

Keener, Craig S. (1992), *Paul, Women and Wives*, Peabody: Hendrickson.

Kennedy, George A. (1984), *New Testament Interpretation through Rhetorical Criticism*, Chapel Hill: University of North Carolina Press.

Keown, Gerald L., Pamela J. Scalise, & Thomas G. Smothers (1995), *Jeremiah 26 – 52*, Dallas: Word.

Kidd, Reggie M. (1990), *Wealth and Beneficence in the Pastoral Epistles: A 'Bourgeois' Form of Early Christianity?*, Atlanta: Scholars.

Kidner, Derek (1964), *Proverbs*, Leicester and Downers Grove: IVP.

—— (1967), *Genesis*, Leicester and Downers Grove: IVP.

Kimball, Charles A. (1994), *Jesus' Exposition of the Old Testament in Luke's Gospel*, Sheffield: JSOT.

Kinukawa, Hisako (1994), *Women and Jesus in Mark*, Maryknoll: Orbis.

Kirk, J. Andrew (1980), *Theology Encounters Revolution*, Leicester: IVP.

Kistemaker, Simon (1980), *The Parables of Jesus*, Grand Rapids: Baker.

—— (1986), *James – I–III John*, Grand Rapids: Baker.

Klein, William W. (1986), 'The Sermon at Nazareth (Luke 4:14–22)', in Kenneth W. M. Wozniak and Stanley J. Grenz (eds.), *Christian Freedom: Essays in Honor of Vernon C. Grounds*, 153–172, Lanham: University Press of America.

Klein, William W., Craig L. Blomberg, & Robert L. Hubbard, Jr (1993), *Introduction to Biblical Interpretation*, Dallas and London: Word.

Knight, George A. F. (1982, 1983), *Psalms*, 2 vols., Edinburgh: Saint Andrew; Philadelphia: Westminster.

Knight, George W., III (1992), *The Pastoral Epistles*, Carlisle: Paternoster; Grand Rapids: Eerdmans.

Knight, Jonathan (1995), *2 Peter and Jude*, Sheffield: Sheffield Academic Press.

Koenig, John (1985), *New Testament Hospitality*, Philadelphia: Fortress.

Kopas, Jane (1986), 'Jesus and Women: Luke's Gospel', *TT* 43: 109–202.

Kosmala, Hans (1964), 'The Parable of the Unjust Steward in the Light of Qumran', *ASTI* 3: 114–121.

Kraybill, Donald B., & Dennis M. Sweetland (1983), 'Possessions in Luke-Acts: A Sociological Perspective', *PRS* 10: 215–239.

Kraybill, J. Nelson (1996), *Imperial Cult and Commerce in John's Apocalypse*, Sheffield: Sheffield Academic Press.

Krodel, Gerhard (1986), *Acts*, Minneapolis: Augsburg.

Kruse, Colin (1987), *The Second Epistle of Paul to the Corinthians*, Leicester: IVP; Grand Rapids: Eerdmans.

Kugel, James L. (1989), 'Qohelet and Money', *CBQ* 51: 32–49.

Kvalbein, Hans (1987), 'Jesus and the Poor: Two Texts and a Tentative Conclusion', *Themelios* 12: 80–87.

Ladd, George E. (1974a), 'The Parable of the Sheep and the Goats in Recent Interpretation', in Richard N. Longenecker and Merrill C. Tenney (eds.), *New Dimensions in New Testament Study*, 191–199, Grand Rapids: Zondervan.

—— (1974b), *The Presence of the Future*, Grand Rapids: Eerdmans, 1974; London: SPCK, 1980.

—— (1993), *A Theology of the New Testament* (rev., 1980 by Donald

A. Hagner), Grand Rapids: Eerdmans; London: Lutterworth (1st ed. 1974).

Lambrecht, Jan (1992), *Out of the Treasure: The Parables in the Gospel of Matthew*, Leuven: Peeters; Grand Rapids: Eerdmans.

Lane, William L. (1991), *Hebrews*, 2 vols., Dallas: Word.

Lang, Bernhard (1985), 'The Social Organization of Peasant Poverty in Biblical Israel', in *Anthropological Approaches to the Old Testament*, 83–99, Philadelphia: Fortress.

Larkin, William J., Jr (1995), *Acts*, Leicester and Downers Grove: IVP.

LaSor, William F., David A. Hubbard, & Frederic W. Bush (1996), *Old Testament Survey*, rev. ed., Grand Rapids and Cambridge: Eerdmans.

Laws, Sophie (1980), *A Commentary on the Epistle of James*, London: Black; San Francisco: Harper and Row.

Lee-Pollard, Dorothy A. (1987), 'Powerlessness as Power: A Key Emphasis in the Gospel of Mark', *SJT* 40: 173–188.

Légasse, Simon (1977), 'The Call of the Rich Man', in *Gospel Poverty: Essays in Biblical Theology*, 53–80 (trans. Michael D. Guinan), Chicago: Franciscan; rev. ed. 1981, New York: Paulist.

——(1994), 'Paul et César – Romains 13, 1–7. Essai de synthèse', *RB* 101: 516–532.

——(1995), 'Paul's Pre-Christian Career According to Acts', in Richard J. Bauckham (ed.), *The Book of Acts in Its Palestinian Setting*, 365–390, Carlisle: Paternoster; Grand Rapids: Eerdmans.

Lemche, Niels P. (1985), *Early Israel: Anthropological and Historical Studies on the Israelite Society before the Monarchy*, Leiden: Brill.

Lenski, Gerhard E. (1966), *Power and Privilege: A Theory of Social Stratification*, New York: McGraw-Hill.

Levenson, Jon D. (1976), 'Poverty and the State in Biblical Thought', *Judaism* 25: 230–241.

Levine, Baruch (1989), *Leviticus*, Jerusalem: Magnes.

Lichtenstein, Murray H. (1982), 'Chiasm and Symmetry in Proverbs 31', *CBQ* 44: 202–211.

Liefeld, Walter L. (1995), *Interpreting the Book of Acts*, Grand Rapids: Baker.

Lincoln, Andrew T. (1990), *Ephesians*, Dallas: Word.

Linnemann, Eta (1992), *Is There a Synoptic Problem?* Grand Rapids: Baker.

Lischer, Richard (1987), 'The Sermon on the Mount as Radical Pastoral Care', *Int* 41: 157–169.

Liu, Peter (1992), 'Did the Lucan Jesus Desire Voluntary Poverty of His Followers?' *EQ* 64: 291–317.

Lochman, Jan M. (1990), *The Lord's Prayer*, Grand Rapids: Eerdmans.

Loewenstamm, Samuel E. (1969), 'נשך and מ/חדביח', *JBL* 88: 78–80.

Lohfink, Norbert F. (1987), *Option for the Poor*, Berkeley: Bibal.

Longacre, Doris J. (1980), *Living More with Less*, Scottdale and Kitchener: Herald.

Longenecker, Richard N. (1981), 'The Acts of the Apostles', in Frank E. Gaebelein (ed.), *Expositor's Bible Commentary* 9: 205–573, Grand Rapids: Zondervan.

—— (1990), *Galatians*, Dallas: Word.

Louw, Johannes P., & Eugene A. Nida (1988), *Greek-English Lexicon of the New Testament Based on Semantic Domains*, 2 vols., New York: United Bible Societies.

Lövestam, Evald (1987), 'Paul's Address at Miletus', *ST* 41: 1–10.

Lührmann, Dieter (1992), *Galatians: A Continental Commentary*, Minneapolis: Fortress.

Lupton, Robert D. (1989), *Theirs Is the Kingdom: Celebrating the Gospel in Urban America*, San Francisco: HarperSanFrancisco.

MacArthur, John F., Jr (1990), 'Faith According to the Apostle James', *JETS* 33: 13–34.

McClay, Wilfred M. (1995), 'Where Have We Come Since the 1950s? Thoughts on Materialism and American Social Character', in Robert Wuthnow (ed.), *Rethinking Materialism*, 25–71, Grand Rapids: Eerdmans.

McCloughry, Roy (1996), 'Basic Stott', *CT* 40 (January 8): 25–32.

McConville, J. G. (1984), *Law and Theology in Deuteronomy*, Sheffield: JSOT.

McGee, Daniel B. (1990), 'Sharing Possessions: A Study in Biblical Ethics', in Naymond H. Keathley (ed.), *With Steadfast Purpose*, 163–178, Waco: Baylor.

McGinn, Bernard (1994), *Antichrist: Two Thousand Years of the Human Fascination with Evil*, San Francisco: HarperSanFrancisco.

McGlasson, Paul C. (1994), *Another Gospel: The Confrontation with Liberation Theology*, Grand Rapids: Baker.

McGovern, Arthur F. (1989), *Liberation Theology and Its Critics*, Maryknoll: Orbis.

McKane, William (1986), *A Critical and Exegetical Commentary on Jeremiah* 1, Edinburgh: T. & T. Clark.

McPolin, James (1989), 'Psalms as Prayers of the Poor', in Kevin J. Cathcart and John F. Healey (eds.), *Back to the Sources: Biblical and Near Eastern Studies*, 79–103, Dublin: Glendale.

Maier, Johann (1993), 'Self-Definition, Prestige, and Status of Priests

Towards the End of the Second Temple Period', *BTB* 23: 139–150.

Malherbe, Abraham J. (1977), *Social Aspects of Early Christianity*, Baton Rouge: LSU Press.

——(1987), *Paul and the Thessalonians*, Philadelphia: Fortress.

——(1996), 'Paul's Self-Sufficiency (Philippians 4:11)', in John T. Fitzgerald (ed.), *Friendship, Flattery and Frankness of Speech*, 125–139, Leiden: Brill.

Malina, Bruce J. (1981), *The New Testament World: Insights from Cultural Anthropology*, Atlanta: John Knox, 1981; London: SCM, 1983.

——(1986), 'The Received View and What it Cannot Do: III John and Hospitality', *Semeia* 35: 171–194.

Maloney, Robert P. (1974), 'Usury and Restrictions on Interest-Taking in the Ancient Near East', *CBQ* 36: 1–20.

Marguerat, Daniel (1993), 'La mort d'Ananiàs et Saphira (Ac 5.1–11) dans la stratégie narrative de Lc', *NTS* 39: 209–226.

Marshall, I. Howard (1978a), *The Epistles of John*, Grand Rapids: Eerdmans.

——(1978b), *The Gospel of Luke*, Exeter: Paternoster; Grand Rapids: Eerdmans.

——(1978c), 'Using the Bible in Ethics', in David F. Wright (ed.), *Essays in Evangelical Social Ethics*, 39–55, Exeter: Paternoster.

——(1980), *The Acts of the Apostles*, Leicester: IVP; Grand Rapids: Eerdmans.

——(1988), *Luke: Historian and Theologian*, 3rd ed., Exeter: Paternoster; Grand Rapids: Zondervan.

——(1990), 'The Christian Life in 1 Timothy', *RefTR* 49: 81–90.

——(1991), *The Epistle to the Philippians*, London: Epworth.

Marshall, Peter (1987), *Enmity in Corinth*, Tübingen: Mohr.

Martin, Francis X. (1972), 'Monastic Community and the Summary Statements in Acts', in M. Basil Pennington (ed.), *Contemplative Community*, 13–46, Washington: Cistercian.

Martin, Ralph P. (1972), *Mark: Evangelist and Theologian*, Exeter: Paternoster, 1972; Grand Rapids: Zondervan, 1973.

——(1986), *2 Corinthians*, Waco: Word.

——(1988), *James*, Waco: Word.

Marty, Martin E. (1995), *Context: A Commentary on the Interaction of Religion and Culture*, 27.11: 1–2.

Marx, Werner G. (1979), 'Money Matters in Matthew', *BSac* 136: 148–157.

Matera, Frank J. (1992), *Galatians*, Collegeville: Liturgical.

Mathews, Kenneth A. (1988), 'John, Jesus and the Essenes: Trouble at the Temple', *CTR* 3: 101–126.

Mathewson, Dave L. (1995), 'The Parable of the Unjust Steward (Luke 16:1–13): A Reexamination of the Traditional View in Light of Recent Challenges', *JETS* 38: 29–39.

May, David M. (1990), 'Leaving and Receiving: A Social-Scientific Exegesis of Mark 10:29–31', *PRS* 17: 141–151, 154.

Mayes, A. H. D. (1979), *Deuteronomy*, London: Marshall, Morgan and Scott; Grand Rapids: Eerdmans.

Maynard-Reid, Pedrito U. (1987), *Poverty and Wealth in James*, Maryknoll: Orbis.

Mayordomo-Marín, Moisés (1992), 'Jak 5, 2.3a: Zukünftiges Gericht oder gegenwärtiger Zustand?' *ZNW* 83: 132–137.

Mays, J. L. (1976), *Micah*, London: SCM; Philadelphia: Westminster.

Meadors, Gary T. (1985), 'The "Poor" in the Beatitudes of Matthew and Luke', *GTJ* 6: 305–314.

Mealand, David L. (1975), 'Community of Goods at Qumran', *TZ* 31: 129–139.

—— (1980), *Poverty and Expectation in the Gospels*, London: SPCK.

Meeks, M. Douglas (1989), *God the Economist*, Minneapolis: Fortress.

Meeks, Wayne A. (1983), *The First Urban Christians*, New Haven and London: Yale.

de Meeus, X. (1961), 'Composition de Lc., xiv, et genre symposiaque', *ETL* 37: 847–870.

Meggitt, Justin J. (1994), 'Meat Consumption and Social Conflict in Corinth', *JTS* 45: 137–141.

—— (1996), 'The Social Status of Erastus (Rom. 16:23)', *NovT* 38: 218–223.

Meier, John P. (1991), *A Marginal Jew: Rethinking the Historical Jesus* 1, New York and London: Doubleday.

Menken, M. J. J. (1992), 'Paradise Regained or Still Lost? Eschatology and Disorderly Behaviour in 2 Thessalonians', *NTS* 38: 271–289.

—— (1994), *II Thessalonians*, London and New York: Routledge.

Menzel, Peter (1994), *The Material World: A Global Family Portrait*, San Francisco: Sierra Club.

Merrill, Eugene H. (1994a), *Deuteronomy*, Nashville: Broadman and Holman.

—— (1994b), *Haggai, Zechariah, Malachi*, Chicago: Moody.

Meyers, Carol L., & Eric M. Meyers (1993), *Zechariah 9 – 14*, New York and London: Doubleday.

Michaels, J. Ramsey (1988), *1 Peter*, Waco: Word.

Millard, A. R., & D. J. Wiseman (eds.) (1980), *Essays on the Patriarchal Narratives*, Leicester: IVP.

Millett, Paul (1991), *Lending and Borrowing in Ancient Athens*, Cambridge: Cambridge Univerity Press.

Miranda, José P. (1982), *Communism in the Bible*, London: SCM; Maryknoll: Orbis.

Mitchell, Alan C. (1990), 'Zacchaeus Revisited: Luke 19, 8 as a Defense', *Bib* 71: 153–176.

——(1992), 'The Social Function of Friendship in Acts 2:44–47 and 4:32–37', *JBL* 111: 255–272.

——(1993), 'Rich and Poor in the Courts of Corinth: Litigiousness and Status in 1 Corinthians 6.1–11', *NTS* 39: 562–586.

Mittwoch, A. (1955), 'Tribute and Land-Tax in Seleucid Judaea', *Bib* 36: 352–361.

Molina, J.-P. (1978), 'Luc 16:1–13: L'injuste *Mamon*', *ETR* 53: 371–375.

Moo, Douglas J. (1985), *The Letter of James*, Leicester: IVP; Grand Rapids: Eerdmans.

——(1996), *The Epistle to the Romans*, Grand Rapids and Cambridge: Eerdmans.

Moritz, Thorsten (1996), 'Dinner Talk and Ideology in Luke: The Role of the Sinners', *EJT* 5: 47–69.

Mott, Stephen C. (1975), 'The Power of Giving and Receiving: Reciprocity in Hellenistic Benevolence', in Gerald F. Hawthorne (ed.), *Current Issues in Biblical and Patristic Interpretation*, 60–72, Grand Rapids: Eerdmans.

Motyer, J. Alec (1993), *The Prophecy of Isaiah*, Leicester and Downers Grove: IVP.

Mouw, Richard J. (1988), 'Toward an Evangelical Theology of Poverty', in Mark Noll and David Wells (eds.), *Christian Faith and Practice in the Modern World*, 218–238, Grand Rapids: Eerdmans.

——(1989), 'Of Households and Economies', in Richard C. Chewning (ed.), *Biblical Principles and Economics: The Foundations*, 140–158, Colorado Springs: NavPress.

Moxnes, H. (1988), *The Economy of the Kingdom*, Philadephia: Fortress.

——(1994), 'The Social Context of Luke's Community', *Int* 48: 379–389.

Mullin, Redmond (1983), *The Wealth of Christians*, Exeter: Paternoster, 1983; Maryknoll: Orbis, 1984.

Munck, Johannes (1959), *Paul and the Salvation of Mankind*, London: SCM; Richmond: John Knox.

Munro, Winsome (1995), 'The Pharisee and the Samaritan in John: Polar or Parallel?', *CBQ* 57: 710–728.

Murchie, David (1978), 'The New Testament View of Wealth Accumulation', *JETS* 21: 335–344.

Murphy-O'Connor, Jerome (1991), *The Theology of the Second Letter to the Corinthians*, Cambridge: Cambridge University Press.

Murray, Michael J., & Kurt Meyers (1994), 'Ask and It Will Be Given to You', *RelStud* 30: 311–330.

Myers, Ched (1988), *Binding the Strong Man: A Political Reading of Mark's Story of Jesus*, Maryknoll: Orbis.

Nash, Ronald H. (1986), *Poverty and Wealth: The Christian Debate over Capitalism*, Westchester: Crossway.

——(1987), 'Economics', in Kenneth S. Kantzer (ed.), *Applying the Scriptures*, 389–406, Grand Rapids: Zondervan.

Nash, Ronald H., & Humberto Belli (1992), *Beyond Liberation Theology*, Grand Rapids: Baker.

Neale, David A. (1991), *None But the Sinners: Religious Categories in the Gospel of Luke*, Sheffield: JSOT.

Nelson, Benjamin N. (1949), *Usury*, Princeton: Princeton University Press.

Neufeld, Edward (1955), 'The Prohibitions against Loans at Interest in Ancient Hebrew Laws', *HUCA* 26: 355–412.

——(1960), 'The Emergence of a Royal-Urban Society in Ancient Israel', *HUCA* 31: 31–53.

Neyrey, Jerome H. (ed.) (1991), *The Social World of Luke-Acts: Models for Interpretation*, Peabody: Hendrickson.

——(1993), *2 Peter, Jude*, New York and London: Doubleday.

——(1994), 'What's Wrong with This Picture? John 4, Cultural Stereotypes of Women, and Public and Private Space', *BTB* 24: 77–91.

Nicholls, Bruce J. (1996), 'Introduction: Priorities in Our Common Task', in Bruce J. Nicholls and Beulah R. Wood (eds.), *Sharing the Good News with the Poor*, 1–10, Carlisle: Paternoster; Grand Rapids: Baker.

Nicholls, Bruce J., & Beulah R. Wood, eds. (1996), *Sharing the Good News with the Poor*, Carlisle: Paternoster; Grand Rapids: Baker.

Nickelsburg, George W. E. (1979), 'Riches, the Rich, and God's Judgment in 1 Enoch 92–105 and the Gospel According to Luke', *NTS* 25: 324–344.

Nickle, Keith F. (1966), *The Collection*, London: SCM; Naperville: Allenson.

Nolland, John (1989, 1993a, 1993b), *Luke*, 3 vols., Dallas: Word.

Nordling, John G. (1991), 'Onesimus Fugitivus: A Defense of the Runaway Slave Hypothesis in Philemon', *JSNT* 41: 97–119.

North, Robert (1954), *Sociology of the Biblical Jubilee*, Rome: Pontifical Biblical Institute.

Nouwen, Henri J. M. (1993), *In the Name of Jesus*, New York: Crossroad.

Nuñez C., Emilio A. (1985), *Liberation Theology*, Chicago: Moody.

Nuñez C., Emilio A., & William D. Taylor (1996), *Crisis and Hope in Latin America: An Evangelical Perspective*, Pasadena: William Carey Library.

Oakman, Douglas E. (1986), *Jesus and the Economic Questions of His Day*, Lewiston and Queenston: Mellen.

——(1992), 'Was Jesus a Peasant? Implications for Reading the Samaritan Story (Luke 10:30–35)', *BTB* 22: 117–125.

O'Brien, Peter T. (1982), *Colossians, Philemon*, Waco: Word.

——(1991), *The Epistle to the Philippians*, Carlisle: Paternoster; Grand Rapids: Eerdmans.

Oden, Robert A. (1984), 'Taxation in Biblical Israel', *JRE* 12: 162–181.

Olson, Mark (1986), 'Open the Border!', *Other Side* 22 (April): 16–21.

Oppenheimer, Aharon (1977), *The 'Am-ha-aretz*, Leiden: Brill.

Osborne, Grant R. (1978), 'Luke: Theologian of Social Concern', *TrinJ* 7: 135–148.

Oswalt, John N. (1980), 'בצע', in R. Laird Harris, Gleason L. Archer Jr, & Bruce K. Waltke (eds.), *Theological Wordbook of The Old Testament*, 1: 122–123, Chicago: Moody.

——(1986), *The Book of Isaiah Chapters 1 – 39*, Grand Rapids: Eerdmans.

O'Toole, Robert F. (1994), 'What Role Does Jesus' Saying in Acts 20, 35 Play in Paul's Address to the Ephesians Elders?' *Bib* 75: 329–349.

——(1995), '"You Did Not Lie to Us (Human Beings) But to God" (Acts 5, 4c)', *Bib* 76: 182–209.

Overman, J. Andrew (1996), *Church and Community in Crisis: The Gospel According to Matthew*, Valley Forge: TPI.

Owen-Ball, David T. (1993), 'Rabbinic Rhetoric and the Tribute Passage (Mt. 22:15–22; Mk. 12:13–17; Lk. 20:20–26)', *NovT* 35: 1–14.

'The Oxford III Conference on Christian Faith and Economics, Agra, India, 1–5 March 1995' (1995), *Transformation* 123: 9–17.

Øyen, Else, S. M. Miller, & Fyed A. Samad (1996), *Poverty: A Global Review*, Oslo: Scandanavian University Press and UNESCO.

Padgett, Alan (1987), 'Wealthy Women at Ephesus: 1Timothy 2:8–15 in Social Context', *Int* 41: 19–31.

Parker, Andrew (1996), *Painfully Clear: The Parables of Jesus*, Sheffield: Sheffield Academic Press.

Parrott, Douglas M. (1991), 'The Dishonest Steward (Luke 16.1–8a) and Luke's Special Parable Collection', *NTS* 37: 499–515.

Pastor, Jack (1997), *Land and Economy in Ancient Palestine*, London and New York: Routledge.

Patterson, Richard D. (1973), 'The Widow, the Orphan, and the Poor in the Old Testament and Extra-Biblical Literature', *BSac* 130: 223–234.

Perkins, John M. (1993), *Beyond Charity: The Call to Christian Community Development*, Grand Rapids: Baker.

Perkins, Pheme (1981), *Hearing the Parables of Jesus*, New York: Paulist.

Peterlin, Davorin (1995), *Paul's Letter to the Philippians in the Light of Disunity in the Church*, Leiden: Brill.

Peterman, Gerald W. (1991), '"Thankless Thanks": The Epistolary Social Convention in Philippians 4:10–20', *TB* 42: 261–270.

—— (1994), 'Romans 15.26: Make a Contribution or Establish Fellowship?', *NTS* 40: 457–463.

—— (1997), *Paul's Gift for Philippi: Conventions of Gift Exchange and Christian Giving*, Cambridge: Cambridge University Press.

Petzer, J. H. (1989), 'Contextual Evidence in Favour of ΚΑΥΧΗΣΟΜΑΙ in 1 Corinthians 13.3', *NTS* 35: 229–253.

Pilgrim, Walter E. (1981), *Good News to the Poor*, Minneapolis: Augsburg.

Pixley, George V. (1987), *On Exodus*, Maryknoll: Orbis.

Pleins, J. David (1987), 'Poverty in the Social World of the Wise', *JSOT* 37: 61–78.

—— (1994), 'Poverty in the Hebrew Bible', *ITQ* 60: 280–286.

Polan, Gregory J. (1986), *In the Ways of Justice Toward Salvation: A Rhetorical Analysis of Isaiah 56–59*, Frankfurt: Peter Lang.

Polhill, John B. (1986), 'Prejudice, Partiality and Faith: James 2', *RevExp* 83: 395–404.

—— (1992), *Acts*, Nashville: Broadman.

Pope, Marvin H. (1977), *Song of Songs*, Garden City: Doubleday.

Porteous, N. W. (1966), 'The Care of the Poor in the Old Testament', in James I. McCord and T. H. L. Parker (eds.), *Service in Christ*, 27–36, Grand Rapids: Eerdmans; London: Epworth.

Porter, Stanley E. (1990), 'The Parable of the Unjust Steward: Irony *Is* the Key', in S. E. Fowl and S. E. Porter (eds.), *The Bible in Three Dimensions*, 127–153, Sheffield: JSOT.

Pratscher, Wilhelm (1979), 'Der Verzicht des Paulus auf finanziellen Unterhalt durch seine Gemeinden: Ein Aspekt einer Missionsweise', *NTS* 25: 284–298.

Prior, David (1985), *The Message of 1 Corinthians: Life in the Local Church*, Leicester and Downers Grove: IVP.

Prior, Michael (1995), *Jesus the Liberator*, Sheffield: Sheffield Academic Press.

Provan, Iain (1996), 'Foul Spirits, Fornication and Finance: Revelation 18 from an Old Testament Perspective', *JSNT* 64: 81–100.

Purdy, John C. (1985), *Parables at Work*, Philadelphia: Westminster.

Rabin, Chaim (1957), *Qumran Studies*, Oxford: Oxford University Press.

Rapske, Brian (1994), *The Book of Acts and Paul in Roman Custody*, Carlisle: Paternoster; Grand Rapids: Eerdmans.

Ravens, D. A. S. (1991), 'Zacchaeus: The Final Part of a Lucan Triptych?' *JSNT* 41: 19–32.

Redford, D. B. (1972), 'Studies in Relations between Palestine and Egypt during the First Millennium BC: The Taxation System of Solomon', in J. W. Wevers and D. B. Redford (eds.), *Studies on the Ancient Palestinian World*, 141–156, Toronto: University of Toronto Press.

Reiner, Erica (1968), 'Thirty Pieces of Silver', *JAOS* 88: 186–190.

Reumann, John (1993), 'Contributions of the Philippian Community to Paul and to Earliest Christianity', *NTS* 39: 438–457.

——(1996), 'Philippians, Especially Chapter 4, as a Letter of Friendship?', in John T. Fitzgerald (ed.), *Friendship, Flattery and Frankness of Speech*, 83–106, Leiden: Brill.

Richard, Earl J. (1995), *First and Second Thessalonians*, Collegeville: Liturgical.

Riches, Graham (ed.), (1996), *First World Hunger: Food Security and Welfare Politics*, New York: St Martin's, 1996; London: Macmillan, 1997.

Riches, John K. (1996), 'The Social World of Jesus', *Int* 50: 383–393.

Ridderbos, H. N. (1987), *Matthew*, Grand Rapids: Zondervan.

Riesner, Rainer (1998), *Paul's Early Period: Chronology, Mission Strategy, Theology*, Grand Rapids and Cambridge: Eerdmans.

Ringe, Sharon H. (1985), *Jesus, Liberation and the Biblical Jubilee*, Philadelphia: Fortress.

——(1995), *Luke*, Louisville: WJKP.

Rodríguez, José D. (1988), 'The Parable of the Affirmative Action Employer', *CTM* 15: 418–424.

Rohrbaugh, Richard L. (1993), 'The Social Location of the Marcan

Audience', *BTB* 23: 114–127.

Ronsvalle, John, & Sylvia Ronsvalle (1990), 'Facts Related to U.S. Wealth from a Global Christian Perspective', in David Neff (ed.), *The Midas Trap*, 151–161, Wheaton: Victor.

——(1992), *The Poor Have Faces: Loving Your Neighbor in the 21st Century*, Grand Rapids: Baker.

Ropes, James H. (1916), *A Critical and Exegetical Commentary on the Epistle of St James*, Edinburgh: T. & T. Clark.

Rosivach, Vincent J. (1991), 'Some Athenian Presuppositions about "the Poor"', *Greece and Rome* 38: 189–198.

Rostovtzeff, M. (1941), *The Social and Economic History of the Hellenistic World*, 3 vols., Oxford: Clarendon.

——(1957), *The Social and Economic History of the Roman Empire*, 2 vols., rev. ed., Oxford, Clarendon.

Roth, S. John (1997), *The Blind, The Lame, and The Poor: Character Types in Luke-Acts*, Sheffield: Sheffield Academic Press.

Rowland, Christopher C. (1993), *Revelation*, London: Epworth.

——(1994), 'Apocalyptic, the Poor, and the Gospel of Matthew', *JTS* 45: 504–518.

——(1995), '"The Gospel, the Poor and the Churches": Attitudes to Poverty in the British Churches and Biblical Exegesis', in John W. Rogerson, Margaret Davies and M. Daniel Carroll R. (eds.), *The Bible in Ethics: The Second Sheffield Colloquium*, 213–231, Sheffield: Sheffield Academic Press.

Rowland, Christopher C., & Mark Corner (1989), *Liberating Exegesis: The Challenge of Liberation Theology to Biblical Studies*, London: SPCK, 1989; Louisville: Westminster John Knox, 1990.

Russell, Ronald (1988), 'The Idle in 2 Thess 3.6–12: An Eschatological or a Social Problem?' *NTS* 34: 105–119.

Rybolt, John S. (1986), *Sirach*, Collegeville: Liturgical.

Ryken, Leland (1987), *Words of Life: A Literary Introduction to the New Testament*, Grand Rapids: Baker.

Safrai, Ze'ev (1994), *The Economy of Roman Palestine*, London and New York: Routledge.

Saldarini, Anthony J. (1988), *Pharisees, Scribes and Sadducees in Palestinian Society: A Sociological Approach*, Wilmington: Glazier, 1988; Edinburgh: T. & T. Clark, 1989.

Saller, Richard T. (1982), *Personal Patronage Under the Early Empire*, Cambridge: Cambridge University Press.

Sampley, J. Paul (1980), *Pauline Partnership in Christ*, Philadelphia: Fortress.

Sanders, E. P. (1985), *Jesus and Judaism*, London: SCM; Philadephia: Fortress.

Sanders, James A. (1975), 'From Isaiah 61 to Luke 4', in Jacob Neusner (ed.), *Christianity, Judaism and Other Greco-Roman Cults*, 75–106, Leiden: Brill.

Sänger, Dieter (1992), 'Recht und Gerechtigkeit in der Verkündigung Jesu: Erwägungen zu Mk 10, 17–22 und 12, 28–34', *BZ* 36: 179–194.

Santa Ana, Julio de (1977), *Good News to the Poor: The Challenge of the Poor in the History of the Church*, Geneva: WCC.

Sarna, Nahum M. (1991a), *Exodus*, Philadelphia and Jerusalem: JPS.

——(1991b), *Genesis*, Philadelphia and Jerusalem: JPS.

Savage, Timothy B. (1996), *Power Through Weakness: Paul's Understanding of the Christian Ministry in 2 Corinthians*, Cambridge: Cambridge University Press.

Scheffler, E. H. (1990), 'The Social Ethics of the Lucan Baptist (Lk 3:10–14)', *Neot* 24: 21–36.

Schluter, Michael, & Roy Clements (1990), 'Jubilee Institutional Norms: A Middle Way Between Creation Ethics and Kingdom Ethics as the Basis for Christian Political Action', *EQ* 62: 37–62.

Schmidt, Thomas E. (1987), *Hostility to Wealth in the Synoptic Gospels*, Sheffield: JSOT.

——(1988), 'Burden, Barrier, Blasphemy: Wealth in Matt 6:33, Luke 14:33, and Luke 16:15', *TrinJ* 9: 171–189.

——(1992), 'Mark 10.29–30; Matthew 19.29: "Leave Houses ... and Region"?' *NTS* 38: 617–620.

Schnackenburg, R. (1992), *The Johannine Epistles: Introduction and Commentary*, New York: Crossroad; Tunbridge Wells: Burns and Oates.

Schneider, John (1994), *Godly Materialism: Rethinking Money and Possessions*, Downers Grove: IVP.

Schneiders, Sandra M. (1991), *The Revelatory Text: Interpreting the New Testament as Sacred Scripture*, San Francisco: HarperSanFrancisco.

Schökel, Luis Alonso (1973), 'James 5, 2 [*sic*] and 4, 6', *Bib* 54: 73–76.

Schöllgen, Georg (1989), 'Die διπλη τιμή von 1 Tim 5, 17', *ZNW* 80: 232–239.

Schottroff, Luise and Wolfgang Stegemann (1986), *Jesus and the Hope of the Poor*, Maryknoll: Orbis.

Schwantes, Milton (1977), *Das Recht der Armen*, Frankfurt and Las Vegas: Peter Lang.

Schweizer, Eduard (1984), *The Good News According to Luke*, Atlanta: John Knox; London: SPCK.

Scott, R. B. Y. (1965), *Proverbs, Ecclesiastes*, Garden City: Doubleday.

Seccombe, David (1978), 'Was There Organized Charity in Jerusalem before the Christians?' *JTS* 29: 140–143.

—— (1983), *Possessions and the Poor in Luke-Acts*, Linz: SNTU.

Segundo, Juan Luís (1985), *The Historical Jesus of the Synoptics*, Maryknoll: Orbis; London: Sheed and Ward.

Seifrid, M. A. (1987), 'Jesus and the Law in Acts', *JSNT* 30: 39–57.

Sider, John (1995), *Interpreting the Parables*, Grand Rapids: Zondervan.

Sider, Ronald J. (ed.) (1980), *Living More Simply: Biblical Principles and Practical Models*, Downers Grove: IVP.

Sider, Ronald J. (1987), *Completely Pro-Life*, Downers Grove: IVP.

—— (1994), *Cup of Water, Bread of Life*, Grand Rapids: Zondervan.

—— (1997), *Rich Christians in an Age of Hunger*, 4th ed., Dallas and London: Word (1st edn., Downers Grove: IVP, 1977; London: Hodder and Stoughton, 1979).

Siker, Jeffrey S. (1992), '"First to the Gentiles": A Literary Analysis of Luke 4:16–30', *JBL* 111: 73–90.

Sim, David C. (1989), 'The Women Followers of Jesus: The Implications of Luke 8:1–3', *HeyJ* 30: 51–62.

Sine, Tom (1991), *Wild Hope*, Dallas: Word.

Skeat, T. C. (1979), '"Especially the Parchments": A Note on 2 Timothy IV.13', *JTS* 30: 173–177.

Skehan, Patrick W., & Alexander A. Di Lella (1987), *The Wisdom of Ben Sira*, New York: Doubleday.

Sloan, Robert B., Jr (1977), *The Favorable Year of the Lord*, Austin: Schola.

Smalley, Stephen S. (1978), *John: Evangelist and Interpreter*, Exeter: Paternoster.

—— (1984), *1, 2, 3 John*, Waco: Word.

—— (1994), *Thunder and Love: John's Revelation and John's Community*, Milton Keynes: Word.

Smick, Elmer B. (1988), 'Job', in Frank E. Gaebelein (ed.), *Expositor's Bible Commentary* 4, 841–1060, Grand Rapids: Zondervan.

Smith, D. L. (1989), *The Religion of the Landless: The Social Context of the Babylonian Exile*, Bloomington, IN: Meyer-Stone.

Smith, R. H. (1980), 'Were the Early Christians Middle Class? A Sociological Analysis of the New Testament', *CTM* 7: 260–276.

Smith, Ralph L. (1984), *Micah–Malachi*, Waco: Word.

Snodgrass, Klyne (1983), *The Parable of the Wicked Tenants*, Tübingen: Mohr.

Soares-Prabhu, George M. (1991), 'Class in the Bible: The Biblical Poor a Social Class?', in R. S. Sugirtharajah (ed.), *Voices From the Margin: Interpreting the Bible in the Third World*, 129–146, London: SPCK; Maryknoll: Orbis.

Sommer, Benjamin D. (1996), 'Did Prophecy Cease? Evaluating a Reevaluation', *JBL* 115: 31–47.

Spenser, F. Scott (1994), 'Neglected Widows in Acts 6:1–7', *CBQ* 56: 715–733.

Spicq, C. (1969), *Les Epitres Pastorales*, Paris: Gabalda.

Stackhouse, Max L. (1987), 'What Then Shall We Do? On Using Scripture in Economic Ethics', *Int* 41: 382–397.

Stafford, Tim (May 19, 1997), 'Anatomy of a Giver', *CT* 41: 19–24.

Stanton, Graham N. (1984), 'The Gospel of Matthew and Judaism', *BJRL* 66: 264–284.

Stegemann, Wolfgang (1984), *The Gospel and the Poor*, Philadelphia: Fortress.

Stein, Robert H. (1981), *An Introduction to the Parables of Jesus*, Philadelphia: Wesminster.

—— (1992), *Luke*, Nashville: Broadman.

Stein, Siegfried (1953), 'The Laws on Interest in the Old Testament', *JTS* 4: 161–170.

Sterling, Gregory E. (1994), '"Athletes of Virtue": An Analysis of the Summaries in Acts (2:41–47; 4:32–35; 5:12–16)', *JBL* 113: 679–696.

Stott, John (1990), *Issues Facing Christians Today*, London: Marshall Pickering.

Strobel, August (1972), 'Die Ausrufung des Jobeljahres in der Nazarethpredigt Jesu; zur apokalyptischen Tradition Lc 4 16–30', in Walther Eltester (ed.), *Jesus in Nazareth*, 38–50, Berlin: de Gruyter.

Stulac, George M. (1990), 'Who Are "The Rich" in James?' *Presbyterion* 16: 89–102.

Suter, Keith D. (1989), 'Christians and Personal Wealth', *AJT* 3: 643–650.

Szesnat, H. (1993), 'What Did the ΣΚΗΝΟΠΟΙΟΣ Paul Produce?' *Neot* 27: 391–402.

Talbert, Charles H. (1982), *Reading Luke*, New York: Crossroad, 1982; London: SPCK, 1990.

—— (1987), *Reading Corinthians*, New York: Crossroad, 1987; London: SPCK, 1990.

—— (1992), *Reading John*, New York: Crossroad; London: SPCK.

—— (1997), *Reading Acts*, New York: Crossroad.

Tamez, Elsa (1990), *The Scandalous Message of James*, New York: Crossroad.

——(1993), *The Amnesty of Grace: Justification by Faith from a Latin-American Perspective*, Nashville: Abingdon.

Tannehill, Robert C. (1970), 'The "Focal Instance" as a Form of New Testament Speech: A Study of Matthew 5:39b–42', *JR* 50: 372–385.

Taylor, John B. (1969), *Ezekiel*, London: Tyndale; Downers Grove: IVP.

Theissen, Gerd (1978), *Sociology of Early Palestinian Christianity*, Philadelphia: Fortress / *The First Followers of Jesus*, London: SCM.

——(1982), *The Social Setting of Pauline Christianity*, Philadelphia: Fortress, 1982; Edinburgh: T. & T. Clark, 1990.

——(1991), *The Gospels in Context*, Minneapolis: Fortress.

Thibeaux, Evelyn R. (1993), '"Known to be a Sinner": The Narrative Rhetoric of Luke 7:36–50', *BTB* 23: 151–160.

Thomas, Carolyn (1994), 'Economic Issues in Paul', *BibTod* 32: 290–294.

Thompson, J. A. (1980), *The Book of Jeremiah*, Grand Rapids: Eerdmans.

Thompson, Leonard L. (1990), *The Book of Revelation: Apocalypse and Empire*, Oxford: Oxford University Press.

Thompson, Michael (1991), *Clothed with Christ: The Example and Teachings of Jesus in Romans 12.1 – 15.13*, Sheffield: JSOT.

Thompson, Thomas L. (1994), *Early History of the Israelite People: From the Written and Archaelogical Sources*, Leiden: Brill.

Thurston, Bonnie V. (1989), *The Widows: A Women's Ministry in the Early Church*, Minneapolis: Fortress.

——(1993), *Spiritual Life in the Early Church*, Minneapolis: Fortress.

——(1995), *Reading Colossians, Ephesians and 2 Thessalonians*, New York: Crossroad.

Tigay, Jeffrey H. (1996), *Deuteronomy*, Philadelphia and Jerusalem: JPS.

Todd, Richard (September 1997), 'Who Me, Rich?', *Worth*: 71–84.

Towner, Philip H. (1994), *1 – 2 Timothy and Titus*, Leicester and Downers Grove: IVP.

Townsend, Michael J. (1994), *The Epistle of James*, London: Epworth.

Tuckett, Christopher M. (1996), *Q and the History of Early Christianity*, Edinburgh: T. & T. Clark; Peabody: Hendrickson.

Vaage, Leif E. (1994), *Galilean Upstarts: Jesus' First Followers According to Q*, Valley Forge: TPI.

Vandana, Sister (1991), 'Water – God's Extravaganza: John 2.1–11', in R. S. Sugirtharajah (ed.), *Voices from the Margin: Interpreting the*

*Bible in the Third World*, 117–128, London: SPCK; Maryknoll: Orbis.

VanderKam, James C. (1994), *The Dead Sea Scrolls Today*, Grand Rapids: Eerdmans; London: SPCK.

Verbrugge, Verlyn D. (1992), *Paul's Style of Church Leadership Illustrated by His Instructions to the Corinthians on the Collection*, San Francisco: Mellen Research University Press.

Verhey, Allan (1984), *The Great Reversal: Ethics and the New Testament*, Grand Rapids: Eerdmans.

Verhoef, Pieter A. (1974), 'Tithing – A Hermeneutical Consideration', in John H. Skilton (ed.), *The Law and the Prophets*, 115–127, Phillipsburg: Presbyterian and Reformed.

——(1987), *The Books of Haggai and Malachi*, Grand Rapids: Eerdmans.

Vermes, Geza, & Martin Goodman (eds.) (1989), *The Essenes According to the Classical Sources*, Sheffield: JSOT.

Verner, David C. (1983), *The Household of God: The Social World of the Pastoral Epistles*, Chico: Scholars.

Via, Dan O., Jr (1985), *The Ethics of Mark's Gospel: In the Middle of Time*, Philadelphia: Fortress.

Vischer, L. (1966), *Tithing in the Early Church*, Philadelphia: Fortress.

Viviano, Benedict T. (1993), 'Eight Beatitudes at Qumran and in Matthew?', *SvExÅrs* 58: 71–84.

Vyhmeister, Nancy J. (1995), 'The Rich Man in James 2: Does Ancient Patronage Illumine the Text?' *AUSS* 33: 265–283.

wa Ilunga, Bakole (1984), *Paths of Liberation: A Third World Spirituality*, Maryknoll: Orbis.

Wacholder, Ben Zion (1973–74), 'The Calendar of Sabbatical Cycles During the Second Temple and the Early Rabbinic Period', *HUCA* 44: 153–196.

Waetjen, H. C. (1989), *A Re-ordering of Power: A Socio-Political Reading of Mark's Gospel*, Minneapolis: Fortress.

Wainwright, John J. (1993), '*Eusebeia*: Syncretism or Conservative Contextualization?' *EQ* 65: 211–224.

von Waldow, H. Eberhard (1970), 'Social Responsibility and Social Structure in Early Israel', *CBQ* 32: 182–204.

Wall, Robert W. (1997), *Community of the Wise: The Letter of James*, Valley Forge: TPI.

Wallace-Hadrill, Andrew (ed.) (1989), *Patronage in Ancient Society*, London and New York: Routledge.

Wanamaker, Charles A. (1990), *The Epistles to the Thessalonians*, Exeter: Paternoster; Grand Rapids: Eerdmans.

Ward, Roy B. (1969), 'Partiality in the Assembly: James 2:2–4', *HTR* 62: 87–97.

Washington, Harold C. (1994), *Wealth and Poverty in the Instruction of Amenemope and the Book of Proverbs*, Atlanta: Scholars.

Watson, Duane F. (1993), 'James in Light of Greco-Roman Schemes of Argumentation', *NTS* 39: 94–121.

Watson, Nigel (1993), *The Second Epistle to the Corinthians*, London: Epworth.

Watts, John D. W. (1985, 1987), *Isaiah*, 2 vols., Waco: Word.

Weber, Beat (1992), 'Schulden erstatten – Schulden erlassen Zum matthäischen Gebrauch einiger juristischer und monetärer Begriffe', *ZNW* 83: 253–256.

——(1993), 'Alltagswelt und Gottesreich: Überlegungen zum Verstehenshintergrund des Gleichnisses vom "Schalksknecht" (Matthäus 18, 23–34)', *BZ* 37: 161–182.

Weinfeld, Moshe (1986), *The Organizational Pattern and the Penal Code of the Qumran Sect*, Fribourg: Editions Universitaires; Göttingen: Vandenhoeck).

Weir, J. Emmette (1988), 'The Poor are Powerless: A Response to R. J. Coggins', *ET* 100: 13–15.

Wenham, Gordon J. (1979), *The Book of Leviticus*, Grand Rapids: Eerdmans.

——(1987, 1994), *Genesis*, 2 vols., Waco and Dallas: Word.

Westbrook, Raymond (1991), *Property and the Family in Biblical Law*, Sheffield: JSOT.

Wheeler, Sondra E. (1995), *Wealth as Peril and Obligation: The New Testament on Possessions*, Grand Rapids: Eerdmans.

White, John (1993), *Money Isn't God: So Why Is the Church Worshiping It?* Downers Grove and Leicester: IVP.

Whybray, R. N. (1989a), *Ecclesiastes*, Grand Rapids: Eerdmans; London: Marshall, Morgan and Scott.

——(1989b), 'Poverty, Wealth, and Point of View in Proverbs', *ET* 100: 332–336.

——(1990), *Wealth and Poverty in the Book of Proverbs*, Sheffield: JSOT.

Wiles, Gordon P. (1974), *Paul's Intercessory Prayers*, Cambridge: Cambridge University Press.

Williams, David J. (1992), *I & II Thessalonians*, Peabody: Hendrickson.

Williams, Francis E. (1964), 'Is Almsgiving the Point of the "Unjust Steward"?' *JBL* 83: 293–297.

Williamson, H. G. M. (1982), *1 and 2 Chronicles*, Grand Rapids: Eerdmans; London: Marshall, Morgan & Scott.

——(1985a), *Ezra, Nehemiah*, Waco: Word.

——(1985b), 'The Old Testament and the Material World', *EQ* 57: 5–22.

Wilson, R. Ward, & Craig L. Blomberg (1993), 'The Image of God in Humanity: A Biblical-Psychological Perspective', *Themelios* 18.3: 8–15.

Wimbush, Vincent L. (1987), *Paul: The Worldly Ascetic*, Macon: Mercer.

Winston, David (1979), *The Wisdom of Solomon*, Garden City: Doubleday.

Winter, Bruce W. (1989), 'Secular and Christian Responses to Corinthian Famines', *TB* 40: 88–106.

——(ed.) (1993–96), *The Book Acts in Its First Century Setting*, 5 vols. Carlisle: Paternoster; Grand Rapids: Eerdmans.

——(1994), *Seek the Welfare of the City*, Carlisle: Paternoster; Grand Rapids: Eerdmans.

——(1997a), 'Gluttony and Immorality at Élitist Banquets: The Background to 1 Corinthians 6:12–20', *Jian Dao* 7: 77–90.

——(1997b), *Paul among the Sophists*, Cambridge: Cambridge University Press.

Wischmeyer, Odar (1994), 'Matthäus 6, 25–34 par – Die Spruchreihe vom Sorgen', *ZNW* 85: 1–22.

Wiseman, P. J. (1977), *Clues to Creation in Genesis*, London: Marshall, Morgan and Scott.

Witherington, Ben, III (1979), 'On the Road with Mary Magdalene, Joanna, Susanna, and other Disciples – Luke 8, 1–3', *ZNW* 70: 243–248.

——(1990), *The Christology of Jesus*, Minneapolis: Fortress.

——(1994a), *Friendship and Finances in Philippi*, Valley Forge: TPI.

——(1994b), *Jesus the Sage*, Minneapolis: Fortress; Edinburgh: T. & T. Clark.

——(1995a), *Conflict and Community in Corinth: A Socio-Rhetorical Commentary on 1 and 2 Corinthians*, Grand Rapids: Eerdmans; Carlisle: Paternoster.

——(1995b), *John's Wisdom*, Louisville: Westminster John Knox.

Witten, Marcia G. (1995), '"Where Your Treasure Is": Popular Evangelical Views of Work, Money, and Materialism', in Robert Wuthnow (ed.), *Rethinking Materialism*, 117–141, Grand Rapids: Eerdmans.

Wittenberg, G. H. (1986), 'The Lexical Context of the Terminology for "Poor" in the Book of Proverbs', *Scriptura* 20: 40–85.

——(1987), 'The Situational Context of Statements Concerning Poverty and Wealth in the Book of Proverbs', *Scriptura* 21: 1–23.

Wood, Beulah R. (1996), 'Ruth: The Story of a Third World Farm Labourer', in Bruce J. Nicholls and Beulah R. Wood (eds.), *Sharing the Good News with the Poor*, 39–43, Carlisle: Paternoster; Grand Rapids: Baker.

Wright, Addison G. (1982), 'The Widow's Mites: Praise or Lament? – A Matter of Context', *CBQ* 44: 256–265.

Wright, Christopher J. H. (1984), 'What Happened Every Seven Years in Israel? Old Testament Sabbatical Institutions for Land, Debt and Slaves', *EQ* 56: 129–138, 193–201.

——(1990), *God's People in God's Land: Family, Land and Property in the Old Testament*, Exeter: Paternoster; Grand Rapids: Eerdmans.

——(1993), 'Biblical Reflections on Land', *ERT* 17: 153–167.

——(1995), *Walking in the Ways of the Lord: The Ethical Authority of the Old Testment*, Leicester: IVP.

——(1996), *Deuteronomy*, Peabody: Hendrickson.

Wright, N. T. (1992), *The New Testament and the People of God*, London: SPCK; Minneapolis: Fortress.

——(1996), *Jesus and the Victory of God*, London: SPCK; Minneapolis: Fortress.

Wuthnow, Robert (1994), *God and Mammon in America*, New York: Free Press.

Yancey, Philip (1990), 'Ecclesiastes: The High Counterpoint of Boredom', *RefJ* 40.6: 14–19.

Yoder, John H. (1972), *The Politics of Jesus*, Grand Rapids: Eerdmans.

Young, Richard A. (1994), *Healing the Earth*, Nashville: Broadman and Holman.

Zimmermann, Frank (1958), *The Book of Tobit*, New York: Harper and Brothers.

# Index of authors

Safrai, Ze'ev 95
Saldarini, Anthony J. 102
Saller, Richard T. 103
Samad, Fyed A. 17
Sampley, J. Paul 206
Sanders, E. P. 143
Sanders, James A. 100
Sänger, Dieter 139
Santa Ana, Julio de 21, 253
Sarna, Nahum M. 34, 42
Satterthwaite, Philip E. 33
Savage, Timothy B. 183
Scalise, Pamela J. 80
Scheffler, E. H. 223
Schluter, Michael 83
Schmidt, Thomas E. 89, 132, 145
Schnackenburg, R. 234, 235
Schneider, John 24, 28, 247
Schneiders, Sandra M. 232
Schökel, Luis Alonso 158
Schöllgen, Georg 210
Schottroff, Luise 102, 114, 215
Schwantes, Milton 82
Schweizer, Eduard 121
Scott, R. B. Y. 58
Seccombe, David 103, 123, 221
Segundo, Juan Luís 22
Seifrid, M. A. 227
Sider, John 112
Sider, Ronald J. 18, 19, 20, 23,
    24, 28, 70, 189, 247, 248, 249,
    250, 251, 252
Siker, Jeffrey S. 134
Sim, David C. 109
Sine, Tom 20, 250-251
Skeat, T. C. 210
Skehan, Patrick W. 93
Sloan, Robert B., Jr 220
Smalley, Stephen S. 214, 235,
    236
Smick, Elmer B. 58
Smith, D. L. 80
Smith, R. H. 219
Smith, Ralph L. 75, 81
Smothers, Thomas G. 80
Snodgrass, Klyne 125
Soares-Prabhu, George M. 90

Sommer, Benjamin D. 91
Spencer, F. Scott 170
Spicq, C. 208
Stackhouse, Max L. 243
Stafford, Tim 20
Stanton, Graham N. 219
Stegemann, Wolfgang 102, 106,
    114, 122, 128, 172, 215
Stein, Robert H. 120, 144
Stein, Siegfried 41
Sterling, Gregory E. 163
Stott, John 25, 194
Streeter, B. H. 214
Strobel, August 134
Stuart, Douglas 163
Stulac, George M. 150
Suter, Keith D. 20
Sweetland, Dennis M. 227
Szesnat, H. 177

Talbert, Charles H. 134, 163, 197,
    223, 233
Tamez, Elsa 148, 150, 159, 199
Tannehill, Robert C. 130
Taylor, John B. 71, 81
Taylor, William D. 22
Theissen, Gerd 135, 182, 185,
    187, 215
Theresa, Mother 126
Thibeaux, Evelyn R. 114
Thomas, Carolyn 194
Thompson, J. A. 79
Thompson, Leonard L. 236
Thompson, Michael 200
Thompson, Thomas L. 51
Thurston, Bonnie V. 161, 174,
    180, 209
Tigay, Jeffrey H. 44
Todd, Richard 253
Towner, Philip H. 206, 209
Townsend, Michael J. 150, 156,
    158
Tuckett, Christopher M. 215

Vaage, Leif E. 215
Vandana, Sister 232
VanderKam, James C. 99